POSIX.4: Programming for the Real World

POSIX.4: Programming for the Real World

Bill O. Gallmeister

O'Reilly & Associates, Inc.

103 Morris Street, Suite A
Sebastopol, CA 95472

POSIX.4: Programming for the Real World
by Bill O. Gallmeister

Editor: Mike Loukides

Production Editor: Clairemarie Fisher O'Leary

Printing History:

       January 1995   First Edition.

ISBN: 1-56592-074-0

To my son, Ian, and my father, who was right.

Table of Contents

PART III: Solutions to Problems

Appendix: Exercise Code   481

Bibliography

Index

List of Figures

List of Tables

Preface

Who and What

This book is about real-world programming: not the part of programming that's about writing tools for creating other programs, but the part that's about interacting with the "real world" outside of the computer. Though you wouldn't know it by looking at a typical university computer curriculum, there's almost certainly more real-world programming going on than general tools programming. Think about it: your VCR is controlled by a microprocessor that has some kind of operating system and software running on it; if your car is under a dozen years old, it's probably littered with microprocessors running everything from the ignition to the brakes, all working together; you routinely get money from automatic tellers. And most attendees of computer shows know about the Internet toaster!

In fact, there are aspects of real-world programming even within a workstation that's used entirely to develop programming tools. That workstation has either a disk drive or a network interface; both disk controllers and network controllers contain their own microprocessors running their own software that deals with hard, mechanical devices (in the case of a disk drive) or electrical impulses running down a wire in measurably non-zero time.

So real-world programs (and real-world programmers) are all around us. What characterizes all of these real-world applications is a critical dependence on time—the messy ingredient that always comes in whenever computers start interacting with the real world. Applications that are formally called "real-time" are only a small part of real-world programming. The brake controller in your car is certainly real-time software, by any definition; if it's late, your car won't stop. But the database software that controls the ATM at your bank has very similar time-oriented requirements, even though they aren't quite as strict. Your ATM shouldn't give you $200 at 3:15, if at 3:14 your bank processed a check that cleaned out your account. And even if you have the money, you'll get awfully nervous if your ATM takes five minutes to give it to you because the mainframe is under a heavy load. (In the much more relaxed world of compilers, editors, and other tools, this is nowhere as significant a problem; it's called a coffee break.)

This book is written to help programmers solve real-world problems in a portable way, using POSIX.1 (the basic operating system interface) and POSIX.4 (real-time, real-world extensions to POSIX.1). The tools needed to solve these problems include process scheduling, interprocess communication, and enhanced I/O. I assume most programmers reading this book will be programming in, or familiar with, the UNIX programming environment, and some (not all) of you will be familiar with POSIX. This is not an introductory book: I assume you know C and are good at it, and you know UNIX programming pretty well, too. In particular, I'm not going to spend much time on basic POSIX.1 functionality: *fork, exec, wait,* signals, pipes, and standard *read/write.*

When people mention POSIX.4, they often speak of POSIX.4a in the same breath. This is understandable, as the two standards were developed by the same working group. They are, however, separate standards, and POSIX.4a is only now completing the balloting process. This book addresses only POSIX.4.

The Rest of the Book

This book starts with an introduction to real-world programming, the POSIX standards, and the problems that POSIX does and doesn't solve.

The next several chapters are an introduction to solving real-world-oriented programming problems, with a special emphasis on UNIX- and POSIX-based solutions. While this book is primarily a guide to POSIX.4, often the solutions to your problems can be found in POSIX.1 or standard UNIX. In Chapter 2, *The POSIX Way,* I'll introduce you to the generalities of POSIX: how you determine what parts of POSIX are present on a system, how to test for compliance, and so forth. This chapter explains the basic operation of a POSIX system—*any* POSIX system—so you should read at least the first part before moving on to the more technical material. On the other hand, the end of Chapter 2 is a detailed discussion of the meaning of POSIX conformance, which may confuse you until you have some grounding in the technical substance of POSIX. You can skim this part, or skip it until later if you want.

Following Chapter 2, we get to the technical substance: Multiple Processes, Better Coordination, Scheduling, and I/O, in that order. Chapter 3, *The Basic of Real-Time: Multiple Tasks,* covers the basics of process creation and signals. Most of this is part of POSIX.1, not POSIX.4 (the exception is signal extensions that POSIX.4 provides—the SA_SIGINFO material). Process basics are required, though, before you can talk about process scheduling or interprocess coordination.

Chapter 4, *Better Coordination: Messages, Shared Memory, and Synchronization*, covers interprocess communication, using pipes and FIFOs (from POSIX.1), message queues, shared memory, and semaphores (from POSIX.4).

In Chapter 5, *On Time: Scheduling, Time, and Memory Locking*, we talk about ways to get things done on time: process priority scheduling, memory locking to prevent unwanted paging, and the clock and timer facilities that allow you to schedule alarms, check the time, and generally perform time-based processing.

Chapter 6, *I/O for the Real World*, covers the I/O enhancements of POSIX.4: synchronized I/O and asynchronous I/O. There's also a short requiem for an I/O enhancement that was kicked out of POSIX.4: real-time files. These would have allowed for contiguous and pre-allocated disk files; we'll discuss your options to achieve this sort of behavior, in the absence of a standard solution.

Finally, in Chapter 7, *Performance, or How to Choose an Operating System*, we'll talk about performance issues; the preceding chapters will have concentrated on functional behavior, ignoring the performance domain that is so critical for real-time applications.

Following the chapters, there are manual pages for all the functions and header files described by POSIX.4. These provide a concise (!) reference to POSIX.4, once you think you know what you're doing.

Throughout the book, I'll refer you to other tomes for more detail on subjects that are peripheral to the topic of discussion. There are complete references in the Bibliography.

Exercises and Sample Code

This book comes with exercises. The purpose of these is to get you thinking about the use of POSIX.4 for solving everyday real-world problems. A secondary purpose is to provide you with more example code. Code for many the exercises is included in the Appendix in the back.

Other code throughout the book is presented in snippet form, not usualy as complete, working programs. These code snippets are there to illustrate and motivate the text, and are not presented in complete form in the Appendix.

Typographical Conventions

The following font conventions are used in this book:

Italic   Names of functions, header names
Courier   Code examples

Acknowledgments

I fell into the POSIX world by accident, starting at Sun Microsystems. Thanks to them for lavishly supporting POSIX.4 work. The environment at Lynx Real-Time Systems allowed me to become POSIX.4 Man. I am still trying to recover from the experience. Thanks to Lynx for the prototype software on which the examples in this book were written and tested. Thanks, on a personal note, to the Bearded White Guys With Glasses for the camaraderie: Chris Lanier, Greg Seibert, Randy Hendry, and, although she has no beard, June Curtis, honorary B(WG)2. Stephe Walli at MKS, Mary Lynne Nielsen at the IEEE, and Hal Jespersen all provided invaluable help on POSIX mechanics and status; Mike Jones at Microsoft provided insight into the status of Windows NT. My reviewers provided invaluable insight; I thank Bob Goettge, Randy Hendry, Dan Hildebrand, David K. Hughes, Andy Oram, Jerry Peek, Claude-Henri Sicard, Stephe Walli, and Steve Watt. Thanks to Mike Loukides, for pointing out that I use "thing" and "stuff" an awful lot (among several billion other useful comments).

Clairemarie Fisher O'Leary copyedited the book and was the production manager, with the able assistance of Sheryl Avruch and Frank Willison. Chris Reilley created the figures, Jennifer Niederst created the interior design of the book, Lenny Muellner and Norm Walsh provided tools support and implemented the design, and Susan Reisler created the index.

PART

I

Programming for the Real World

CHAPTER

1

Introduction

This book is written to help people who are trying to use UNIX (or any other POSIX-supporting system) for real work.

Real work includes database systems, transaction managers, and navigation systems. It includes applications for automating a factory floor, as well as applications for controlling jet engines and your VCR, software controlling robots, the ATM from which you get cash, and telephone networks.

While UNIX has been a popular operating system, its applicability to the real world has been rather more problematic. Many vendors have made many attempts to add the features and performance that UNIX needs in order to be truly useful in the real world. These attempts are now coming to fruition with the availability of industrial-strength UNIX from major software vendors. With the increasing availability of these new features, UNIX is now capable of supporting true real-time, real-world applications. The question is, how do you use these new facilities for your real-world applications?

In the UNIX world, real-world functionality has come from two often contradictory camps: System V Release 4 UNIX (as described by the System V Interface Definition, or SVID), and recently, IEEE POSIX.4 (also known as PASC 1003.4). Other specifications, including COSE (Common Operating Software Environment), XPG4 (X/Open Portability Guide), FIPS 151-2 (Federal Information Processing Standard 151) and so forth, really are just calling out either SVR4 or POSIX functionality. This book concentrates on the features of POSIX.4 for a couple of reasons:

- POSIX.4 is newer than SVR4, and fewer people know about it. More to the point, there are no books about it.

- POSIX.4 has wider applicability than SVR4, since POSIX is not a UNIX standard *per se.*

1

Although I'll spend most of my time here touting POSIX.4, I'll also cover other possible solutions to real-world problems where they are available.

What's POSIX?

POSIX, the Portable Operating System Interface,[*] is an evolving, growing document that is being produced by the IEEE and standardized by ANSI and ISO. The goal of POSIX is the source-code portability of applications: in the best of al you to to move an application from one operating system to another by simply recompiling it. This goal is unattainable since most applications, especially the real-world ones, require more operating system support than you can find in any particular standard. However, POSIX has achieved a less apocalyptic version of this goal: reducing the amount of effort in a port. POSIX-conformant applications can be easily ported to systems as diverse as SVR4 UNIX, LynxOS and MVS.

"POSIX" refers to a couple of different things. The most important meaning of POSIX is the POSIX standards. These are the end products of the POSIX working groups. These groups, composed of computer vendors, applications writers, government representatives, and a modicum of hangers-on, meet quarterly in IEEE-sponsored meetings in exotic locales such as Parsippany and Utrecht. The overall POSIX working group is composed of many smaller groups with names like "POSIX-dot-something." For instance, POSIX.4 is the working group concerned with real-time operations. These working groups put out proposed standards, which are often eponymously named (The '.4 working group put out the '.4 proposed standard); however, this naming is just coincidental ('.4 also put out the '.13 proposal). So what you have is many small groups all working towards the standardization of their small (but crucially important) sectors of the universe.

As these small proposals pass balloting,[†] POSIX grows. The first such standard was POSIX.1, which specified many of the basic calls that UNIX programmers have come to expect. Several amendments to POSIX.1 have also been approved. POSIX.4, approved in September, 1993, is a set of real-time extensions to POSIX.1, and is the standard we are most concerned with here. This growth, though, results in additional complexity for you, the user of POSIX. You need to know which version of POSIX your system supports, in order to tell what features you have. Do you have the shiny, new, real-time features of September, 1993? Or are you stuck with the old, reliable basics of POSIX.1 (September, 1990)? Luckily, this information is encoded in header files and formal POSIX conformance statements, so you do not need to rely on some salesperson's word for what is actually in an operating system you may be considering buying. In Figure 1-1, you can see the basic structure of POSIX: mandatory parts, and extra optional behavior.

---

[*] And what's an OS without an "X" on the end of it?

[†] The ballot process is a standard mechanism the IEEE has set up for the adoption of standards.

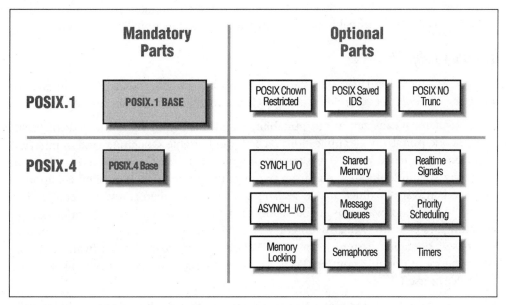

Figure 1-1. Mandatory and optional parts of POSIX.1 and POSIX.4

As POSIX grows, it becomes more and more useful; it also becomes more complex and harder to understand. The POSIX.1 facilities formed a nucleus of common operating system functions that could be used to create programs that were portable from one UNIX system to the next, and even to non-UNIX systems, like VMS, LynxOS, QNX, CTOS, MVS, and MPE/ix. As such, it's like the chassis of a car. POSIX.1 gives you portable versions of functions you need for writing applications, but there's little question that you need *more* than POSIX.1 for most applications. Now, a new chapter of the POSIX book has emerged: POSIX.4. POSIX.4 adds real-time (I like to call it real-world) functionality to the chassis of the car: shared memory, priority scheduling, message queues, synchronized I/O, and so forth. POSIX.4 is the wheels of the car. If you need POSIX.1, then you probably need POSIX.4, as well.

In a recent debate on the Internet, for instance, there was some question as to how usable POSIX is for "real work." The opinions went two ways. A bunch of the GNU tools (GCC, Emacs, etc.) are written for the POSIX.1 environment, as are the tools provided by Mortice Kern Systems for DOS and several other operating systems. Therefore, POSIX.1 in and of itself is useful, since these obviously useful programs can be built using only—or mostly—POSIX.1. The other opinion holds that editors and compilers do not constitute "real work." Various anti-free-software pejoratives get stirred into the mix, and the debate continues. However, I was intrigued to see that some folks share my feeling that there's more to computer programming than programming tools. I mean no disrespect to the people at MKS or the Free Software Foundation—the examples in this book were all written and tested using GCC, a real product if ever there was one. However, you have to admit that, at some point, computers are supposed to be used for something besides writing computer programs. For these applications, POSIX.1 probably does not provide all the functionality you need.

Is POSIX Useful?

"Real work" includes database systems, transaction managers, factory floor automation programs, jet engines controllers, etc. This is the real world! Is POSIX useful for it?

"Useful," here, means "an aid to portability," and this brings us to the goal of POSIX: source-code portability of applications. POSIX, the Portable Operating System Interface, is supposed to make it easier to write a program that you can easily move from one operating system to another, and from one machine to another. Portability is important because hardware lifetimes are decreasing at a rate faster than software lifetimes. That means that old software has to be made to run on new hardware. In addition, old operating systems are regularly retired. Who'd have thought Sun would throw out their BSD-based operating system in favor of Solaris? Given changing hardware and software, the more portable your applications are, the more successful they're likely to be. So, is POSIX useful?

Well, you know what *I'm* going to say. Of course it's useful! Nothing could be *more* useful than POSIX! POSIX is the best thing to come along since high level languages! POSIX is the mythical silver bullet!*

Well, maybe it's not all that. POSIX is an incremental step towards a standard, useful operating system interface. If you use "the POSIX way," as Don Lewine puts it, for those things which POSIX specifies, then they will be portable from one POSIX system to the next. Until POSIX specifies a "way" for all things, it won't provide a total portability solution. And who are we kidding? Total portability is probably unattainable, and certainly undesirable for a lot of programs. Portability entails generality and flexibility, and generality and flexibility cost time and space. For any given problem, a non-portable program is going to be smaller and faster, right? When you're building your applications, you need to balance the need for portability against the need for reasonable efficiency. In all likelihood, every program built for the real world is going to have some non-portable component. That's okay! By using the POSIX way for the *rest* of your application, you avoid having to look at that part. Portability becomes easier, not trivial—that's the point.

---

* "No Silver Bullet: Essence and Accidents of Software Engineering," Dr. Fred Brooks, in *IEEE Computer*, April 1987. In this article, Dr. Brooks describes the mess we're in, software-wise, and how we software engineers can get out of it. He didn't mention POSIX, but I'm sure that was accidental, not essential...

The Limits to POSIX

Another recent thread of discussion concerns the suspicion that POSIX (the working group) is out of control, producing more and more ill-considered standardese at a snowballing rate that will inevitably lead to an unusable mass of documentation.

There is some substance to this fear. Certain POSIX working groups have on occasion veered off into some fairly treacherous weeds, like language-independent specifications and poorly-planned profiling expeditions. My personal opinion is that a lot of the later efforts of the POSIX.4 working group itself were pretty esoteric and really not ready to be standardized—much of the POSIX.4b (Yet More Real-Time) and POSIX.13 (Real-Time Profiles) proposals, in particular.

However, I don't see much evidence that the working groups are going to go hog-wild and inflict a bunch of useless functionality on the world. More likely, as the working group finds itself doing weirder and weirder work, the people doing said work will find better things to do, and the balloting groups will find themselves either unwilling to approve the results, or too bored to proceed with the ballot at all. In other words, I think POSIX (the working group) is bound to snuff itself out after its real useful work is done.

When people raise this "out-of-control" fear, though, they usually mention POSIX.4—my group, my standard—as a prime example. To this, I can only say they're wrong. Real-time has been around for a while, and the functionality you'll find is not particularly bizarre. It's based on real experience with existing operating systems, although these are often real-time systems, not traditional UNIX boxes. Much of this *is* new to a standard UNIX system, and I suppose that's why we hear the occasional sour grapes from UNIX purists.

The Grand Renumbering

One example of the advancing senility of the POSIX working group may be found in The Grand Renumbering. After years of work on POSIX.4, POSIX.6 and so forth, the working group decided to renumber a great many of the documents. The documents that were amendments to 1003.1 (POSIX.1) were given numbers that built upon the "1003.1" prefix. So POSIX.4 became 1003.1b, POSIX.6 became 1003.1e, etc.[*] I suppose the new numbering makes it easier to understand the published documents, since now all the "operating system" documents will be 1003.1-something, all the commands are 1003.2-something, and so on. Remember this: wherever you see a 1003.1x, it used to be POSIX.y. 1003.1x numbers are strictly a result of The Grand Renumbering, and are an attempt to confuse you.

---

[*] It was called POSIX.4—IEEE 1003.4—throughout its development and balloting. As a result of The Grand Renumbering, it is now also known as POSIX 1003.1b-1993. For the remainder of the book, I'm going to refer to POSIX.1 and POSIX.4 because those terms are much easier to differentiate than "1003.1-1990" and "1003.1b-1993." They're also easier to say.

Doing More the POSIX Way

So what can we do "the POSIX way"? Until recently, only very basic and general operations were specified by POSIX.1, the first edition of POSIX. These included mechanisms for process creation and demise (*fork, exec, exit, wait*), signals, basic I/O and terminal handling, and some other miscellaneous basics. POSIX.1 is essential. It is the basis on which the rest of POSIX resides. Without POSIX.1 there is nothing. POSIX.1 is necessary, but not sufficient for real-world applications.

POSIX.4 (the *Real-Time Extensions to POSIX*) was approved in September, 1993. It is an amendment and addition to POSIX.1, providing additional facilities necessary for real-world applications. These include process scheduling, access to time, a couple of interprocess communication mechanisms, and enhanced I/O operations.

Another standard, POSIX.4a (renumbered as 1003.1c) provides the ability to run multiple, concurrent *threads* of execution within a single POSIX process. The 1003.1c standard is completing balloting as this book goes to press, and should be an IEEE standard within the year. POSIX.4a is a different standard than POSIX.4, and discussion of threads would fill up another book.

POSIX and Its Amendments

POSIX is both a set of standards and an ongoing effort of standards development. As such, it can sometimes be unclear what we're talking about when we refer to POSIX, because there are so many things that go by that name! Table 1-1 is a quick listing of most of the proposed standards, either in progress or approved as of this writing. Obviously the status of the standards will change as time goes by. This snaphot is as of April, 1994. Several of the documents (like POSIX.4) have been renumbered to be part of the POSIX.1 (1003.1) standard. For these documents, I've mentioned the new number.

Table 1-1: Status of POSIX standards as of April, 1994

Standard	What is It?	Status as of April, 1994
POSIX.1 (1003.1-1990) (ISO 9945-1 (1990))	Basic OS interfaces	Approved (IEEE and ISO)
POSIX.1a	Miscellaneous extensions	Completing ballot
POSIX.2	Commands (sh and the like)	Approved (IEEE and ISO)
POSIX.3	Test methods	Approved by IEEE
POSIX.4 (1003.1b-1993)	Real-time extensions	Approved by IEEE
POSIX.4a (1003.1c-1994)	Threads extensions	Completing ballot

Table 1–1: *Status of POSIX standards as of April, 1994 (continued)*

Standard	What is It?	Status as of April, 1994
POSIX.4b (1003.1d)	More real-time extensions	In ballot
POSIX.5	ADA binding to POSIX.1	Approved by IEEE
POSIX.6 (1003.1e)	Security extensions	In ballot
POSIX.7	System administration	In ballot
POSIX.8 (1003.1f)	Transparent file access (Network)	In ballot
POSIX.9	FORTRAN-77 binding to POSIX.1	Approved by IEEE
POSIX.10	Supercomputing profile	In ballot
POSIX.11	Transaction processing	Project withdrawn
POSIX.12 (1003.1g)	Protocol-independent communication (sockets)	Completing ballot
POSIX.13	Real-time profiles (Subsets of POSIX)	In ballot
POSIX.14	Multiprocessor profile	Early drafts
POSIX.15	Batch/supercomputer extensions	In ballot
POSIX.16	Language-independent POSIX.1	Early drafts
POSIX.17 (IEEE 1224.2)	Directory/name services (Network)	Approved by IEEE
POSIX.18	Basic POSIX system profile	In ballot
POSIX.19	FORTRAN-90 binding to POSIX.1	Project withdrawn
POSIX.20	Ada binding to POSIX.4	Early drafts
POSIX.21	Distributed real-time	Early drafts

The POSIX Environment

The documents comprising POSIX together define a computing environment that you can count on being present for your programs to use. The technical definition of what it means to "be POSIX" is currently a topic of debate, and is getting more obscure by the minute. The confusion arises because there's a market share for any vendor who can attach POSIX to their product, which means that different people mean different things when they say "we're POSIX compliant." We'll discuss what it means to "be POSIX" in Chapter 2, *The POSIX Way*, since the issues are complex and you need to be aware of them. For now, suffice it to say that POSIX refers to a *UNIX-like, standard* computing environment. We'll elaborate on each of these features, then we'll talk briefly about a few things that POSIX *isn't*.

POSIX Is Like UNIX

Because POSIX is based on UNIX, the solutions we bring to bear on our technical problems will be based on UNIX. We'll be forking processes and sending signals, reading with *read* and writing with *write*. UNIX has generally had a problem with the sorts of real-world problems we'll discuss below, so the real-time features of POSIX may be unfamiliar. That's another reason for this book; the facilities of POSIX.4 are not as familiar as those in other parts of POSIX.

POSIX Is Standard

The second characteristic of the environment is that it is standard, and based on common practice. Those of you who've been following, or been immersed in, the UNIX wars between Berkeley and AT&T, and later OSF, and UI (and later, Berkeley and AT&T and OSF and UI and Novell and X/Open and Ted and Alice), are probably scratching your heads cynically now. "What does it mean to be standard?" There are lots of so-called standard UNIX versions, and none of them are the same. What makes POSIX any different?

There are two reasons I see why POSIX will become more of a standard than the other contenders. The first reason is pure goodness and light: POSIX has been developed by independent, industry-wide committees with representatives of all sides, including Berkeley, AT&T, OSF, and UI, as well as operating systems producers and consumers. POSIX was developed using a consensus process and balloted among all interested parties. And POSIX is an ISO standard that is not owned by anyone in particular, so no one gets any fast-track advantage if a procurement calls for POSIX.

Yeah, yeah, yeah. If you ask me, the real reason is that governments buy a lot of computers. Governments specify "open systems" (meaning UNIX) and conformance to a thing called The FIPS (FIPS-151, an American government shopping list for what ought to be in a computer system the government buys). The FIPS is an American document, but other countries have their own documents which are basically the same (Canada's is called TBITS 7.1; other countries point to X/Open's XPG4, which in turn points to POSIX). The FIPSes of the world specify POSIX. So guess what Big OS Vendor X (and Small OS Vendor Y) is going to support if it wants to do business with the governments? You guessed it. POSIX allows any vendor to play in the government market, and that's important.

Whatever the reason, you can already see POSIX becoming the common nucleus of just about any UNIX system you look at. As of this writing, UNIX SVR4 specifies POSIX.1 facilities already, as well as several portions of POSIX.4, and claims it will evaluate the rest of POSIX.4 when it becomes available. Today, you can get a FIPS-certified POSIX.1 on Digital's VMS and IBM's MVS (VMS, in fact, was the *first* system to pass the FIPS 151-2) systems. You can get POSIX.2 support now for DOS, VMS, MVS, HP-RTE, CTOS, and a host of other non-UNIX operating systems. You can get POSIX.1 on UNIX boxes, machines running LynxOS and QNX, and many other vendors are claiming POSIX Real Soon Now. Even Windows NT, the *bête noire* of the UNIX world, has been certified against FIPS 151-2.

POSIX runs on nearly all the UNIX variants, and it runs on lots of non-UNIX systems. I maintain that POSIX will become the standard operating system interface. And for maximum portability, that's what you want to write your application for.

The Applications Are Varied

So, what are these applications that POSIX.4 is so good for? What are the real-world problems that POSIX.4 was built to address?

There are a lot of different kinds of applications that can take advantage of the POSIX.4 interfaces. POSIX.4 was built, however, to address the requirements of real-time applications. These are the applications where the *timing* of the answer, not just the answer itself, is an integral part of the correctness of the application. We can talk about real-time applications in a number of ways. We can split them up by the requirements the application has, or by the sort of application it is.

Real-time applications fall into two broad categories: hard real-time and soft real-time. Hard real-time is the world of metal, speed, and danger: software controlling steel mills, jet engines, precision medical equipment, and electric bullet trains. In hard real-time, a late answer is of no use at all. It doesn't do you any good if the signal that cuts fuel to the jet engine arrives a millisecond after the engine has exploded. In fact, a late response may make a bad situation even worse.

In soft real-time, by contrast, there's more gradation. The answer that is on time is definitely the best one, but a late answer still has some value, so long as it's not too late. Online databases generally fall into this category, such as the software running program trades on the stock exchange or the software that runs your credit card through "the machine." The faster, the better. You might get annoyed waiting for your credit card to be approved, but nobody is going to die if it takes thirty seconds instead of fifteen.

Most real-time applications, whether hard or soft, have a couple of common characteristics. First, speed is of the essence. Second, these applications tend to be in touch with the real world, through robot arms in the steel mill or the magnetic stripe on your credit card. Third, real-time applications tend to do a lot of juggling, controlling many activities at once. When you think about it, most real-time applications are naturally concurrent because they must conform to the natural parallelism of the world outside the computer.

Sample Real-Time Applications

I describe a few typical real-time applications below, some hard real-time and the others soft. We'll use these application "templates" in the rest of the book to explain how the functions of POSIX.4 might be best used. In the figures, the boxes indicate processes, and the arrows are lines of communication or coordination.

Real-time control loops

A very common real-time application is the software control of a particular piece of hardware. In this application, shown in Figure 1-2, input from a sensor, together with the past state of the device under control, are combined into a control output to the device. The application operates in a loop, continually sensing input, computing, and outputting control to the device. Usually a control-loop application falls into the hard real-time category: you must provide control output to the device in a timely fashion, or the device will go nuts. For example, consider a program controlling something robotic, such as a motor or something which must be constantly "steered" lest it, literally, crash. I saw another example recently that you may be familiar with: a SCSI controller chip. This particular chip is used for controlling the disk and tape drives on a workstation-class machine, and it had the unfortunate characteristic of going out to lunch if you didn't keep up a steady stream of conversation with it. In other words, the SCSI controller on this machine needs to be controlled in a timely fashion—a perfect example of a hard real-time application inside your workstation! Both the robot and the SCSI controller are hard real-time applications, requiring constant, on-time responses.

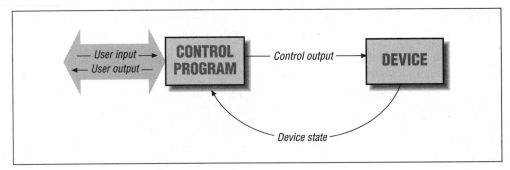

Figure 1-2. Real-time control loop—one device

Not all control-loop applications must be so stringent, though. In a video game, for example, input comes from a variety of knobs and buttons attached to the machine, and the application's job is to combine these inputs with the previous state of the game to determine a next state (the sounds and lights) in a timely fashion. In this case, the world's not going to come to an end if a few noises are delayed, but it makes for a better game if everything happens on time.

The application pictured above requires only one process, since there is only one input to be received and one output to be generated. However, if you add multiple inputs and outputs, as shown in Figure 1-3 operating at different frequencies and with differing response requirements, you quickly come to the point where you need to split processing into multiple processes for your own sanity. This example comes close to describing what a real, real-time application might look like.

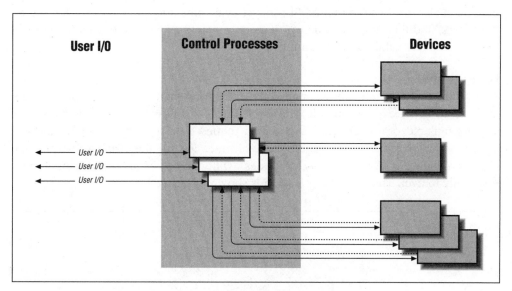

Figure 1–3. Real-time control loop—multiple devices

Terminals and server

The control loop real-time application described above is presumably hard real-time: you must provide outputs to the controlled devices at the right times, or the system will fail. Our next example, shown in Figure .4 is a soft real-time application: a server of some sort, communicating online with users at terminals. In this application, a slow response is not the end of the world, although it is to be avoided if at all possible.

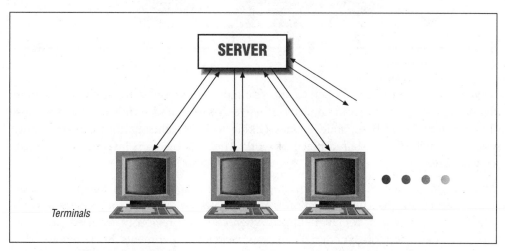

Figure 1–4. Terminals and server

Terminals and a server separate an application into two very distinct parts, which communicate with each other. In this sort of application, the server is pretty much eternal, existing at all times. The terminals, in contrast, will come and go as humans log on, do their work, and then log off again. An important point to make here is the concept of separate entities "talking" to one another.

Database servers

Abstracting the example above, there may be more than one server process, for instance, to better exploit multiple processors or disks. In this example, the "server" is actually multiple processes, each servicing a request from one of the terminals. The servers must coordinate their actions to avoid messing up the database. Again, the client terminals are more transitory processes, while the server processes hang around essentially forever. This sort of application is shown in Figure 1-5.

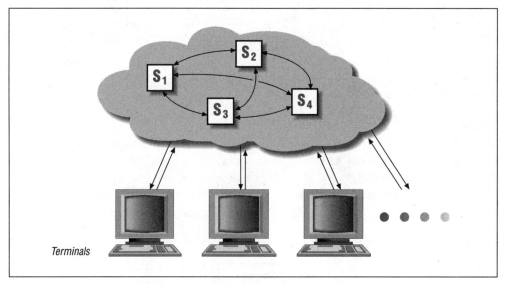

Figure 1–5. Multiple servers

Servers of this sort often cooperate and communicate amongst themselves in a more free-form way than the communication between server and terminal. That's because they are not so much separate entities talking to each other as they are one entity, working together on a shared piece of work. Their cooperation involves sharing data very closely.

Another important sort of real-time application is data acquisition and replay. Data acquisition means that the application is storing data somewhere as it receives it, probably for later analysis or replay. Replay is when you use previously-acquired data as an input for some sort of experiment analysis. Science experiments often involve data acquisition and replay, as do multimedia systems (video and audio capture and playback). Acquisition and replay generally lean towards the *hard* side of real-time. They require I/O performance and control which can stress the capabilities of many systems, especially standard UNIX systems. We'll see how the POSIX.4 standard aids in this area when we get to Chapter 6, *I/O for the Real World.*

The examples presented above represent a wide range of applications: video games, robots, databases, online terminal systems, data acquisition systems, and multimedia systems. The applications have a number of things in common.

The Problems Are the Same

Real-time applications and their real-world brethren face the same problems as other programs: algorithm design numeric accuracy, user interface design and so on. However, real-world applications also face completely different kinds of problems that arise from their dealings with the real world.

Problems Technical...

If you're trying to solve real-time sorts of problems, you are dealing with some fairly thorny technical issues. Here's a short list of some of the things you might be wrestling with:

How to Do a Lot of Things at the Same Time

In real-world applications, you often find yourself doing a lot of things at once. In a robotics application, there are a bunch of motors that have to be independently controlled, sensors to be polled, and so forth. In avionics, you have to keep an eye on the fuel mix, the engines, the heading, and oh yes, you also have to check on what the pilot wants the plane to do. In a database system, the complexity comes from controlling the access of multiple users to the data.

There are a couple of ways to get many things done at once. The most general and robust way is to use a dedicated computer for each one. Failing that, you can run multiple virtual computers, or processes, on your one computer. Each process can independently deal with its own little piece of the problem. Of course, since there is really only one computer, you need to deal with the fact that these processes have to be scheduled so that they all get their jobs done on time. You also need to worry about the processes stepping on each others' data.

What Time is It?

Getting things done on time means knowing what time it is, and being able to set things up so that something happens at some specific point in time.

Deadlines

Once you have access to the time, you need to worry about those multiple processes. You need to ensure that every deadline your application has is met, in both the average and the worst case. This is where scheduling comes in. Scheduling is the art (or science; it depends who you ask) of getting things to happen on time. It's hard. Sometimes it's impossible. If it's impossible, you'd like to know that ahead of time, too!

How to Get Things Done Predictably On Time

Real-time means time, first and foremost. Things need to be done, and they need to be done on time *every time*. You wouldn't be comfortable if, when you pressed on your car's brake pedal, there was only a 95% chance that the brake processor would react in time!

Making Sure the Important Task Gets the Resource

Related to scheduling is the question of general resource allocation. Normally you think of scheduling as how the processors get multiplexed among multiple processes. Computers are made up of more than processors, though. There are also memory, disk drives, peripheral devices, and so forth, and they all need to be scheduled. It doesn't help to give the most important process one of the resources it needs (e.g., the CPU) if some other process is still hogging another required resource (e.g., the disk drive). Making sure the important process has what it needs when it needs it is another difficult issue.

How to Cooperate

When you are using these dedicated virtual machines to solve the various parts of your real-world problem, you need to worry about how the machines cooperate with each other. They don't just all go off on their own without talking to each other. They need to share data, coordinate their actions with each other, and, in general, let each other know what's going on. How do you do that? Do you use signals? Pipes? Message queues? Shared memory? Semaphores? Mutexes? Condition variables? Rendezvous? Monitors? Each solution to the cooperation problem has its uses, and each solution is poorly suited to other uses. Each solution also carts along its own share of problems, for instance:

- **How to avoid dropping signals**: If you decide to use signals to communicate between processes, you need to worry about how those signals are queued, and whether signals can be lost on the way.

- **How to avoid overflowing message queues**: Likewise, message queues can overflow. What happens then?

How to Do I/O in a High-Performance, Predictable Way

Real-world applications make a lot of demands on a computer's I/O system. You want to get your data in from, or out to, the disks and data collection devices as fast as possible, yet with some sort of predictability. Going the other way, if some unimportant process has I/O going on, you don't want it to get in the way of your most important process running. How do you do all this?

These are all hard problems. Coincidentally, they are also all things that standard, garden-variety UNIX has generally had a very difficult time doing. When POSIX.4 provides interfaces to address these issues, therefore, don't be surprised if the facility doesn't look like anything that has existed in UNIX before. Sometimes, the facility is very familiar. Sometimes it's not.

...And Logistical

Aside from the strictly technical issues of how to get your application running correctly in Environment X and on Machine Y, there are some higher-level, logistical issues relating to your application.

How Can I Make My Real-Time Application Portable?

Real-time applications tend to have a fairly long life, either because they are part of a physical plant that doesn't go away, or for political and bureaucratic reasons. This fact, coupled with the steadily decreasing life cycles of computer hardware, means that porting your real-time application from the original platform to another platform is something you will likely have to do. Portability frees you from vendors' proprietary solutions and allows you to make the best hardware choice for your solution; you don't have to contend with artificial constraints like "will the software run on this hardware?"

Portability, Performance, and Determinism

Portability of code is tricky, especially since every vendor in the world is out to make you think their system is portable and standards-conformant without actually having to do all that work. There are hidden secrets and gotchas out there just itching to break your code when you move it from system X to system Y.

In real time, the timing dimension makes this problem even stickier. Despite all the calculations and scheduling theory, you know your real-time application meets its timing constraints on a given system because you've run the application on that system. Another box, another set of performance problems. How can you easily achieve real-time performance that will port from one machine to the next? That's a whole other monkey wrench thrown into the works for you.

How do I Compare Computer Systems?

Finally, from a procurement standpoint, you need to be able to make apples-and-apples comparisons of systems. This is a realm where real-time has lagged behind the rest of the computer industry. Although their metrics are still pretty awful, workstation vendors can at least quote the same SPECmarks and Whetstones. In real time, however, you have to compare one vendor's average interrupt latency with another's worst-case interrupt dispatch; one vendor's context switching time with another's task dispatch time. Given this, how can you hope to make a fair comparison of various real-time systems?

Some Solutions to These Problems

POSIX.4 provides portable solutions to the problems mentioned above. From the technical side, POSIX.4 has priority-preemptive scheduling, usually considered necessary for deterministic, real-time response. POSIX.4 specifies memory locking, to avoid the non-determinism that is inevitable when some part of your memory can get swapped out to disk. There are higher-resolution timers and improvements to signals, so you can use time and signal mechanisms that improve on those of POSIX.1. There's the ability to do I/O asynchronously, and to bypass the system buffer cache for guaranteed I/O completion. In the area of interprocess communication, shared memory, message queues, and semaphores are specified.

From the logistical side, POSIX.4's advantages are less cut-and-dried. Because POSIX.4 facilities are portable, the procurement question is made simpler. You can compare one POSIX system to the next, rather than comparing a VMS box to a UNIX box to an MVS box. And, in doing things "the POSIX way," you can increase the portability of your application. However, POSIX.4 does not give you any performance guarantees; you'll have to check performance yourself. Of course, since you're comparing POSIX systems, you can at least compare apples and apples; but you still have to make the effort yourself. Vendors are still going to try and play games with benchmarks to make themselves look better than everyone else. This is expected.

The thorniest logistical problem is that POSIX.4 is structured, unlike POSIX.1, as a set of options. When a vendor trumpets, "we have POSIX!" it means, "we have POSIX.1, and some (possibly empty) subset of POSIX.4!" And when a vendor proclaims, "we have POSIX.4!" it is pretty meaningless. Just about every facility in POSIX.4 is a separate option. Luckily, it's easy to tell what parts any particular vendor has, by looking in system headers or in the POSIX Conformance Statement for the operating system. Again, though, you have to look. You have to be a crafty consumer: ask the questions, kick the tires.

What POSIX Does Not Do

POSIX won't solve all your problems. Heck, it won't even solve all your computer-related problems! Here are a few things that you might have been wondering about: It sounds obvious when written down here, but some expect that code written for one POSIX system will be immediately and trivially portable to another POSIX system. Just press the F1 key and a new version of your application pops out, right? Wrong. First of all, POSIX does not provide interfaces for all the things you may want to do in your application: windowing, networking, and other facilities are either not standardized yet, or not planned to be standardized in POSIX. Second, POSIX is not an airtight specification. There are options, implementation-defined behaviors, and undefined behaviors, all of which your application may rely on. Other machines will differ in those aspects. And finally, there are assumptions built into POSIX, and probably built into your application, that will make it non-portable. You can use portable interfaces to write non-portable code. A typical example is an implicit reliance on process scheduling order. Write your application on a uniprocessor and it works fine. Try and run it on a multiprocessor—it explodes!* Given what I've said above, it should be even more obvious that POSIX is not a binary compatibility standard. POSIX is for the *source-code* portability of applications. There are POSIX systems running on 80×86s, SPARCs, MIPSes, Precisions, Motorolas, IBM 370s, and so forth. You're *at least* going to recompile your code to run it on all those machines. Finally, as mentioned above, POSIX doesn't standardize everything. I already said that POSIX doesn't address window systems. Device characteristics are not standardized; neither are the vagaries of machine booting and system configuration, nor development environment. As you use these standard systems, you'll see more and more that they are not all the same, by any stretch of the imagination. The trick is to use the standards when they're available, and encapsulate the code where you require non-standard features. It will help to use additional standards outside of POSIX: X and Motif, for instance, TCP/IP or RPC for networking, SCSI devices for I/O.

But enough discussing what POSIX can't do. Let's dive into some real issues: figuring out what any particular POSIX implementation does, or doesn't support. That's what we cover in Chapter 2, *The POSIX Way*.

---

* That said, you can achieve pretty easy portability if you work very hard at it. The Free Software Foundation people have worked hard at it, and as a result, some of their software is quite easily, often automatically, portable (Emacs and GNU C are the examples I'm thinking of here). But still, it's often a non-trivial task to bring up GNU software on a new machine.

2

The POSIX Way

This chapter is a brief, overall introduction to the structure of POSIX on a running operating system. We'll cover what is present in all POSIX systems, what functionality is optional, and how you can check for what a particular system supports.

You may check for the presence or absence of POSIX features either when your application is compiled, or when it runs. In embedded real-time environments, compile-time checks are generally sufficient, because you control the exact operating system that will be loaded into the embedded machine. You basically check that the OS provider has the necessary components, and then build your application without run-time checks. Run-time checks are useful in those cases where it's possible that the underlying machine environment is going to change. A desktop UNIX environment, where the kernel may be easily reconfigured, is a good example of such an environment.

What POSIX Is

POSIX is a standard to allow applications to be *source-code portable* from one system to another. On a system conforming to a particular version of POSIX (as measured by the test suite it passed), you should be able to just compile and run those applications which use the POSIX (and only the POSIX) functions.[*] That, in turn, dictates what POSIX is. On any given system, POSIX support consists of:

- **A Compilation System**: A compiler, basically. Real live POSIX systems are supposed to support a standard language. For our purposes, we'll assume that the language is ANSI C. In fact, vendors may support K&R[†] C in addition to or maybe even instead of ANSI C. In any event, your system has to have some way of compiling

---

[*] A real application is not generally going to be this portable; it's bound to need *something* that the standards do not provide.

[†] Kernighan and Ritchie: *C Classic*.

code, namely, a compiler and the proper options to get POSIX support linked into your application. For instance, under LynxOS one invokes the compiler (GNU C) with **gcc -mposix1b**, and under QNX the POSIX.4 facilities are available by default. Using the compilation system in the approved fashion makes the POSIX environment available to your program. This application consists of *headers* used when compiling source code into object code, and *libraries* used when linking objects into executables.

- **Headers**: A set of headers that defines the POSIX interface supported on the particular system. These are usually files in */usr/include*, but they could be elsewhere, especially when you're cross-developing (building programs on one machine with the intention of running them on another, totally different machine); they might not even be files in the traditional sense. All you really need to know is that a line like #include <unistd.h> will include the information from that header into your application, if you use the compiler the way you're supposed to. Of course, if you actually need to *look* at a header (I find the code to be the ultimate documentation, personally), you will want to know where the header files really are. That information should be available from your vendor.

- **Libraries**: Libraries are pre-compiled, vendor-supplied objects that implement the POSIX functionality for you. The libraries are linked into your application when you build it, or in the case of dynamically-shared libraries, when you run the program. Usually, you won't need to inspect a library, however, you may want to know *which* libraries are being used to build your application, and *in what order* they are included, in case your application won't link for some reason. Generally this won't be necessary unless you're trying to do something tricky. You might also want to see what is in a particular library. An archiver tool like *ar* and a symbol-table utility like *nm* are useful in such instances. Both tools are part of the development environment option described in POSIX.2 (1003.2-1992).

- **A Run-Time System**: Once you've built your program, the run-time, or operating system, allows you to run your application. For most of you UNIX folks, the run-time system is the same system under which you built the application. You compile the application and then you run it, just like that. However, it's important to realize that you may compile your application in one place and run it in an entirely different environment. Especially in the real-time world, it's common to build an application in a more user-friendly environment, such as SunOS on a SPARC or HP-UX on a Precision machine—or even MS-DOS (everything's relative). Once the application is built, it is then *downloaded* to a target machine running the run-time system. This scenario is shown in Figure 2-1. The real run-time system is often a very light-weight, bare-bones environment, with few amenities (or none). This target may be another workstation-class machine, a VME board in a nuclear accelerator, or a PC embedded in a hospital bed. The distinction between compilation environment and run-time environment is crucial, because often the code you build will not be run on the machine you build it on.

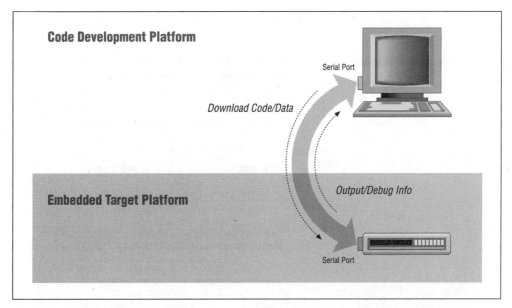

Figure 2-1. Cross development

Now that we know how POSIX support is going to be structured, we can move on to the contents of a particular POSIX system. Different systems support different levels of POSIX functionality. It is important that you know what all vendors *must* support, what's optional, and how you can determine what a particular vendor has.

POSIX has taken care to encapsulate most of its various options within header file constants and features you can test from a program. Using the features described below, you can automatically query a system for its degree and quality of POSIX support, as shown in Figure 2-2.

POSIX Is Options

As I mentioned before, POSIX is not a single standard. It is several separate standards, corresponding to different parts of a computer system. There are standards for the OS interface to programs, for different languages, like ADA and FORTRAN, for user commands, and for test methods. For this book, we're only concerned with the programmatic OS interface, and we're only worried about it in C. But even within this hunk o' POSIX, there are separate, optional parts.

Prix Fixe to the Chinese Menu

So what do you have on your POSIX system? Originally, POSIX was a pretty monolithic chunk of standardese. The first POSIX standard, POSIX.1, is a set of functionality that pretty much *all* has to be present before a vendor can claim conformance. POSIX.1

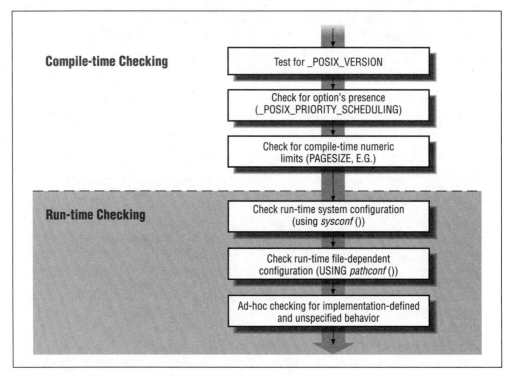

Figure 2–2. POSIX conformance checking—basic outline

defines basic, required operations that all operating systems need in order to be useful. Other POSIX standards extend this basic functionality.

The only optional parts of POSIX.1 are capabilities that were present in some UNIX systems, but not in others. The basic, monolithic chunk is still at the core of any POSIX system, and you can count on it being there. The minor optional pieces are listed in Table 2.1. (I'll explain what the option names mean and how to look for them in the next section, "Compile-Time Checking.")

Table 2–1: The Menu for POSIX.1 Functionality

Option Name	Functionality
_POSIX_JOB_CONTROL	The ability to suspend and resume process groups *setpgid, tcsetpgrp, tcgetpgrp*
_POSIX_CHOWN_RESTRICTED	Who can do a *chown*, and how they can do it, are more restrictive than usual
_POSIX_SAVED_IDS	Processes maintain a "shadow," or saved *set-user-id* and *set-group-id*. Semantics of *fork, kill, setuid, setgid* are somewhat affected.

Table 2-1: The Menu for POSIX.1 Functionality (continued)

Option Name	Functionality
_POSIX_NO_TRUNC	Overlong pathnames generate an error, rather than being silently truncated. An extra error condition is introduced for functions taking pathnames as arguments.
_POSIX_VDISABLE	The ability to disable some terminal special characters.
NGROUPS_MAX	The presence of supplementary group IDs, per process, which can be used to determine file access permissions. *getgroups*, a mandatory function, returns 0 unless there are supplementary groups. In any event, *setgroups* is not defined by POSIX.1.

The option names are called *feature test macros* in POSIX terminology because you use them to test for features. Actually, they are preprocessor constants (#defines) you can test for in your program in order to determine what is on your system. More on this in the next section. As you can see, the options present in POSIX.1 are tiny, referring almost exclusively to fringe behavior of the system.

POSIX.4 on the other hand, is not considered to be basic functionality that all systems need in order to be useful (regardless of my personal opinion). Therefore, POSIX.4 is structured as a set of well-defined options that a vendor can support, or not. The only parts of POSIX.4 that aren't optional are some additions to the basic POSIX.1 signal mechanism. Table 2-2 lists the POSIX.4 options:

Table 2-2: The Menu for POSIX.4 Functionality

Option Name	Functionality
Not Optional	Real-time, queued signals (SA_SIGINFO, SIGRTMIN, SIGRTMAX)
_POSIX_REALTIME_SIGNALS	Additional signal functions: *sigwaitinfo, sigtimedwait, sigqueue*
_POSIX_PRIORITY_SCHEDULING	Process scheduling control: *sched_setparam, sched_getparam, sched_setscheduler, sched_getscheduler, sched_yield, sched_get_priority_max, sched_get_priority_min, sched_rr_get_interval*
_POSIX_TIMERS	Clocks and timers: *clock_settime, clock_gettime, clock_getres, timer_create, timer_delete, timer_settime, timer_gettime, timer_getoverrun, nanosleep*
_POSIX_ASYNCHRONOUS_IO	Asynchronous I/O: *aio_read, aio_write, lio_listio, aio_suspend, aio_cancel, aio_error, aio_return, aio_fsync* (if and only if _POSIX_SYNCHRONIZED_IO)

Table 2-2: The Menu for POSIX.4 Functionality (continued)

Option Name	Functionality
_POSIX_PRIORITIZED_IO	Prioritized asynchronous I/O: modifies asynchronous I/O queueing.
_POSIX_SYNCHRONIZED_IO	Guarantees that a file's data is always out on disk: *fdatasync, msync* (if and only if _POSIX_MAPPED_FILES), *aio_fsync* (if and only if _POSIX_ASYNCHRONOUS_IO), additions to *open* and *fcntl*
_POSIX_FSYNC	The *fsync* function
_POSIX_MAPPED_FILES	Files mapped as memory: *mmap, munmap, ftruncate, msync* (if and only if _POSIX_SYNCHRONIZED_IO)
_POSIX_MEMLOCK	Lock all memory to avoid paging/swapping: *mlockall, munlockall*
_POSIX_MEMLOCK_RANGE	Lock memory ranges: *mlock, munlock*
_POSIX_MEMORY_PROTECTION	The ability to set memory protections: *mprotect*
_POSIX_MESSAGE_PASSING	Message Queues: *mq_open, mq_close, mq_unlink, mq_send, mq_receive, mq_notify, mq_setattr, mq_getattr*
_POSIX_SEMAPHORES	Counting Semaphores: *sem_init, sem_destroy, sem_open, sem_close, sem_unlink, sem_wait, sem_trywait, sem_post, sem_getvalue*
_POSIX_SHARED_MEMORY_OBJECTS	Shared Memory: *mmap, munmap, shm_open, shm_close, shm_unlink, ftruncate*

As you can see, there are a lot of choices when it comes to POSIX.4, and a vendor can legitimately say that it complies with POSIX.4 by telling you that all the options are unavailable in a standard way. Aside from the abuses of marketing hype, this is actually pretty valuable. Ideally, even non-real-time systems would comply with POSIX.4 (and all the other POSIXes); if you ask for a real-time feature it will tell you, "Sorry, no can do," in some standard way. The problem now is, how do you determine what your vendor gives you?

Compile-Time Checking

If you control the operating system environment in which your application is going to run, then you can check an operating system's POSIX support at compile time, either from code in your application or in a totally separate conformance-checking application that you run at the same time. A generic conformance checker is a useful program because it's not tied to a particular application.

Each optional piece of POSIX comes with a constant which defines its existence, and perhaps other symbols which define its size and shape. Existence is defined in *<unistd.h>*, and the numeric parameters (size and shape) for each option are given in *<limits.h>*. We can determine what we need to know by looking in these header files.

If you like reading header files, that's fine. Since they are header files, though, we can take the easier route and write a program that does our checking for us.

_POSIX_C_SOURCE and _POSIX_SOURCE

Since every system supports more than just POSIX, you need some way to tell your system that you are using the POSIX definitions for your application. To do this, you define a symbol (kind of a reverse feature-test macro) that tells the system you are compiling POSIX source code. This symbol is called _POSIX_C_SOURCE, and you give it a value that indicates which revision of POSIX you are conforming to. For instance, for the definitions of POSIX.4 (approved in September, 1993), you'd say:

```
#define _POSIX_C_SOURCE 199309
```

This definition tells your system that you want the POSIX definitions that were in effect for the September, 1993 version of POSIX. You don't care about POSIX work that happened after that, and you don't care about anything other than POSIX.

The description above sounds okay, but in fact there's a problem. Earlier versions of POSIX did not use this reverse feature-test macro; they used another one, and they used it in a simpler (and less powerful) way. They had you define _POSIX_SOURCE, not _POSIX_C_SOURCE, and you didn't have to give it a value. You just said:

```
#define _POSIX_SOURCE
```

Now, a system that does not define _POSIX_C_SOURCE does not conform to the September, 1993 version of POSIX, i.e. POSIX.4. For the purposes of us real-world, real-time applications developers, then, we really should only need to define _POSIX_C_SOURCE. If that doesn't give us the symbols we need, then the system doesn't have what we want. However, it can provide an interesting extra piece of information if _POSIX_C_SOURCE has no effect, but _POSIX_SOURCE does. That tells you that you have a system corresponding to the 1990 version of POSIX, POSIX.1 (since the '93 version of POSIX is a superset of the '90 version, anyone who supports _POSIX_C_SOURCE would also support _POSIX_SOURCE).

The _POSIX_C_SOURCE definition also, unfortunately, tells your compiler that you're not interested in *any* symbols other than those defined by POSIX or ANSI C. If you are a POSIX True Believer, you think that you can do anything using only POSIX and ANSI C, and you won't be needing anything else from your operating system. However, you may be needing psychiatric evaluation. *Of course* you're going to need more for a real application! In that case, those modules that need additional definitions from your system should *not* define _POSIX_C_SOURCE (or _POSIX_SOURCE, for that matter). This can be clumsy when you need both POSIX and non-POSIX functionality in the same module.

The lesson here is, POSIX makes your application more portable—not totally, utterly, trivially portable.

What Pieces Do I Have?

When you are considering a new operating system, the first order of business is to find out what you have, and then to find out how much of it you have. Correspondingly, we'll first look at *<unistd.h>*, which defines the POSIX pieces a given operating system supports.

The first order of business is to determine whether or not POSIX is even present on your system. _POSIX_SOURCE and _POSIX_C_SOURCE alone do not tell you that; *you* defined those symbols, remember? The real test is to define _POSIX_C_SOURCE, and see what that definition buys you. The feature test macro _POSIX_VERSION tells you this information. This symbol has a numeric value that tells you what version of POSIX is present on your system. A value of 198808 (August, 1988, when POSIX.1 was approved as an IEEE standard) means that your system conforms to the 1988 version of POSIX.1. Usually, this implies that the system passes U.S.A. FIPS 151-1. A _POSIX_VERSION of 199009 tells you that the system conforms to the 1990, ISO version of POSIX. This is not significantly different from the 1988 version, but the test suite, U.S.A. FIPS 151-2, is better and harder to pass. Either value means you have the base POSIX.1, with no real-time functionality. Nuts! On the other hand, a value of 199309 (for September, 1993, the month when POSIX.4 was approved) tells you that the basic POSIX.1 facilities, *and* the POSIX.4 functions as well, are present. Values greater than 199309 indicate a version of POSIX more recent than September, 1993. These versions should also support POSIX.4, since they will be supersets of the 1993 edition.

Since POSIX.4 is mostly options, the fact that _POSIX_VERSION is greater than or equal to 199309 does not tell you a lot. Speaking academically, this condition is necessary, but not sufficient, for all the functions of POSIX.4 to be present. Table 2-3 shows the currently meaningful values of _POSIX_VERSION.

Table 2–3: _POSIX_VERSION Possible Values

Value	Meaning
(not defined)	POSIX is not supported on this system!
(long)198808	Only POSIX.1 is supported (FIPS 151-1).
(long)199009	Only POSIX.1 is supported (FIPS 151-2).
(long)199309	POSIX.1 and POSIX.4 are both supported.
Greater than 199309	POSIX.1, POSIX.4, and some additional functions are present.

You could use this in a small test program as follows:

```
#define _POSIX_SOURCE
#define _POSIX_C_SOURCE 199309
#include <unistd.h>

#ifndef _POSIX_VERSION
printf("POSIX is not supported!\n");
#else    /* _POSIX_VERSION */
```

```
#if _POSIX_VERSION == 199009
printf("POSIX.1 is supported but not POSIX.4\n");
#else
#if _POSIX_VERSION >= 199309
printf("POSIX.1 and POSIX.4 are supported\n");
#else
printf("Strange: POSIX VERSION value is between 199009 and 199309!\n");
#endif
#endif
#endif  /* _POSIX_VERSION */
```

Now, say that _POSIX_VERSION is 199309. You still need to find out which optional parts of POSIX.4 are supported. It's actually legal for a vendor to claim _POSIX_VERSION is 199309 when none of the optional POSIX.4 facilities are supported!

Since every optional part of POSIX.4 is flagged under a separate feature-test macro, you can write a small program to check out the configuration of a supposed POSIX.4-conformant machine. For instance, if you wanted to check whether POSIX.4 asynchronous I/O was supported, you might include some code like this:

```
#define _POSIX_SOURCE
#define _POSIX_C_SOURCE 199309
#include <unistd.h>

#ifdef _POSIX_ASYNCHRONOUS_IO
printf("POSIX Asynchronous I/O is supported\n");
#else
printf("POSIX Asynchronous I/O is not supported\n");
#endif
```

This sample gives you the flavor of the sort of checking you need to do for POSIX options, but conformance testing is far more complex than this. There are levels of checking to be done. First, there's *#ifdef*: whether _POSIX_ASYNCHRONOUS_IO is defined at all. There may be dependencies between multiple *#ifdefs*, for instance, checking on asynchronous I/O involves the definition and values of two constants: _POSIX_ASYNCHRONOUS_IO and _POSIX_ASYNC_IO. Then, we check the system run-time configuration using *sysconf* (discussed further on), to determine whether the system's run-time configuration agrees with the constants. Next, we interrogate the limits to our functionality, both by checking constants in *<limits.h>* and also by run-time checking (using *sysconf* again). Finally, we can perform ad-hoc checks to verify some functionality whose behavior may vary from one system to the next. As an example, the I/O functionality of POSIX.4 may be supported on some files (e.g., disk files) and not others (e.g., special device files).

The Limits to Functionality

<unistd.h> tells you what chunks of POSIX.1 are present on your system. However, there's more to the menu than that. Each chunk may also have some numeric parameters associated with it. For semaphores, for instance, how many can I create at once? For message queues, what is the largest message priority I can specify? These sorts of

limits are given in, logically enough, *<limits.h>*. Table 2-4 shows you which limits are defined, what they mean, and the minimum value that's allowed in a legitimate POSIX.4 implementation. The descriptions may not mean much to you now, since they apply to POSIX.4 functions you haven't learned about yet. We'll revisit these limits in each chapter.

Table 2-4: POSIX Feature Limits: Maxima

POSIX Feature	Limits for this System	Minimum	Description
Asynchronous I/O	AIO_LISTIO_MAX	2	Maximum number of operations you can supply in one call to *lio_listio*
	AIO_MAX	1	Maximum concurrent asynchronous I/Os
Prioritized I/O	AIO_PRIO_DELTA_MAX	0	Maximum amount you can decrease your AIO priority
Message queues	MQ_OPEN_MAX	8	Maximum number of message queues per process
	MQ_PRIO_MAX	32	Maximum number of message priorities
Real-time signals	RTSIG_MAX	8	Maximum real-time signals
	SIGQUEUE_MAX	32	Maximum outstanding real-time signals sent per process
Semaphores	SEM_NSEMS_MAX	256	Maximum number of semaphores that one process can have open at a time
	SEM_VALUE_MAX	32767	maximum semaphore value
Clocks and timers	TIMER_MAX	32	Maximum number of timers a process can have at one time
	DELAYTIMER_MAX	32	Maximum number of times a timer can overrun and you can still detect it.

This table says that the limit for AIO_LISTIO_MAX must be *at least* two. It can have a higher value—in fact, if you're interested in list I/O at all, you'd hope it has a higher value—which is why your program should test it. However, the POSIX standard guarantees that if list I/O is present at all (and it might not be—you need to check _POSIX_ASYNCHRONOUS_IO), AIO_LISTIO_MAX will be at least two.

We can now begin to flesh out our conformance tester for asynchronous I/O, adding static limit interrogations.

```
#define _POSIX_SOURCE   /* Define old-style feature selector */
/* Use 9/93 POSIX.1, .2, and .4 definitions only */
#define     _POSIX_C_SOURCE 199309L
```

```
#include    <unistd.h>   /* For POSIX definitions */
#include    <stdio.h>
#include    <errno.h>


/**********************************************
 Testing for POSIX Asynchronous I/O
 **********************************************/

#ifdef _POSIX_ASYNCHRONOUS_IO
#include    <limits.h>
#include    <fcntl.h>

int have_asynchio(void)
{
    int i, res, num_ok;

    printf("System claims to have POSIX_ASYNCHRONOUS_IO.\n");
    printf("AIO_LISTIO_MAX = %d\n", AIO_LISTIO_MAX);
    printf("AIO_MAX = %d\n", AIO_MAX);
}
#else   /* _POSIX_ASYNCHRONOUS_IO */
int     have_asynchio(void) { return 0; } /* Not supported at all */
#endif  /* _POSIX_ASYNCHRONOUS_IO */
```

In addition to the limits described above, there are also some interesting, but pretty useless, numbers given in *<limits.h>*. These are the smallest values that *any* POSIX system can provide for the facility. These values are fixed by the POSIX standard, and are not going to change on your system. Why do you need these values in a header file, if they're invariant? I don't know. But they're there. The values are listed in Table 2-5.

Table 2-5: POSIX Feature Limits: Minimum Requirements

Limit (All Systems)	Description	Value
_POSIX_AIO_LISTIO_MAX	Number of operations in one listio	2
_POSIX_AIO_MAX	Number of simultaneous asynchronous I/Os	1
_POSIX_MQ_OPEN_MAX	Number of message queues for one process	8
_POSIX_MQ_PRIO_MAX	Number of message priorities	32
_POSIX_RTSIG_MAX	Number of real-time signals	8
_POSIX_SIGQUEUE_MAX	Number of real-time signals a process can queue at once	32
_POSIX_SEM_NSEMS_MAX	Number of semaphores per process	256
_POSIX_SEM_VALUE_MAX	maximum semaphore value	32767
_POSIX_TIMER_MAX	Number of timers per process	32
_POSIX_DELAYTIMER_MAX	Number of times a timer can overrun	32

Run-Time Checking

Remember that the run-time system and the compilation environment may be completely distinct. In particular, their levels of POSIX support may differ! That's because most real-time operating systems are configurable, to support varying memory requirements and hardware environments. In the workstation environment, it's easy enough to solve all kinds of problems by buying more memory. In an embedded, real-time system, though, memory, and its cost, are at a premium.

Say you've built your application to use POSIX.4 asynchronous I/O (_POSIX_ASYNCHRONOUS_IO). The header and library support are present, and your application builds with no problem. In fact, you run and test your application on a fully-loaded version of your target machine. No problem. Then, in a configuration management phase of your project, some other developer tries to reduce memory usage by removing parts of the run-time system. Say he doesn't realize that you used asynchronous I/O, and he removes it from the run-time system. What's going to happen? Your asynchronous I/O calls are going to fail mysteriously when you run your application on this new system!

To get around this problem, POSIX provides functions you can call to determine your machine's configuration at run-time. These functions are called *sysconf, fpathconf,* and *pathconf,* and are used to determine the presence, absence, and numerical limits of options on a per-system and a per-file basis, respectively. These functions are summarized as follows:

```
#include    <unistd.h>

long sysconf(int name);
long pathconf(const char *pathname, int name);
long fpathconf(int fd, int name);
```

Real-World Costs

Costs come in different varieties: monetary cost, cost in physical space, and energy cost. In one project I was involved with, my team was chosen over a competing system because (among other reasons) our operating system used less power than the competition! We were referred to as a "half-watt operating system" while the other system weighed in at a hefty three watts. A peculiar way of comparing software, to be sure!

---

sysconf

For system-wide options, like the number of asynchronous operations that can be outstanding at once (_POSIX_AIO_MAX), use *sysconf* as follows:

```
long val = sysconf(_SC_AIO_MAX);
```

The function is simple. You pass it a particular option, and it returns to you the value associated with that option on the current running system. For options that have numeric values (limits), *sysconf* returns the value of that limit.

For binary values, where the support is either there or not there (for instance, POSIX_PRIORITY_SCHEDULING), the return value from *sysconf* gets more complex. If you pass in a bogus option number, you will get back –1, with *errno* set to EINVAL. But say your system just doesn't support the _POSIX_PRIORITY_SCHEDULING option. In that case, and for all options which are not supported, *sysconf* returns –1 without changing *errno*. Thus, it's better to initialize *errno* before calling *sysconf*:

```
errno = 0;
val = sysconf(_SC_PRIORITY_SCHEDULING);

if ((val == -1) && (errno)) {
        printf("Bad option number %d (POSIX_PRIORITY_SCHEDULING)\n", option);
        printf("System does not conform to POSIX_VERSION 199309\n");
} else if ((val == -1) && (! errno)) {
        printf("_POSIX_PRIORITY_SCHEDULING not supported\n", option);
} else {
        /* Any return means POSIX_PRIORITY_SCHEDULING is supported */
        printf("_POSIX_PRIORITY_SCHEDULING is defined (value %d)\n", val);
}
```

The currently-defined *sysconf* options are given in Table 2-6; true options are binary, while numeric limits are not:

Table 2-6: sysconf Options

sysconf option name	System Value Returned	Standard
_SC_JOB_CONTROL	_POSIX_JOB_CONTROL (binary)	POSIX.1
_SC_SAVED_IDS	_POSIX_SAVED_IDS (binary)	POSIX.1
_SC_VERSION	_POSIX_VERSION (binary)	POSIX.1
_SC_ARG_MAX	ARG_MAX	POSIX.1
_SC_CHILD_MAX	CHILD_MAX	POSIX.1
_SC_CLK_TCK	clock ticks per second (a.k.a. HZ)	POSIX.1
_SC_NGROUPS_MAX	NGROUPS_MAX	POSIX.1
_SC_OPEN_MAX	OPEN_MAX	POSIX.1
_SC_STREAM_MAX	STREAM_MAX	POSIX.1
_SC_TZNAME_MAX	TZNAME_MAX	POSIX.1
_SC_ASYNCHRONOUS_IO	_POSIX_ASYNCHRONOUS_IO (binary)	POSIX.4
_SC_MAPPED_FILES	_POSIX_MAPPED_FILES (binary)	POSIX.4
_SC_MEMLOCK	_POSIX_MEMLOCK (binary)	POSIX.4

Table 2-6: sysconf Options (continued)

sysconf option name	System Value Returned	Standard
_SC_MEMLOCK_RANGE	_POSIX_MEMLOCK_RANGE (binary)	POSIX.4
_SC_MEMORY_PROTECTION	_POSIX_MEMORY_PROTECTION (binary)	POSIX.4
_SC_MESSAGE_PASSING	_POSIX_MESSAGE_PASSING (binary)	POSIX.4
_SC_PRIORITIZED_IO	_POSIX_PRIORITIZED_IO (binary)	POSIX.4
_SC_PRIORITY_SCHEDULING	_POSIX_PRIORITY_SCHEDULING (binary)	POSIX.4
_SC_REALTIME_SIGNALS	_POSIX_REALTIME_SIGNALS (binary)	POSIX.4
_SC_SEMAPHORES	_POSIX_SEMAPHORES (binary)	POSIX.4
_SC_FSYNC	_POSIX_FSYNC (binary)	POSIX.4
_SC_SHARED_MEMORY_OBJECTS	_POSIX_SHARED_MEMORY_OBJECTS (binary)	POSIX.4
_SC_SYNCHRONIZED_IO	_POSIX_SYNCHRONIZED_IO (binary)	POSIX.4
_SC_TIMERS	_POSIX_TIMERS (binary)	POSIX.4
_SC_AIO_LISTIO_MAX	AIO_LISTIO_MAX	POSIX.4
_SC_AIO_MAX	AIO_MAX	POSIX.4
_SC_AIO_PRIO_DELTA_MAX	AIO_PRIO_DELTA_MAX	POSIX.4
_SC_DELAYTIMER_MAX	DELAYTIMER_MAX	POSIX.4
_SC_MQ_OPEN_MAX	MQ_OPEN_MAX	POSIX.4
_SC_MQ_PRIO_MAX	MQ_PRIO_MAX	POSIX.4
_SC_PAGESIZE	PAGESIZE	POSIX.4
_SC_RTSIG_MAX	RTSIG_MAX	POSIX.4
_SC_SEM_NSEMS_MAX	SEM_NSEMS_MAX	POSIX.4
_SC_SEM_VALUE_MAX	SEM_VALUE_MAX	POSIX.4
_SC_SIGQUEUE_MAX	SIGQUEUE_MAX	POSIX.4
_SC_TIMER_MAX	TIMER_MAX	POSIX.4

fpathconf and pathconf

You use *sysconf* to find out what your system supports. For options that are not file- or directory-related, that's fine. But for options that are applied to files, like synchronized I/O or asynchronous I/O, the *system* may support the option, but any given *file* might not. Some options are only meaningful for certain kinds of files, and some options are interpreted differently depending on the type of file that you're working with.

Therefore, you need a version of *sysconf* that tells you whether a given option is supported for a particular file. POSIX gives you two such functions: *pathconf* and *fpathconf*. These perform the same function, but *pathconf* takes a pathname string, while *fpathconf* takes the file descriptor of a file you have already successfully opened:

```
#include        <unistd.h>

int val, opt, fd;
char *pathname;

pathname = "/random/path/in/which/i/am/interested";

opt = _POSIX_SYNCHRONIZED_IO;
val = pathconf(pathname, opt);          /* Use the pathname... */
```

```
fd = open(pathname, O_RDWR);          /* ...or open the file... */
val = fpathconf(fd, opt);             /* and use the descriptor! */
```

You can pass the options listed in Table 2-7 to *pathconf*. There are fewer options than for *sysconf*, however, their interpretation is rather more complex, as we'll go into later in this section. Several of the POSIX.1 options are rather complex, but that's not the focus of the book. For more detail on these you'll want to refer to the *POSIX Programmers' Guide*, by Donald Lewine (O'Reilly & Associates, 1991) or the POSIX.1 standard itself.

Table 2-7: pathconf and fpathconf Options

pathconf option name	System Value Returned	Standard
_PC_CHOWN_RESTRICTED	_POSIX_CHOWN_RESTRICTED (binary)	POSIX.1
_PC_NO_TRUNC	_POSIX_NO_TRUNC (binary)	POSIX.1
_PC_VDISABLE	_POSIX_VDISABLE	POSIX.1
_PC_LINK_MAX	LINK_MAX	POSIX.1
_PC_MAX_CANON	MAX_CANON	POSIX.1
_PC_MAX_INPUT	MAX_INPUT	POSIX.1
_PC_NAME_MAX	NAME_MAX	POSIX.1
_PC_PATH_MAX	PATH_MAX	POSIX.1
_PC_PIPE_BUF	PIPE_BUF	POSIX.1
_PC_ASYNC_IO	_POSIX_ASYNC_IO (binary)	POSIX.4
_PC_PRIO_IO	_POSIX_PRIO_IO (binary)	POSIX.4
_PC_SYNC_IO	_POSIX_SYNC_IO (binary)	POSIX.4

Call *pathconf* or *fpathconf* with these names and you will get the value of the associated _POSIX symbol for that particular file. The POSIX.4 options do not allow you to pass in a directory name; some of the POSIX.1 functions do.

The return value from *pathconf* can get strange, like *sysconf*. If the functions return –1, but do not set *errno*, then there is *no limit* for the symbol. In other words, the functionality is supported. Since all the POSIX.4 options are binary, you'd expect this return if the functionality were there. It's also possible, though, that the functions will return a value other than –1 for the POSIX.4 options. This is okay, too. It means that the functionality is supported for the file.

Here's some further detail on the meaning of each of these options:

_PC_LINK_MAX

This option returns the maximum link count for the file you pass in.

_PC_MAX_CANON, _PC_MAX_INPUT, _PC_VDISABLE

These limits and the special VDISABLE character refer to terminal characteristics. It only makes sense to pass in a terminal special file to *pathconf* for these options.

_PC_NAME_MAX, _PC_NO_TRUNC

These values are the maximum length of a filename, and whether the name will be truncated if it exceeds that length (the alternative is to return an error). These options make sense only when you pass in directories, because they refer to creation or access characteristics of files. (If you think about it, you'll see that these options don't make any sense when applied to files: for example, why would you ask, "What's the maximum name length for the file *foobarbazzot.c*?" It already has a name.) The values returned refer to files within the named directory.

_PC_PATH_MAX

This value is the maximum length of a relative pathname in your current working directory.

_PC_PIPE_BUF

This value is the largest number of bytes you can write to a named pipe (or FIFO) at one time. FIFOs live in the file system and have pathnames. If you pass in the name of a FIFO, this option refers to that FIFO; if you pass in a directory, the option refers to FIFOs created in that directory.

_PC_POSIX_CHOWN_RESTRICTED

If this option returns true for a regular file, it means that you cannot do arbitrary *chown*s of files; you must have appropriate permission (either be owner of the file, or be root), and you can only *chown* the file to your group's ownership—you cannot give it away to another group ID, unless you're root. If you pass in a directory, then this property applies to files created within that directory.

_PC_SYNC_IO, _PC_ASYNC_IO, _PC_PRIO_IO

These options indicate whether synchronized I/O, asynchronous I/O, and prioritized I/O are supported for a particular file. Don't pass in directory or FIFO names; the effect of that is not specified by POSIX.4.

We can now complete our example test for asynchronous I/O conformance:

```
#define _POSIX_SOURCE    /* Define old-style feature selector */
/* Use 9/93 POSIX.1, .2, and .4 definitions only */
#define     _POSIX_C_SOURCE 199309L

#include    <unistd.h>  /* For POSIX definitions */
#include    <stdio.h>
#include    <errno.h>


/**********************************************
 Testing for POSIX Asynchronous I/O
 **********************************************/

#ifdef _POSIX_ASYNCHRONOUS_IO

#ifdef _POSIX_ASYNC_IO
/*
 * If this symbol is defined in <unistd.h>, then it implies
 * system-wide support or lack thereof.  Otherwise, we must go check on
 * the files in which we are interested
 */
#if _POSIX_ASYNC_IO == -1
```

```
int     have_asynchio(void) { return 0; } /* Not supported at all */
#else
int     have_asynchio(void) { return 1; } /* Supported everywhere */
#endif
#else   /* _POSIX_ASYNC_IO is NOT defined */

/*
 * must check on individual files using pathconf
 */
#include    <limits.h>
#include    <fcntl.h>

char *asynch_io_files[] = {
    "/tmp/fu",
    "/fu",
    "./fu",
    "/mnt/fu",
    "/dev/tty",
    "/dev/dsk/c2t0d0s0",
    NULL
};

int have_asynchio(void)
{
    int i, res, num_ok;

    /* Interrogate limits: compile- and run-time */
    printf("System claims to have POSIX_ASYNCHRONOUS_IO.\n");
    printf("AIO_LISTIO_MAX = %d\n", AIO_LISTIO_MAX);
    printf("AIO_MAX = %d\n", AIO_MAX);

    printf("Runtime value of AIO_LISTIO_MAX is %d\n",
        sysconf(_SC_AIO_LISTIO_MAX);
    printf("Runtime value of AIO_MAX is %d\n", sysconf(_SC_AIO_MAX);

    /* Use pathconf to check for functionality on a per-file basis */
    for (i=num_ok=0; asynch_io_files[i]; i++) {
        printf("Checking on path %s\n", asynch_io_files[i]);
        errno = 0;
        res = pathconf(asynch_io_files[i], _PC_ASYNC_IO);
        if ((res == -1) && (! errno)) {
            printf("\tAsynch. I/O is allowed!\n");
            num_ok++;   /* No limit here */
        } else if (res < 0) {
            printf("\tAsynch. I/O is NOT allowed! (%s)\n",
                strerror(errno));
        } else {
            printf("\tAsynch. I/O is allowed\n");
            num_ok++;   /* No limit here */
        }
    }
    if (num_ok == i)
        return 1;
    else
        return 0;
```

```
     }
     #endif   /* _POSIX_ASYNC_IO */
     #else    /* _POSIX_ASYNCHRONOUS_IO */
     int      have_asynchio(void) { return 0; } /* Not supported at all */
     #endif   /* _POSIX_ASYNCHRONOUS_IO */
```

Notice that we have two levels of constant checking: for _POSIX_ASYNCHRONOUS_IO and for _POSIX_ASYNC_IO. The I/O options of POSIX are special in that they each have two constants defining their existence. The first, longer constant is defined if the functionality is there *at all*. The second constant is there to save you the effort of calling *pathconf* for many files. If that constant is defined, its value tells you whether the support is system-side or not.

Headers and Namespace Pollution

All the functionality of POSIX.4 is declared via header files, as described in Table 2-2. Some of these headers are standard ones you've seen before, *<signal.h>*, for example. Other headers may be new to you, e.g., *<aio.h>*.

Likewise, the functions and constants of POSIX.4 are either existing facilities, like *fsync* and *mmap,* or they are new, like *sched_setscheduler.* The new functions and macros stand out because they all use standard prefixes in their names. For instance, all the asynchronous I/O functions start in *aio_* or *lio_*; all the *#defines* start with either AIO_ or LIO_. This peculiar naming discipline was used to avoid a curious phenomenon known as *namespace pollution.*

Imagine an application you've written which you want to be portable to many different systems. How do you know that the symbols you define for your application won't conflict with symbols that will be defined by some system you may be porting to some day? For example, what if I'd written a program, several years ago, that defined a new function, called *mmap.* Now, my *mmap* does nothing like what the standard UNIX *mmap* does. In fact, my *mmap* predates the existence of UNIX *mmap* by several years. My application is easily portable for years, until certain Berkeley-UNIX-based systems start coming out with their own version of *mmap.* Suddenly, I can't link my application on these systems because of a duplicate name definition. Or worse, the application links, but I get the wrong *mmap* function!

When vendors name their new functions whatever they want, it's called *namespace pollution.* Usually, it's very unlikely that this "pollution" will have any effect at all; you're not generally going to name your functions just like some other, system-supplied function, just by random chance. However, these conflicts do sometimes occur. And when they occur, it's as big a problem for operating system vendors as it is for programmers. For instance, early versions of POSIX.4 called their asynchronous I/O facilities *aread, awrite,* and so on—conflicting with the names chosen by Sun for their own implementation of asynchronous I/O in SunOS 4.1.

The solution to this problem is imperfect, but it works well for now. POSIX posts advisories, called *reserved namespaces*, that tell you where they are likely to define new names for functions. These namespaces are listed in Table 2-8. Each header file in POSIX declares that a certain set of names is off-limits. These sets of names are those names which begin with the reserved prefixes: AIO_, sched_, and so forth. When you write an application, you are admonished not to name any of your own constants or data structures with those prefixes. That way, you know that you won't conflict with the definitions of the facility itself. Some operating systems have also adopted this policy. For example, QNX calls have a standard prefix of *qnx_*. Another common practice is for system vendors to name their calls and variables with an underscore as the first character. This namespace is reserved by POSIX, as well.

The reserved names fall into two categories: those that are declared (functions, variables, and so on), and those that are *#defined*: constants, macros, and so forth. The namespaces for declared objects are just plain forbidden territory. POSIX says you can't use those names. The namespaces for the *#defined* things are a little more lenient: if you *must* use one of these names (they are the ones that start with all capital letters), you should *#undef* the name first. For instance, if you absolutely *had* to have a constant AIO_MYCONSTANT in your code using asynchronous I/O, you'd *#define* it as follows:

```
#include    <aio.h>      /* Reserves aio_, lio_, AIO_, LIO_ */

#undef AIO_MYCONSTANT
#define AIO_MYCONSTANT 3
```

Now, I don't know about you, but I'd be a bit leery about undefining the symbols that the system may be using to support the asynchronous I/O that I needed. I'd rename my symbol. You should do the same. Your code will be more portable if you stay away from all these restricted namespaces.

Table 2-8: POSIX Reserved Namespaces

Header file	Namespace	Type	Reserved By
<aio.h>	aio_	declared	POSIX.4
	lio_	declared	POSIX.4
	AIO_	#defined	POSIX.4
	LIO_	#defined	POSIX.4
<dirent.h>	d_	declared	POSIX.1
<fcntl.h>	l_	declared	POSIX.1
	F_	#defined	POSIX.1
	O_	#defined	POSIX.1
	S_	#defined	POSIX.1
<grp.h>	gr_	declared	POSIX.1

Table 2-8: POSIX Reserved Namespaces (continued)

Header file	Namespace	Type	Reserved By
<limits.h>	_MAX (suffix)	#defined	POSIX.1
<locale.h>	LC_[A-Z]	#defined	POSIX.1
<mqueue.h>	mq_ MQ_	declared #defined	POSIX.4 POSIX.4
<pwd.h>	pw_	declared	POSIX.1
<sched.h>	sched_ SCHED_	declared #defined	POSIX.4 POSIX.4
<semaphore.h>	sem_ SEM_	declared #defined	POSIX.4 POSIX.4
<signal.h>	sa_ si_ sigev_ sival_ SA_ SI_ SIG_	declared declared declared declared #defined #defined #defined	POSIX.1 POSIX.4 POSIX.4 POSIX.4 POSIX.1 POSIX.4 POSIX.1
<sys/mman.h>	shm_ MAP_ MCL_ MS_ PROT_	declared #defined #defined #defined #defined	POSIX.4 POSIX.4 POSIX.4 POSIX.4 POSIX.4
<sys/stat.h>	st_ S_	declared #defined	POSIX.1 POSIX.1
<sys/times.h>	tms_	declared	POSIX.1
<termios.h>	c_ V I O TC B[0-9]	declared #defined #defined #defined #defined #defined	POSIX.1 POSIX.1 POSIX.1 POSIX.1 POSIX.1 POSIX.1
any	_t (suffix) _	declared (types) declared	POSIX.1 POSIX.1

Who's Got What?

Since POSIX is structured as a set of options, the amount of POSIX functionality supported by different "POSIX systems" can vary tremendously. In addition, POSIX is not usually sufficient for a total application. You're going to need some additional facilities, whether for networking, screen handling, or just performing operations that POSIX hasn't standardized yet. I'm thinking in particular of functionality that is provided on all reasonable UNIX systems: *select, ioctl, curses, X,* and so forth. The only way to determine presence or absence of these features is to ask.

As far as POSIX goes, though, you can do a little better. The National Institute of Standards Technology maintains an Internet mail daemon you can contact to determine who's been certified against the FIPSes, and which options they support. It's enlightening to see that vendor S supports all the POSIX options, while vendor M supports nothing it doesn't absolutely have to in order to get the check on the Government list!

To contact the NIST mail daemon, send email to *posix@nist.gov* with the following text:

```
send help
send 151-1reg
send 151-2reg
```

These three requests will send you complete information on how to use the mail server, and the current lists of who has passed FIPS 151-1 and FIPS 151-2. As a POSIX.4 FIPS becomes available, an additional list should start.

Conclusion

So what does all this mean? POSIX defines a standard interface for a large and useful operating system, one you can use to get real work done. The headers and functions provided allow you to determine your configuration at compile time (via *<unistd.h>* and *<limits.h>*), or at run time (via *sysconf, pathconf,* and *fpathconf*). The rules for what names you are supposed to use for your symbols are explicitly laid out (and to be honest, you're probably not going to run into these restrictions, as OS variable names tend to be obscure by design!). If the information I've presented seems a bit thick at the moment, then just let it go for now, go on to the rest of the book, and then come back to this. In the meantime, the next several chapters cover the real substance of real-world problem solving on POSIX systems. Take a look at that stuff and then maybe come back to this once you're more fully immersed.

The Basics of Real-Time: Multiple Tasks

This chapter discusses the ground-level basics of real-time applications: the use of multiple tasks. You'll find, or you already know, that real-time applications are inherently multitasking because they conform to the inherent concurrency of the real world. The use of multiple tasks for real-time applications is therefore essential. This chapter introduces the subject and explains the rudimentary uses of POSIX processes that are typically used to perform *tasks*.* If you are well-acquainted with *fork, exec, exit,* and *wait,* the first part of this chapter will be review for you. Following that, I'll talk about the POSIX signal model, which may differ from the traditional UNIX signal model you're used to. At the end of the chapter, I'll talk about the POSIX.4 extensions to signals.

You'll find, once you're creating multiple processes, a significant need for some good interprocess communication mechanisms, as well as the need for deterministic scheduling of those multiple processes. Those topics are covered in Chapter 4, *Better Coordination: Messages, Shared Memory, and Synchronization,* and Chapter 5, *On Time: Scheduling, Time, and Memory Locking.*

Doing Everything at Once

Real-world applications are different from other applications in a very important way: they deal with the real world, rather than with just a keyboard, graphics tube, and a disk. An application in the real world may be talking to communication lines, robot arms, disk farms, engine controllers, heat sensors, altitude sensors, impact detectors, and so on.

An important aspect of this communication is that it is in general all happening at the same time. Take, for example, a vehicle control application that might be driving some

---

* A *task* is an abstract concept meaning, "a job that has to be done." Often, there's a one-to-one mapping between the tasks and processes, although, as we'll see, that is not necessarily the case.

sort of autonomous vehicle somewhere, for instance, the Mars rover. At any given time, this software might be:

- Taking in the surrounding terrain for path mapping
- Getting input from various sensors telling it whether its wheels are touching ground
- Controlling the power being put out to any and all of several different motors
- Sampling the air, temperature, and light, and scooping up little pieces of Mars
- Getting input from the humans back on Earth, telling it to unjam the silly antenna

The job of your software, in an application like this, is to provide timely-enough response to multiple inputs, all at once. The inputs may be completely unrelated. For instance, it's unlikely that air sampling has much to do with the status of the wheels on the Mars rover. Conversely, the inputs may be closely related. Engine control is dependent on the speed of the vehicle, the incline the vehicle is ascending, the status of the wheels (one's in a pothole, so deliver more power to the rest), and the course laid out for the vehicle.

So, you are writing a real-time application, whether it is a soft real-time application or a hard real-time application. The job of your application is to provide timely response, via some set of outputs, to some other set of inputs. The outputs may very well affect the next wave of inputs. How are you going to structure your application to meet these constraints? How are you going to do all these different, maybe-related things at the same time? There are a few alternatives:

- Use one process. You could service all your various inputs and outputs using a single process. This method avoids the overhead of multiple processes, but may result in complex code for more than a few, simple tasks. The maintenance of such a system can become extremely difficult as new features and support are added. Sometimes merely switching the hardware will cause such an application to fail!

- Use many processes. At the other end of the scale, you could use a separate, dedicated process for every different activity required by your application. This method can avoid the complexity of a single process, but introduces the problem of how the multiple processes coordinate their actions. In addition, this solution has a problem with performance (processes come with a weight that must be borne by the operating system and you), as well as scalability issues (you can't run an infinite number of processes, because of that same weight).

- Use not quite so many processes. If one process per activity is too much, you can combine like activities into single processes. Of course, you have to choose carefully which activities get combined, to avoid excessive complexity in any one process. The right choice of processes can greatly simplify your programming effort.

For mission-critical real-time systems, complexity often hides bugs. Simplicity is good.

- Use signals to emulate multiple processes (we'll cover signals in detail in the "Signals" section later in this chapter). A signal handler can almost be thought of as an independent, asynchronous flow of control within a process, awakened only in response to a particular signal. If you can hook up all your inputs and outputs so they generate signals, you might be able to use this asynchronous behavior to emulate the behavior of multiple processes, without the extra weight of processes. The problem with signals is that, while they may feel like separate flows of control from the main program, they're not.

- Use threads. POSIX.4a threads, or *pthreads*, are a means of supporting multiple tasks within a single process address space. Threads provide an easier and more efficient means of dealing with multiple, related tasks. The POSIX.4a standard is not quite approved as of this writing, so *pthreads* are not really accessible to you, and I will not cover them any further in this book. However, there are other threads packages, like Sun's LWPs and Mach's C-threads, and *pthreads* will certainly be supported on many systems soon.

Each alternative has its place; however, we'll see that the first and last alternatives both have serious limitations that restrict how big, and how portable, your solution can be.

Running in Cycles

Imagine a control-loop sort of real-time application which needs to read data from a port or two, and in response to that input, update a display appropriately and maybe send off a couple of outputs. In other words, consider a video game. How would you structure it?

As a first approximation of the right solution, you'd put it in a big *while* loop. (My strategy would be to use the *while* loop approach, and if that didn't work, then to try something else. With experience, of course, you'll know when the big *while* loop isn't going to work, right off.) Let's assume you start off with a game that uses the keyboard for input, and sends its output to the screen. Your code might end up looking like this:

```
while (1) {
        /* Read Keyboard */
        /* Recompute Player Positions */
        /* Update the display */
}
```

Now, this is a perfectly fine little program, and for small real-time applications it will work well. You need to figure out some way to convince the read operation not to block; instead, it should just check for input from the keyboard and immediately return, so that if the user doesn't press any keys, the display will continue to be updated. Conversely, you need to make sure that the display update is fast enough, so that no keystrokes are lost (serial ports usually buffer their input, but they can only buffer so much). There are methods for doing this, called *select*, *poll*, and O_NONBLOCK. We'll cover the facilities POSIX provides for I/O in that chapter.

The Cyclic Executive Approach

The "big *while* loop" approach to real-time programming (you can call it the "cyclic executive" approach if you want to sound smarter) can be made to work for small, simple, real-time applications, especially where the need for real-time response is not too stringent, and where the things going on in the loop are basically happening in synch with each other.

One immediate problem we need to deal with, though, is that the big loop *is* an infinite loop, and as set up in the example above, it's going to spin as fast as possible. This may be neither socially acceptable (other people may want to use the machine for useful work) nor necessary. In fact, you only need to run the loop fast enough to service the input or output with the highest frequency. You need to find some way of running the loop at exactly that frequency, usually by using a device interrupt (if one is available), or by setting a timer to go off periodically. We'll see how to do that in the scheduling chapter, when we talk about access to time. Remember that you only need to run the loop as fast as the highest frequency task, assuming that all the tasks are in synch. In fact, you only *want* to run the loop that fast, because otherwise you're monopolizing the CPU. Not only is that a pain on a system that may be doing other things, it's also sloppy and inefficient programming. You want to use the least number of cycles you can get away with.

When I say that the tasks are "in synch," I really mean something very specific: the tasks all have harmonic frequencies. That is, the frequencies of the various tasks are all multiples of the shortest (highest) frequency.[*] When this happens, you can structure your tasks in a cyclic structure (a "big *while* loop") without a lot of pain. For instance, if you need to read user input 60 times a second, and you must update the screen 30 times a second for (somewhat) smooth animation, then you can run your loop at 60 Hz (the highest frequency), only updating the screen every other time through the loop. In contrast, imagine that you had to get user input 50 times a second, and update the screen 30 times a second. 50 Hz is 20 milliseconds, while 30 Hz is 33.333... milliseconds. If you ran the loop at 50 Hz, you'd have to update the screen every one and two-thirds times through the loop—not a really pleasant thing to code up! Your other alternative is to run the loop at a higher frequency, and do both the keyboard input and the display update every M and N iterations, respectively (M and N would be factors of that higher frequency). Determining that higher frequency can be painful. Furthermore, if it's too high, then you cannot do all the processing you need to do in one cycle of the loop (each iteration must become shorter in order to run at a higher

---

[*] Technically, the frequencies could all be multiples of another frequency, like half or a third the period of the highest-frequency task.

frequency), and you'll need to deal with the fact that you'll overrun your cycles. Clearly, the "big *while* loop" has its disadvantages.

So there are a few simple problems to be overcome with the cyclic executive approach: harmonic frequencies, finding an appropriate timing base, and using counters to figure out what needs to be done with each iteration of the loop. The *real* problems come in when we begin adding features to the game. As more and more work needs to be done in the loop, the timing becomes progressively more complex. A bit more computation *here* and all of a sudden, you're missing keystrokes *there*. For instance, let's add mouse support and sounds:

```
while (1) {
        /* Synchronize to Highest Frequency */
        /* Read Keyboard */
        /*    AND read mouse */
        /* Recompute Player Positions */
        /* Update the display */
        /*    AND emit sounds */
}
```

Your keyboard and mouse inputs have to be fast, and everything has to be non-blocking. Still, you can probably deal with it, especially since this application isn't hard real-time. Just about any modern computer can be made to go fast enough to stay ahead of mere human responses. That is, unless the graphics are really sophisticated or there are a lot of human responses to be dealt with. Let's take this game off the UNIX box it's been prototyped on, and try it out on the video game hardware.[*] Now, we're going to have a lot more output to do, because it's one of those new force-feedback games where the game setup moves in response to what the user's doing. There's also a lot of ancillary peripherals to be dealt with: flashing lights, and, literally, bells and whistles.

```
while (1) {
        /* Synchronize to Highest Frequency */
        /* Read Keyboard */
        /*    AND read mouse */
        /* Recompute Player Positions */
        /* Update the display */
        /*      AND all the other lights */
        /*    AND emit sounds */
        /*      AND more sounds */
        /*      AND move the game physically */
}
```

All of a sudden, the application is getting complex.

---

[*] This is another reason why you want to use as few cycles as possible. A video arcade game is an example of an embedded system, that is, a computer embedded in some real-world appliance. In this sort of marketplace, you'll want to use the slowest, smallest, most energy-efficient parts you can, to save both watts and money. If your application can run on a slower processor, you'll want to be able to use it!

This assumes, as well, that all these jobs can still be done within a single loop without compromising your performance. A long computation, like for course planning (often used in robotics applications, and requiring time-consuming artificial intelligence techniques) or perhaps software video decompression (as in Intel's Indeo) may need to be broken up across multiple iterations of a loop. Another technique that is used is to periodically poll for other work from within a long computation. This is the classical Macintosh programming model.

At this point, a poorly-structured application may begin to show some strain. And again, it is important to point out here that we're just talking about human responses. A video game is a soft real-time application. A hard real-time application will be much more stringent in its requirements. A video game might seem sluggish if keyboard input or a video frame gets dropped, whereas a jet engine may explode or a radar tear itself off its mount.

Tuning a cyclic executive for performance involves moving parts around, splitting computations, literally tuning the application for its hardware. This may be quite difficult, and gets you into fun tricks like maintaining the state of a computation across multiple iterations of the loop. Furthermore, the tuning relies on the performance of your machine not changing, or else the speed of the various things in the loop changes, and your timing goes off. So much for portability! Given all that, you may find yourself wondering, "Gee. Wouldn't it be easier if I just used a multitasking operating system like UNIX?"

Pretending to Multitask with Signal Handlers

An alternative to the "big *while* loop" is the use of signal handlers, to emulate multitasking in your application. A POSIX signal is a software analogue to a hardware interrupt; when a process gets a signal it vectors off from whatever it was doing to the signal handler function that it set up for that signal. When the signal handler completes, the process goes back to what it was doing. When you can arrange for signals to be delivered for many of the important events in your application, it can sometimes seem that you have achieved the look and feel of true multitasking.

Unfortunately, even if you have the look, you don't really have the feel. As anyone who's written an interrupt handler knows, one is very limited in what one can do from within such a handler. Specifically, the signal handler cannot synchronize its execution with any of the other signal-simulated tasks. Why? Because there aren't really any other tasks. There's just this one, going off and handling various signals. Any time the signal handler blocks, the entire process blocks. The result is one hung application.

For many uses, though, signal handlers are just what you need, and they are certainly widely used to respond to various external events (like I/O completion and timer expiration). We'll return to this multitasking subject after I've described how signals work. That way, you'll have a little more basis for understanding the benefits and limitations of signal handlers that try to emulate multitasking.

Multiple Processes

As we've seen, the cyclic executive approach can be successfully used for small, harmonic sets of tasks, but it doesn't deal terribly well with the whole range of real-time problems. If you were to try and split computations across multiple invocations of the loop, saving all the necessary state of each computation, you would eventually find yourself doing something very similar to what a multitasking operating system does when it switches between tasks or processes. Why not let the operating system do the work?

The advantage of using multiple processes is clear from the discussion of cyclic executives—simplicity. Each process is a distinct entity, separately scheduled by the operating system. You no longer need to manhandle the interactions between the various tasks within your single big *while* loop. Instead, you have a whole bunch of "little *while* loops," each running at its own frequency, doing what it needs to do for its particular job. This solution is much simpler to code, and, therefore, much more robust. It is also much more portable. In fact, for large real-world systems where portability (to newer machines or other operating systems) is important, multitasking is the only reasonable alternative.

Other advantages include:

- **Scalability.** An application that is split into multiple processes is not locked into a single process model (duh!). You can run multiple processes on multiple processors, either on a multiprocessor computer, or in a distributed environment. There's a bit more work to be done than just splitting the process into multiple processes, especially if the processes want to communicate. However, at least the *model* is right!

- **Modularity.** You can add or subtract processes from your application to configure it for different target environments and workloads. This can be quite difficult with a cyclic executive.

- **Protection.** Processes live in isolated, protected virtual address spaces, separated from nasty, errant processes that might tromp their memory with broken pointers and bad algorithms. This protection leads to more robust applications than a single, large application running in a single chunk of memory. This is important for mission-critical applications. Modern computers come with MMUs. You should use them when you can.

What are the problems? There are a number.

- **Processes cost more.** They are supported by the operating system as generalized schedulable entities, complete with state information that may be irrelevant to your application. That state takes up memory.

- **Processes are slower.** It's been claimed that processes, because of this extra weight, are slower than other methods for multitasking (like the big *while* loop). This is not the case. Processes are slower because the operating system has to get involved in the scheduling decisions, and the operating system makes general choices based on a generalized scheduling scheme, not the highly tuned system you may have had to devise in your big *while* loop.

- **Processes have to be scheduled.** Nothing happens for free. Just because you're running all your jobs in separate processes, that doesn't imply that the operating system can magically cause all your tasks to always make all their deadlines. Remember that the operating system is still just slicing up time on a single machine. In all but the most trivial cases, you'll need to give the operating system some clues as to which jobs are more important and which are less important. In other words, you'll still have to deal with the scheduling of the jobs, albeit in a much more palatable way than the cyclic executive forced upon you!

- **Processes are alone.** Each process in the POSIX model executes in a protected, distinct address space, sharing no variables or other communication channels with any other processes. Any coordination needs to be programmed explicitly.

We'll discuss the first two issues below, along with a fast review of how to use multiple processes. Some interprocess communication is possible using signals, which we'll cover in the "Multitasking with Signal Handlers" section of this chapter. Better communication mechanisms are covered in Chapter 4. Process scheduling is the subject of Chapter 5.

Making Processes

For a concise example of most every facility in POSIX.1 for process creation and destruction, we can turn to the terminal-server application I described in Chapter 1, *Introduction*. Here is the server end of the application, absent everything except the process-related functions.

```
#define POSIX_C_SOURCE 199309

#include    <unistd.h>
#include    <stdio.h>
#include    <sys/types.h>
#include    <sys/wait.h>
#include    <signal.h>
#include    <errno.h>
#include    "app.h"      /* Local definitions */

main(int argc, char **argv)
{
```

```
        request_t r;
        pid_t terminated;
        int status;

        init_server();            /* Set things up */

        do {
            check_for_exited_children();
            r = await_request();       /* Get some input */
            service_request(r);     /* Do what the terminal wants */
            send_reply(r);          /* Tell them we did it. */
        } while (r != NULL);

        shutdown_server();           /* Tear things down */
        exit(0);
    }


    void
    service_request(request_t r)
    {
        pid_t child;
        switch (r->r_op) {
            case OP_NEW:
                /* Create a new client process */
                child = fork();
                if (child) {
                    /* parent process */
                     break;
                } else {
                    /* child process */
                    execlp("terminal", "terminal application",
                        "/dev/com1", NULL);
                    perror("execlp");
                    exit(1);
                }
                break;
            default:
                printf("Bad op %d\n", r->r_op);
                break;
        }
        return;
    }
```

The terminal end of the application looks like this:

```
#define POSIX_C_SOURCE 199309

#include    <unistd.h>
#include    <stdio.h>
#include    <sys/types.h>
#include    <sys/wait.h>
#include    <signal.h>
#include    "app.h"      /* Local definitions */

char *myname;
```

```
main(int argc, char **argv)
{
    myname = argv[0];
    printf("Terminal \"%s\" here!\n", myname);
    while (1) {
        /* Deal with the screen */
        /* Await user input */
    }
    exit(0);
}
```

The server operates in a loop, accepting requests, servicing those inputs, and then sending a response message to the original requestor. One possible request is to create a new terminal process. This is the code in the case statement which handles OP_NEW (that's my definition, and has no meaning beyond this application).

To create a new terminal, the server calls *fork,* which duplicates the process so that there are two, called the original (or parent) process and the child. The parent process returns from the function and continues servicing user requests. The child process calls one of the *exec* functions to overlay itself with a new process image (one stored in the file "terminal" in this case).

The child process, transformed into the terminal program, does whatever it is that it does (presumably something user-related), and eventually ceases to exist by calling *exit.*

More Details on fork, exec, and exit

The POSIX process creation, transformation, destruction and cleanup functions are defined in POSIX.1. The *POSIX Programmer's Guide* has a good introduction to the use of *fork* and the *exec* functions. Here's a summary:[*]

```
#include         <sys/types.h>

pid_t fork(void);
int execl(const char *file, const char *arg0, ... NULL);
int execv(const char *file, char *const argv[]);
int execle(const char *file, const char *arg0, ... NULL, char *const envp[]);
int execve(const char *file, char *const argv[], char *const envp);
int execlp(const char *file, const char *arg0, ... NULL);
int execvp(const char *file, char *const argv[]);

void exit(int status);   /* Terminate the process, cleaning up ANSI C stuff. */
void _exit(int status);  /* Terminate the process, cleaning up POSIX stuff. */

#include         <sys/types.h>
#include         <sys/wait.h>
```

---

* The syntax in this summary is not exactly ANSI C. I have taken liberties with it in the interest of clarifying the arguments.

```
pid_t wait(int *status);    /* Wait for a child, any child, to die */
pid_t waitpid(pid_t which, int *status, int options);
```

One process calls *fork*, but two return. Each of these processes is a unique, individual process in a protected, separate virtual address space; the processes just happen to look the same. The *fork* call returns, to the original process, the process ID of the new process, while the new process is returned a 0. These different return values enable the two processes to do different things based on which one is which.

A new process costs memory. Each process consists of a number of kernel data structures, running from a couple of hundred bytes to a few (as much as, say, fifteen) kilobytes if you include file pointers, MMU context and room for a supervisor stack (if the operating system requires one—QNX does not require a separate kernel stack per process). In addition, the new process has its own user memory: an exact duplicate of the address space of the parent process, including the user stack and data areas. These days, most operating systems fault in the user context for a new process. The new guy starts out without any memory, and then, as it tries to use its memory, the operating system detects memory faults and supplies the required memory at that time. This has the advantage that memory not used by the new process is not wasted. In a real-time context, though, you do not want time-consuming memory faults happening at random times, so you will probably want to fault in all your memory as soon as you *fork*.

You can do this by touching everything you plan to use, assuming you can figure out where "everything" is. A simpler solution is to lock your memory down. If you lock memory in the parent process, don't expect it to be locked in the child. You'll have to lock it, explicitly, in each new process. Memory locking is part of POSIX.4, and is covered when we talk about how to do things On Time in Chapter 5.

Fork makes new processes, but they're duplicates of each other. The *exec* family of functions loads in new code—a new program—to be *exec*uted. The *exec*'d process is actually the same process. It has the same process ID, and some files may be left open across an *exec*. The newness comes from the fact that the process memory space is reinitialized with a new executable program; this new program starts running at *main* (in C), or wherever it is that programs start running (in other languages). Memory locks are lost when a process successfully calls an *exec* function. There are many variants of *exec*. Each provides a somewhat different interface to the same functionality. The *exec* functions are *execl, execv, execle, execve, execlp,* and *execvp*. The functions with an *l* in the suffix take a *list* of arguments, a variable number terminated by NULL, as in the server example. The functions with a *v* take a vector, or array of pointers to characters, which again is terminated by a NULL pointer. The presence of an *e* in the suffix indicates that a second list or vector can be passed to set up the environment of the new executable image. (Unless one of these functions is called, the new executable image inherits the environment of the caller.) Finally, a *p* in the suffix specifies that the environment variable PATH should be used for looking up the executable file, so you do not need to specify a fully-rooted pathname.

Regardless of which *exec* variant you decide to use in your applications, the basic usage is the same. The first argument to any *exec* function is the name of the file containing the executable image (whether fully rooted or not). The rest of the arguments form the *argv* argument with which *main* in the new program is invoked. The first element in this array, *argv[0]*, is traditionally the last component of the pathname to the executable file. However, it can be anything. *argv* is interpreted by the new program, and you can do anything you want with it.

Hints and notes for using processes

Here's a gotcha that I've seen enough times that I'd like to warn you about it. When you are using *execlp* or *execvp*, make sure that your executable file name is different from the name of any utility that may already be in your path! This is because the PATH is searched from beginning to end, according to POSIX.1. Depending on the order of your PATH variable, you might find the program you are trying to execute, or you might find a totally unrelated version in some other directory! This really happened to a guy who was working with me from halfway across the country. He called me on a Tuesday, having already tried for an entire day to figure out what was going on. A test program he was writing was giving completely bizarre results—stuff he hadn't even put in the program at all! He was testing semaphore creation and deletion, I think, but the test program kept saying, "Argument expected." It turns out that he had named his test program "test", and there is also a standard utility called *test*, a general comparator that can be used for determining file states, doing numeric comparisons and the like. It was this general utility that he'd been executing all this time!

But Wait! There's More

There are two *exit* calls (*exit* or *_exit*) that are used to terminate a process. Once a process exits, the parent process can determine its exit status by using one of the *wait* functions. The *_exit* function is defined by POSIX.1, whereas *exit* was defined by ANSI C. Both of these functions will have the desired effect of terminating your process. In general, you want to use the ANSI function because it cleans up more than the POSIX function does. Usually, but not always, *exit* is implemented as a sequence of cleanup steps, followed by a call to *_exit*. Neither call ever returns. It's tedious to refer to both functions by name, so when I refer to *exit*, please take that to mean "*exit* or *_exit*."

The *wait* calls are more than just nice for determining the manner of passing of child processes. Once a process has exited, most of its memory and other resources will usually be returned to the system (although POSIX is silent on the subject). Some resources, however, remain occupied after the process is gone. Notably, the supervisor stack of a process is often not freed at the time of *exit* (because it is difficult to free a stack the process is currently using), and, in addition, some subset of the process control data structures will also be left out to store the exit status of the deceased process.

The *status* value passed to *exit* and *_exit* becomes the exit status of the process. This value can be retrieved by the parent process if it so desires, by use of *wait* or *waitpid*. In the POSIX documents, *wait* is described as an interface that can be used to retrieve the exit status of deceased processes. It's more than that. The *wait* functions serve the important purpose of freeing the leftover resources associated with a deceased process. Historically, a process is called a "zombie" from the time it calls *exit* until the time the parent process *wait* s for it. During the zombie period, the process is still occupying system resources. If the parent process never calls *wait,* then it is possible that the system will clog up with zombies and be unable to proceed. So, it is important that parent·processes *wait* (or *waitpid)* for their children, even though POSIX doesn't say they have to.* Not all systems require a *wait* for each terminated child, but most do, so you should program with the assumption that *wait* calls are necessary. Alternatively, the parent process itself can exit. In this case, the child processes are cleaned up by the system. Zombie processes are only a problem when a parent process remains alive, creating child processes indefinitely but not waiting for their demise.

The simple *wait* function blocks until a child process terminates. It returns the process ID of the deceased child and status information encoded in the parameter passed to it. *waitpid* is the version of *wait* with the racing stripes, chrome hubcaps, and the dingle balls in the window. You can set it to wait for only one child, or any. You can cause it to block, or not, by setting flags in the *options*.

In the terminal/server example, the server had a function call that checked for deceased child processes. This function uses the *waitpid* call:

```
void check_for_exited_children(void)
{
    pid_t terminated;
    /* Deal with terminated children */
    terminated = waitpid(-1, &status, WNOHANG);
    if (terminated > 0) {
        if (WIFEXITED(status)) {
                printf("Child %d exit(%d)\n",
                    terminated, WEXITSTATUS(status));
        } else if (WIFSIGNALED(status)) {
                printf("Child %d got signal %d\n",
                    terminated, WTERMSIG(status));
        } else if (WIFSTOPPED(status)) {
                printf("Child %d stopped by signal %d\n",
                    terminated, WSTOPSIG(status));
        }
    }
}
```

The first argument to *waitpid,* called *which,* specifies the set of processes you want to wait for.

---

* This is most likely because POSIX, as an interface standard, isn't allowed to talk much at all about the operating system resources required for running processes.

- If *which* is -1, then *waitpid* will wait for any process that is a child of the calling process, just like *wait* does.

- If *which* is 0, then *waitpid* will wait for any process that is a child of the calling process that has the same process group ID as the calling process.*

- If *which* is positive, then *waitpid* will wait only for that process, which had better be a child of the calling process (or else an errno, ECHILD, will be returned).

- Finally, if *which* is less than -1, then the absolute value of *which* specifies a process group ID. In this case, *waitpid* will wait for any process that is a child of the calling process that has that process group ID.

The last argument, *options*, can have two flags set in it: WNOHANG and WUNTRACED. WNOHANG, which we are using, tells *waitpid* not to wait for processes to exit. If there is a dead process handy, then WNOHANG returns its status. Otherwise, an error is returned, indicating that no processes had exited when *waitpid* was called. If WUNTRACED is set, and if _POSIX_JOB_CONTROL is supported, then *waitpid* will return the status for stopped, as well as terminated, child processes. _POSIX_JOB_CONTROL does not really concern us here.

The status information for the exited process can be decoded using the macros you see in *check_for_exited_children*. These macros are:

WIFEXITED(status_info)

    This call returns a true value if the child process exited normally (via a call to *exit, _exit,* or by falling off the end of its *main* routine).

WIFSIGNALED(status_info)

    This macro returns true if the child was killed by a signal. Usually this means the process got a segmentation fault, bus error, floating point exception, or some other processor fault. It may also mean that a signal was explicitly sent to the child process. Signals are a leading cause of process death, in addition to their other uses (like stopping processes, *faux* asynchrony and low-bandwidth, asynchronous interprocess communication). We'll discuss signals below.

WIFSTOPPED(status_info)

    This macro returns a true value if the process has not terminated at all, but is, instead, just stopped (this only happens if *waitpid* is used, with WUNTRACED set in the *options* parameter). Stopped processes are usually in that state because they received a stop signal. That implies the application is exercising some sort of job control of its own (like a shell does), or is being debugged. The POSIX-standard job control features are supported only if _POSIX_JOB_CONTROL is defined in

---

* Process group ID is inherited by child processes, and is generally not changed. The process group has to do with job control—the running of multiple applications (jobs) from a single terminal. However, if _POSIX_JOB_CONTROL is defined, processes can change process groups using the *setpgid* call.

<unistd.h>. Job control does not concern us here, and I'll say no more on the subject.

WEXITSTATUS(status_info)

If *WIFEXITED(status_info)* returned true, then this macro returns the exit status for the process. Only the least significant 8 bits of the exit status are returned by this macro. The rest are lost.

WTERMSIG(status_info)

If *WIFSIGNALED(status_info)* returned true, then this macro tells you which signal was responsible for the child's termination.

WSTOPSIG(status_info)

If *WIFSTOPPED(status_info)* returned true, then this macro tells you which signal was responsible for the child's being stopped.

Signals

Signals are an integral part of multitasking in the UNIX/POSIX environment. Signals are used for many purposes, including:

- Exception handling (bad pointer accesses, divide by zero, etc.)
- Process notification of asynchronous event occurrence (I/O completion, timer expiration, etc.)
- Process termination in abnormal circumstances
- Emulation of multitasking (see below)
- Interprocess communication

A complete multitasking application has to deal with signals properly, because POSIX systems use them for so many purposes. We'll begin by covering the basics of signals, and finish up by examining communication between processes. As we'll see, signals are not always the best interprocess communication mechanism, and that conclusion will lead us into the next chapter, discussing other means of communicating.

The following synopsis shows the POSIX-conformant signal functions. The first section consists of functions that must be present on all POSIX (not just POSIX.4) systems. The POSIX.4-specific facilities are required only if _POSIX_REALTIME_SIGNALS is defined (in *<unistd.h>*, remember). *<unistd.h>* is not required for signal definitions themselves; only for the definition of _POSIX_REALTIME_SIGNALS.

```
#include        <unistd.h>
#include        <signal.h>
/* The following are all required in all POSIX-conformant systems */
/* Manipulate signal set data structures */
int sigemptyset(sigset_t *set);
int sigfillset(sigset_t *set);
int sigaddset(sigset_t *set, int sig);
```

```
int sigdelset(sigset_t *set, int sig);
int sigismember(sigset_t *set, int sig);

/* Set the process's signal blockage mask */
int sigprocmask(int op, const sigset_t *set, sigset_t *oldset);

int sigaction(int this_signal, const struct sigaction *sa,
    struct sigaction *old_response);

/* Wait for a signal to arrive, setting the given mask */
int sigsuspend(const sigset_t *new_mask);

/* Send a signal to a process */
int kill(pid_t victim_id, int this_signal);

/*
 * The remainder of the functions are part of POSIX.4, and conditional
 * on _POSIX_REALTIME_SIGNALS.
 */
#ifdef _POSIX_REALTIME_SIGNALS
int sigqueue(pid_t victim_id, int this_signal, union sigval extra_info);
int sigwaitinfo(const sigset_t *one_of_these_signals, siginfo_t *addl_info);
int sigtimedwait(const sigset_t *one_of_these_signals, siginfo_t *addl_info,
        const struct timespec *timeout);
#endif _POSIX_REALTIME_SIGNALS
```

There are two layers to a POSIX.4 signals implementation. Most of the signal behavior is dictated by POSIX.1. The second layer consists of extensions to the POSIX.1 model which were made by POSIX.4. The next several sections discuss the POSIX.1 signals model. Following that, I'll tell you about some of the problems with signals, and what POSIX.4 has done about them. Finally, I'll tell you what problems still remain, even with the POSIX.4 extensions.

What Is a Signal?

A POSIX signal is the software equivalent of an interrupt or exception occurrence. When a process "gets" a signal, it signals (pardon the pun) that something has happened which requires the process's attention.

As a simple example, let's go back to the terminal/server application. Say that the server has created a number of terminal processes, and then gets a command to shut down. It really *should* shut down all its terminals as well. A signal, sent from the server to the terminals, serves the purpose nicely. The appropriate code in the server is a single line added to *shutdown_server*:

```
#define SIG_GO_AWAY SIGUSR1      /* An available signal */

void shutdown_server(void)
{
    printf("Shutting down server\n");
```

```
    /* Kill all children with a signal to the process group */
    kill(0, SIG_GO_AWAY);
}
```

This modification has the result of delivering a signal to every process in the process group of the server when the server exits. On the terminal side, we can simply let the signal kill the process, or we can arrange for a more graceful *exit* by handling the signal, as follows:

```
void
terminate_normally(int signo)
{
    /* Exit gracefully */
    exit(0);
}

main(int argc, char **argv)
{
    struct sigaction sa;
    sa.sa_handler = terminate_normally;
    sigemptyset(&sa.sa_mask);
    sa.sa_flags = 0;
    if (sigaction(SIG_GO_AWAY, &sa, NULL)) {
        perror("sigaction");
        exit(1);
    }
    ...
}
```

In this example, the child process sets up a signal handler using *sigaction*. When the signal arrives, the function *terminate_normally* will be called. It, in turn, can do whatever is necessary to deal with the signal. In this case, it just *exits*. In a real application, it would probably clean up the terminal screen again so it could be used for something else.

When do signals occur?
In the example above, the signal was used as an interprocess communication mechanism. However, that's not what signals are best at. Signals occur when:

*   A machine *exception* occurs: a page fault, a floating point exception, and so forth. These are the *synchronously-generated* signals, because they happen in immediate or near-immediate response to something the process itself does.

*   Something happens, asynchronous to the process's execution, to *interrupt* that process's execution. For instance, job control (someone typed CTRL-Z at the keyboard to stop the process) or user interruption (someone typed CTRL-C to terminate the process), or asynchronous I/O completion, timer expiration, or receipt of a message on a message queue.

*   Some other process explicitly decides to send a signal to the process.

Should you use signals for interprocess communication?

Because a process can send a signal to another process, signals can be used for inter-process communication. Signals are almost never the appropriate choice as a communication mechanism; they're too slow, too limited, the queuing is insufficient, and they asynchronously interrupt your process in ways that require clumsy coding to deal with. However, there are occasions when signals *are* an appropriate communication mechanism, either alone or in combination with a secondary means. In our example, for instance, the signal was a simple means of notifying the terminals of a simple occurrence. The mechanism interrupts the terminal's normal processing without requiring a lot of coding on either side—exactly what we want!

Signals are mostly used for other reasons, like the timer expiration and asynchronous I/O completion mentioned above. A real application needs to know how to deal with signals, even if it's not using signals to pass messages. Signals are generated for a number of reasons, but in the discussions that follow, I'm going to concentrate on signal-based interprocess communication: processes sending signals to each other as a sort of message-passing. We'll cover signals delivered for other reasons in the chapters that discuss those reasons.

There are legitimate reasons for using signals to communicate between processes. First, signals are something of a lowest common denominator in UNIX systems—everyone's got signals, even if they don't have anything else! If you want a technical reason, signals offer an advantage that other, higher-performance communication mechanisms do not support: signals are asynchronous. That is, a signal can be delivered to you while you are doing something else. In the case of POSIX.4, signals allow you to perform I/O asynchronously, to set timers to expire some time in the future, or to be notified when a message queue enters a particularly propitious state. In contrast, if you're using synchronous functions, you must explicitly go look to see whether a service you want is available, and possibly block, awaiting for your service. You wait to read data from the disk, wait on a semaphore, and wait for a message to be delivered on a queue. The advantages of asynchrony are:

- **Immediacy**. You are notified immediately (for *some* value of immediately) when something occurs.

- **Concurrency**. You can be off doing something else while other processing goes on concurrently with your application. When that other processing completes, you are notified via a signal.

There are also disadvantages to asynchrony:

- **Complexity**. If your application must prepare for the possibility of a signal at any point in its execution, the application is going to become more complex. With complexity comes a lack of robustness, difficulty in understanding and maintaining, and so on.

- **Non-determinism**. You don't really know when a signal is going to arrive, relative to other signals or even to the event that caused the signal to be delivered. Signal delivery happens "under the hood" of the operating system, and isn't very well specified at all. This is as it should be, since different operating systems implement signals in different ways.

- **Lower performance**. Signals are slower than the synchronous mechanisms for communication, because asynchrony costs. It takes time to stop an application, set up an appropriate environment in which to call the signal handler, and then actually call the handler. None of that overhead is required when one is just synchronously waiting for an occurrence.

That said, signals definitely have their place. In our server/terminals application, using signals for communication from the server and the terminals allows the terminal to be off doing something else, like responding quickly to user keystrokes, while the database server is off humming on some humongous request submitted earlier. At the completion of the request, the server sends a signal to the terminal process, interrupting whatever it was doing. The terminal can then paint a particular area of the screen with a message that request #86 is now completed and ready for perusal. This basic asynchrony is visible to the terminal user as the ability to do multiple jobs at once—a feature that "power users" generally love.

Crush, kill, destroy

One process sends a signal to another process by using the ominously-named *kill* call. To send a signal, all that the sender has to know is the process ID of the victim. There are also some permission checks done: we can't have arbitrary processes killing off other, unrelated processes, now can we? *kill* is so named because the result of this action is usually the abrupt and abnormal termination of the target process, unless the other process has done something special, like set up a handler, in preparation for the signal.

Back to the permission-checking issue: you can send a signal to another process if your process has the same real or effective user ID as the victim process. One of the sender's IDs has to match one of the victim's IDs. Usually, this means that the user who created the sender process also needs to create the victim process. Getting the permissions right can be difficult, especially in an asynchronous environment like that of the terminal/server application. One possibility is to have an "overlord" process that spawns all terminal *and* server processes. This setup is also generally useful for managing software failures: the overlord can monitor its children and deal with unexpected failures. Another possibility is to use the *setuid* capability to artificially set the effective user ID of any process to that of a particular user. You would do this by setting the S_ISUID mode bit for the executable file. Since this is an issue marginally related to real time, and is as much a system configuration issue as anything else, I'm going to leave its discussion to those volumes. Suffice it to say here, that you may have permission problems in sending signals in all but the most obvious cases (parent spawns child, parent can *kill* child, for instance).

Signals are identified by their number. Each POSIX-conformant system supports a variety of signal numbers, usually more than POSIX itself requires. Each number has a particular meaning and effect on the process that gets the signal. For portability, you never use the actual number of the signal; you never send signal 13 to a process. That's because 13 means something on one system, but may mean something else entirely on another system. Instead, you include the header *<signal.h>* and use the symbolic names for signals which are defined in that header. Most signal numbers are used for particular system-dictated actions, and you shouldn't go around sending them from one process to another, because the system may also send those signals for important reasons of its own. As Table 3-1 shows, POSIX requires several different signals, but only two are avilable for your application to use: SIGUSR1 and SIGUSR2. POSIX.4 defines many more application-available signals, which are detailed in Table 3-2. I recommend that you encapsulate your use of signals into a small section of code, so that if you need to change signal numbers from one platform to another, you can do so easily. In our example, you saw how I defined my own constant, SIG_GO_AWAY. In practice, I'd put that definition in a header file that both the terminal and the server included.

Table 3–1: Signals Required by POSIX (Default Action Termination)

Signal Name	Used For
SIGABRT	Abnormal termination, abort
SIGALRM	Alarm clock expired (real-time clocks)
SIGFPE	Floating point exception
SIGHUP	Controlling terminal hung up (Probably a modem or network connection)
SIGILL	Illegal instruction exception
SIGINT	Interactive termination (usually CTRL-C at the keyboard)
SIGKILL	Unstoppable termination (signal 9 on most UNIX systems)
SIGPIPE	Writing to a pipe with no readers
SIGQUIT	Abnormal termination signal (interactive processes)
SIGSEGV	Memory access exception
SIGTERM	Terminate process
SIGUSR1	Application-defined uses
SIGUSR2	Application-defined uses

Table 3-2: POSIX Optional Signals

Signal Name	Default Action	Used For
Option: _POSIX_JOB_CONTROL		
SIGCHLD	Signal Ignored	Child died or stopped
SIGSTOP	Stop the process	Stops process (uncatchable)
SIGTSTP	Stop the process	Stops process (from terminal)
SIGCONT	Continue process	Continues stopped process
SIGTTOU	Stop the process that tries to write to the terminal	Stop a background process
SIGTTIN	Stop the process that tries to read from the terminal	Stop a background process
Option: _POSIX_REALTIME_SIGNALS		
SIGRTMIN-SIGRTMAX	Termination	Application-defined uses

Dealing with Signals

kill itself is not enough to build a complete communication interface between processes. They don't call it *kill* for nothing. If your terminal process does not set itself up properly to deal with the arrival of SIGUSR1, the result will be that the process that gets the signal will be terminated—killed. How's *that* for communication? In order to avoid this abrupt termination, you need to prepare the target process (also known as the victim) for the signal.

There are three ways in which you can deal with a signal.

1. You can *block* the signal for a while, and get to it (by unblocking it) later. Blocking signals is only a temporary measure.

2. You can *ignore* the signal, in which case it is as if the signal never arrives.

3. You can *handle* the signal, by setting up a function to be called whenever a signal with a particular number (e.g., SIGUSR1) arrives.

The terminal/server example *handles* the signal by calling *sigaction*.

Signal handlers and ignoring signals

The *sigaction* is used to set all the details of what your process should do when a signal arrives. The *struct sigaction* encapsulates the action to be taken on receipt of a particular signal. *struct sigaction* has the following form (element order may vary):

```
struct sigaction {
    void (*sa_handler)();
    sigset_t sa_mask;
    int sa_flags;
    void (*sa_sigaction)(int, siginfo_t *, void *);
};
```

The most important member is *sa_handler,* which takes a pointer to a function. This function will be invoked whenever the process gets a particular POSIX.1 signal. The signal handler function is declared like this:

```
void handler_for_SIGUSR1(int signum);
```

The handler is passed the number of the signal as its sole argument. This allows you to use one handler function for a number of different signals, and still handle the different signals differently (of course, you could use different functions for different signal numbers, too).

POSIX.1 does not use an ANSI C function prototype for *sa_handler* in the *sigaction* structure. That means that no compile-time checking of the arguments passed to your handlers will be done. In the future, though, an ANSI C prototype may be used. In that case, you'd better make sure that your signal handlers all take a single, integer argument. It's also important to note that many signal handlers take *more* than the single, integer argument. In particular, POSIX.4 queued signals take additional arguments, as described later in this chapter. These signal handlers would break under ANSI prototyping for the old-style, single-argument signal handlers. The solution is to use a *new, different* field of the *sigaction* for these sorts of handlers. For handling POSIX.1 signals, use *sa_handler.* A system-defined constant, SIG_IGN, can be assigned to *sa_handler* to indicate that, for this particular signal, the system should just ignore it and not deliver it to the process. This is different than merely blocking a signal. If a process has blocked a particular signal, and that signal is delivered to the process, then that signal occurrence will remain pending until you unblock the signal. At that point you can expect the signal to be delivered to you. SIG_IGN, in contrast, is essentially a null handler, a handler function that just returns, having done nothing at all. If you wanted to reset the action for a signal to the default action (terminate the process), you could do so by specifying SIG_DFL as the *sa_handler* field in a call to *sigaction.*

A problem that often arises with signals is that your handling of a particular signal may interfere with some other software component's handling of the same signal. For instance, if your signal uses SIGUSR1, and you build your application using some outside party's libraries that also use SIGUSR1, you may end up in a situation where your handler gets replaced by the third-party library's handler for SIGUSR1. Instant program failure! Alternatively, you may find yourself in the converse situation: if you are writing code to be used by diverse application writers, they may unknowingly interfere with your signal handling. For instance, our "database server and terminals" example application may be a generic library of routines you're trying to sell to people, to build into their own specific on-line database applications. You need to take this possibility into account. One of the things you can do in your code is use the *old_action* parameter to *sigaction* to remember what the previous signal state was, and, when you are done handling that particular signal, to restore the old signal action. In other words, clean up after yourself. You can successfully use this strategy for synchronously generated signals. For instance, if you write some code that may possibly get a floating point error, you could bracket it with signal handling:

```
#include <signal.h>
/* Handler for floating point exceptions */
extern void handler_for_SIGFPE(int);
struct sigaction action, old_action;
int i;

action.sa_flags = 0;
sigemptyset(&action.sa_mask):
action.sa_handler = handler_for_SIGFPE;

/* Install temporary signal handling mechanism */
i = sigaction(SIGFPE, &action, &old_action);

/* Perform calculations, possibly generating SIGFPE */

/* Put old signal handler back */
i = sigaction(SIGFPE, &old_action, (struct sigaction *)NULL);
```

Unfortunately, this is only a partial solution and it really doesn't solve the problem, especially when the signals may be generated asynchronously. In that case you need to leave your handler installed all the time. Really, what is required is that components of an application have to advertise which signals they expect to be able to use. Again, try to keep your use of signals into contained code areas, in case you need to switch signal numbers when you port from one system to another. It's a very good idea to define your own signal names in header files, so you can easily switch signals when porting. Finally, document the signals you rely on for your application's correct behavior. You, and users of your code, will be thankful for such documentation later.

The second member of the *struct sigaction* is *sa_mask,* which defines the set of signals to be blocked from delivery while your handler is executing. The mask in effect while a signal is being handled is calculated by taking the mask currently in effect for the process, adding in the signal being delivered (SIGUSR1 in our example), and then adding in all the signals in the set indicated by *sa_mask.* (The signal being delivered is added to the mask because you usually don't want *another* occurrence of a signal happening while you're in the middle of handling the first one.) None of the signals in the resulting signal mask will be delivered for the duration of the signal handler.*

The *sa_flags* field can have special flags set in it to indicate to the system that it should handle the signal in various special ways. The only flag value defined by POSIX.1 is SA_NOCLDSTOP. This flag has to do with _POSIX_JOB_CONTROL and stopping processes. Basically, the SIGCHLD signal is sent to a parent process when a child process terminates. Optionally, systems that support job control may send SIGCHLD to the parent process when a child process stops. If this flag is set, then the system knows *not* to send this signal to the parent process when and if the child processes stop. This flag is

---

* Two signals are defined as unstoppable: SIGKILL and SIGSTOP. Attempts to block, ignore, or handle these signals will be silently ignored by the operating system.

generally of concern when you are writing command shells and other sorts of applications that are intertwined with job control.

For SIGRTMIN through SIGRTMAX (the POSIX.4 standard's new signals), you set *sa_sigaction*, not *sa_handler*. This is a heads-up to you; we'll discuss these enhanced handlers later in this chapter.

Blocking signals and signal masks

You may want to deal with a signal in different ways depending on where you are in your code. Think about the terminal example. In general, we can just set up a handler for SIGUSR1 and deal with the signal when it arrives. The only exception will be when the terminal is doing something that the signal handler code itself might also want to do. For instance, the signal handler may paint an area of the screen, or clean it up entirely. It may be error-prone, therefore, to get that signal when the terminal process is in the middle of updating the screen for some other reason. Thus, the terminal process may also want to block SIGUSR1 for various sections of code. Signal blocking is usually a temporary measure, because you can always unblock the signal and let it through. But there are times in your application when you *really don't want* to have a particular signal arrive.

Each POSIX process has associated with it a signal mask that dictates which signals will be passed through to the process, and which will be held pending, or blocked, until that signal number is removed from the mask.

Signal Sets and Masks

You'll hear about the signal mask, and about signal sets, pretty much interchangeably. You might be confused by that, since "mask" seems to indicate a bit mask, and "set" seems to indicate an abstract data structure. POSIX tries hard to talk about sets of signals, rather than signal numbers and masks. That's to allow for an extensible *sigset_t*. One vendor may implement the *sigset_t* as a short, 16-bit quantity that will only really allow you to deal with 16 signals. Another vendor might support 64 signals by using two 32-bit-long integers. A particular signal, like SIGUSR1, is a number (like 13); the system usually adds that signal to a set by ORing the corresponding bit into a bit vector. This explanation is for your edification; you really do need to use the POSIX "signal set" facilities, explained below, to achieve portable signal handling.

Where does the initial signal mask come from? A process's signal mask is inherited from its parent process when the parent *forks*. On *exec*, the process's signal mask is *unchanged*. Be sure to explicitly set it before you *exec*. You change the process's mask using the *sigprocmask* call, or by having a new signal mask installed as part of a signal handler invocation (see above discussion of *sigaction.sa_mask*).

```
#include <signal.h>

sigset_t newset, oldset;
int i;

i = sigprocmask(SIG_BLOCK, &newset, &oldset);
i = sigprocmask(SIG_UNBLOCK, &newset, &oldset);
i = sigprocmask(SIG_SETMASK, &newset, &oldset);
```

Using *sigprocmask*, you can add signals to be blocked, subtract signals from the mask, or set the mask, depending on whether the value of the first argument is SIG_BLOCK, SIG_UNBLOCK, or SIG_SETMASK, respectively. The signals in the argument *newset* are those that are added, subtracted, or become the process's signal mask. The final argument, if it's not NULL, will have the previous signal mask of the process stored into it by the system when you call *sigprocmask*. This allows you to nest calls to *sigprocmask*, restoring previous masks as you leave nesting levels.

The second argument can also be NULL. If that's the case, then the system will just store the current signal mask into *oldmask*. (If that parameter is also NULL, then the call doesn't do anything.)

When you have blocked a signal, and that signal is sent to your process, it remains *pending* for you until you unblock the signal. When you do unblock a signal that is pending, you should immediately expect to receive the signal.

Now, we need to know how to set up these signal sets we're passing in to *sigprocmask*. POSIX defines a whole set of functions for manipulating the signal sets.

*sigemptyset(sigset_t *s)*

  This function initializes a signal set to be empty, no signals in it.

*sigfillset(sigset_t *s)*

  This function initializes a signal set to be full; all the signals defined by POSIX will be in the set.

  You must always initialize a signal set by calling either *sigemptyset* or *sigfillset* (or by passing the set as the *oldset* argument to *sigprocmask*). Then, you can add or subtract signals from the initialized set with the following two functions:

*sigaddset(sigset_t *s, int signum)*

  This function adds the signal numbered *signum* to the set *s*.

*sigdelset(sigset_t *s, int signum)*

  This function removes the signal numbered *signum* from the set *s*.

*sigismember(sigset_t *s, int signum)*

  Finally, you can use this function to tell you whether the signal *signum* is in the set *s*.

All of the *sigset_t* manipulation functions described above may return -1 and set *errno* to EINVAL if you pass them a bad signal number, but they don't have to. In the usual implementation, all these functions are macros that expand to a shift and logical operation (OR or AND), and adding a check for a bogus signal number would greatly slow down the function. Use the symbolic signal names defined by POSIX, not actual numeric values, and you'll be okay.

Synchronizing with signals

Signals interrupt whatever your application is doing, but what if your application runs out of things to do? For example, our terminal process runs in an infinite loop. At the bottom of that loop, it may well wish to pause and wait for a signal returned from the server process. Perhaps this new signal indicates something else, like the completion of some piece of work the terminal has earlier submitted. POSIX supports this requirement with another call, *sigsuspend:*

```
#define SIG_GO_AWAY       SIGUSR1
#define SIG_QUERY_COMPLETE  SIGUSR2

void query_has_completed(int signo)
{
  ...
}

main(int argc, char **argv)
    struct sigaction sa;
    sigset_t wait_for_these;

    sa.sa_handler = query_has_completed;
    sigemptyset(&sa.sa_mask);
    sa.sa_flags = 0;
    if (sigaction(SIG_QUERY_COMPLETE, &sa, NULL)) {
        perror("sigaction");
        exit(1);
    }
    sigemptyset(&wait_for_these);
    sigaddset(&wait_for_these, SIG_QUERY_COMPLETE);
    sigprocmask(SIG_BLOCK, &wait_for_these, NULL);
    ...
    while (1) {
        /* Deal with the screen */
        /* Await server response */
        (void)sigsuspend(&wait_for_these);
    }
    ....
```

sigsuspend takes the signal mask you pass in, installs it as the signal mask of the process, and then halts execution of the process until an unblocked signal arrives. When that happens, the signal handler for that signal is invoked. When the handler is done, *sigsuspend* will return; it always returns -1 with *errno* set to EINTR. You may as well just ignore this return code.

You'll notice that we've also added some signal blocking calls. In fact, the new signal, SIG_QUERY_COMPLETE (a.k.a. SIGUSR2), is *always* blocked except for when *sigsuspend* is called. This is necessary, but why?

Imagine that, in your process, SIGUSR2 is not blocked. That means, at any point, it could arrive. You would probably have some sort of indicator that the signal has occurred. For instance, you could use a global variable, as in the following (buggy!) code:

```
int sigusr2_occurred = 0;

void handler_for_SIGUSR2(int signo)
{
        ...
        sigusr2_occurred = 1;
        ...
}

main
{
        ...
        /* SIGUSR2 can be delivered at any time */
        while (! sigusr2_occurred) {
                sigsuspend(mask);
        }
        ...
}
```

When you look at *sigusr2_occurred* in the main routine, if may be zero. So you decide to block. In the instant *after* you look at *sigusr2_occurred* and *before* you call *sigsuspend,* SIGUSR2 gets delivered, the handler goes off, and *sigusr2_occurred* is set to 1. Now, your *sigsuspend* call will sleep arbitrarily long, waiting for a signal *that has already occurred!*

In order to repair this race condition, you must check *sigusr2_occurred* while SIGUSR2 is blocked from arrival, and then atomically unblock SIGUSR2 and wait for it by calling *sigsuspend:*

```
main
{
        sigset_t block_sigusr2;

        sigemptyset(&block_sigusr2);
        sigaddset(&block_sigusr2, SIGUSR2);
        sigprocmask(SIG_BLOCK, &block_sigusr2, NULL);

        /* SIGUSR2 is blocked */
        while (! sigusr2_occurred) {
                (void)sigsuspend(mask);
        /* Atomically unblock and wait for SIGUSR2 */
        }
        ...
}
```

Problems with POSIX.1 Signals for Communication

POSIX.1 signals provide one basic mechanism for asynchronous communication between processes. However, they are not ideal for this purpose. Imagine, for instance, that we want to use signals between our server and terminal processes to indicate the completion of queries that the terminal had earlier sent to the server. Using signals for this purpose would enable the terminal to continue processing, while the server fulfilled an earlier request. However, there are some serious problems if you want to use the POSIX.1 signals. These problems include:

- Lack of signals for application use
- Lack of signal queueing
- No signal delivery order
- Poor information content
- Asynchrony
- Speed

POSIX.4 addresses a few of these problems, so we'll discuss those problems below as a lead-in. POSIX.4 does *not* address the more serious problems with signals-as-communication-mechanism, so we'll talk about those problems after we've discussed the POSIX.4 signals extensions.

Lack of signals

There aren't enough distinct signal numbers available for application use. SIGUSR1 and SIGUSR2, defined by POSIX.1 and most standard UNIX systems, are simply not enough. It's easy to see that our simple application could easily want to use more signals than POSIX.1 provides.

Signal queueing

Imagine our application fires off five queries. The server processes these, then sends back five signals (all SIGUSR2, say) to indicate query completion. How may signals does the terminal receive? Unfortunately, it may receive as few as two.

In traditional UNIX systems, signals are not queued. When a signal occurs and cannot be immediately delivered to the process (because it's blocked, for instance), most signal implementations register the fact that the signal is there by setting a bit corresponding to that signal. When the signal is actually delivered, the bit is cleared. Thereafter, another signal will cause the bit to be set again.

But what happens when a second signal is delivered *before* the first signal can be handled? In general, the system treats it just like the first signal: it sets the same bit as was set for the first signal's arrival. When the process finally gets around to handling the signal, there is only the memory of one signal having happened!

This lack of queueing capability is why signals are considered to be an unreliable means of communication between processes. Messages can be lost if the messenger is a signal.[*]

Signal delivery order

If there are multiple signals pending for a process, POSIX.1 doesn't say anything about the order in which these signals are delivered to the process. This can be a problem in some applications. You might want to use some signals for high-priority messages, and other signals for less-important uses. You'd like to know that the high-priority messages always get delivered before the low-priority messages. Using just POSIX.1 signals, there's no way of assuring that sort of delivery order for signals.

Information content of signals

The information content implicit in a signal delivery is minimal, really almost binary. The target process only knows that, for example, SIGUSR1 happened. Any additional information must be transmitted by ad-hoc means. For our terminal example, for instance, the terminal process must know implicitly that a SIGUSR1 means that a transaction has completed, and that it should go and check which transaction is done. This almost always implies some more communication than the mere signal has to happen between the terminal and the server. Clearly, the low bandwidth of information transfer in a signal is an impediment to using signals for serious communication.

Asynchrony

Signals can arrive at any time in a process's execution. This means that your code must be prepared for the possibility of a signal arriving at any spot in your code. If you are modifying a data structure that a signal handler also touches, for instance, you must go to special extremes to be sure that the signal does not occur at exactly the wrong time—while you're in the middle of modifying your data structure. This enforced paranoia in your code leads to additional complexity and opens the door for a whole new class of bugs: race conditions between your process and its own signal handlers. In contrast, synchronous, event driven applications can be much simpler to design, code, and debug.

POSIX.4 Extensions to POSIX.1 Signals

POSIX.4 has made a set of changes to the POSIX.1 signals model. The presence of the POSIX.4 signals extensions is indicated by the constant _POSIX_REALTIME_SIGNALS being defined in *<unistd.h>*. These changes address, with varying degrees of success, all the problems mentioned above (except for asynchrony, which is a necessary evil implicit in the nature of signals). In making these changes, POSIX.4 walked a tightrope.

---

[*] In POSIX.1 (ISO 9945-1 (1990)), it's stated that the queueing, or lack thereof, of signals is implementation-defined (page 53, lines 463-464). That means that somewhere in the conformance statement for a particular system, it will tell you whether or not signals are queued. Some systems *do* queue signals. However, you certainly cannot count on it.

On the one hand, the existing signal functions, inappropriate though they were for communication, could not be wholly abandoned,* nor could they be altered so that existing (non-real-time) code would no longer work. The approach that POSIX.4 took was to define a new set of signals, and then to change the semantics for this new set of signals. That way, old code would continue to function correctly using the old signals, but code using the new signals could reap the benefits of the POSIX.4 modifications.

As an example, here is code for our client/server application that communicates between the server and the client using POSIX.4's real-time extended signals. The server simply sends a signal, using the new function *sigqueue*:

```
#define SIG_QUERY_COMPLETE SIGRTMIN

void
send_reply(request_t r)
{
    union sigval sval;

    /* Send a notification to the terminal */
    sval.sival_ptr = r->r_params;
    if (sigqueue(r->r_requestor, SIG_QUERY_COMPLETE, sval) < 0)
        perror("sigqueue");
}
```

The client-side code is slightly more complicated, requiring a signal handler be set up:

```
#define SIG_QUERY_COMPLETE SIGRTMIN

void
query_has_completed(int signo, siginfo_t *info, void *ignored)
{
    /* Deal with query completion.  Query identifier could
     * be stored as integer or pointer in info. */

    void *ptr_val = info->si_value.sival_ptr;
    int int_val = info->si_value.sival_int;

    printf("Val %08x completed\n", int_val);
    return;
}

main(int argc, char **argv)
{
    struct sigaction sa;

    sa.sa_handler = terminate_normally;
    sigemptyset(&sa.sa_mask);
    sa.sa_flags = 0;
```

---

* The POSIX.4 working group tried this approach first, and got large numbers of ballot objections. People, it seems, like using a single general mechanism for diverse needs. I can't say that I blame them.

```
    if (sigaction(SIG_GO_AWAY, &sa, NULL)) {
        perror("sigaction");
        exit(1);
    }

    sa.sa_sigaction = query_has_completed;
    sigemptyset(&sa.sa_mask);
    sa.sa_flags = SA_SIGINFO;    /* This is a queued signal */
    if (sigaction(SIG_QUERY_COMPLETE, &sa, NULL)) {
        perror("sigaction");
        exit(1);
    }
    ...
```

The example above points out many of the differences between POSIX.1 signals and the new, real-time extended signals:

- A new set of signals is used: SIGRTMIN through SIGRTMAX.

- The signal handler is set up with a new flag, SA_SIGINFO, which turns on queueing of the signal.

- The signal handler is defined as a new sort of function, taking more arguments than the normal signal function. These arguments are used to pass extra data.

There are more signals

The first, biggest perceived problems with signals were the dearth of signals for use by an application, and the lack of signal queueing. To address this problem, POSIX.4 defines a new set of signals. The new signal numbers begin with SIGRTMIN and proceed up through SIGRTMAX, inclusive. There must be at least RTSIG_MAX real-time signals between SIGRTMIN and SIGRTMAX. SIGRTMIN and SIGRTMAX come from *<signal.h>*, while RTSIG_MAX comes from *<limits.h>*. RTSIG_MAX must be at least 8. The new features described below apply only to these new signals, so don't expect them to work for SIGUSR1 and SIGUSR2.

When you use the POSIX.4 real-time signals, refer to them in terms of SIGRTMIN and SIGRTMAX, rather than using actual numbers. That is, your code should use SIGRTMIN+1 as the second real-time signal number. Again, it's an even better idea to define your own signal names, for easy redefinition during a port. That's what I've done with SIG_QUERY_COMPLETE.

Although SIGRTMIN and SIGRTMAX *look* like your basic constants (they're in all caps, and that's usually the way I indicate a constant), they may not be constants. In particular, an implementation is free to resolve these symbols at runtime in whatever way it chooses. All this really means is that you cannot use your compiler for automatic error detection. For instance, the following code will not work:

```
#include <signal.h>

#if SIGRTMIN+300 > SIGRTMAX
ERROR--Not enough real-time signals!
```

```
#else
#define HIGH_PRIORITY_MESSAGE_SIGNAL (SIGRTMIN + 300)
#endif
```

Instead, you'd need to put a check in your application, preferably in the beginning section of code where you do all your conformance testing:

```
#define HIGH_PRIORITY_MESSAGE_SIGNAL (SIGRTMIN + 300)

if (HIGH_PRIORITY_MESSAGE_SIGNAL > SIGRTMAX) {
        fprintf(stderr, "ERROR--Not enough real-time signals!\n");
        exit(1);
}
```

Real-time signals are queued and carry extra data

The queueing behavior of POSIX.4 signals, as well as the additional information-carrying capability of these signals is enabled by setting a new bit in the *sa_flags* field of the *sigaction* structure. This bit is called SA_SIGINFO. It indicates that the corresponding signal number is going to be carrying a little more information than a normal signal, and so it should be queued to the process rather than being registered, as before, by the setting of a bit.

There are two important parts to this example. One, you must set SA_SIGINFO in *sa_flags* in order to get queued signal behavior. An additional, subtle point is that, for queued signals, one uses *sa_sigaction*, not *sa_handler*! POSIX.4 has defined an additional "field" in *struct sigaction,* and this field is used only to register the handler for a queued signal. This handler field is an ANSI C prototype, and will allow for compile-time argument checking. Be very careful in your application to use the proper field for the proper signal. If you are queueing signals, use *sa_sigaction*. Otherwise, and for normal signals, use *sa_handler.** When SA_SIGINFO is set for a particular signal, multiple occurrences of the signal are queued to the process. If SIGRTMIN is generated twenty times, then it will be delivered to the process twenty times. Period.

SA_SIGINFO also increases the amount of information delivered by each signal. Remember that a POSIX.1 signal handler is invoked with a single parameter, the signal number. If SA_SIGINFO is set, then the signal handlers have three parameters:

```
void handler_for_SIGRTMIN(int signum, siginfo_t *data, void *extra);
```

The *signum* parameter is as before, and the *extra* parameter is undefined by POSIX.4 (it has meaning in several standard UNIX systems, however, generally referring to the machine context at the time of the signal; POSIX.4 defines it so as not to gratuitously break the function prototypes used in those implementations). The real addition is the

---

* The existence of two different handler fields is something that you may find slightly odiferous (I do). After thinking about it for a little while, though, it seems to have been the easiest and cleanest way out of this issue of ANSI C prototyping of signal handlers. That is precisely why there are two different fields. In fact, a clever-enough system can use the same storage in the *struct sigaction* for both fields! So, there is not necessarily any hit taken in extra space required—but there is a price to be paid in interface complexity. *C'est la guerre.*

data parameter, which allows an additional piece of information to piggyback on a signal's delivery. The extra data is a pointer to a structure called a *siginfo_t,* defined as follows:

```
typedef struct {
    ...
    int si_signo;
    int si_code;
    union sigval si_value;
    ...
} siginfo_t;
```

The most important field of the *siginfo_t* is the extra data value, passed to the handler in *si_value.* In our example, the server passed a value to *sigqueue* in *sval.* That same value is the value that would appear in the client's signal handler as *info->si_value!* This field is a union, so that it can contain numerous different sorts of values. The POSIX.4 definition of *sigval* requires the following members:

```
union sigval {
    ...
    int sival_int;        /* Integer data value */
    void *sival_ptr;      /* Pointer data value */
    ...
};
```

This union allows either an integer or a pointer data value to be passed along with the signal number. In most code, you'll use one or the other, not both, as in my example.

The *si_signo* field is the signal number, which will always be the same as the first parameter to the signal handler.

si_code yields more information about the cause of the signal, in case you are delivering one signal for various different uses. Other sections of POSIX.4 exploit these signal extensions for their own uses: asynchronous I/O, message passing, and timers all use signals. The *si_code* field tells you which POSIX facility was responsible for the signal. It may have one of the following values:

SI_QUEUE

  The signal was sent by the *sigqueue* function, as in our example.

SI_TIMER

  The signal was delivered because of timer expiration (see *timer_settime* in the clocks and timers section).

SI_ASYNCIO

  The signal was delivered as a result of asynchronous I/O completion (see *aio_read, aio_write, lio_listio,* in the section on asynchronous I/O).

SI_MESGQ

  The signal was delivered as a result of a message arriving to an empty message queue (see *mq_notify* in the section on message passing).

SI_USER

The signal was sent by *kill,* or some other *kill*–like function such as *abort* or *raise*.

Our example code did not use the *si_code* field, both for clarity of the example and because there was no possibility of the signal having been sent by anything other than *sigqueue*.

Sending a real-time signal

The *kill* function is used to send a normal POSIX.1 signal, but it will not suffice for sending real-time signals. That's because there's no way to pass that extra signal value argument along. POSIX.4 defines *sigqueue*, which adds another data parameter to the signal to be sent. *sigqueue* looks a lot like *kill,* on which it is modeled. The only real difference, aside from the name, is the third parameter, a *union sigval*. Notice that the *sigval* is passed by value, not by address. The value is passed to the victim's signal handler as the *si_value* field of the *siginfo_t*. In most other respects, *sigqueue* is identical to *kill*.

There is one additional failure mode for *sigqueue*. Each signal queued to a process requires some amount of system resources. Eventually, the system can reach a state where no more signals can be queued, either by this process, or perhaps even in the system as a whole. POSIX.4 defines a per-process limit on the number of signals that can be *sigqueued* by a single process but not yet received by the target process(es). This limit is given in *<limits.h>* by SIGQUEUE_MAX. I find it more probable that the limit will be system-wide, rather than per-process. In either case, *sigqueue* will return EAGAIN when there are not enough system resources left to *sigqueue* another signal.

You might be wondering how the application determines *which* field of the *union sigval* should be used, pointer or integer. The answer is that the application has to figure it out. Unlike other unions (the UNIX version of *union wait*, for instance), there is nothing that can be used to determine which version of the *union sigval* has meaning. Generally, applications know this by convention. You wrote the sender, you wrote the receiver. You should know.

The real-time signals are delivered in order ·

There is no defined delivery order for POSIX.1 signals. If multiple signals are pending, you don't know which one will be delivered first. Not so with POSIX.4's queued signals. These signals are delivered lowest-numbered signal first. Thus, the higher-priority communications should be given the lower-numbered signals (SIGRTMIN is highest priority; SIGRTMAX is lowest).

The ordering of POSIX.1 signal delivery is not specified by POSIX.4, nor is the order of queued signals relative to the basic POSIX.1 signals. (In most cases, you'd imagine that the POSIX.1 signals would be delivered first. Notification of a segmentation fault or a floating point error should generally take precedence over a communication signal!)

Other real-time signals and the sigevent structure

So far, we've talked about real-time signals sent by the *sigqueue* function. However, most POSIX.4 signals are sent as a result of three other facilities in POSIX.4. We'll cover these facilities in detail in their own chapters, but for now, you need to know that real-time signals can be generated as a result of expiration of a POSIX.4 timer, completion of asynchronous I/O, and by arrival of a message on an empty message queue.

In these three cases, there's no server process to *sigqueue* a signal; there's no way for that data value to be set. Instead, the data value is set as part of initialization of the timer, the asynchronous I/O or the message queue, by using a structure called a *sigevent*. This structure totally encapsulates all the information needed for the system to send a signal later, when necessary. The *sigevent* structure is described below, and we'll talk about where it's used when we talk about the individual facilities (asynchronous I/O, messages, and timers) concerned.

The *sigevent* structure is used to encapsulate and contain all the parts that are required to describe a signal (or some other means of asynchronous notification). This structure has three fields:

```
struct sigevent {
        ...
        int             sigev_notify;   /* Asynchronous mechanism being used */
        ...
        int             sigev_signo;    /* Number of signal to be delivered */
        ...
        union sigval    sigev_value;    /* Value for real-time signal */
        ...
};
```

First, the field *sigev_notify* defines which asynchronous notification mechanism is being described by this structure. POSIX.4 defines only one such mechanism, the signal. That makes this field seem just a little silly at first glance. However, there are other mechanisms that could be used instead of signals, which might be much faster than signals. POSIX.4 did not want to rule out the capability of using such mechanisms, whenever they become available. So, for now, *sigev_notify* is there for future extensibility.[*] At the moment, you can set it to two possible values:

- SIGEV_SIGNALS: use signals for asynchronous notification.
- SIGEV_NONE: don't use anything for asynchronous notification.

If you set *sigev_notify* to SIGEV_NONE, you basically turn off the asynchronous notification for whatever you're using this *sigevent* for. If you set it to SIGEV_SIGNALS, you're using signals. We'll assume you're going to set it to SIGEV_SIGNALS. In that case, the

---

[*] In fact, another POSIX document has already extended it. POSIX.4a—threads—defines a new delivery mechanism, SIGEV_THREAD, which causes a function to be called upon completion of the asynchronous operation. Although it sounds sort of like a signal handler function, this function might be called in any process's context, leading to better performance due to a lack of signal-handling overhead.

two other fields describe the signal you want delivered whenever the system decides it has to send you a signal (because asynchronous I/O completed, a message was received, or a timer expired).

Two members completely describe a signal. First, *sigev_signo* indicates the number of the signal to be delivered. If the number is between SIGRTMIN and SIGRTMAX, and you've set SA_SIGINFO for the signal action for that signal, then there is also an associated data value to be passed to your signal handler. That value is given by the *union sigval* in the *sigev_value* field. When the signal is delivered, that is the value that will be used for the *si_value* field of the *context* argument to the signal handler.

As usual, implementations are allowed to define additional fields in this structure. In this case, they almost certainly will, to support additional implementation-defined notification mechanisms besides signals.

Faster response to signals

The other thing which POSIX.4 added to the standard signals interface was another way to wait for signals to arrive. (It's not the waiting part that's sped up, but rather the speed with which a blocked process can be awakened when an awaited signal arrives.)

Remember how *sigsuspend* works. You call it, and your process is blocked until an unmasked signal arrives. When the signal arrives, the process must first go off and handle the signal by executing the signal handler, and then, after the handler has returned, the system will return the process from its blocked state.

Well, why do you need this clumsy approach? The whole reason for a handler function is so that the process can asynchronously do something in response to the signal. In this case, though, you are already *waiting* for the signal to arrive! There's no need for asynchrony. If *sigsuspend* just told you which signal had arrived, you could probably call the handler yourself, faster than the system could. The problem with *sigsuspend* is speed. It takes a long time to set up the dispatch out to a user signal handler. It takes a while to execute the handler. And it takes a long time to clean up after the handler. All this has to happen before *sigsuspend* returns. The result is that *sigsuspend* does not provide a very fast response to signal arrival.

To solve the problem of fast synchronous signal-waiting, POSIX.4 defined a new function, *sigwaitinfo*. This function performs the wait for signals, but does not go through the hassle (and the time-consuming overhead) of calling the signal handler for the signal that arrives. It just tells you which signal arrived. Our terminal process could use *sigwaitinfo* much like it earlier used *sigsuspend*:

```
main(int argc, char **argv)
{
    int i;
    sigset_t look_for_these;
    siginfo_t extra;
```

```
    sigemptyset(&look_for_these);
    sigaddset(&look_for_these, SIG_QUERY_COMPLETE);
    sigprocmask(SIG_BLOCK, &look_for_these, NULL);

    while (1) {
        /* Deal with the screen */
        /* Await server response */
        i = sigwaitinfo(&look_for_these, &extra);
        if (i < 0)
            perror("sigwaitinfo");
        else {
            printf("Waited for sig %d, val %x\n",
                i, extra.si_value.sival_int);
        }
    }
...
```

sigwaitinfo returns the number of the signal it received, and sets the additional real-time information in the second parameter for which you pass it the address. *sigwaitinfo* may also wait for non-real-time signals, in which case that second parameter is just ignored.

If there is a signal pending when *sigwaitinfo* is called, it will immediately return. Otherwise, it will block until one of the awaited signals arrives. When that signal arrives, *sigwaitinfo* will immediately return with that signal and its data value. The signal will not cause a signal handler to be invoked. Hopefully, that will allow *sigwaitinfo* to be much more speedy than *sigsuspend*.

When using *sigwaitinfo,* you definitely *must* have the signals blocked. If they do arrive and are *not* blocked, then they are handled by the handler functions, *not* passed to *sigwaitinfo*. In other words, the old-style handlers take precedence. However, with *sigwaitinfo* you may find there is no *need* for an old-style handler—just block the signal forever, and check for it occasionally using *sigwaitinfo*!

If you are uncomfortable with a wait that may take arbitrarily long, *sigwaitinfo* also comes in a model with a timeout. Modifying our example above to wait for no more than a second is easy:

```
    struct timespec timeout;

    timeout.tv_sec = 1;
    timeout.tv_nsec = 0;

    while (1) {
        /* Deal with the screen */
        /* Await server response, with timeout */
        i = sigtimedwait(&look_for_these, &extra, &timeout);
        if (i < 0) {
            if (errno == EAGAIN)
                printf("Timed out.\n");
    ...
```

We'll discuss more about time and the *struct timespec* in Chapter 5. For now, all you need to know is that it specifies a time interval in seconds and nanoseconds, and *sigtimedwait* interprets that interval as relative to the time at which you called the function. Thus, if you set the timeout to one second, you'll wait for no more than one second. Simple.

The same signal delivery order is enforced for *sigwaitinfo* and *sigtimedwait* as for asynchronous delivery of the queued signals. The lowest-numbered pending queued signal gets delivered first.

Remaining Problems with Signals for Communication

Even with the POSIX.4 signal extensions, signals remain a clumsy and inefficient method for interprocess communication. What are some of the problems that still remain?

Speed

Signals are generally slow to deliver. This is because signals carry a lot of baggage with them: handlers, masks, interaction with system calls. But by far the worst speed problem is the asynchrony of signals. Setting up an asynchronous trap out to user mode, and then returning from it, is a complex activity for the operating system to perform. It takes time, more time than is really necessary for this sort of operation, and certainly more time than is necessary for a communication and coordination mechanism!

Asynchrony

Asynchrony is a problem all its own. I've already mentioned how asynchrony makes things slower. It also makes code less robust, more error prone. That's because of the possibility of a signal arriving *at any time*. If signals arrived only at set times, you could write simpler code that didn't need to deal with the possibility of signals arriving in the middle of something. You *can* code your application that way, by masking off all signals and waiting for them when you want them. but why should you have to? If you want to do communication and coordination, the asynchrony is pure baggage.

Lack of Bandwidth

Finally, signals, even queued, data-carrying signals, suffer from a lack of bandwidth. Each signal carries a maximum of little more than 32 bits of information. That's a piddly number of bits for a message transfer between processes. There are much faster ways of transferring data.

On the other hand, however, signals still do have their pluses:

Asynchrony

Perhaps the most distinguishing characteristic of signals is that they are asynchronous, interrupting whatever the target process was doing. Thus, a terminal process could be waiting for user input when a signal arrives, and go immediately to a screen update to reflect input from the server. With a message queue, in contrast, the message from the server would sit in the queue until the terminal process explicitly fetched it by reading the queue.

Little Setup

Delivering a signal requires little prior setup: one merely needs to know the ID of the victim. On the victim's side, the signal handlers and masks must be installed, but that's pretty simple.

Directed at a Particular Process

A signal is targeted towards a particular process. This may be a behavior you desire. Other mechanisms, in contrast, are directed at any process that happens to be listening.

Not Terribly Restrictive

Limits on signal usage are usually less-restrictive than those on other mechanisms. Every process simply has the ability to send and receive signals, with no particular system configuration required. In contrast, many UNIX systems limit the number of message queues or shared memory areas (described further on) that you can have on a system. In the terminal/server example, you might want a message queue per terminal. You might easily run out of system resources by adding more and more terminals in such a scenario. In this case, you might consider using signals as a communication mechanism between the servers and the terminals, especially since response to the terminals is soft real-time.

The conclusion is this: signals definitely have their uses, mostly in non-communication areas (flagging exceptions, asynchronous I/O completion, timer expiration, etc). Even for communication, though, signals do have their place. That place is where information bandwidth and determinism are not terribly important, or where resource limitations rule out other forms of communication, or where the process-specific or asynchronous nature of signals is explicitly required. As we've seen, our online terminal-and-server example is a good example of such an application. It's not terribly real-time, but it *is* real-world.

Multitasking with Signal Handlers

As I mentioned earlier in this chapter, you might consider using signal handlers to achieve a degree of multitasking in your single-process application. This is especially possible because the other interfaces of POSIX.4 (asynchronous I/O, timers, and message queues in particular) all deliver signals upon completion of various asynchronous processing. In the cyclic executive we were discussing earlier in this chapter, there was a need to read the keyboard and the mouse, and that operation needed to be a non-blocking, polling sort of operation to avoid getting in the way of the rest of the loop. What if you could set up your application so that the system was reading the mouse and the keyboard *for* you, so you didn't have to do it in the loop? What if the system just sent you a signal whenever it had actually read in data from either source? In that case, your loop would be simpler, and the data input operations would be handled essentially in parallel, by a combination of the operating system and the signal handlers you set up. Using asynchronous I/O, you can achieve that sort of multitasking look and feel. Asynchronous I/O is covered in Chapter 6, *I/O for the Real World*. Here, I'm just going to provide the code to pore over.

```
extern void mouse_handler(int);
extern void keyboard_handler(int);

/*
 * Set up the signal catching functions for the mouse
 * and keyboard signals.  Which signal was actually used for
 * SIGMOUSE and SIGKEYBOARD would be up to you, the programmer.
 * That topic is covered in our discussion of the POSIX.4 real-time
 * signals extensions.
 */
sigemptyset(sa.sa_mask);
sa.flags = 0;
sa.handler = mouse_handler;
sigaction(SIGMOUSE, &sa, NULL);          /* Mouse handling function */
sa.handler = keyboard_handler;
sigaction(SIGKEYBOARD, &sa, NULL);       /* Keyboard handling function */

/* Fire off mouse asynchronous I/O request (one asynchronous read) */
mouse_acb.aio_fildes = mouse_fd;
mouse_acb.aio_offset = (long)0;
mouse_acb.aio_buf = mousebuf;
mouse_acb.aio_nbytes = 1;
mouse_acb.aio_reqprio = 0;
mouse_acb.aio_sigevent.sigev_signo = SIGMOUSE;
mouse_acb.aio_sigevent.sigev_sigval.sival_ptr = (void *)&mouse_acb;
aio_read(&mouse_acb);

/* Fire off keyboard I/O request (one asynchronous read) */
keyboard_acb.aio_fildes = keyboard_fd;
keyboard_acb.aio_offset = (long)0;
keyboard_acb.aio_buf = keyboardbuf;
keyboard_acb.aio_nbytes = 1;
keyboard_acb.aio_reqprio = 0;
keyboard_acb.aio_sigevent.sigev_signo = SIGMOUSE;
keyboard_acb.aio_sigevent.sigev_sigval.sival_ptr = (void *)&keyboard_acb;
aio_read(&keyboard_acb);

while (1) {
        /* Synchronize to Highest Frequency */
        /* Recompute Player Positions, using
         * asynchronously-read mouse and keyboard input */
        /* Update the display */
}

mouse_handler(int signo, siginfo_t *info, void *context)
{
        /* Handle mouse I/O which has just completed. */
        /* Restart the mouse I/O. */
```

```
        aio_read(&mouse_acb);    /* Do it exactly the same, again */
}


keyboard_handler(int signo, siginfo_t *info, void *context)
{
        /* Handle mouse I/O which has just completed. */
        /* Restart the mouse I/O. */
        aio_read(&keyboard_acb);        /* Do it exactly the same, again */
}
```

I've added a great deal of detail to the signal-handling and asynchronous I/O portions of this example to show you how these facilities work in practice. Now, what we would seem to have created is a program with three separate "flows" of control. There's the main flow, which is just the big *while* loop. Then, there are two asynchronous flows, one for each I/O channel. On each of these channels, the flow is:

- System performs asynchronous I/O
- System notifies application of I/O completion via a signal
- Application handles signal
- Application submits another asynchronous I/O

The two I/O "flows" are not really totally asynchronous, of course. A signal handler operates as an asynchronous transfer of control from what the main program *was* doing, to the signal handler. Whatever the main loop is doing, it can be interrupted at any time by our signal handlers. When the signal handlers terminate, the main loop is resumed exactly where it was before.

So we have successfully moved the I/O out of the *while* loop, at least kind of. What's the problem?

The problem is that the signal handlers cannot do everything a true, separate flow of control can do. The I/O flows are not true parallel tasks. They are merely interruptions of what the main loop was doing so it could do something else. As an example, think of how you would "handle the mouse I/O," as I mentioned in my example. Well, you'd probably want to use the mouse data to update the player's position on the "screen." Meanwhile, the main loop may be using the "screen" for updating the display. You may have interrupted it right in the middle of using the old player position. By just changing the position now, you'll risk leaving some screen garbage lying around from the old display position. This is a basic illustration of the need for synchronization between multiple tasks. Essentially, if one task (the main loop) is reading some information, another task (the mouse handler) cannot be allowed to change that information until the first task is done. The main loop has to get a coherent snapshot of the data. How can these tasks synchronize? The flow of control that got to the data last is going to have to wait for the first flow of control to finish its work. And there's your problem. The signal handler is a temporary interruption of the main thread. It cannot let the main thread proceed and still hope to get back control!

Signal handlers are definitely useful in real-world applications, but they are not true asynchronous flows of control, so there are important limitations on what they can do. For true asynchronous operation, you need separate flows of control that can successfully coordinate their actions with each other.

Conclusion

Given the basic process primitives of POSIX.1, we can begin to construct real-world applications. POSIX signals are essential to any real application, but not sufficient to meet your needs for high-bandwidth interprocess communication. In the next three chapters, we'll cover the functionality you need for the real-world: better coordination, time and resource control, and I/O extensions.

Exercises

The solutions to problems that require programming can be found in the Appendix, in the section listed in parentheses after each such problem.

I said a couple of times that signals are a "low-bandwidth" means of communication. That means you can't send a great deal of information in a short time using signals. Quantify this number by writing a program that forks, then sends signals from one process to the other repeatedly for a period of time. How many signals can your machine send in a minute? What bandwidth (bytes per second) does this come out to?

Above, I suggested a program where one process repeatedly *kills* the other process. This will not give a complete picture of interprocess communication bandwidth. To see why not, instrument your program to tell how many signals were received, as well as how many were sent. How do the numbers compare? *(sigs_sent_noswtch.c)*

To get a real picture of IPC bandwidth, you need for the two processes to context switch on each signal delivery. One way of doing that is by both processes sending and receiving signals repeatedly. Try this approach. What is the signal bandwidth now? *(sigs_sent_swtch.c)*

A complete information transfer via signal delivery consists of the following steps:

1. Process 1 sends signal to Process 2.

2. Context switch to Process 2.

3. Process 2 executes its signal handler function.

How would you go about measuring each of these components?

Extend your program to benchmark POSIX.4 real-time extended signals passing data values back and forth. Has the number of signals per minute changed? What is the bandwidth for POSIX.4 real-time extended signals? *(sigs_sent_swtch.p4.c)*

If the number of signals per minute is less for POSIX.4 signals than for POSIX.1 signals, explain why.

How many POSIX.4 queued signals can you send to a particular process? Write a program that sets up a child with a POSIX.4 real-time signal blocked, and then blast POSIX.4 real-time signals at it until you get an error. What's the error message? What is the root cause of it?

How many bits of information are transferred by a regular signal? How many by a POSIX.4 real-time extended signal? Which mechanism transfers more data per second on your system?

Better Coordination: Messages, Shared Memory, and Synchronization

Communicating Between Processes

So now we know how to create processes and terminate them, and we know how to wait for processes that are terminated. We've seen how signals operate and how you can try to use them for interprocess communication. Although signals provide asynchrony which you may desire in your application, they're really not an appropriate means for communicating between processes, due mostly to their speed (or lack thereof). In the example from Chapter 3, *The Basics of Real-Time: Multiple Tasks*, we were able to pass a signal—32 bits of information—from one process to another, but that's not sufficient for actually passing a query from a terminal to a server, or a meaningful response from the server back to the terminal. The next thing to figure out, then, is how to do some *real* communication between processes.

Communication and coordination are synonyms here, and synchronization is a closely related term. Communication refers to the transfer of information between multiple processes. When communicating, synchronization is usually required, as one process or another is going to have to wait for the communication to occur. In many cases, the synchronization is the important activity, and there is no other communication. Coordination is a vague term that seems to cover both communication and synchronization. That's why I used it in the chapter title.

There are a lot of coordination mechanisms you may have used, or heard of being used. The mechanisms vary in the amount of setup required, the flexibility of the service provided, the performance capabilities (transaction rate and bandwidth), reliability, and the functionality provided. If we can leave the UNIX realm behind for a moment, we can see there are a lot of coordination mechanisms in the abstract, including:

- Message passing
- Shared memory
- Semaphores (binary and counting)
- Mutexes and condition variables
- Readers/writers locks
- Tasking and rendezvous
- Event flags

Moving into the UNIX/POSIX realm, the mechanisms provided seem even more diverse:

- Signals
- Pipes and FIFOs
- File locking
- System V messages
- System V shared memory
- System V semaphores
- POSIX.4 message queues
- POSIX.4 shared memory
- POSIX.4 semaphores
- POSIX.4 extended signals

It will help for us to try and categorize all these mechanisms. They really boil down to four categories, as shown in Table 4-1.

Table 4-1: Coordination Mechanisms

Name	Reliable?	Flexible?	Fast?
Signals	Sometimes	Very	No
Messages	Yes	Not very	Not particularly
Semaphores	Yes	Very	Very (use w/shared memory)
Shared Memory	Yes	Very	Very (use w/semaphores)

Signals

Signals are used for different things, most not related to communication or coordination. We've already seen that signals are also usable as a means for passing small, limited messages between processes. I list them as a separate category because the interface to signals is so different from the interface to the other communication interfaces.

Messages

Probably the most general and abstract form of communication is message passing. The terminal/server application generally communicates from server to terminal, and back again, via messages. In fact the majority of all applications are probably formulated in terms of messages going back and forth between tasks, whether or not the implementation of those applications uses actual message passing. People just seem to think in terms of small, manageable packets of information flowing between entities. Perhaps that's because it's how people themselves communicate.* In POSIX.1, pipes and FIFOs provide a means of passing messages between processes. In POSIX.4 and System V both, there are actual interfaces to different sorts of message queues. Signals, both POSIX.1 signals and the POSIX.4 variety, are used for passing messages. Message queues can be made network transparent in a fairly straightforward manner, by extending the idea of "machine" to encompass the network.

Shared memory

Shared memory is an extremely low-level way for processes to communicate with each other. It is more difficult to use than signals or message queues, because all synchronization of access to the shared memory must be through an additional mechanism (usually semaphores, mutexes, or condition variables). All reliability must be added by the application itself, since the facility is so primitive (it's *memory*! Store stuff in it! What's there to be reliable about?). It's unlikely that a shared-memory interface will perform terribly well in a distributed (networked) system, while it's very conceivable that network-transparent message queues will offer reasonable performance. The advantages of shared memory are its incredible flexibility and its great speed. Because shared memory is a basic building block of interprocess communication, the application can use it in just about any way it chooses. And, since the data you write into shared memory is immediately† available to the other processes sharing memory, it's very fast. Both POSIX.4 and System V define shared memory interfaces. The example of multiple server processes would certainly benefit from allowing the multiple servers to operate on a single, shared copy of the data in the database.

Synchronization

If our multiple server processes *were* sharing their data, they would need a mechanism to ensure that no two processes were changing the same data at the same time. Without such a mechanism, the database would become corrupted. Shared memory in general requires additional mechanisms for synchronizing accesses to that memory. However, synchronization itself is very useful even when shared

---

* At least that's how speech usually works. Occasionally, I'd swear I was listening to someone's raw Ethernet interface...

† "Immediately" is a bit of an oversimplification. I should say, "immediately, subject to the whims of the processor-memory interconnection scheme in use on the particular machine." Particularly on multiprocessors, there's an issue of when memory updates by one processor appear to other processors. We'll talk about this issue when we discuss shared memory in more detail.

memory is not involved. Synchronization is a low-bandwidth communication mechanism, so I suppose you could say it's of lower performance than the other communication mechanisms. Usually, though, one uses synchronization mechanisms not so much for communicating as for just getting processes into the proper lock-step with each other. POSIX.4 provides counting semaphores as a synchronization mechanism, and System V provides a semaphore facility that is a world unto itself. In addition, POSIX.1 provides file locking, which can be misused, in my opinion, as a perfectly fine synchronization mechanism. (I won't cover file locking, since semaphores serve the same purpose and are a more general mechanism). Finally, the message passing and signals mechanisms can be used for synchronizing, since receiving a message usually entails some synchronization.

At this point, I should say a brief word about distributed, networked systems. POSIX.4 explicitly does not address either multiprocessor or distributed systems. It is defined as an interface for uniprocessors. Be that as it may, multiprocessors and networked systems exist, and particularly in the area of interprocess coordination, you'll find that some mechanisms are better suited for being networked than others. In particular, message queues extend well to a network model, and the other mechanisms do not extend so well. Some implementations, QNX in particular, support distributed POSIX.4 message queues, but I'm aware of none that support distributed POSIX.4 shared memory or semaphores or signals. This is an additional factor to consider if a distributed system is in your future.

First, we'll discuss message passing interfaces, including both pipes, FIFOs, and POSIX.4 message queues. In a follow-on to message passing, I'll cover shared memory, and that will bring us to the section on synchronization, which covers POSIX.4 semaphores.

POSIX.1 Communication: Pipes and FIFOs

POSIX.1 provides a possibility for interprocess communication with the *pipe* and its named cousin, the FIFO. As a communication channel, pipes are more appropriate than signals. Pipes are built for doing communication between processes. This means that they don't come with the extra baggage of signals (asynchrony, handler functions, masking). They also queue data internally, unlike the majority of POSIX.1 signals. However, pipes have their limits, too, as we'll see. FIFOs, a variation of pipes, remove one of the pipe's restrictions, but the others still remain.

```
/* Pipes and fifos are required in all POSIX-conformant systems */
int pipe(int fds[2]);

#include        <sys/types.h>
#include        <sys/stat.h>
char *name_of_fifo;
mode_t permissions;
int mkfifo(const char *name_of_fifo, mode_t permissions);
```

A pipe is actually two file descriptors. One of those descriptors is the *writing* end of the pipe, and the other descriptor is the *reading* end of the pipe. You use these file descriptors just like you use basic POSIX.1 files: you read and write data in them, using *read* and *write*. The communication aspect of these two descriptors comes from the fact that you can cause these file descriptors to remain open in processes you create via *fork* and *exec*. The new processes can then read data you write, and write data for you to read!

As an example, we could use a pipe to communicate results from our server process to its terminals. In the server, we need to create a pipe before *forking* the child process.

```
/* Create a new client process */
if (pipe(pipe_ends) < 0) {
    perror("pipe");
    break;
}
global_child = child = fork();
if (child) {
    /* parent process */
    break;
} else {
    /* child process */
    /* Make the pipe ends be fds 3 and 4. */
    (void)close(3);
    (void)close(4);
    if (dup2(pipe_ends[0], 3) < 0)
        perror("dup2");
    if (dup2(pipe_ends[1], 4) < 0)
        perror("dup2 2");
    (void)close(pipe_ends[0]);
    (void)close(pipe_ends[1]);
    execlp(CHILD_PROCESS, CHILD_PROCESS,
        "/dev/com1", NULL);
    perror("execlp");
    exit(1);
}
```

The server process simply *writes* data to the write end of the pipe (the second file descriptor), which the child process can then *read* from the read end of the pipe (the first file descriptor). Here's the relevant code for the child terminal process:

```
#include <fcntl.h>

char buf[MAXBYTES];

/* Set pipe in non-blocking mode to avoid waiting for input. */
if (fcntl(channel_from_server, F_SETFL, O_NONBLOCK) < 0) {
    perror("fcntl");
    exit(2);
}
while (1) {
    /* Deal with the screen */
```

```
/* Check for server input */
nbytes = read(channel_from_server, buf, MAXBYTES);
if ((nbytes < 0) && (errno != EAGAIN))
    perror("read");
else if (nbytes > 0) {
    printf("Message from Server: \"%s\"\n", buf);
}
...
```

The *pipe* call is simple. It opens up two file descriptors for the pipe ends. You read from the first file descriptor, *pipe_ends[0]*, and you write into *pipe_ends[1]*. The data you write into the pipe is read in a First In, First Out manner, like a simple queue of bytes.

Plumbing Hints for Working with Pipes

The example above shows a complete setup for using a pipe between two processes. There are several steps involved in getting the pipe to work between two processes. Here's a blow-by-blow summary:

1. First, you call *pipe* to create the pipe.

2. Then, you *fork*. Both the child and the parent now have access to the pipe.

3. Because the child process is going to *exec* a new process, you need to make sure the new child image can *find* the two pipe ends you've created (*pipe_ends*, the data structure, will not exist in the *exec*ed process, even though the pipe ends will be open).

4. The easiest method for placing file descriptors in a well-known location is to use *dup2* to duplicate the file descriptors into values agreed upon by both client and server. In this case, we use file descriptors 3 and 4, which we first *close* to make sure they are available.

5. The child *execs*. In the new process, file descriptors 3 and 4 will remain open, because pipes are defined to be created with FD_CLOEXEC cleared.

6. By default, a *read* on a pipe end will block until data appears in the pipe. To avoid this blocking, the child terminal process uses *fcntl* to set the O_NONBLOCK flag on the file descriptors. This causes reads that would normally block to fail with an *errno* of EAGAIN, instead (we'll cover O_NONBLOCK again in Chapter 6, *I/O for the Real World*).

Limitations of Pipes

Pipes are set up between processes at the time when processes are *fork*ed and *exec*ed, and are mostly used for communication in a "pipelined" manner: one process to the next, to the next, to the next. This matches the shell syntax you are familiar with for the use of pipes:

```
% prog1 | prog2 | prog3 | prog4
```

This linear arrangement of processes may not be exactly what you need, but by using *dup2* and *close*, you can probably create just about any topology you want. One problem, though, with the pipe is that it is only one-directional. In our example, we set up a pipe down which the server could *write*, and the child *read*. The child cannot turn around and *write* into the pipe itself, because its writes will be intermingled with the server's into one FIFO stream. For bidirectional communication, two pipes are needed.

The pipe also requires that you set it up in a parent process and then *fork* a child. This rigid hierarchy can be cumbersome. For instance, our terminals-and-server example is to use pipes for communication between the server and the terminal processes. That means that either the terminal processes are children of the server, the server process is the child of the terminals, or both the server *and* the terminals are children of some overlord process. All these approaches have their difficulties. First, the server process cannot be the child of the terminals. A process can have only one parent, and there are presumably many terminals. Furthermore, since the server is presumed to be in existence at all times, while terminals come and go, it will be difficult for an overlord process to create all the pipes necessary for all the terminals, and see to it that the server gets access to all these pipes. No, the only alternative which makes any sense at all is to have the server process fork off the terminal processes. Even this solution has its problems: first, it adds more functionality to the server, and slows it down from its business of, well, *serving*. Second, this solution only works if there is one server. What if there are several? They cannot *all* be parents of the terminal process! For this example, the parent-child hierarchy required by pipes does not work out very well.

FIFOs

If the limited topology of pipes is a problem for you, you can use FIFOs. A FIFO is simply a pipe that has a name in the file system. That means that any process with the appropriate permissions can access the pipe. That removes restrictions on how you can lay out your processes.

One opens a FIFO using the standard *open* call. Obviously, in this case, you don't get two file descriptors back, like you did by calling *pipe*. You get either the *read* end, or the *write* end of the pipe, depending on whether you *open* the FIFO for reading (O_RDONLY) or writing (O_WRONLY). You cannot open a FIFO for both reading and writing (O_RDWR); POSIX says the results are undefined. FIFOs would provide a dandy solution for our terminal-and server dilemma above. Any old terminal could open up FIFOs; the server could open as many as it could deal with. End of problem!

A FIFO, or named pipe, as it is also known, is very simple. Once created, it exists in the file system awaiting your call to *open*. The only additional thing you may need to know is how to create a named pipe in the first place. A special POSIX.1 call is provided for this, *mkfifo*.

```
#include        <sys/types.h>
#include        <sys/stat.h>

int mkfifo(const char *fifo_name, mode_t mode);
```

This call creates a FIFO named /usr/fifos/my_fifo, assuming that all the permissions and so forth are correct for creating such a file. The second argument to the function encodes file permission bits. On a normal UNIX system, you would specify *read* and *write* permission for the owner with the number 0600. Now, it's not the best coding practice to use constants like that. POSIX defines macros for the various permissions. These macros are defined in <sys/stat.h>, and encode read, write and execute permission (R, W, and X), for three sets of processes: those with the same user ID as the caller (USR), those with the same group ID as the caller (GRP), and all the others (OTH). You form the symbolic constants by sticking the permission together with the group, and adding the magic S_I to the beginning:

- S_IRUSR: Read permission for processes with the same user ID

- S_IRGRP: Read permission for processes with the same group ID

- S_IROTH: Read permission for others

- S_IWUSR: Write permission for processes with the same user ID

- S_IWGRP: Write permission for processes with the same group ID

- S_IWOTH: Write permission for others

- S_IXUSR: Execute permission for processes with the same user ID Execute permissions are not important for FIFOs, and are only included here for the sake of completeness.

- S_IXGRP: Execute permission for processes with the same group ID

- S_IXOTH: Execute permission for others

- S_IRWXU: Read, write, and execute permission for the user

- S_IRWXG: Read, write, and execute permission for the group

- S_IRWXO: Read, write, and execute permission for everyone else

One final note: FIFOs have filenames and exist in the file system until you unlink them. In this respect, they're just like normal disk files.

More Limitations of Pipes

We've seen that pipes have topological limitations that can be overcome with FIFOs. But there are other limitations that apply to both pipes and FIFOs. Here are a couple of the problems:

Prioritization

One problem with the pipe stems from its very FIFOness, that is, the fact that data sent to the pipe is read in a strictly First In, First Out fashion. This mechanism assumes that all messages sent to a pipe are of equal importance. In fact, when processes are sending messages to one another, some messages are of low importance (please log this mildly interesting event in the event log), while others are critical (the temperature in the reactor is rising rapidly, so you'd better drop the control rods). Some means of prioritizing messages is required, and pipes provide no such means. Such a mechanism *could* be built at the application level, by using separate pipes for different priorities, and then using *select* to determine which pipes have data on them before reading any data from any pipe at all. Unfortunately, this requires a great deal of application overhead, and *select* is not a part of POSIX.1 *or* POSIX.4—it's a standard UNIX function.[*]

Asynchronous operation

It would be nice to provide the ability to write messages into a pipe without having to wait for someone to read them. In general, this is possible by using O_NONBLOCK on the file descriptor. However, there is a certain amount of kernel buffer space the operating system uses to implement the pipe: when you write data to the pipe, it ends up in this buffer space, and when you read data from the pipe, it comes out. Unfortunately, there's no portable way to control (or even to know) the amount of buffer space available for a given pipe. When the kernel buffer space fills up, the process writing to the pipe ends up blocked, waiting for a reader process to take enough data *out* of the pipe so the write can finish.

Lack of control over pipe structure

Often, an application will be interested in finding out a little more about the state of its communication channel. In particular, you may want to know how many bytes are currently in the pipe. Pipes offer no way to determine this information. Furthermore, applications may want to size their pipes differently (e.g., to allow differing amounts of data in the pipe). In our terminal-server example, we might want the server's request queue to hold the average number of requests that may be pending at any given time. There is no way to control the depth of a pipe.

Lack of structure in the data stream

The pipe is a fairly pure example of the powerful UNIX file abstraction. A pipe is nothing more than a stream of bytes. You can read, or write, as many bytes at a time as you wish. This may, however, be a problem if you are trying to pass messages back and forth using pipes. You need to make sure that each "message" sent is read with the correct number of bytes, otherwise you end up with partial messages in the pipe, and so forth. This is not a big problem if every message going

---

[*] This is why many of the operating systems that support POSIX also support non-POSIX UNIX functionality—because it's useful. In contrast, an operating system that conforms to POSIX only as a checkoff item on a government list may not be so interested in its usability. See Chapter 2, *The POSIX Way*, for more detail on this issue.

down a pipe is of one fixed size. If variable-sized messages are being passed, then the situation becomes a little more complex.

Limited numbers of pipes and FIFOs

A file descriptor is required for each FIFO and for each end of each pipe. Processes are limited as to the total number of files they can have open. Imagine a server process trying to have a different FIFO open for each of 300 terminal processes! Many UNIX systems have substantially raised the number of open files a process may have, but many have not. Furthermore, many non-UNIX POSIX systems are subject to file limitations that would come up fairly quickly in the server-and-terminals example.

For many uses, the pipe is probably a fine solution, but it lacks the features needed to serve as a general message-passing facility. For that reason, POSIX.4 specifies message queues.

System V Message Queues

There *is* another message queue option in UNIX systems, and that is the message queue facility provided by System V UNIX. POSIX.4 message queues are not related at all to System V message queues. In fact, POSIX.4 semaphores are not like System V semaphores, nor is POSIX.4 shared memory anything like System V shared memory.

What are these three interprocess communication facilities from System V UNIX? I think of them as an evolutionary oddity. They *do* provide the desired IPC facility, sort of; but they are clumsy to use. System V message queues are named by numbers, rather than strings. An entirely separate "namespace" for these IPC objects is maintained by the utilities *ipcs* and *ipcrm*. Another major failing of System V messages is that they are very slow. Their interface basically requires an in-kernel implementation, with a system call being made for each message operation. That is not the case with the POSIX.4 offering.

When the POSIX.4 working group considered message queue interfaces, System V messages *were* mentioned as an area of existing practice. However, their well-known failings—especially the performance issue—caused the working group to decide to abandon them in favor of something new. The same decision was reached for semaphores and shared memory, as you'll see in the rest of this chapter.

POSIX.4 Message Queues

Let's return to our example: terminals communicating with a server process. Remember the problems we had trying to use a pipe or FIFO to communicate with the server? The topology problem was solved by using a named pipe. However, we still had problems related to the lack of structure in a pipe and lack of control over that structure. Message queues are named objects which operate basically as pipes do, with readers and writers. In addition, a message queue has more structure than does a pipe; a message queue is a priority queue of discrete messages. POSIX.4 message queues offer a certain, basic amount of application access to, and control over, message queue geometry. If your application is passing messages back and forth, a message queue, obviously enough, is what you want to use!

Here's a summary of the POSIX.4 message queues facility (defined under the option _POSIX_MESSAGE_PASSING):

```
#include        <unistd.h>
#ifdef _POSIX_MESSAGE_PASSING
#include        <mqueue.h>

mqd_t mymq;
struct mq_attr my_attrs;
mode_t permissions;
char *mq_name;
char *msgbuf;
int msgsize;
unsigned int msgprio;

/* The last two arguments are needed only when creating the message queue. */
mqd_t mq_open(const char *mq_name, int oflag,
    mode_t create_mode, struct mq_attr *create_attrs);
int mq_close(mqd_t mqueue);
int mq_unlink(const char *mq_name);

/* Send a message to a message queue */
int mq_send(mqd_t mymq, const char *msgbuf,
    size_t msgsize, unsigned int msgprio);

/* Receive a message (oldest, highest-priority) from a message queue */
i = mq_receive(mymq, msgbuf, &msgsize, &msgprio);

/* Get status information regarding a message queue */
int mq_getattr(mqd_t mymq, struct mq_attr *mq_attrs);
/* Set (a subset of) attributes on a message queue */
int mq_setattr(mqd_t mymq, const struct mq_attr *new_attributes,
    struct mq_attr *prev_attributes);

/* Receive notification when a message arrives on a queue */
int mq_notify(mqd_t mymq, const struct sigevent *notify_spec);
#endif _POSIX_MESSAGE_PASSING
```

POSIX.4 message queues were designed as a fairly efficient means of communicating message data between multiple processes. The POSIX.4 interface attempts to strike a balance between the different ways people can use message queues (flexibility) and the need for efficiency (simplicity). In trying to achieve this goal, the interface leans a bit more in the direction of simplicity, leaving more exotic bits of functionality for vendor extensions or future standardization efforts.

As a bit of history, consider the message passing interface that went out to ballot in earlier drafts of POSIX.4. This interface attempted to satisfy all the various ways in which people might possibly use message queues. It had bells. It had whistles. It had a million little parameters that could be set to alter this functionality or that, and it allowed you, *in theory*, to do all sorts of neat, high-performance stuff. For instance, you could pass messages without copying them from one process to another (by mapping them from address space to address space), and small messages were specially optimized. Unfortunately, the complexity of this early draft weighed it down so much that its implementation was, to use the vernacular, way slow. Early versions of message queues were shouted down by the balloting group. What emerged to take its place in later drafts is a pared-down, simple interface. It lets you send messages. It lets you get messages. It tells you a little bit about the message queue itself, and it does the message prioritization that many, many applications desire. A lot of the additional functionality has been stripped out of it. For instance, the asynchronous capability I spoke of in the section on pipes is not in this interface. It would be nice, but it would add to the complexity of the facility, so it went away after those early drafts ran into resistance. As a result, POSIX.4 message queues are not the ultimate do-everything message interface. On the other hand, they should be fast.

The presence of POSIX.4 message queues are indicated by the constant _POSIX_MESSAGE_PASSING being defined in *<unistd.h>*.

Creating and Accessing Message Queues

The first step in using a message queue is to create or open it. Message queues use a set of interfaces that parallel UNIX file interfaces very closely. As a simple example, here's how our terminal processes might access an already-existing message queue:

```
#include        <mqueue.h>
mqd_t child_mq;                  /* Descriptor of opened message queue */


child_mq = mq_open("/terminal.0", O_RDWR);
if (child_mq == (mqd_t)-1)
    perror("mq_open");
```

As you can see, it looks an awful lot like opening a file that already exists. In fact, the only real difference is that, with *open*, you'd get back an integer file descriptor value, while *mq_open* returns a value of type *mqd_t*. In fact, the *mqd_t* is even required to be some sort of type that can be cast into an integer (a long, a short, a char, or, on most sane machine architectures, a pointer), because *mq_open* returns a value of –1 on error. The values that can be ORed into *oflags* control how the message queue is opened. The values that can be used are a subset of the flags that can be used for regular *open*. First, you must set one of the following values to tell the system how you will be using the message queue:

- O_RDONLY: Open the message queue for reading (i.e., receiving messages) only.

- O_WRONLY: Open the message queue for writing (sending messages) only.

- O_RDWR: Open the message queue for both sending and receiving messages.

You may optionally also specify O_NONBLOCK in *oflags*. O_NONBLOCK tells the system not to suspend your process when you try to receive on an empty queue or send to a queue where there's no space. Instead, the system returns an error code telling you that the operation would have blocked (EAGAIN).

Naming a message queue

Now, we get to a part that's a little weird: the naming of the message queue. To get at a message queue, like all other operating system objects, you need some sort of name for that object. In most of UNIX, names are character strings—filenames, for instance. As the message queue interface parallels files very, very closely, message queues are also named by character strings, something like files. However, you must be very clear that message queues *are not files*. Message queues use a set of interfaces that are parallel to the standard file interfaces of POSIX.1. Instead of *open, mq_open* is used. Likewise, *close* is replaced by *mq_close,* and *mq_unlink* is used to destroy a message queue, instead of *unlink*. Rather than using *write* and *read* to put data in and take data out of a message queue, you use *mq_send* and *mq_receive.*

Unlike FIFOs, pipes, and device special files, message queues are not accessed using *open, read,* and *write*. If you do an *ls* to look at a directory, do not expect to see message queues. They may not be there.

Why did POSIX.4 adopt this strange "kind-of-like-a-file" naming for message queues (and shared memory, and semaphores, as we'll see later)? It all boils down to efficiency. The file system in UNIX has a certain amount of overhead associated with it. In particular, *open, read,* and so on are all system calls, and take a lot of time compared to library calls. Because communications and synchronization are so important to real-time applications, the real-time community wants these functions to be as fast as possible. There are ways of implementing message passing and semaphores without requiring system calls. Thus, it is possible for a vendor to implement a message-passing scheme that is significantly faster if that vendor is not forced to use the overhead of the UNIX file system. This parallel naming scheme allows vendors to achieve higher-performance message passing than would otherwise be possible. At the same time, the POSIX.4 working group still allows vendors to implement message queues, etc., as simple calls to *open, read,* and so on—provided that the vendor feels that his or her version of *read* is fast enough to be used as an effective means for message-passing.

Exactly how do you have to form a message queue name for POSIX.4? File names look like this: */usr/bog/tmp/filename*. That's an *absolute* pathname, because it begins with /. A relative pathname doesn't begin with /, and is interpreted relative to the current working directory of the process, i.e., *tmp/filename*. In the case of message queues, a limited form of the same pathname construction is supported. Here are the details:

Build the name like a pathname

Message queue names are a subset of normal UNIX pathnames, and must be constructed like pathnames: */part1/part2/part3*.

Further rules all have to do with the presence or absence of the "/" character in your message queue names. If you follow the next two rules, your message queue names will work the same on all POSIX.4-conformant systems. The interpretation of *components* of a message queue name is the issue. Some systems will treat the "/" as a special character, and separate components as directories. Other systems will not treat the "/" character differently at all. Based on this choice, your message queue behavior can be radically different. Unfortunately, there is no compile-time or run-time symbol that you can check to determine the behavior of your system (e.g., there is no _POSIX_LEADING_SLASHES_REQUIRED). The good news is that the interpretation of "/" is implementation-defined, which means that each POSIX.4 system must tell you what they do with "/" in a message queue name. You can, if you want, use "/" characters, and run your application on the POSIX.4 systems that support the functionality you require.

Start the name with a /

Imagine an implementation where message queues existed in the file system namespace. In such an implementation, a name that did not start with a slash would be interpreted *relative to the current working directory* of the process. If your application was in directory */usr/bog*, and you opened the message queue named *my_message_queue*, then you'd actually get */usr/bog/my_message_queue*. Interpreting the name that way has some advantages for structuring applications. You could run multiple copies of the same application, in different directories, without the multiple invocations interacting with each other. But such an implementation would require an interaction with the UNIX file system, and that's heavyweight. Most existing real-time systems, in contrast, would rather just use the string *my_message_queue* as a hash key into a single, flat namespace of message queues. Such a system would probably be faster than a system using the UNIX file system namespace. However, in such a system the current working directory would be irrelevant—wherever you were, if you opened *my_message_queue*, you would get the *one* message queue of that name on the system. For total portability, start off your name with a "/" character. Then all the processes that open the message queue will open the same one—regardless of whether message queue names are implemented using file system semantics or using simple hashing.

Don't use any other / characters

You only have a totally portable message queue name if the single slash in the name is the very first character. Additional slash characters have an effect that may vary by implementation. In other words, some implementations may do a full, filesystem type pathname lookup, complete with all the permission checks and so forth that a file-system operation entails. This has advantages for security and application structure. On the other hand, other implementations might just treat the whole string, "/" characters and all, as a unique string of characters that can be used to hash to a particular message queue. In that case, there would be no interpretation of the additional "/" characters at all. For total portability, you should leave out all but the first "/".

Creating a message queue

We now know how to name message queues, and we know about the *oflags* argument as well. This allows us to open existing message queues. How about creating message queues in the first place? Our server process would need to create the message queue before the terminal could use it. Here's how:

```
#include    <mqueue.h>
struct mq_attr mq_attr;
mqd_t mymq;

/* Create a message queue for terminal/server communication */
mq_attr.mq_maxmsg = 100;
mq_attr.mq_msgsize = 128;
mq_attr.mq_flags = 0;
mymq = mq_open(GLOBAL_MQ_NAME, O_CREAT|O_RDWR, S_IRWXU, &mq_attr);
if (mymq == (mqd_t)-1)
    perror("mq_open");
```

As with files, you create a message queue by using a special flag to *mq_open:* O_CREAT. When O_CREAT is ORed into *oflags,* then the system will create the named message queue if it doesn't already exist. The semantics of O_CREAT are the same as for files. The permissions on the created queue are set appropriately, as are the owner and group ID of the message queue. As you can see, message queues really do behave a lot like files, even if they're not necessarily in the file system. The parallelism between files and message queues extends to the ability to use the O_EXCL flag in conjunction with O_CREAT. As I said above, O_CREAT causes the system to create a message queue if one does not already exist. If one *does* already exist, then calling *mq_open(..O_CREAT..)* would simply open the existing message queue. It wouldn't actually create anything. Now, you might be interested in knowing if there was already a queue there. Specifically, the queue might have been there as a result of a previous application that failed. It might have stale messages in it that need to be discarded. It might even be all wrong for your application, and need to be removed and remade. If, instead of just using O_CREAT, you call *mq_open* with O_CREAT and O_EXCL both set in *oflags,* then the system will return −1 and set errno (to EEXIST) if the message queue existed prior to the call to *mq_open.*

When you are creating a message queue, you need additional arguments to *mq_open* to further describe the queue to be constructed. The two new arguments are *mode,* which is almost the same as the *mode* argument to *open(..O_CREAT..),* and a *struct mq_attr,* which describes a few attributes of the message queue.

First the mode. This is used for files, to define the permissions on a file when it is first created. We saw creation modes used also during the description of *mkfifo*. There are nine values which can be ORed into the mode parameter: S_IRUSR, S_IWUSR, S_IXUSR, S_IRGRP, S_IWGRP, S_IXGRP, S_IROTH, S_IWOTH, and S_IXOTH. As for FIFOs, these bits encode read, write, and execute permission for the user who creates the message queue, members of the group that created the message queue, and everyone else (the others). No other bits can be specified for the mode of a message queue.

Now, let's talk about the *mq_attr* structure. This structure is used in calls to *mq_open,* as well as a couple of other calls we'll see later on. It has more fields than are used for the *mq_open(..O_CREAT..)* call; those fields are used for the other calls.

```
struct mq_attr {
        ...
        long mq_maxmsg;    /* Maximum number of messages "in the queue" */
        ...
        long mq_msgsize;   /* Maximum size of a single message */
        ...
        long mq_flags;     /* Modifies behavior of the message queue */
        ...
        long mq_curmsgs;   /* Number of messages currently in the queue */
        ...
};
```

The first two fields together describe the size of the message queue. The first tells how many messages can be in the queue at one time; that is, this is the maximum number of messages that have been sent by a process, but not yet received. The second attribute tells how large each individual message can be. Multiplying these numbers tells you the minimum total data storage the system needs for message data on this queue. In our example above, we set up the message queue for 100 messages of size 128 bytes apiece. When you call *mq_open(..O_CREAT..),* you should set these two values in the *mq_attr* structure so the system will create a properly-sized message queue. If you send a single message larger than *mq_msgsize* bytes, you'll get an error. If you send a message to a message queue that already has *mq_maxmsgs* enqueued on it, you may either block, or get an error back, depending on whether you opened the message queue with O_NONBLOCK.

The *mq_flags* field is not used by *mq_open*. O_NONBLOCK is the only flag defined for *mq_flags,* but the *mq_flags* field is used only by *mq_getattr* and *mq_setattr,* described below. This flag is *not* consulted when you create a message queue. Instead, the O_NONBLOCK flag in the *oflags* parameter is used, for parity with normal file *open*. It can be a bit confusing that you can set O_NONBLOCK in two different places when you create a message queue. Just remember that the *mq_flags* field is *ignored* when a message queue is created. The reason the flags field, and the bit, are there is to per-form the function that *fcntl* would normally perform if message queues were files. Since message queues are not files, special functions (*mq_getattr* for *fcntl(F_GETFL)* and *mq_setattr* for *fcntl(F_SETFL)*) are provided.

Finally, *mq_curmsgs* tells you, the application, how many messages are currently on a message queue. This field is not set by the application. Rather, it's filled in as part of another call (*mq_getattr*) that retrieves information about message queues. Obviously, when you first create the message queue, there are no messages on it. Equally obvi-ously, the number of messages currently enqueued is not a constant; any value you get for *mq_curmsgs* reflects reality at some instant during the call to *mq_getattr*.

You don't *need* to specify an *mq_attr* structure at all when you create your message queues. If you don't particularly care what the geometry of the message queue is, you can just pass a NULL to *mq_open* as your pointer to the *mq_attr* structure. In this case, the system creates a message queue, with implementation-defined default attributes. These attributes, being implementation-defined, will appear in the POSIX conformance statement for the system you're using. In my opinion, you should always specify the attributes of your message queues. Even if the number of messages you can have in the queue is unimportant to you, the maximum message size probably *is* important, unless your messages are all one byte long.

Cleaning Up After Yourself

Where there is a function to open something, there is also a function to close it again. And, when you can create something, you also must be able to delete it. Two func-tions, *mq_close* and *mq_unlink*, provide these abilities. Each function mimics its corre-sponding file-based call, *close* and *unlink* respectively.

```
#include        <mqueue.h>

mqd_t my_message_queue;
int i;

/* Obtain access to message queue */
my_message_queue = mq_open(...);


/* Release access to message queue */
i = mq_close(my_message_queue);
```

mq_close releases your access to the message queue described by the message queue descriptor you pass in. Calling *mq_close* has no effect on the contents of the message queue, unless the message queue has been unlinked with *mq_unlink* (more on that later). In other words, all the messages that were in the queue remain in the queue, even after everyone has closed their message queue descriptors. You can open a mes-sage queue, send ten messages to the queue, close the queue, go home, have dinner, come back to work, open the message queue and retrieve all ten messages from the queue again. *mq_close* also removes any notification request you may have attached to the message queue with *mq_notify* (described later). All message queues a process has open are closed automatically when the process calls *exit, _exit,* or one of the *exec* functions. This is somewhat different from files, where you can clear the FD_CLOEXEC flag (using *fcntl*) to keep a file from being closed when you call one of the *exec s.*

```
#include        <mqueue.h>

char *message_queue_name;
int i;

/* Remove message queue name from the system */
i = mq_unlink(message_queue_name);
```

mq_unlink does for message queues what *unlink* does for files. If no one has the named message queue open when you call *mq_unlink,* then the message queue is immediately obliterated. Any messages that may have been in it are lost. That message queue will then be inaccessible to any other process.

If there are processes that have the message queue open when *mq_unlink* is called, then the destruction of the message queue is delayed until the last such process closes it. When no process has the unlinked message queue open, then the message queue will be removed. Meanwhile, the name of the message queue *is* removed. This makes it impossible for any other process to *mq_open* the message queue. After calling *mq_unlink,* the only processes that can access this message queue are the ones that had it open before *mq_unlink* was called (and, if those processes *fork,* their children can also use the message queue because message queues are inherited across *fork,* just like files).

Since message queues do not exist in the file system, it is possible to leave them lying around with no way for you to get rid of them unless you know their names (*ls* and *rm* do not work with message queues, at least not portably). A good, portable application should therefore be careful to unlink its message queues when it is done with them. Unless you really need the ability to leave messages in the queue when no processes are running, I suggest you unlink your message queues as soon as all your processes have opened them. That way, if your processes terminate prematurely, you won't have an extra message queue floating around. (Alternatively, you may want the message queue left around for debugging. It's critical to realize that the queue can be left floating in the system unless you take special measures, though.)

Sending Messages

Now that you've created and opened the message queue, you can send messages to it. The interface for this is *mq_send:*

```
#include        <mqueue.h>

int mq_send(mqd_t message_queue, const char *message_data,
    size_t message_data_length, unsigned int priority);
```

Except for the *priority* parameter, sending a message looks a lot like writing to a file. This call sends a single message, *message_data,* of length *message_data_length,* to the message queue indicated by *message_queue.* Simple enough. In our terminal/server code, you could take the *pipe*-based code and convert it over to using message queues by changing the *write* calls to *mq_sends,* and the *read* calls to *mq_receives* (described later).

There are a few complications to remember. First, remember that when we created the message queue, we created it with a maximum message size. If *message_data_length* exceeds that length (*mq_msgsize* in the *mq_attr* structure), then the call to *mq_send* will fail.

Now let's talk about *priority*. Unlike pipes, message queues are not strictly FIFOs. Each message has a priority, from 0 to MQ_PRIO_MAX. MQ_PRIO_MAX, like all other numeric parameters of a POSIX system, is to be found in *<limits.h>*, and must be at least 32. Messages are inserted into the message queue in order of their priority. Higher-priority messages get sent to the front of the queue, and will be pulled off the queue before lower-priority messages are. This prioritization supports two different requirements:

- The ability to send "emergency" messages down a message queue. These should be delivered before the normal, everyday messages. In our terminal/server example, normal messages might have a priority of zero, and a particularly urgent message could be flagged with a high priority. Such a request should get priority service, and that starts with the message going to the head of the queue.

- The ability to prioritize all system services is essential in a real-time system. Imagine that we are using a message queue to communicate between a number of hard real-time tasks at differing priorities and some sort of centralized server. The higher-priority real-time tasks should get their messages handled before the lower-priority tasks. The cardinal rule of real-time prioritization is that a high priority task should never be unnecessarily delayed by a low priority task.

Sending prioritized messages down the queue is not a complete solution to this overall prioritization problem, since the server process itself may be a low-priority process. There are mechanisms that help address this problem (such as priority inheritance by message passing as implemented in QNX), but they are not widely enough used to be part of the POSIX.4 standard. A kludge you might consider using in your application is to run your server at maximum priority while it waits for messages, then have it lower its priority to match that of the message it receives. This solution gets you closer to the ideal of total system synchronization, but still suffers from timing holes.

At a single priority level, messages are still put on the queue in FIFO order. You have to give your messages a priority. If you do not care about prioritization, you can just set this parameter to 0. If you specify a number greater than MQ_PRIO_MAX, *mq_send* will fail.

Finally, let's discuss blocking. If there is room on the message queue for this message, then the message will be added to the queue without blocking the calling process. No problem. But it is possible that the queue will be full when you call *mq_send*. In other words, there may already be *mq_maxmsg* (the value you set when creating the queue) messages sent to the queue but not yet received—in transit, as it were. If there is no room for this message, then the call to *mq_send* may block. It will block unless you set O_NONBLOCK in the *mode* argument when you called *mq_open*.

Receiving Messages

The other half of the message-passing interface, *mq_receive,* looks sort of like *read,* just as *mq_send* looks sort of like *write:*

```
#include        <mqueue.h>

size_t mq_receive(mqd_t message_queue, const char *message_buffer,
    size_t buffer_size, unsigned int *priority);
```

This call removes the message at the head of the *message_queue,* and places it in *message_buffer. buffer_size* advises the system how large *message_buffer* is. Upon return from this function, the system will fill in *priority* with the priority of the message pulled off the queue, and will return the number of bytes that were actually in the message. Of course, the function also stores the received message in the buffer pointed to by *message_buffer.* Notice that the *priority* parameter is a *pointer* to an unsigned *int,* not an unsigned *int* itself.

Now, the complications. First, the buffer you pass to the system must be at least as large as the maximum message size for the message queue. That's the number you supplied as *mq_attr.mq_msgsize.* If you pass in a buffer that is too small, the system will return an error and not give you any message off the queue.

And again, unless you have set the message queue into non-blocking mode (by using O_NONBLOCK at *mq_open* time or by setting O_NONBLOCK in *mq_flags* in a call to *mq_setattr*), you will block waiting for a message on an otherwise-empty message queue. In fact, this was the very behavior desired in our terminal/server example. We didn't *want* the terminal to block awaiting a message from the server, we just wanted it to *check* for one.

Message Queues and fork, exec, and exit

Message queues behave pretty much like files where *fork, exec,* and *exit* are concerned. Files are inherited when a process *forks;* so are message queues. Likewise, when a process calls *exit* or *_exit,* both files and message queues are closed implicitly. The *exec* functions behave differently for files and message queues. All message queues are closed when a process calls one of the *exec* functions. In contrast, files are, by default, left open when you *exec*.[*] In our terminal and server example, then, we need to change things a little bit to move from pipes to message queues. Rather than the server *piping, dup2ing,* and the terminal just inheriting the layout, we need to call *mq_open* in both the parent and the child process. In this sense, using a message queue is more akin to using a FIFO, or named pipe.

Additional Message Queue Facilities

Once you can create and open message queues, and send and receive messages, you're pretty much ready to start using message queues in your applications. There are a couple of other functions in the POSIX.4 interface that you may find useful.

Determining and changing the status of the message queue

You may want to know how many messages are on the queue at a particular moment. Or you may want to be reminded of the features of a given message queue: for example, your process may not have created the message queue, and you need to know *mq_maxmsg* and *mq_msgsize*. In our terminal server example, the server probably creates the queues when it starts, and the terminals come along later. The terminal processes could use *mq_getattr* to discover a queue's attributes (for instance, to see whether any messages were present on the queue):

```
channel_from_server = mq_open(GLOBAL_MQ_NAME, O_RDWR);
if (channel_from_server == (mqd_t)-1)
    perror("mq_open");
else {
    /* Set MQ access into non-blocking mode. */
    mqa.mq_flags = O_NONBLOCK;
    if (mq_setattr(channel_from_server, &mqa, NULL) < 0)
        perror("mq_setattr");
    /* Get current MQ status */
    if (mq_getattr(channel_from_server, &mqa) < 0)
        perror("mq_getattr");
    else {
        printf("MQ: %s has %d msgs (max %d, max size %d, %s mode)\n",
            GLOBAL_MQ_NAME, mqa.mq_curmsgs, mqa.mq_maxmsg,
            mqa.mq_msgsize, (mqa.mq_flags & O_NONBLOCK) ?
            "non-blocking" : "blocking");
    }
}
```

mq_getattr writes the attributes of the named message queue into the attributes structure you pass in. This is the same *mq_attr* structure as was used when the message queue was first created. *mq_maxmsg* and *mq_msgsize* and *mq_flags* all reflect the underlying attributes of the message queue. In addition, the *mq_curmsgs* field now

---

[*] You can explicitly force a file descriptor to be closed whenever you call *exec*, by setting the file descriptor flag FD_CLOEXEC with *fcntl*. By default, that flag is clear for every file you have open. Since *fcntl* is applied to file descriptors, and message queues are not file descriptors, *fcntl*, as well as the FD_CLOEXEC flag, are irrelevant to message queues.

takes on a value which is the number of messages currently on the queue (sent, but not yet received). Of course, that value is just a snapshot and can change at any moment as processes call *mq_send* and *mq_receive*. The value is guaranteed, though, to reflect the state of the message queue at *some* instant during the call to *mq_getattr*.

There is also a *mq_setattr* function, but this function sets only *one* attribute of the message queue: the blocking/non-blocking nature of the queue. Other attributes, like the depth and message size of the queue, are create-time attributes that are too difficult to change after the queue is created. If you need to change these attributes, you should create a new queue and remove the old one. In our example, again, the terminal process uses *mq_setattr* to make sure their message queue access is queued to be non-blocking. (Okay, they could do this at *mq_open* by specifying O_NONBLOCK, but then I wouldn't have an example, now would I?) *mq_setattr* stores the old attributes of the message queue in *previous_attributes* (if it is not NULL), and then changes the attributes of the message queue in accordance with the new attributes passed in *new_attributes.* You can only change the *mq_flags* attribute. The only defined flag for *mq_flags* is O_NONBLOCK. The effect of setting O_NONBLOCK is the same as if you had set O_NONBLOCK in *oflags* when you first opened the message queue: it puts the message queue into non-blocking mode. You won't wait for message arrival, and you won't block waiting space to free up when you send messages.

Receiving notification when a message is on the queue

Now, we get to a strange function. Every message queue has the ability to notify one (and only one) process whenever the queue's state changes from empty (no messages) to nonempty. This ability means that a process doesn't need to check for messages. Instead, it can arrange to get poked when a message arrives. This is especially useful when messages must be retrieved quickly after they're sent, as when some critical condition has caused the sender to send the message, and it needs a fast response from the receiver. In such a case, periodically polling the message queue may have too high a latency.

For instance, our server might set up a special, separate queue to handle administrative requests (like "shut down the database"). There are generally no messages on such a queue, but when they come in, they are very important and must be dealt with promptly. An asynchronous notification of message arrival on such a queue is handy. Here's how the server could set this up.

```
#include        <mqueue.h>
#include        <signal.h>
/* Asynch. notification of an important message arriving! */
void emergency_handler(int signo, siginfo_t *info, void *ignored)
{
    mqd_t mq_notifying;
    ssize_t nbytes;
    unsigned int prio;
```

```
    char buf[MAXBYTES];
    struct sigevent se;

    /* We passed along the MQ descriptor as signal data */
    mq_notifying = (mqd_t)info->si_value.sival_ptr;
    nbytes = mq_receive(mq_notifying, buf, MAXBYTES, &prio);
    /* Deal with emergency message stored in 'buf' */

    /* re-attach notification request */
    se.sigev_notify = SIGEV_SIGNAL;      /* send me a signal */
    se.sigev_signo  = SIG_EMERGENCY;     /* send me THIS signal */
    se.sigev_value.sival_ptr = (void *)mq_notifying;
    if (mq_notify(emergency_mq, &se) < 0)
        perror("mq_notify");
}

void init_server()
{
    struct mq_attr mq_attr;
    struct sigaction sa;
    struct sigevent se;

    mq_attr.mq_maxmsg = 10;
    mq_attr.mq_msgsize = 128;
    mq_attr.mq_flags = 0;
    emergency_mq = mq_open(EMERGENCY_MQ_NAME, O_CREAT|O_RDONLY|O_NONBLOCK,
        S_IRWXU, &mq_attr);
    if (emergency_mq == (mqd_t)-1)
        perror(EMERGENCY_MQ_NAME);
    /* Set up an asynchronous notification request on this message queue */
    sa.sa_sigaction = emergency_handler;
    sigemptyset(&sa.sa_mask);
    sa.sa_flags = SA_SIGINFO;   /* real-time signal */
    if (sigaction(SIG_EMERGENCY, &sa, NULL) < 0)
        perror("sigaction");
    se.sigev_notify = SIGEV_SIGNAL;      /* send me a signal */
    se.sigev_signo  = SIG_EMERGENCY;     /* send me THIS signal */
    se.sigev_value.sival_ptr = (void *)emergency_mq; /* with this data */
    if (mq_notify(emergency_mq, &se) < 0)
        perror("mq_notify");
}
```

Calling *mq_notify* arranges for the process to get asynchronous notification, described by the *sigevent* structure, when a message arrives on the given message queue (*emergency_mq*) and there is not already a process blocked waiting for the message. Only one signal is sent, and after that, your notification request is de-registered and another process can attach its own notification request. You must re-attach your notification request if you want notification whenever there is a message for you on the queue. We do this from the signal handler for the notification signal (*emergency_handler*).

The *sigevent* structure, which was described in the signals section, describes the signal that will be sent to the process when your message arrives. We set up an extended, queued, data-carrying signal by setting SA_SIGINFO in the call to *sigaction*. In this case, *se.sigev_value* will be passed to your signal handler as the data value for that signal. It's generally useful to set that value to the *mqd_t* that describes this particular message queue, or, alternatively, a pointer to a data structure of your own invention that more fully describes your use of the message queue. The *sigev_value,* remember, is a union that can contain either an integer value (to which the *mqd_t* can be cast), or a pointer to *void* (to which another pointer type can be cast). In our example, we pass the message queue descriptor along, so that we can differentiate *mq_notify* signals coming from multiple queues.

If any other process then attempts to attach its own notification request to the queue, it will fail. Only one process can have a notification request attached to a message queue at a time. In fact, you cannot even replace your original notification request with another one!

What you can do, though, is remove your notification request. Do this by passing in NULL for the *notification_request* argument to *mq_notify*. That frees up the notification request "spot" for that message queue, enabling any process (including you) to attach a new notification request.

When are you notified? If a message is sent to a queue, and there are no receivers blocked in *mq_receive* at the time, a signal will be sent to notify you that a message is waiting. If there is a process blocked waiting for a message to arrive, then that process will get the message, and you will not be notified. After all, the purpose is to let you know when there's a message *for you.*

When you close the message queue (by calling *mq_close,* or by calling one of the *exit* or *exec* functions), your notification request, if you attached one to the message queue, is removed and the "slot" is freed up for another process to attach its own notification request.

Message queues are inherited across a *fork.* Notification requests are not. Only one process can have a notification request attached to a message queue at a time. The child of a process that forks should not expect to be notified as the result of its parent's notification requests.

Using Message Queues

There are certain guidelines that you should always follow when using message queues. These include the following.

Clean Up Your Queues

As I mentioned above, message queues do not have to exist in the file system namespace. They might, but then again, they might not. That means it is possible to leave a queue lying around in your system after your application has terminated. To make things worse, you probably can't see the message queue by typing *ls.* Eventually, you may run into resource problems because of "dead" queues left lying around. The operating system can fill up its available space for message queues and you'll start getting error messages when you try to create more.

Even more insidious, the messages in a queue remain there, even when the queue is not being used by anybody! That may be what you want—the message queue can be used as temporary storage. This behavior may not be what you desire. Imagine that you have an application you're trying to debug. It sends some messages, say ten of them. It receives nine messages, then bombs out. You debug it and try it again. What you may have forgotten is that there's an extra, leftover message from the last time you ran the application. The first message you receive (at that priority level, of course) will be a left-over from the previous run—probably not what you expected!

The lesson is that every application must have a shutdown phase where it cleans up and empties its message queues. It may also be appropriate to remove its message queues from the system. Especially while you are developing, make sure that your application cleans up its queues when it terminates.

Always Create Your Queues

A corollary of the above rule is that your application must create its message queues when it starts. There are two reasons for this. The first reason is the stylistic one that I mentioned above: you should be removing your queues when you're done with your application, and that implies you have to create them when you start the application again.

The second reason to create your message queues is more important. Message queues are understood to be fleeting in their existence. Unlike files, they generally do not survive a system crash or reboot, because they live entirely in the memory of your machine, which gets wiped at system startup. Many applications, particularly embedded ones, run in environments where the power gets turned off from time to time. Or you may be prototyping on a system that crashes frequently. Or maybe the machine gets turned off every night to save the phosphor on the screen. Whatever. When you fire up your application, it's simply good practice to call all your initial *mq_open*s with O_CREAT set.

Verify That Queue Creations/Opens Did What You Expect

While you're at it, it's probably also useful to set O_EXCL. For any given *mq_open,* you know what you expect—that the message queue must be created, or that it's already there. Using O_EXCL gives you confirmation of your expectations in the return value from the system. If you expected to have to create a queue, and it was already there, you should check for old messages left in the queue. You may want to call *mq_getattr* to verify that the message queue sizing information is correct.

Problems with Message Queues

Message queues are measurably better than pipes as a means of interprocess coordination. They give you more structure and control over that structure, the ability to send messages without knowing the ID of the target, and a boost in performance. Another very important advantage of message queues is that they can be easily extended across machine boundaries into a distributed application. (Assuming, of course, that a distributed message passing facility exists in your target system). In contrast, an application using shared memory is more tightly tied to a single-machine model, because distributed shared memory is not widely available, nor is it terribly efficient.

Message queues have some limitations. The most basic is that they're queues. Many applications are naturally structured using queues, especially those applications that fit into the overall mold of "entities talking to one another." Say, though, that you want to communicate in some way that's not queue-based. You may want communication based on a stack, or you may want to share some data that multiple processes can operate on concurrently. You may want a shared pool of bits that a number of processes can get at concurrently. Message queues are clumsy at best for such applications.

The other limitation is efficiency. POSIX.4 message queues require data to copied from the sender into the operating system, and then copied from the operating system into the receiver (this is because the *mq_receive* call specifies the location of the received data, rather than letting the operating system decide where the received message is). These two copy operations take time. The larger the message, the greater the time required.

There are variations on the abstract message queue (not the POSIX version) that can use the MMU to *map* the message from one process into another, thus avoiding all that copying overhead. This requires, though, that a message buffer be appropriately aligned, usually to a page boundary. A better alternative is to allow the operating system to pass a pointer back as the result of an *mq_receive*, rather than having the application specify where the received data is to go. Neither alternative is present in POSIX.4.

For total flexibility, as well as the highest possible performance on a uniprocessor, you must use shared memory.

POSIX.4 Shared Memory and File Mapping

When two or more processes share some memory, that memory is in two (or more) places at once. It's mapped into the address spaces of all processes concerned. If one process writes a value into a particular byte of shared memory, the other processes see it immediately.* Any data structure you want can be embedded in a shared memory area, and thus be made accessible to multiple processes. This gives you the flexibility to create any communication structure you desire.

For example, let's imagine that our database example needs the ability to log data collected by other real-time processes. This is a fairly demanding application, in which a stream of information needs to be processed as it appears. Say our data-collection process reads its data into memory, then writes it to a pipe or message queue. This would involve a copy into system space (the system's internal buffers), and then a copy out again into the space of the database server. Two copies is two too many. Instead, the application and the database server could share several pages of memory, cooperating on which pages are being actively used for data gathering and which are being logged into the database by the server.

If you already know the generalities of shared memory (how it works, why you want it, the need for synchronization when using it), you can safely skip forward to the "Memory Is A File ... Sort Of" section, where there are step-by-step instructions for using the POSIX.4 shared memory mapping facilities. The following section provides some additional background information on shared memory.

Complications: Synchronization

The free-form, low-level nature of shared memory also gives you the freedom to hang yourself pretty badly. You have to be careful when you use it, because the operating system is not involved in your use of this memory. That's one reason for its speed. You don't have to call the operating system to do anything for you; you just operate on memory.

In particular, when using shared memory there is no implicit synchronization going on between processes. Unless you explicitly synchronize your process's accesses to shared memory, you can run into problems based on the process's concurrent access to the same data structure.

For instance, say you've implemented a circular, doubly-linked list in shared memory (one of my own personal favorites). The list can be a list of anything you want: say it's a list of free pages for our process to use in its real-time data collection. The collection process removes pages from this free list, fills them, then queues them to the database server. The server empties the pages and returns the page to the free list. There are

---

* Well, almost immediately. The instantaneous sharing of memory is subject to the physical characteristics of the underlying hardware memory coherence system. In particular, it may take several cycles for memory writes on one processor to wend their way through caches, out onto the memory bus, and back up into the cache of a neighboring processor. POSIX does not address multiprocessors at all; in fact, the scope of the POSIX.4 working group explicitly ruled out multiprocessor considerations. That's unfortunate, because multiprocessors are increasingly common.

two basic operations for a queue: *enqueue* and *dequeue*. Here's the basic doubly-linked list *dequeue* operation; it takes an element, assumed to be on a queue, off it:

```
dequeue(element *e)
{
        e->prev->next = e->next;
        e->next->prev = e->prev;
        e->next = e->prev = NULL;
}
```

This operation accesses three queue elements: the one being dequeued, the one before that (*e->prev*), and the one after it (*e->next*). Imagine that two processes simultaneously try to dequeue two *adjacent* elements. In other words, *e1* is the predecessor of *e2*, and these two processes try to dequeue both elements at the same time. Figure 4-1 shows what will happen if one process is preempted by the other halfway through the operation.

The end result is that the list is totally torn apart, and a traversal of the list, either backwards or forwards, will certainly lead to a NULL pointer access and a probable core dump. When you use shared memory, you must explicitly synchronize accesses to shared data structures. In the example above, you'd need to put some sort of lock on the queue itself so that only one process at a time could get at it. There are many ways to synchronize process execution. That's the subject of the next section.

Complications: File Mapping

Another complication we face is a result of the way POSIX.4 standardized shared memory. Shared memory is intertwined with another facility, called file mapping. File mapping, known mostly by the name of its most important interface, *mmap,* allows the application to map *any* file, not just shared memory, into its address space and then access it as if it were memory. Figure 4-2 illustrates this. Shared memory is a particular case of the more generic file mapping operation. This is a standardization of a widely available UNIX function (*mmap*). However, it does complicate the shared memory interface somewhat, because the options covering file mapping and shared memory have overlapping requirements.

As a simple, introductory example of the complexity of the shared memory interface, consider how you'd determine whether your system supports shared memory. As with the rest of POSIX, you'd look in *<unistd.h>*, where all the _POSIX_ constants are. However, part of the shared memory facility can be present, even if you do not have full shared memory.

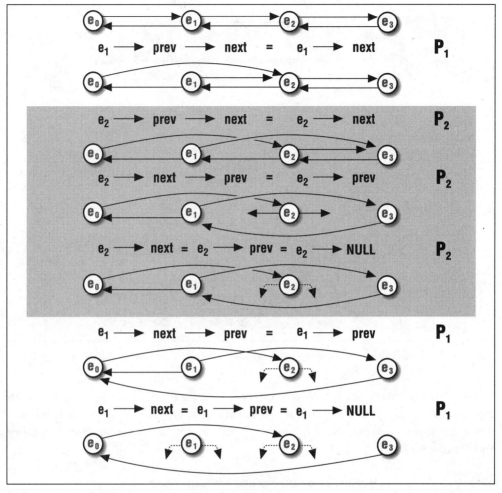

Figure 4–1. Result of simultaneous dequeue by two processes

The reason for this is the presence of file mapping. Operating system vendors may not be interested in real-time: they don't care about POSIX.4 shared memory, but they are *really* interested in file mapping. As a result, _POSIX_SHARED_MEMORY_OBJECTS is defined if all the shared memory functions are present. In addition, *mmap* and its related functions can also be defined under _POSIX_MAPPED_FILES, even if _POSIX_SHARED_MEMORY_OBJECTS is *not* defined. If _POSIX_SHARED_ MEMORY_OBJECTS is defined, you have shared memory, including the *mmap* interface necessary to actually use shared memory. If just _POSIX_MAPPED_FILES is defined, then you have *mmap*, but not shared memory. For the purpose of real-time coordination, just look for _POSIX_SHARED_MEMORY_OBJECTS. Other functions in this area are intertwined with other _POSIX_-constants: _POSIX_MEMORY_PROTECTION describes whether MMU protection bits can be set to enforce memory protections, and

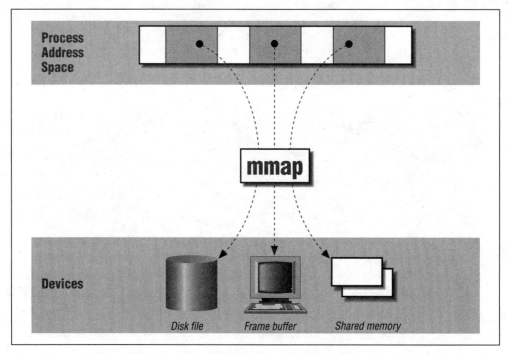

Figure 4–2. mmap is used for mapping differing sorts of objects, including shared memory

_POSIX_SYNCHRONIZED_IO is required for one of the memory functions (*msync*, which synchronizes a mapped file with the underlying disk file. *msync* is the last function described in this section). Table 4.2 summarizes the options affecting shared memory and file mapping.

Table 4–2: How to Get Various Shared Memory and File Mapping Facilities

Function	Present According to Which Options?
mmap	_POSIX_MAPPED_FILES or _POSIX_SHARED_MEMORY_OBJECTS
munmap	_POSIX_MAPPED_FILES or _POSIX_SHARED_MEMORY_OBJECTS
shm_open	_POSIX_SHARED_MEMORY_OBJECTS
shm_close	_POSIX_SHARED_MEMORY_OBJECTS
shm_unlink	_POSIX_SHARED_MEMORY_OBJECTS
ftruncate	_POSIX_MAPPED_FILES or _POSIX_SHARED_MEMORY_OBJECTS
mprotect	_POSIX_MEMORY_PROTECTION
msync	_POSIX_MAPPED_FILES and _POSIX_SYNCHRONIZED_IO

Did the working group go a little crazy here with the options? You be the judge.

Memory Is a File . . . Sort Of

Shared memory and message queues (and, as we'll see in the next section, semaphores as well) are all cousins in the POSIX.4 specification. Each uses a similar scheme for initializing (opening), de-initializing (closing), and so forth. In addition, each facility follows similar rules for naming the object, be it a message queue, shared memory object, or semaphore. Each individual interface is different from the others because each of the interfaces has unique and special characteristics. Message queues, for instance, are simple: open the queue, send a message. As we'll see below, shared memory is more complex, because you have the additional flexibility (and responsibility) to explicitly *place* shared memory (*map* it in) at a particular location in your address space. Finally, semaphores are complicated by the desire to place them, as well, in shared memory segments, for reasons we'll discuss later. So, message queues are the simplest of the three coordination interfaces in POSIX.4. Shared memory, while similar in its basics, requires additional steps.

Setting up shared memory is a two-step process because it is a special case of file mapping. As a result, shared memory is even more like a file than message queues are. The two steps to map shared memory are:

* Open the shared memory object (using *shm_open*).

* Use the resulting descriptor to map the object into your address space (using *mmap)*.

First, let's discuss the easy part. Opening a shared memory object is very much like opening a message queue: the same "sort of like a file, but not quite" interface is supported, and the same naming rules must be followed. The functions for working with shared memory therefore look a lot like the functions for message queues. We'll cover this part first, and then move on to the truly new ground of *mmap.*

Opening and creating shared memory objects

Shared memory objects are opened and created using a function that is very similar to *open: shm_open.*

```
#include        <sys/mman.h>

int shm_open(const char *shared_memory_name, int oflag, mode_t mode);
```

shm_open takes exactly the same arguments as *open,* and even returns the same sort of object: a file descriptor. In this, *shm_open* is different from *mq_open:* the message queue open routine returns an object of type *mqd_t,* which is not necessarily a file descriptor. The descriptor returned from *shm_open,* on the other hand, is definitely a file descriptor, and you can even use a couple of the normal file operations on it! Remember, though, that *shm_open* operates on a *name* that may not exist in the file system. Like message queues, shared memory may not show up in the output of a command like *ls.* Although the name of a shared memory object looks like a normal filename, it may be different. That's why a separate interface is required. Just for review, here are the rules for naming a POSIX.4 shared memory object:

- The shared memory object name must be constructed like a normal file pathname.
- To run on all systems, the name should start with a "/".
- To run on all systems, the name should contain no other "/" characters.

The conformance document for your implementation must tell you what happens when you do not start the shared memory object's name with a "/", and when you use more "/" characters in the name.

Also like message queues, you cannot perform most of the usual file operations with a shared memory descriptor—even though, in this case, you have a real, live file descriptor as a return value from *shm_open*! In particular, you cannot call *fstat, read, write,* or *lseek* with the file descriptor you get back from *shm_open*. There *are* two normal file functions that are defined to work correctly with shared memory objects: *ftruncate*, which sets the object's size, and *close*. It's a *special* descriptor. Just keep repeating that to yourself.

That is the only real difference between *shm_open* and *open.* This function opens the named shared memory object, using the flags given in *oflag.* As before, *oflag* contains the read/write mode of access. This flag must have either O_RDONLY (read-only access to the shared memory is desired) or O_RDWR (both read and write access to the shared memory is desired) set in it. By contrast, with files and message queues, an additional access mode, O_WRONLY (write-only access) is allowed. Because of the need for synchronization, and also because some MMUs don't support write-only memory, O_WRONLY is not allowed in *oflag* for *shm_open.* If you need to write the memory, open it with O_RDWR, and then refrain from reading the memory, if you can. Generally, shared memory is used in both read and write mode. In the database-server and real-time data acquisition example above, note that the data acquisition program would only be writing data to the pages of shared memory (and maybe reading those pages if there were control data structures embedded in them), while the database server would only be reading the data. Therein is a perfect example of when differing memory protections might be used.

O_CREAT and O_EXCL can be specified in *oflag* to cause the shared memory object to be created if necessary. These flags operate as expected. O_CREAT will create the shared memory object, using the given *mode* to set access permissions for the shared memory object as for message queues. O_EXCL, used in conjunction with O_CREAT, causes the interface to complain if the shared memory object already exists. If O_EXCL is not specified, then O_CREAT will silently fail to re-create a shared memory object that already exists.

Unlike message queues, no additional parameters are needed to describe the shared memory you create. All the relevant parameters for shared memory are set at the time you map the shared memory object into your address space, with *mmap*. There are no particularly relevant attributes of shared memory that are implicit to the shared memory object itself. When you call *shm_open(..O_CREAT..),* you get a shared memory object with default attributes—period.

There *are* attributes to shared memory, of course. Each shared memory region, for instance, has a size. When first created, that size is zero.[*]

Setting shared memory size

shm_open and *mmap* provide access to shared memory, but one important feature is not yet present. Every shared memory has a certain size. How is that size set? With files, the file size is automatically extended when you *write* to the file. Since one does not use *write*, or any system call at all, for modifying shared memory, there's no immediately obvious way of setting the size of a shared memory region. POSIX.4 provides the confusingly-named *ftruncate* function to set the size of a file or shared memory region.

A shared memory area has zero size when it's first created, or after someone opens it with the O_TRUNC flag set in *oflag*. When you truncate an existing shared memory area, any data that was in the truncated area will be lost. This is something like letting the air out of a balloon. The balloon's still there, but it's not as full.

To inflate the shared memory object after you truncate it (or when it's first created), you use *ftruncate:*

```
#include        <unistd.h>

int ftruncate(int fd, off_t total_size);
```

ftruncate actually works on all files, but we're interested in it because it operates on shared memory objects, too—even though shared memory objects *are not files*. In fact, POSIX defines *ftruncate*'s behavior only if the function _POSIX_MAPPED_FILES or _POSIX_SHARED_MEMORY_OBJECTS is defined.[†] *ftruncate* works both ways. You can use it to lengthen a shared memory object, oddly enough, but you can also use it to shrink a shared memory object. Whatever size you pass in to *ftruncate* becomes the size of the shared memory object. That size, by the way, is the size for *all* users of the

---

[*] Usually, a shared memory region also has a *default mapping* where the system will try to place it in your address space. The desire here is to map the same object at the same address in multiple processes. If the object is at the same address everywhere, it is easier for cooperating processes to use pointers to access the shared memory. Otherwise, all access to the shared memory object must be carefully scaled and shifted by the location of the shared memory object in that particular process. This attribute, and any others that may be associated with the shared memory object, are usually set by *mmap*. Attributes such as the default mapping are not explicitly visible to the application. But they are, regardless, attributes of the shared memory object.

[†] *ftruncate* is a standard UNIX function used for setting file sizes. POSIX doesn't require *ftruncate* unless shared memory is being supported. The reason is that *ftruncate* for normal files is not really a necessary part of a basic operating system; you can emulate its behavior with other functions if you need to.

shared memory. Only one process needs to do the *ftruncate*; all processes will see the result.

Close for shared memory objects

Of course, where you have an *open* routine, you must have a corresponding *close*. Because *shm_open* returns a file descriptor, it does not need a special close operation. Normal POSIX.1 *close* operates correctly on file descriptors for shared memory objects, as in the following example:

```
#include        <sys/mman.h>

int fd; /* FILE descriptor for shared memory object */
int i;

/* Initialize name, oflag, and mode if necessary */
fd = shm_open("/shared_memory", O_RDWR);

  ...
  ... map shared memory into your address space using mmap
  ... (discussed below -- don't worry about it just yet)
  ...

/*
 * Close the shared memory object
 * (does NOT unmap the shared memory!)
 */
i = close(fd);
```

I mentioned that shared memory setup is a two-step process. Opening the shared memory object is just the first stage. The open object must also be mapped into your address space using *mmap* (I'm getting to it, I promise!). The important point to remember for *close* is that it only recycles the file descriptor for the shared memory object: it only undoes the first of the two steps required to get shared memory. Once you've mapped the memory in, you can safely *close* the descriptor. In fact, you should close it for tidiness if no other reason. The shared memory remains mapped in your address space until you explicitly unmap it (with *munmap*).

Destroying shared memory objects

Completing our special shared memory functions, there is a function to remove shared memory objects. Since shared memory objects may not be in the file system, it makes sense that we use *shm_unlink* instead of *unlink*.

```
int i;

i = shm_unlink("/shared_memory");
```

Unlinking shared memory has the same semantics as unlinking a file or a message queue. If any processes are using the shared memory when it is unlinked, then those instances of the shared memory object remain viable and stable until each individual process ceases to use the shared memory. In the case of shared memory, of course, that means that each process must *close*, and also *munmap*, their shared memory before it truly ceases to exist. *exit* and *exec* implicitly close shared memory instances, just like they close files and message queues.

Mapping in shared memory

Finally. We've discussed how to create, set the size of, and destroy shared memory objects, and how to open and close them. None of this actually gets us memory to share. To get the memory into the address space of a process, you need to take the file descriptor returned from *shm_open*, and map it into your address space using *mmap*.

```
#include         <sys/mman.h>

void * mmap(void *where_i_want_it, size_t length, int memory_protections,
            int mapping_flags, int fd, off_t offset_within_shared_memory);
```

My first thought on looking at *mmap* was, "Holy Smokes! That's a lot of arguments!" You may be thinking the same thing. *mmap* is a fairly complex function. Here's a very basic description. *mmap* maps in the *length* bytes of shared memory at *off-set_within_shared_memory* in the shared memory object associated with file descriptor *fd. mmap* will try to place the mapped memory at the address you tell it in *where_i_want_it*, and will give it the memory protection you specify in *memory_protections*. The address you pass in to *mmap* may not be available for mapping memory. The address used by *mmap*, where it actually put the shared memory, is returned as the return value of the function. Finally, *mapping_flags* affects the way the mapping is done. These arguments are illustrated in Figure 4-3.

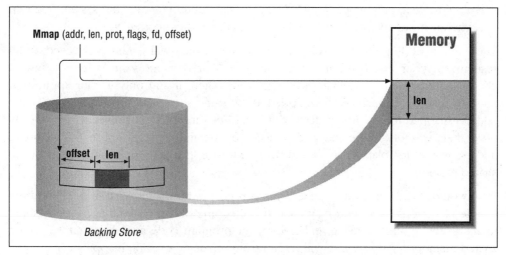

Figure 4-3. How mmap's arguments refer to the mapped region

Now, here's some more detail on each argument. Keep in mind that *mmap* works on all sorts of files. I'm going to talk mostly in terms of shared memory objects that have been opened by *shm_open*. Where the behavior for other sorts of files is different, I'll flag it.

fd, offset_within_shared_memory, and *length*

These define the region of the shared memory object to be mapped into your address space. *fd* is obviously the file descriptor you got back from *shm_open*. The *offset_within_shared_memory* refers to an offset within that shared memory object. (If you're mapping regular files, it is the offset in the file where mapping should start.) *length* is the number of bytes to be mapped in. Generally, you're going to want to map an entire shared memory region into your address space, so the *offset* will be zero and the *length* will be the entire size of the shared memory region. However, if you want to map a particular chunk of a shared memory object, you can do so by setting the *offset_within_shared_memory* and *length* parameters appropriately.

where_i_want_it (and where you get it)

The return value from *mmap* tells you the address at which your shared memory has been mapped in. You can try and tell the system where to put the shared memory, by passing in an address as a hint. That's *where_i_want_it*. The system is supposed to use your hint and try to place the shared memory near that address. A conforming POSIX system, though, can utterly disregard your hint and place the shared memory wherever it wants, unless you specify a particular flag, described below, that makes the system place the shared memory at the address you give it if at all possible. If you pass a hint of zero in, then the system is given free rein to place the mapping wherever it sees fit. I recommend you give the system free rein whenever possible, as it's tricky to use the hint address correctly.

There is one fairly portable way of using the hint, which will generally succeed on all systems. In your first mapping of a particular shared memory area, let the system choose an address by specifying a hint of zero. Then, if and only if your application requires that shared memory be mapped at the same spot in all processes, specify the address mapped for the first process as the address at which all subsequent processes want their memory to be mapped. Since the operating system chose the mapping address in the first place, you should be able to use it in subsequent mappings of the shared memory.

Why wouldn't the system use the address you give it, no matter what it is? There are a couple of reasons. One, you may have specified an address range that overlaps some memory you're already using, either for your program code and data or for another shared memory region. *mmap* will refrain from replacing existing mappings. Two, you may have specified a region that the particular system just doesn't support. Most systems only allow you to put shared memory in particular address ranges. For instance, you can't overwrite the mappings for the operating system. Generally, the operating system will also prevent you from overwriting your process's own executable code and data regions.

Let's assume, though, that you've managed to avoid those addresses where you and the operating system already exist, and that you are in the area where your operating system supports shared memory mappings. Why else might the system modify the address you give it? Usually, this will be because of page granularities. A memory management unit operates in chunks of memory called pages. You cannot map in shared memory at any old address. You have to start it on a page boundary. Most mainstream architectures use a page size that is 4096 or 8192 bytes—the constant PAGESIZE, from *<limits.h>*, tells you exactly what it is. For portable use of *mmap*, you really want to make sure that any mapping address you specify, as well as any file offset and length, are aligned modulo PAGESIZE. If they are not, the system either aligns its mapping appropriately without complaining or returns an error. Some systems (the sane ones, in my view) make sure that the offsets, lengths, and addresses you pass in are aligned to PAGESIZE multiples. That way no alignment happens without you being explicitly aware of it.

As an example of silent alignment, though, take the following. Say you ask for your file mapping to begin at offset 5 within the file, for 10 bytes of the file, and PAGESIZE is 4096. If the system does not return an error, you are going to get back a pointer that is going to be equal to 5, modulo PAGESIZE (e.g., 5001, 8197, etc.). Say the system returns 5001 to you. That means that the bytes from 5001 to 5011 are your shared memory. Be aware, though, that the 5 bytes from 4096 to 5001 are also going to be mapped in. The system cannot help but map those bytes in as well. Furthermore, there is memory mapped in from 5011 up to 8192. Assuming that your shared memory area is bigger than 15 (5 + 10) bytes, those additional bytes mapped in also reflect the shared memory area. If you modify them, other processes will be able to see the changes!

So, if all these restrictions and alignments are going on, how can you possibly use the address hint in a meaningful fashion? Well, there's generally only one reason you need shared memory to be at a particular address. That is, because your processes are using absolute pointer values to access the shared memory. If this is the case, then you need your shared memory to be in the same spot in each of the processes sharing memory. But notice! You don't need the memory to be at any particular spot. *All you need is for the memory to be in the same spot in each process.* Now, that's simpler. All you need to do is map the memory into your first process, letting the system choose the address. Then, each subsequent process can specify the address the system chose to put the first process's mapping at. That address is quite likely to be available, appropriately aligned, and otherwise generally O.K. for all cooperating processes to use. To force subsequent mappings (in other processes) to use *where_i_want_it*, set MAP_FIXED in *mapping_flags*.

mapping_flags

These flags control how the mapping is done. There are three flag values defined: MAP_SHARED, MAP_PRIVATE, and MAP_FIXED. MAP_SHARED specifies that you want this mapping to be shared with all other processes who map in this particular segment of the shared memory object. This is the desired behavior for shared memory: *of course* you want to share it! For other objects, like files, which you may be mapping, you may not want to share your mapping with anyone else. For this reason, MAP_PRIVATE is provided as the second flag value. MAP_PRIVATE need only be supported if the _POSIX_MAPPED_FILES option is supported, because it's not very useful if all you have is shared memory.

MAP_SHARED and MAP_PRIVATE really control how memory writes to the mapped object are reflected in the object itself. In the case of MAP_SHARED, your writes are propagated down to the object, and from there they find their way up into everyone else's mappings of the same object. Likewise, other processes that have mapped MAP_SHARED will have their changes propagated through the underlying object (shared memory, file, or whatever) to become visible to you.

MAP_PRIVATE causes any changes you make to your mappings to be visible only to you. Other processes sharing the same object never see your changes. MAP_PRIVATE provides you with a shadow copy of the object, which you can modify without having to worry about any other process seeing the changes. This functionality is not proper or desirable for shared memory. However, it is perfect for mapping in a shared library of code and data into your address space. Multiple processes using the same shared library can share the instructions in that library—those are never changed. But the data area from the shared library remains private to each process that uses it. This sort of use for *mmap* is why MAP_PRIVATE exists. Chances are, you'll never use it.

The third flag is MAP_FIXED. Implementations do not have to support MAP_FIXED. If you find a system that supports it, it tells the system to use your address hint as the address at which to place the shared memory—period. No alignment or adjustment is allowed. The system either puts the memory at the address you give it, or *mmap* fails. If MAP_FIXED is specified, then your hint, and the offset, must have the same value modulo PAGESIZE (5, in the example above). Furthermore, the system may require that both the offset and the hint address you pass in be aligned exactly to a PAGESIZE boundary.

memory_protections

Finally, you must specify the permissions for the mapping. Now, you already specified the permissions you wanted when you opened the file (O_RDWR or O_RDONLY). You need to specify permissions again here, to set the memory protection bits in the MMU. Memory_protections is a bitwise OR of any of the following: PROT_READ, PROT_WRITE, PROT_EXEC, PROT_NONE. If you only want to read the shared memory, specify PROT_READ. If you want to read and write, specify PROT_READ|PROT_WRITE. The system will check these permissions against the permissions you have for the file. Specifically, you must have opened the file (or shared memory object) with O_RDWR in order for PROT_WRITE to be allowed. And you must have opened the file with O_RDONLY or O_RDWR in order for PROT_READ to be allowed.

What about the others? PROT_EXEC means that you can execute the memory that you map in. That assumes that the memory you map contains instructions that make sense on your machine. Some machines also require you to set PROT_READ before you can execute code. PROT_EXEC is especially useful for implementing shared libraries, and is not particularly useful for much else. I suppose you could use it to implement a user-level overlay manager and relive the glory days of the 1970s, if you want. PROT_NONE means you can't read, or write, or execute the memory you map in. Now *that's* useful.

Some hardware cannot support the protections you may specify. For this reason, there is a separate option in POSIX, called the Memory Protection Option (_POSIX_ MEMORY_PROTECTION). If this option is defined in *<unistd.h>*, then the protections you set up will be enforced. If you try to change a value in an area that was not mapped with PROT_WRITE, you'll get a SIGBUS signal. I imagine that _POSIX_MEMORY_PROTECTION will be supported on all of the workstation-type architectures, although some embedded variants come without the required MMUs. If _POSIX_MEMORY_PROTECTION is not defined, then the protection may not be enforced. In this case, your application has to be careful not to write where you said you were only going to read.

File and shared memory mapping are obviously a little bit tricky. The following example shows everything required to create a shared memory area in one process and then map it in another.

```
#include    <sys/mman.h>
#define     SHM_AREA_NAME   "/shmarea"
#define     MYSHMSIZE   1048576
void *      shm_area;
char        shm_addr[32];
int     shm_descr;



shm_descr = shm_open(SHM_AREA_NAME, O_CREAT|O_RDWR, S_IRWXU);
if (ftruncate(shm_descr, MYSHMSIZE) < 0)
    perror("ftruncate");
if ((shm_area = mmap(0, MYSHMSIZE, PROT_READ|PROT_WRITE, MAP_SHARED,
    shm_descr, (long)0)) == NULL) {
        perror("mmap");
}
/* Make a printable version of the SHM addr */
sprintf(shm_addr, "%d", (unsigned long)shm_area);
close(shm_descr);   /* Done with this file descriptor */

/* Create a new process and pass the SHM address to it */
```

```
if (! fork()) {
    execlp(CHILD_PROCESS_PATH, CHILD_PROCESS_PATH, shm_addr, NULL);
}
```

The code in the child process would be:

```
int main(int argc, char **argv)
{
    void *shm_area;

    /* Get SHM address used by parent */
    shm_area = (void *)atol(argv[1]);

    shm_descr = shm_open(SHM_AREA_NAME, O_RDWR);
    if (shm_descr == -1)
        perror("shm_open");
    /* Map in shm at the same address as in the server--we will be using
     * pointers! */
    if (mmap(shm_area, MYSHMSIZE, PROT_READ|PROT_WRITE
        MAP_SHARED|MAP_FIXED, shm_descr, (long)0) != shm_area) {
            perror("mmap");
    }
    close(shm_descr);
    ...
```

There are a few things to notice in this example. First, notice how the parent allows the system to choose the mapping address, then the child performs a MAP_FIXED mapping to that same address. In this way, both processes have the same memory at the same address, and pointers into that region can be easily passed back and forth. Second, notice the method in which the shared memory address was passed to the child—as a command line argument. This is a pretty grungy way of getting that address publicly known, but it works. Finally, notice that both processes *close* the shared memory file descriptor as soon as the memory is mapped. Once the mapping is performed, the file descriptor is irrelevant and can be recycled.

What can I map besides shared memory?
The POSIX.4 specification never comes out and says which files a conforming implementation *must* allow *mmap* to work on. It certainly requires that *mmap* work for shared memory objects, and it seems to hint that regular files and other files may be supported. On the other hand, special devices are never mentioned, except to say that an error can be returned if you try to map something that it makes no sense to map (like a terminal). The meaning of "sense" is left up to the operating system vendor. Standard UNIX systems today support file mapping of just about any device on the system. When you're using systems that aren't based on UNIX code, though (real-time operating systems, for instance), you want to be careful to make sure that the system supports the mapping you require.

When you're done: unmapping your shared memory

As I've mentioned above, once you've *mmap*ed in your object (shared memory, frame buffer, disk file, or whatever), you can close the file descriptor and still retain the mappings you've set up. The mappings are inherited across a *fork*, so your child processes will have exactly the same mappings as you. The mappings are removed when you call *exit* or *exec*.

You may want to unmap your shared memory explicitly when you are done with the mappings you've set up. *munmap* is the function which unmaps memory you've previously mapped with *mmap*. It is much simpler than *mmap*:

```
#include        <sys/mman.h>

/* Unmap memory previously mapped with mmap */
int munmap(void *begin, size_t length);
```

munmap removes the mappings you've set up for the pages containing the address range *begin* through *begin* + *length*. Note that it is pages, multiples of PAGESIZE, for which the mappings are removed. Further references to these pages will result in an exception, just like accessing a bad pointer: you'll get a SIGSEGV signal, and if you're not prepared for that, you'll get a nice core dump to pore through. The operating system might require you to give it an address that's a multiple of PAGESIZE, although any value of *length* will be accepted. As with *mmap*, I recommend that you make sure the arguments to *munmap* are multiples of PAGESIZE. That way, you know exactly what memory you are mapping and unmapping, and that the system isn't rounding and truncating addresses for you.

When you *munmap* your mappings, it signifies you're done with the object. If your mappings were made with the MAP_PRIVATE flag set, any changes you made to this memory will be lost forever.

Remember how *close* and *unlink* work together? When you *unlink* a file that processes have open, the processes are allowed to continue using that file, but no other processes can open the file. When the last process closes the file, it finally, irrevocably disappears. Something analogous happens with *munmap*. An unlinked file, or a *shm_unlinked* shared memory object, will persist in any processes that currently have established mappings via *mmap*. When these processes remove their mappings (via *munmap*, *exit*, or *exec*), the object finally ceases to exist.

Do I need to say it? *Don't* call *munmap* for memory that you didn't *mmap* in the first place. It will probably fail. Worse yet, it might succeed!

So what happens to your shared memory when you've unmapped it? More importantly, what happens when everyone has unmapped it? POSIX.4 shared memory is persistent: it remains around in the system until it is explicitly removed (generally, shared memory also disappears if the system crashes or is rebooted). That means that you can unmap shared memory buffers full of interesting data and get that data back later. For example, you can do the following:

```
main()
{
    shm_descr = shm_open(SHM_AREA_NAME, O_CREAT|O_RDWR, S_IRWXU);
    if (ftruncate(shm_descr, MYSHMSIZE) < 0)
        perror("ftruncate");
    shm_area = mmap(0, MYSHMSIZE, PROT_READ|PROT_WRITE, MAP_SHARED,
        shm_descr, (long)0);
    sprintf((char *)shm_area, "Hello, there!");
    exit(0);
}
```

Followed by:

```
main()
{
    shm_descr = shm_open(SHM_AREA_NAME, O_RDONLY);
    shm_area = mmap(0, MYSHMSIZE, PROT_READ, MAP_SHARED,
        shm_descr, (long)0);
    }
    printf("Shared Memory says, \"%s\"\n", (char *)shm_area);
    exit(0);
}
```

The second process will successfully print Shared Memory says, "Hello, there!"

This persistence also means you must be careful, when your application first maps in some shared memory, to be sure the contents of that memory are valid. I recommend unlinking, then re-creating shared memory regions whenever your application first starts up. Such an activity should not take too long, and application startup is not generally time-critical anyway. Modifying the example given above, we'd have code like this in the *first* process, which is the one that creates the shared memory:

```
/* Remove shared memory object if it existed */
(void)shm_unlink(SHM_AREA_NAME);
/* Create the object */
shm_descr = shm_open(SHM_AREA_NAME, O_CREAT|O_RDWR, S_IRWXU);
if (ftruncate(shm_descr, MYSHMSIZE) < 0)
    perror("ftruncate");
if ((shm_area = mmap(0, MYSHMSIZE, PROT_READ|PROT_WRITE, MAP_SHARED,
    shm_descr, (long)0)) == NULL) {
        perror("mmap");
}
```

More memory protection

When I was explaining the *memory_protections* used by *mmap*, I mentioned that the protections were only enforceable on certain machines. For such machines, a separate option, _POSIX_MEMORY_PROTECTION, indicates that protection works, and unauthorized accesses to memory will be dealt with by delivery of SIGBUS.

_POSIX_MEMORY_PROTECTION means that the permissions you set when pages are *mmapped* will actually be enforced. Say, however, that you want to change the permissions of pages you have previously *mmapped* in. I do this when I suspect a process is performing an incorrect write to a memory area it shouldn't be touching. I'll turn off memory write permissions for that page in the section where the damage seems to be occurring, then wait for the SIGBUS to happen. This is a useful, if forceful, debugging mechanism. POSIX.4 supports it. If _POSIX_MEMORY_PROTECTION is defined, a function is provided for changing the protections of mappings you've already made:

```
#include        <unistd.h>

#ifdef _POSIX_MEMORY_PROTECTION
#include         <sys/mman.h>

void *begin;
size_t length;
int i, memory_protections;




/* Change the protections on memory previously mapped with mmap */
i = mprotect(begin, length, memory_protections);
#endif _POSIX_MEMORY_PROTECTION
```

The protection bits you can specify for *mprotect* are the same as for the original *mmap*: PROT_NONE, or some combination of PROT_READ, PROT_WRITE, and PROT_EXEC. Again, you may need to have your address aligned to PAGESIZE, and I recommend you align both the address and the length appropriately. Finally, the protections you try to set here are also checked against the permissions with which you opened the file. You cannot exceed the permissions with which you opened the file (or *shm_open*ed the share memory object).

You don't have to change the protections for an entire mapping; you can set the protections of individual pages within a mapping you've made. For example, if you *mmap* in three pages with PROT_READ and PROT_WRITE protection, you could turn off writability for just the middle page.

```
#include <sys/mman.h>

int fd, i;
void *addr;
/* Open and map in three pages of shared memory */
fd = shm_open("/my_shm", O_RDWR);
addr  = mmap( 0, 3*PAGESIZE, PROT_READ|PROT_WRITE, MAP_SHARED, fd, 0);
/* Set the protection of the middle page to be just PROT_READ. */
i = mprotect(addr + PAGESIZE, PAGESIZE, PROT_READ);
```

For regular files: backing store

Finally, let's talk about backing store. Backing store is the underlying object which you have mapped into your address space. Think of your mappings as kind of a shadow image of the underlying object. In the case of shared memory, the shadow image and the underlying object are one and the same: the physical memory being used to share information. With a disk file, on the other hand, there is a definite dichotomy. There's this file out on a disk, rotating at a measly 3600 RPM, with an access time in the milliseconds. And then, there's a memory image of a part of that file, mapped into your, and maybe some other process's, address spaces. This memory is fast. You can change it in nanoseconds. Obviously, the system is not going to keep the disk file updated with the contents of the memory image at all times: that would make your accesses to the shared memory unacceptably slow. When *mmap* is used to map a regular file, the contents of memory and the disk contents are synchronized at undefined times. In fact, the only times that POSIX says the disk and the memory are synchronized are when you remove your mappings, via *munmap*, or when you explicitly synchronize the mapping and the disk by using a special function, *msync*.

Because *msync* is useful only for files with slow backing store, like disk files, it's provided under the _POSIX_MAPPED_FILES option rather than under the option _POSIX_SHARED_MEMORY_OBJECTS. And, because functions that synchronize the disks are provided under their own separate option (you'll see more of this in Chapter 6), *msync* also requires another option be present: _POSIX_SYNCHRONIZED_IO. It works like this:

```
#include        <unistd.h>

#ifdef _POSIX_MEMORY_PROTECTION
#ifdef _POSIX_SYNCHRONIZED_IO
#include        <sys/mman.h>

void *begin;
size_t length;
int i, flags;

/* Synchronize mapped memory with the underlying file. */
i = msync(begin, length, flags);
#endif /* _POSIX_SYNCHRONIZED_IO */
#endif /* _POSIX_MEMORY_PROTECTION */
```

One more time: the address and length should, and may have to, be aligned to PAGE-SIZE. *msync* ensures that the mapped memory in the range *begin* through *begin + length* is updated on the disk or whatever underlying permanent media you are using to store your file on. You don't need to call *msync* for memory other than that you mapped with *mmap*, and you shouldn't, because the effects are undefined.

msync is pretty simple, except for the *flags* parameter. *flags* can be set with various bits to influence the exact way in which *msync* updates the disk. First, you can set either MS_SYNC or MS_ASYNC (not both) to synchronously, or asynchronously, update the underlying disk. As a rule, you'll want to use MS_SYNC. In this case, the call to *msync* will block until the data has gotten out to disk successfully. If MS_ASYNC is set, the system merely queues the I/O operations to be done, and then returns immediately. The synchronization will be done concurrently with your continued execution, and will complete at an unknown time in the future. Meanwhile, while the asynchronous I/O is going on, you can do something else—in particular, you can modify the mapped area that you're synchronizing. However, changes you make to the mapped object may or may not find their way into the ongoing synchronization. Given that you don't really know when the synchronization is done, or what exactly was synchronized, the use of MS_ASYNC doesn't really give me a warm fuzzy feeling about the coherence of the disk and the mappings. I'd stick to MS_SYNC.

One more flag is defined for *msync*, and you probably should use it. When you set MS_INVALIDATE, this flag will cause all copies of the mapped object (in other process's address spaces, for instance) to be invalidated, so that the next time those other processes access the shared memory, they'll get a copy which is guaranteed to reflect the stuff which you have just updated on the disk with *msync*. Many systems will keep cached copies of data up to date with very little latency, so MS_INVALIDATE is not strictly necessary on those systems. The details of how multiple copies of cached mappings are kept consistent is not something you can count on from one operating system to the next, or even from one revision of an operating system to the next! I recommend using MS_INVALIDATE for the portability it gives you. It may be a bit slower, since it forces other processes to get updated copies of the mapped data. But heck. You've already committed to going out to that slow old 3600-RPM disk drive anyway! A little more time taken, in an operation that's already dog slow, is not a big price for improved portability.

Synchronizing Multiple Processes

When you are using shared memory, or a mapped file between two or more processes, you must take care that each process does not step on another process's work in the shared memory area. If one process is modifying a data structure in shared memory, other processes should wait until the first process is done before reading. That way, they get a consistent picture of what's going on. Obviously, you don't want two or more processes changing the same data structure at the same time. And finally, if a process is reading a data structure, you want any process that decides to modify the data structure to wait until the first process finishes reading.

Synchronization, in General

How do you synchronize multiple processes? Dozens of ways are in use today. This introductory section covers a number of the alternatives you may find or hear discussed. The POSIX solution I'm going to describe is the counting semaphore. If you are only interested in the specifics of counting semaphores, you can skip to the next section. POSIX.1 supplies another mechanism, file locking, which can be used to mimic the behavior of semaphores. Since semaphores provide more basic and general functionality than file locking, I will stick to semaphores.

One method of synchronization is to use programmatic solutions, where you simply *know* that any process accessing a particular data structure is alone. This solution relies on your application structure. For instance, maybe you have an application where only one process is awake at a time and the rest are sleeping. Another example is most UNIX kernels, where it is an invariant condition that there is at most one process in the kernel at any given time. This sort of solution requires a careful analysis—and the problem is that your analysis might be wrong.

Alternatively, you must do some sort of explicit synchronization around accesses to the data structure that needs protection. A lot of synchronization mechanisms are in use today. The most common are:

- Counting semaphores
- Mutexes and condition variables
- Readers/writer locks

POSIX provides interfaces for most of these, believe it or not. Counting semaphores are provided in POSIX.4 and are one of the most primitive synchronization mechanisms you can have. Mutexes and condition variables are part of POSIX.4a, the proposed Threads standard. POSIX.1's file locking is a textbook readers/writer lock.

So, what *are* these synchronization mechanisms? Here are quick, abstract descriptions of each mechanism. Each mechanism is separate from all the rest, and you cannot mix-and-match them. Don't get any bright ideas about using a counting semaphore with a mutex, or a rendezvous with file locking—it won't work.

Counting Semaphores.

A semaphore can be used to guard accesses to a resource, or, alternatively, just to let processes wait for something to happen. Processes *wait on* and *post* a semaphore. These operations decrement and increment an integer count associated with the counting semaphore (hence the name). When a process waits on a semaphore whose count is positive, then the process just continues, having decremented the semaphore count possibly to zero. If the semaphore count is zero, then the waiting process is blocked, added to the pile of processes waiting on the semaphore, and not allowed to proceed until another process posts the semaphore. If a process comes along and posts the semaphore, and there is no process waiting for the semaphore, then the semaphore value is just incremented. Otherwise, one of the processes waiting for the semaphore is released and allowed to proceed. Anyone with access to the semaphore can wait on it or post it. Figure 4-4 shows one possible sequence of several processes, using a semaphore.

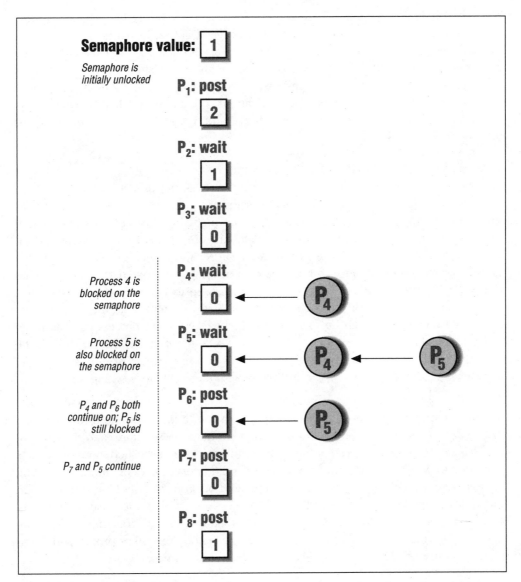

Figure 4–4. A counting semaphore over time

Notice that I have not talked about the semaphore value becoming negative. Rather, it just goes down to zero, and then we start stacking up blocked processes. Conversely, until all processes are released, a post operation will not increment the semaphore value. Some systems maintain a negative count, which then indicates the number of blocked processes. Depending on how the semaphore is implemented, though, the negative count may not be possible. So, for an abstract discussion, we don't talk about negative semaphore values.

The other thing about counting semaphores is the Dutch Connection. The semaphore was invented by the Dutch (a fellow named Edsger Dijkstra, in particular), who took the initiative of naming the operations *wait* and *post* in Dutch. The Dutch words are *proberen* (to test) and *verhogen* (to increment), *P* and *V* for short. Nowadays, we (in the United States at least) are moving away from *P* and *V* towards more descriptive (and English) names for the semaphore operations. I don't know what the Dutch position is on all this. But now you know what *P* and *V* are; in case anyone mentions them, you can play smart.

Mutexes and Condition Variables

Mutexes and condition variables are not part of POSIX.4, but they are part of POSIX.4a (threads), which should become a POSIX standard pretty soon now. A mutex, as shown in Figure 4-5, is something which provides mutual exclusion (processes excluding each other) for access to a particular data structure. Mutexes are closely tied up with the idea of *critical sections* of code. A critical section is a part of code that needs to be protected—for instance, when you're modifying a shared data structure. One talks about being *in* a critical section. A mutex is used to guard the critical section. I think of the critical section of code as a room, with the mutex as the door to that room. The mutex, then, can be locked or unlocked. Only one process can be in the room at a time. The process that locks the mutex is the one that has to unlock the mutex. This is unlike semaphores, where any process can post the semaphore. Mutexes have the idea of an owner associated with them, whereas semaphores do not.

Where do condition variables come into all this? A mutex is a very simple facility, and the condition variable is used in conjunction with it to add a little more functionality. Say you enter the critical section of code, look at your data structure, and then realize that it is not to your liking yet. Some condition has not been satisfied, and that means you need to wait for another process to come in and create that condition. By waiting on a condition variable, you unlock the mutex and wait on the condition atomically, in one uninterruptible action. When the other process comes along, it satisfies the condition, and then signals the condition variable, waking you up. You then re-lock the mutex, check that your condition was, indeed, satisfied by this other process, and continue on your way. The important features of the condition variable are:

- That it is associated with a particular mutex
- That the release of the mutex and waiting on the condition variable are atomic, thus preventing race conditions
- That you always re-lock the mutex, preserving the invariant that there be only one process in the critical section at a time

Figure 4–5. Mutex and condition variables

Readers/Writer Locks

This is a lock that allows any number of readers (processes looking at the shared data, but not changing it) at once, but forces a process that wants to change the data (a writer) to wait until there are no readers. Conversely, if there is a writer changing the data, then all the readers who come along are blocked until the writer finishes his work. There are two different sorts of locks associated with a readers/writer lock, a read lock and a write lock. A readers/writer lock is somewhat less primitive than either a mutex/condition variable pair or a semaphore.

Because POSIX.4a is not available yet, I'm not going to go into detail about the mutex/condition variables provided. And because there are plenty of Ada texts around, and the focus of this book is C, I'm not going to discuss the rendezvous. File locking *can* be used for pure synchronization (just ignore the file associated with the lock, and *voila!*, there you are). That's a rather clumsy way to do synchronization, and semaphores provide a more general solution. That leaves us with the counting semaphores of POSIX.4.

POSIX Counting Semaphores

There are two uses for most synchronization mechanisms: mutual exclusion and general waiting. The semaphore can do both, although it cannot do mutual exclusion as well as a mutex.

In mutual exclusion, a process "locks a door" by waiting on a semaphore. The process then enters a critical section of code where it modifies a shared resource. During the critical section, the data structure or resource may be in an inconsistent state. For instance, if the data structure is a doubly-linked list, and the critical section is an enqueue operation, then there are points where the "prev" pointer has been set up, but the "next" pointer is not yet set up. When the critical section is completed, the data structure is once again in a consistent state. At this point, the process posts the semaphore. The same process both posts the semaphore and waits on it. A mutex is arguably better than a semaphore for mutual exclusion because, with a mutex, you *know* that the ownership property is going to hold, whereas with a semaphore that's not always the case. When an implementation knows the owner of a synchronization object in advance, it can perform some optimizations to facilitate real-time processing. These optimizations are known as priority inheritance and priority ceiling, and are used to prevent priority inversions. Priority inheritance and the priority ceiling protocol are discussed in Chapter 5, *On Time: Scheduling, Time, and Memory Locking*, in the context of rate-monotonic analysis.

For general waiting, the process that needs to await something simply waits on the semaphore associated with that condition. Whenever another process comes along and satisfies the condition, it *posts* the semaphore, allowing the waiting process to continue. For instance, say two processes are cooperating in an area of shared memory. One process is transferring data into the shared memory area (from, say, a data collection device), and the other is transferring the data out again (logging it to a disk). The disk process must wait until the other process has transferred an entire page to the shared area before it writes anything to disk. This application might use a semaphore to show the state of the page. The logging process would wait on the semaphore while it was writing the page, thus forcing the disk process to wait until the logging was done. When logging was finished, the logging process would post the semaphore, allowing the disk process to proceed.

The POSIX.4 semaphores facility is encapsulated in the _POSIX_SEMAPHORES option. Here's a summary:

```
#include <unistd.h>
#ifdef _POSIX_SEMAPHORES
#include <semaphore.h>

/* Memory-based (unnamed) semaphores */
int sem_init(sem_t *semaphore_location, int pshared,
    unsigned int initial_value);
int sem_destroy(sem_t *semaphore_location);
```

```
/* Named semaphores */
sem_t *sem_open(const char *semaphore_name, int oflags,
    mode_t creation_mode, unsigned int initial_value);
int sem_close(sem_t *semaphore);
int sem_unlink(const char *semaphore_name);

/* Semaphore operations (both named and unnamed) */
int sem_wait(sem_t *semaphore);
int sem_trywait(sem_t *semaphore);
int sem_post(sem_t *semaphore);

int sem_getvalue(sem_t *semaphore, int *value);
#endif /* _POSIX_SEMAPHORES */
```

sem_open: creating and accessing semaphores

Before using a semaphore, one must create or open it. There are two ways to create semaphores. The first method creates "named" semaphores that obey all the same naming rules as message queues. The second method creates *memory-based* or *unnamed* semaphores, and will be covered later in this chapter.

To open an already-existing semaphore, use the *sem_open* function, with the semaphore's name and the normal flags as arguments:

```
#include        <unistd.h>
#ifdef  _POSIX_SEMAPHORES
#include        <semaphore.h>
char *sem_name;                 /* Name of semaphore to be opened */
int oflags;                     /* Open flags--NOT like for open!   */
sem_t *sem_des;                 /* Descriptor of opened semaphore */

sem_des = sem_open(sem_name, oflags);
#endif  /* _POSIX_SEMAPHORES */
```

The POSIX semaphore functions are conditional on _POSIX_SEMAPHORES being defined in *<unistd.h>*.

The *sem_open* call accesses and optionally creates a named semaphore, returning a pointer to the semaphore as its return value. The standard says that if *sem_open* fails, it returns –1, even though the function is defined to return a pointer type. NULL might have been a better choice, but that's not what's in the standard.

The restrictions on the semaphore name parallel the restrictions on message queue and shared memory object names:

- *sem_name* must be constructed like a normal file pathname.

- To run on all systems, *sem_name* should start with a "/".

- To run on all systems, *sem_name* should contain no other "/" characters.

The conformance document for your implementation must tell you what happens when you do not start the semaphore name with a "/", and when you use more "/" characters in the name. Most systems support one of two alternatives. These are:

- The implementation treats the semaphore name exactly like a path name, with associated directory traversal, use of current working directory, and permission checks. This alternative corresponds to an operating system implementing semaphores on top of mapped files.

- The implementation treats the semaphore name like a string of characters, without regard to the file system namespace, directories, or anything like that. This would be the case when the underlying system is not using the file system code for naming the shared memory regions. This is often the case on smaller, embedded real-time kernels.

Note that *oflags* is not used like it is for the *open* call. Usually, you'd set O_RDONLY, O_WRONLY, or O_RDWR in *oflags*, depending on whether you wanted to read, write, or read *and* write the object. Since semaphores are always used in the same way, there's no need to clue the system in as to your intentions. If you're opening a semaphore, the assumption is that you're going to use it. Also, in the name of simplifying the interface, other flags that might otherwise be set in *oflags* (O_NONBLOCK, O_SYNC, whatever) are not supported for *sem_open*. There are basically only two flags you can set, both relating to semaphore creation: O_CREAT and O_EXCL. These flags indicate that *sem_open* should create a new named semaphore:

```
#include          <semaphore.h>
char *sem_name;                  /* Name of semaphore to be opened/created */
sem_t *sem_des;                  /* Descriptor of opened semaphore */
mode_t mode;                     /* Mode for the created semaphore */
unsigned int initial_value;      /* Initial semaphore value */

sem_des = sem_open(sem_name, O_CREAT, mode, initial_value);
```

Semaphore creation takes two additional arguments to *sem_open*: the mode, which is the normal UNIX-style file permission, and an initial value for the semaphore. Notice that the semaphore value can only be zero (a locked semaphore with no waiting processes) or positive (an unlocked semaphore). A negative initial value for a semaphore would imply that the semaphore had processes waiting on it. This cannot be the case for a semaphore you have just created! The semaphore value must also be less than SEM_VALUE_MAX, defined in *<limits.h>*. This value is usually no less than the maximum signed integer value. The smallest value SEM_VALUE_MAX is allowed to have is 32767.

You can also set O_EXCL in *oflags* to cause the call to fail if the named semaphore already exists. If O_EXCL is not specified, then O_CREAT will silently fail to re-create a semaphore that already exists.

There is a hole in the standard regarding the *mode* in which you create the semaphore and the permission checking that goes on when someone calls *sem_open* on a created semaphore. The access mode to the semaphore is implicit, remember—you don't specify O_RDONLY, O_WRONLY, or O_RDWR. So, what permission bits is the system going to check when you *sem_open* a semaphore? Read, write? Execute? Maybe all three? The standard missed this specification. Luckily, the work-around is easy. For a semaphore there is no distinction between "read," "write," and "execute" permissions. There's just access, or the lack thereof. So set *all permissions* for whomever you want to be able to access the semaphore There are handy macros in *<sys/stat.h>* that serve this purpose: S_IRWXU, S_IRWXG, and S_IRWXO specify read, write, and execute permissions for user, group, and others, respectively. You should use these macros rather than the other S-macros in *<sys/stat.h>*. That way, you know your permissions will work appropriately, no matter how the underlying system performs its permission checks.

sem_close and sem_unlink: the usual suspects

Just as *sem_open* is similar to *mq_open*, the interfaces for closing and destroying a semaphore are similar to the message queue variants. *sem_close* removes the process's connection to the semaphore described in *sem_des*:

```
#include         <semaphore.h>

sem_t *sem_des;
int i;

/* Obtain access to semaphore */
sem_des = sem_open(...);


/* Release access to semaphore */
i = sem_close(sem_des);
```

Likewise, *sem_unlink* destroys a semaphore:

```
#include         <semaphore.h>

char *sem_name;
int i;

/* Remove semaphore name from the system */
i = sem_unlink(sem_name);
```

The normal caveats apply to *sem_close* and *sem_unlink*. *sem_close* renders the semaphore referenced by *sem_des* inaccessible, so the process that has called *sem_close* can no longer use that semaphore. The *exit* and *exec* functions also have the side effects of closing all open semaphores in a process. Finally, a semaphore that has been *sem_unlink*ed will not be removed until the last process that has it open closes it (by calling either *sem_close*, or one of the *exit* or *exec* functions).

Waiting and posting semaphores

Now that you know how to create and destroy semaphores, we can get on to the real functionality: using semaphores for synchronization. Whether you create your semaphores using *sem_open* or the memory-based interface *sem_init* (described later in this section), you still use the semaphores identically: with *sem_wait*, *sem_post*, and *sem_trywait*. *sem_wait* and *sem_post* do what you would expect: wait on, and post, a semaphore. *sem_trywait* is a variant of *sem_wait* that tries to wait on a semaphore, but never blocks. If the operation would require the process to block (i.e., if the semaphore value was zero or negative), *sem_trywait* fails, rather than blocking.

```
#include        <semaphore.h>

sem_t *sem_des;
int i;

/* Open the semaphore first... */

/* Wait on a semaphore */
i = sem_wait(sem_des);

/* Post a semaphore */
i = sem_post(sem_des);

/* Try and wait on a semaphore, but do not block */
i = sem_trywait(sem_des);
```

There's not much more to say about the actual use of the semaphores. You wait on them, you post them. If the semaphore is locked when you wait on it, you block until someone else comes along and posts it. There is one important detail you should know. That's the queueing order of blocked processes on a semaphore. Assume that you, and a pile of other processes, are all waiting on a particular, locked semaphore. When one process comes along and posts the semaphore, which process gets awakened? Well, if the waiting processes are all running under the POSIX real-time schedulers (described in Chapter 5), then those processes are queued highest-priority first. The POSIX real-time scheduling disciplines apply not just to processor scheduling, but also to the queueing of processes for just about everything in the system.[*] Semaphores (and file locks, and mutexes, and condition variables) are the most obvious spots in an application where priority queueing should take place. Less obvious locations are: when multiple processes are waiting for I/O on a message queue or pipe; when I/O is queued down to devices; and when multiple processes are contending for the various locks inside an operating system that protect its own shared data structures.

---

[*] The POSIX committee would have liked to say that everything in a system is done based on scheduling priority, but that was overstepping the committee's bounds as an operating system interface committee. Since I can say it here, I will: any real-time system worth its salt should perform priority queueing for every resource in the system, unless there's a good reason not to. If such a reason exists, you should hear it!

If your processes are not running under the real-time scheduling disciplines, then what happens? There are two levels of answer to this question.

- **What if my system supports _POSIX_PRIORITY_SCHEDULING, but I happen to be running under a scheduler other than SCHED_FIFO or SCHED_RR?** In this case, the standard says that the queueing shall be done in a manner appropriate to the scheduling algorithms involved. What exactly does this mean? Strictly speaking, it doesn't mean anything. However, the implementor of new scheduling algorithms can certainly be expected to document how the new algorithm impacts queueing for semaphores. Furthermore, if the process is running under SCHED_OTHER (the third scheduling algorithm in POSIX.4, kind of an implementation-defined, trapdoor scheduler), the implementation is expected to provide complete documentation of how this algorithm works.

- **What if _POSIX_PRIORITY_SCHEDULING is not supported at all?** You're toast. A system that doesn't support priority scheduling at all can hardly be expected to document its scheduling algorithms. Of course, if you're running on such a system, then your application is probably not that dependent on proper scheduling, and in this case, queueing order may not be important to you. For many so-called "real-time" applications, fast enough is okay, and actual priority scheduling may not be required. These are the squishiest of all "soft real-time" applications, like online transaction processing at an ATM or a grocer's checkout counter. You want it fast, but no jet engines are going to explode if it's delayed a little bit. This is the case in our terminals-and-servers example. As long as the delay isn't great, it'll be okay.

Debugging semaphores

Until now, we've discussed semaphores pretty much in terms of their abstract, clean, high-level definition. That is the best way to understand semaphores. However, when we talk about debugging applications that use semaphores, things get a little bit more complicated, because we need to talk about how semaphores may actually be implemented. Bear with me. Above, I described a counting semaphore as having a value that is either positive or zero. The value of the semaphore indicates another attribute of the semaphore: its state. A zero value means a locked semaphore, and a positive value corresponds to an unlocked semaphore. Each locked semaphore has a queue of blocked processes (maybe an empty queue) associated with it. And each post operation removes one process from that queue until the queue is empty. Then the value gets incremented. (If you're wondering about the semaphore value ever going negative, read on.)

So far, so good. What if your application has a bug in it, though? Imagine that you have made a subtle error in your code. You have a bunch of processes cooperating in a shared memory area, and when you run the application, it goes for a while and then "locks up." None of the cooperating processes are running anymore. Through the insertion of various ingenious debugging hints, you've discovered that the processes are all piling up on a particular semaphore which never gets unlocked. You'd really like to see how many processes are waiting on this semaphore at any given time. If the number goes over, say, two, then you know something has gone wrong.

In order to support this sort of debugging, the function *sem_getvalue* is provided to get the value of a semaphore at any particular time. You could use *sem_getvalue* to implement a monitor process that checks all your application's semaphores:

```
#include        <semaphore.h>

sem_t *sem_des;
int val;
int i;

/* Open the semaphore first */
sem_des = sem_open(...);

/* What is the semaphore's value? */
i = sem_getvalue(sem_des, &val);
```

sem_getvalue stores the semaphore's current value in the integer pointed to by the second argument. Seems pretty simple. But notice that the second argument is a pointer to a plain old integer, not an unsigned integer! That implies that a negative value can be stored in it. And some systems will store a negative number in the value if they can. In such systems, a negative value means that the semaphore is locked, and there are blocked processes waiting on the semaphore. The number of blocked processes will be the absolute value of the semaphore value. This number can be highly informative for debugging your application, although it is less useful in a running, presumably debugged system.

So why don't all systems return this negative number, if it's so useful? Some systems can't, that's why. There are two basic ways to implement a semaphore. One way uses an increment/decrement solution. In such a solution, *sem_wait* decrements the semaphore value, and then decides, based on the resulting value (negative or not) whether to block. *sem_post* increments the value and then decides whether or not anyone needs to be awakened. In such a system, the semaphore's value can be positive, negative, or zero.

Other systems implement semaphores with a test-and-set instruction. On these systems, *sem_wait* writes a single number (say zero) into the semaphore, while testing the semaphore's previous state. The post operation just writes another number (one, for instance) into the semaphore.* With this implementation, the first process doing a *sem_wait* will write a zero into the semaphore, see that the previous value was one,

---

* The actual values written to memory by the test-and-set are machine dependent. Some architectures can only write certain values. For instance, the SPARC processor has a test-and-set instruction that tests the memory location, and loads the value −1 into the location. One and zero are the values most people assume for "unlocked" and "locked," but an implementation may use other numbers to represent these states if it wishes.

and proceed. The other waiters will "spin" on the lock, continually executing the test-and-set instruction until another process executes a *sem_post*. This sort of solution is more applicable to machines made up of multiple processors, since the waiting processes each occupy a processor. These systems never generate a negative count of the number of waiting processes, because the semaphore implementation on such machines is not capable of providing such a count! Because this solution is common on multiprocessors, it would have been irresponsible to outlaw it. Unfortunately, that means that on some systems, *sem_getvalue* can return a negative value, and on others, it only returns zero for a locked semaphore. The implementation must indicate what it does in its POSIX conformance statement.

Memory-based semaphores

Earlier, we said that *sem_open* isn't the only way to create a semaphor. Now, we'll discuss the other interface: memory-based semaphores. But first, a few words on why you might find *sem_open* a problem.

Like *shm_open* and *mq_open*, *sem_open* requires a semaphore name, and returns something like a file descriptor (a pointer to a *sem_t*). The use of names has its disadvantages. For example, let's think about our database server. Databases often require very fine granularity for locking: locking individual rows and columns in a database is not uncommon. For data sets of reasonable size, we may need thousands of semaphores! The operating system may not be able to allocate that many semaphores for a process. And even if the operating system can create all those semaphores, someone has to come up with all those names.

sem_open's cousin, *sem_init*, eliminates these problems. With *sem_init*, you provide an address, and the operating system just initializes a semaphore for you at that address. No name is required; the address is enough for the operating system. These are called *memory-based* semaphores, as opposed to the *name-based* scheme I've explained previously. Memory-based semaphores represent another school of thought about how semaphores should be created. This school has its advocates and adherents, just as the name-based semaphores have their fans. You can use whichever scheme suits you. The memory-based semaphores offer more flexibility, allowing you to embed semaphores in shared memory-based data structures. Memory-based semaphores also parallel the interfaces for mutexes and condition variables which you will find in the POSIX.4a (threads) standard. The disadvantage of memory-based semaphores is additional complexity for the developer; you have to place the semaphore somewhere explicitly, rather than letting the system do it for you. Memory-based semaphores must be placed in shared memory to be useful between processes, so this interface also requires _POSIX_SHARED_MEMORY_OBJECTS.

```
#include        <unistd.h>
#ifdef _POSIX_SEMAPHORES
#include         <semaphore.h>
int i, inter_process;
```

```
unsigned int initial_value;
sem_t *my_semaphore;

inter_process = 1;      /* Use this semaphore between processes */
initial_value = 1;      /* Unlocked.  0 would mean locked */
my_semaphore = (sem_t *)...;     /* Where you want the semaphore located,
                                  * presumably in shared memory */

i = sem_init(my_semaphore, inter_process, initial_value);
/* Use semaphore with sem_wait, sem_post, sem_trywait, sem_getvalue */
i = sem_destroy(my_semaphore);   /* De-allocate semaphore when done */
#endif _POSIX_SEMAPHORES
```

sem_init and its converse, *sem_destroy*, are parallel to *sem_open*, *sem_close*, and *sem_unlink. Do not mix and match these two interfaces on one semaphore!* If you use *sem_open* to create a semaphore, then you have to use *sem_close* and *sem_unlink* to get rid of it. If you use *sem_init* to initialize a semaphore in memory, then you must use *sem_destroy* to remove it. Both interfaces yield semaphores on which you can use *sem_wait, sem_trywait*, and *sem_post.*

You must initialize *sem_init*'s first argument as a pointer to the location where you want the semaphore. The system then fills this location with whatever initialization is required to create a semaphore in that spot.

The second argument, *inter_process*, is a flag that tells the system whether this semaphore will be used between multiple processes. This flag should always be one if you are using multiple processes and wish to synchronize them. A value of zero indicates that the semaphore is to be used only within this process. That's not very useful, unless you have multiple threads of execution within a single process. Multiple threads is part of POSIX.4a, the threads standard, which specifies how the semaphore should behave under these circumstances. In the context of this book, you'll always set the *inter_process* argument to one.

The third argument, *initial_value*, specifies the initial value of the semaphore. This value can be zero for a locked semaphore, or positive for an unlocked semaphore. Negative values are not permitted, as that would imply a number of waiting processes.

sem_destroy

When you are done using a particular memory-based semaphore, you should call *sem_destroy* on that semaphore to let the system know that the semaphore is no longer being used; the system then frees any resources associated with the semaphore. The semaphore must be unused when you call *sem_destroy*. It may be either unlocked or locked, but if it's locked, there can be no blocked processes waiting on it.

If you do not call *sem_destroy* for a semaphore, then it is implicitly destroyed when the memory in which the semaphore resides is deallocated. If you have a semaphore in non-shared memory, then the semaphore is destroyed implicitly when your process calls *exit* or *exec*. If your semaphore is in shared memory, then it is destroyed when the shared memory is destroyed, after the last process has closed and unmapped the shared memory, and the shared memory object has been removed using *shm_unlink*.

Setting up a memory-based semaphore for inter-process use

There is more to creating a memory-based semaphore than just calling *sem_init*. You must make sure that the memory in which your semaphore resides is memory that is shared between the processes that need to synchronize. In the usual case, that means placing your semaphore in a shared memory area. What I'd recommend is that you embed your semaphores in data structures which you place in shared memory. For example, let's go back to the example of the circular, doubly-linked list in shared memory, which I used earlier in this chapter. There are two basic operations on this data structure: *enqueue* and *dequeue*. Both must be guarded against concurrent access by another process. I would tend to create a data structure that encapsulates all the relevant parts—the head of the list, any flags or whatever—associated with the list, and also the semaphores necessary for synchronizing access to the list. This example maps in a region of shared memory in which to store the list elements, and initializes a semaphore to guard access to the list.

```
#define POSIX_C_SOURCE 199309
#include    <unistd.h>
#include    <stdio.h>
#include    <errno.h>
#ifdef _POSIX_SHARED_MEMORY_OBJECTS
#include    <sys/mman.h>
#else /* _POSIX_SHARED_MEMORY_OBJECTS */
ERROR: _POSIX_SHARED_MEMORY_OBJECTS is not present on this system!
#endif

#define SHM_NAME    "/dblinks.shm"
#define NELEMENTS   500

#define ROUND_UP_TO_A_PAGE(s)   ((s & (PAGESIZE-1)) ? \
                (s & ~(PAGESIZE-1)) + PAGESIZE : s)

struct element {
        struct element  *prev;
        struct element  *next;
    void        *data;  /* A pointer to some informative bits */
};

struct dblq {
        struct element head;    /* List head */
        sem_t guard;        /* Semaphore to guard same */
};

struct whole_thing {
    void *proper_shm_address;
    struct dblq h;
    struct elements e[NELEMENTS];
};
```

```
#define MYSHMSIZE    ROUND_UP_TO_A_PAGE(sizeof(struct whole_thing))

struct whole_thing *shm_area;    /* Shared memory pointer */
struct whole_thing *my_list;     /* List w/in SHM. */

/* Initialize the data structure */
void init_structure(void)
{
    int shm_descr;
    struct element *e;
    int i;


    /* Create a shared memory area */
    shm_descr = shm_open(SHM_NAME, O_CREAT|O_RDWR, S_IRWXU);
    if (ftruncate(shm_descr, MYSHMSIZE) < 0)
        perror("ftruncate");
    /* Map in the shared memory */
    if ((shm_area = (struct whole_thing *)mmap(0, MYSHMSIZE,
        PROT_READ|PROT_WRITE,
        MAP_SHARED, shm_descr, (long)0)) == NULL) {
            perror("mmap");
    }
    close(shm_descr);

    shm_area->proper_shm_address = (void *)shm_area;

    my_list = &shm_area->h;
    /* Initialize list header and semaphore */
    my_list->head.prev = my_list->head.next = &(my_list->head);
    /* Initialize sem. as Process-shared, init. value 1. */
    if (sem_init(&my_list->guard, 1, 1) < 0)
            perror("sem_init");
    else {
            /* Put all elements on queue */
            e = bits->e;
            for (i=0; i<NELEMENTS; i++) {
                    dblink_enqueue(e);
                    e++;
            }
    }
    return;
}

void shutdown_structure(void)
{
    /* Destroy the semaphore */
    if (sem_destroy(&my_list->guard) < 0)
        perror("sem_destroy");
    /* SHM file descriptor was closed as soon as we mapped the memory in */
    if (shm_unlink(SHM_NAME) < 0)
        perror("shm_unlink");
    (void)shm_unmap((void *)shm_area, MYSHMSIZE);
}
```

```
/* Put element at tail of list */
dblink_enqueue(struct element *e)
{
        sem_wait(&my_list->guard);
                e->prev = my_list->head.prev;
                e->next = &(my_list->head);
                e->prev->next = e;
                my_list->prev = e;
        sem_post(&my_list->guard);
}

/* Remove element from list */
dblink_dequeue(struct element *e)
{
        sem_wait(&my_list->guard);
                e->prev->next = e->next;
                e->next->prev = e->prev;
                e->next = e->prev = NULL;
        sem_post(&my_list->guard);
}
```

Things to note about this example:

1. The *struct whole_thing* is present just for sizing the shared memory area conveniently.

2. The shared memory area size is rounded up to a number of pages.

3. The *init_structure* function shows how the entire data structure is instantiated in the first place. Other processes need to merely map in this shared memory area, *at the exact address* because we are using pointers into the shared memory area.

4. Only one routine should *shm_unlink* the shared memory and *sem_unlink* the semaphore. The rest can just unmap the relevant memory.

5. The technique used earlier to pass a shared memory address to an *exec*ed program will not work here, because we do not know who's *exec*ing when. Therefore, I've taken the liberty of storing the proper address of the shared memory area as the first word in the shared memory area. Processes attaching to the structure then map in the area, and if it is not at the appropriate address, they unmap it and try again. The *attach* routine is given below.

```
/* Attach to the (already initialized) data structure */
int attach_structure(void)
{
    int shm_descr;
    struct whole_thing *shm_area;
    void *exact_address;


    /* Open a shared memory area */
    shm_descr = shm_open(SHM_NAME, O_RDWR);
    if (shm_descr < 0) return -1;
```

```
        /* Map in the shared memory */
        if ((shm_area = (struct whole_thing *)mmap(0, MYSHMSIZE,
            PROT_READ|PROT_WRITE,
            MAP_SHARED, shm_descr, (long)0)) == NULL) {
                close(shm_descr);
                return -1;
        }

        if (shm_area->proper_shm_address != (void *)shm_area) {
            /* Not mapped at proper address.  Try again. */
            exact_address = shm_area->proper_shm_address;
            shm_unmap((void *)shm_area, MYSHMSIZE);
            if ((shm_area = (struct whole_thing *)mmap(exact_address,
                MYSHMSIZE, PROT_READ|PROT_WRITE,
                MAP_SHARED|MAP_FIXED, shm_descr, (long)0)) == NULL) {
                    close(shm_descr);
                    return -1;
            }
        }

        close(shm_descr);
        my_list = &shm_area->h;
        return 0;
    }
```

Conclusion

POSIX supports an entire spectrum of interprocess communication facilities, including standard UNIX mechanisms like signals and pipes, and building upon these with message queues, shared memory, and semaphores.

There are some shortcomings. An owned synchronization object, like a mutex, is required in order to avoid priority inversions (mutexes and condition variables are part of the upcoming POSIX.4a standard). The namespace of message queues, shared memory objects, and semaphores may be tricky.

Even so, these building blocks allow for a wide variety of process coordination to suit just about any need. We can now create and coordinate multiple processes. The next step is finer control over the timing of processes: processor and memory scheduling, and access to the time.

Exercises

Several of the exercises below build on the signals work done in Chapter 3, to compare the performance of the various methods of interprocess communication. In addition, we explore the persistent nature of POSIX.4 shared memory, message queues and semaphores.

The solutions to problems that require programming can be found in the Appendix, in the section listed in parentheses after each such problem.

Pipes and FIFOs

Each POSIX.4 real-time signal passes one pointer's worth of data (plus six or so bits of information implicit in the signal number and signal code themselves). Earlier we wrote a program to discover the bandwidth of signals on your machine. Modify that program so that it sends data, one pointer's worth at a time, between two processes using a pipe, or a FIFO. What is the bandwidth of pipes passing pointers on your machine? How does it compare to signals? *(fifo.c)*

Message Queues

Rather than using pipes, try using message queues to transfer a pointers' worth of data at a time. Set up the message queues with *mq_maxmsg=1*. How many bytes per second can you send this way? *(msg.c)*

So far, we've compared signals, pipes, and message queues for sending "messages" as big as a pointer's worth of data. Let's see what happens when we scale up the message size. Modify both the pipe and the message queue benchmarks so you can specify a message size to be sent down the message queue or pipe. How does the number of bytes per second change as you scale up the message size? At what point (if any) on your system do pipes outperform message queues? When do message queues outperform pipes? How large a message can you send using each mechanism? When you reach your upper size limit, how does each mechanism fail?

What happens to message performance as you increase *mq_maxmsg*? Under what circumstances would you want to use a small value for *mq_maxmsg*? Under what circumstances would you use a large value?

Shared Memory

Write an application that shares a page of memory between two processes. Just for interest, try to make the processes different executables, not just one process being the child of the other (i.e., do a *fork* and an *exec*, and get the shared memory to still work!). *(shm.c)*

In our earlier benchmarks, we relied on the fact that one process will block waiting for a "message" (a signal, a pipe, or a bona-fide message on a queue). With shared memory, any such synchronization is up to us. Without using semaphores, come up with a few mechanisms for ensuring that one of the processes waits for the other to put something (a variable amount of data, for easy comparison with the other programs we've been writing) into the shared memory. Implement some of these mechanisms. How does the bandwidth of shared memory compare to that of pipes, message queues, and real-time signals under this scenario? Any surprises? *(shmmutex_flock.c)*

Semaphores

Now, alter your shared memory program to use a semaphore for synchronization instead of your ad-hoc methods from before. Use *sem_open* to create and open the semaphore. How does the bandwidth of shared memory look now? How does it scale up for larger "messages"? *(shmmutex_sem.c)*

Try and run your program twice. Have you correctly closed and unlinked the semaphores when you are done with them? What if you terminate your program with a signal (by typing CTRL-C, for instance)?

Modify your test program so that it uses *sem_init* and *sem_destroy* instead of *sem_open*, *sem_close*, and *sem_unlink*. Which style of interface do you prefer? *(shmmutex_semembed.c)*

Persistence

Write a program that creates a named semaphore and then exits without *sem_unlink*ing the semaphore. *(mksem.c)*

After the program runs, try to use *ls* to find your semaphore. Does it exist in the file system of your machine? On some implementations it will. On others, it will not. How would you go about removing a semaphore left over from a program that did not unlink its semaphores? Implement your cleanup method, if your system does not support semaphores in the file system. Keep this program around—you may need it! You may also wish to create variants for shared memory and message queues. *(rmsem.c)*

5

On Time:
Scheduling, Time, and
Memory Locking

Trying to Make Things Happen On Time

Real-time applications are concerned with *when* things happen, not just how they happen. A car company is advertising nowadays their sophisticated new braking system, "which checks road conditions 300 times a second and adjusts brake pressure accordingly." Now, there's a real-time system, and a fairly typical one. Say you're driving that car, and I bet a few of you are, by now. Will you be happy if those computations miss their deadlines? I hope you're wearing your seatbelts, and that the real-time application that deploys the airbags also runs on time!

Scheduling concerns can be placed into several broad, somewhat overlapping categories. Generally, you will want to do one or more of the following:

- Make sure something happens at or before a specific time.
- Make sure something happens before something else.
- Make sure your important job is not delayed if that delay is not a part of the application (for instance, you don't want your important job delayed because someone else has caused your job to be swapped out to disk, or someone else is using a resource, like a file, that your job needs).
- Provide guarantees as to the schedulability of a given task set. (This objective is more academically-inclined than most people generally operate, but it is a very important objective, as we'll see later.)

Why is this a problem? Probably the easiest answer I can give here is to ask you the following. Say you had a computation that had to happen at a certain time. How would you make it happen at the right time? You could use *cron*, if the timing restriction were very loose (minutes or hours).* You could also use the *sleep* command, again if the timing were loose (on the order of seconds). But now, imagine the timing requirement is on the order of milliseconds. That is the case with most real-time applications, and some applications are even *more* stringent, requiring timing on the order of microseconds. This problem isn't going to get any easier for you! High resolution timing means you cannot use a command like *cron* or *sleep* anymore; the overhead of running one program, then another, is too high. For example, it takes your average disk drive about 10 milliseconds just to seek to the location of one of the blocks comprising a program. You have to program your timing into the application, using the sleep system call or interval timers. Even interval timers have a maximum resolution of 10 or 20 milliseconds. That's generally enough resolution for a real-time application, but you may need even more precision.

Say you have set things up so your one computation actually does happen on time. Now, what do you do if you have *two* things that have timing requirements? What if you have 10 or more? What if some of them are not dependent on clock times, but rather on sporadically interrupting devices?

The area of getting lots of things to run at the right times is a science unto itself. Some scheduling problems are unsolvable, and those that are solvable are pretty difficult. The decision as to *how* to schedule things is not even decided yet: there is still debate, mostly academic at this point, as to which scheduling algorithm is the best. Meanwhile the real world, as usual, has settled upon a fairly primitive scheme for scheduling that generally works for what you need it to do. The official scheduling solution of the real world is preemptive, priority scheduling. Priority scheduling works by assigning a set priority to each thing that needs to happen, and runs the highest-priority things first. "Preemptive" means that the system will interrupt a running task to run another task, if that other task is higher priority and suddenly becomes runnable. The timing aspects—the "when?"—are left to the application itself, using interval timers or whatever other means is appropriate. Other, future, scheduling algorithms may incorporate timing into their scheduling decisions, and that may well be a better way to solve the scheduling problem. In the meantime, though, we have real-world problems to solve, and priority scheduling for solving them.

First, I'll talk about the *how* and *why* of scheduling: how different requirements dictate different scheduling decisions, and why the separate processes in our example programs need to run with different scheduling parameters. After that, we'll examine how standard UNIX scheduling operates, and determine whether any of the standard UNIX scheduling mechanisms (*nice*, and SVR4 UNIX's *priocntl*) can help us out. Then we'll cover the POSIX.4 scheduling facilities. As a second part to this chapter, we'll examine two other facilities that relate to scheduling and schedulability of your applications.

---

* *cron* is described in *Essential System Administration*, by Æleen Frisch (O'Reilly & Associates, 1991).

First, the timer facilities of standard UNIX and POSIX.4 allow the application, with varying degrees of accuracy, to tell the time, wait for a time interval, or wait until an absolute time (11:11 A.M., November 11, 2011, for instance). Second, we'll talk about how demand paging and swapping can mess up all your scheduling decisions, and how to avoid paging and swapping by locking your application's memory down. Finally, when all the pieces are introduced, we'll spend some time on the details of how priorities should be assigned, and more survival tips for real-time applications programming.

Rates and Responses

As we saw earlier in the book, many real-time applications are naturally structured as multiple processes. For instance, imagine, as in Figure 5-1, that we are gathering data for a scientific experiment, or monitoring some piece of equipment. In this application, we may be taking input from a device that interrupts sporadically, and also from a device which does not interrupt but which must be sampled 10 times a second. In addition, we must log the data to disk. We have to provide a real-time graphical display of the ongoing process to a console. And, in response to both the current device state and to user inputs, we must feedback control information to the device under test.

These processes have different performance requirements, which fall into two broad categories: rate requirements and response requirements. A rate requirement is when a task must provide service at a particular rate: X times a second. Response requirements are generally more sporadic in nature, merely requiring that, when event Y occurs, the task responds to it within a certain amount of time. Here's some more detail on where rate and response requirements come from.

Hardware Inputs and Outputs

These are tasks getting real-time input data from data sources, or sending control data to output devices. These tasks are constrained by the performance requirements of the outside world. In particular, if the device is providing input 33 times a second (33 Hz), the input task had better be able to deal with that data rate, or it's either going to screw up or drop data. Conversely, we have tasks outputting control data to devices in the real world. Sometimes, a real-world control task runs at a certain frequency required to keep the real-world device under control. For instance, on the Space Shuttle, output tasks, controlling the engines during ascent, run at a rate of 100Hz, adjusting various parameters needed to keep the motors from cutting out, exploding, or otherwise malfunctioning.

In other cases, the output task is invoked only sporadically, as a device needs readjustment or special-case service. Such a task still needs to respond to its hardware within a certain, critical time frame. For example, the SCSI controller chip on my workstation issues phase change interrupts which must be serviced within a

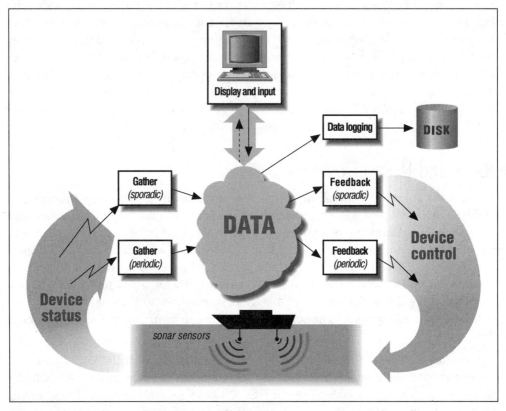

Figure 5–1. Real-time device monitoring and control

small number of milliseconds, or else the SCSI chip goes out to lunch. Phase change interrupts are sporadic, since they rely on the rate of requests to the SCSI bus and individual device characteristics. The interrupt, when it comes in, must be serviced quickly. For analyzing the behavior of sporadic tasks, you'll generally want to know the worst-case arrival rate of interrupts. This will allow you to determine how fast your task will need to run in the worst case.

Data Logging

Real-time data logging must run at a particular frequency in order to keep data streaming to or from the underlying logging device (a disk or tape, presumably). This requires the logging task to run periodically to keep poking the I/O along.

User I/O

These tasks convey information to the users of the application, and may allow the users to adjust parameters of the real-time system while it's operating. For instance, the terminal tasks in our terminal-database example, or a user interface hooked up to our real-time control example. Humans are pretty slow and nondeterministic I/O devices in the scheme of things; user interface tasks accordingly don't have as stringent performance requirements. Usually, faster is better, but humans can afford to wait—a little—while the hardware tasks keep the machines from blowing up.

Background Computation Tasks

Finally, we may have background computations that don't explicitly affect either hardware or wetware. An example comes from the use of artificial intelligence in real-time systems. Many cutting-edge systems incorporate some artificial intelligence techniques to perform motion planning or some other sort of solution generation. These jobs are very intense, long computations which take the input data, chew on it, and eventually produce some very sophisticated sort of output for the real-time system under control. For instance, a robot may take video input to be massaged by an expert course planning system, which will decide on the high-level course the robot should take.

While the computation *must* be done by some point in time, it cannot interfere with the running of the system *while* the computation is proceeding. This sort of task, again, has performance requirements that are dictated by *who* it's doing the job for. Furthermore, long computations may have partial value for partial results, so their requirements may vary with time. If time is plenty, you may let the computation continue. However, if time is short and you have an answer that's "good enough," you may just terminate the computation, or have it start on a new iteration.

If you have a clear requirement of rate or response, your real-time scheduling needs are usually correspondingly clear: higher rates, and tighter responses, require higher priorities than other tasks. Of course, it's not always that simple. You may have requirements which are unclear, as in the case of the ongoing AI computations, or which vary with time or the job at hand, as with database servers. The job of correctly assigning real-time scheduling parameters is difficult. We'll talk about how to do it right in the "Assigning Priorities" section in the chapter. Right now, let's get down to the mechanisms you'll want to use for running different tasks with different scheduling parameters.

Standard Scheduling Solutions Under UNIX

Standard UNIX, either from AT&T or Berkeley, has never solved the real-time scheduling problem in a comprehensive way. However, there are a couple of facilities that can be used in standard UNIX to attack the scheduling problem. One of these facilities is ineffective. The other facility is effective, but is complex and only works on SVR4 UNIX boxes. The POSIX facilities, on the other hand, do the same thing more simply and will be available on more platforms where you are likely to need to support real-time applications.

Being Nice—or Not

The standard UNIX system until now has run a time-sharing scheduler whose behavior is undefined by any standard; however, this scheduler does a respectable job in running time-sharing applications. The crucial item for any time sharing scheduler is to balance the needs of interactive or I/O-bound tasks (quick response for people at terminals) and the needs of compute-bound tasks (as much CPU time as possible, please). This is done by constantly adjusting each process's scheduling priority depending on what the process is doing. Processes that do a lot of waiting get their priority bumped up, so that they're responsive when they finally finish waiting. Processes that would monopolize the processor are penalized for this antisocial behavior. The ebb and flow of various process priorities is dictated by a couple of algorithms and computations.[*] One additional parameter inserted into these algorithms is the *nice* value associated with each process. To manipulate the *nice* value for each process, there's a *nice* system call, and a *nice* command as well.

nice is a number that indicates how "nice" the process wants to be in competing for the CPU. A process has a *nice* value of 0 by default. When you have a big kernel build on a loaded machine, you might *nice* it +20 (make it very nice to other processes) so as not to unduly affect other users. On the other hand, if you had a deadline and the other users weren't supposed to be using your machine in the first place (dammit!), you could *nice* your job -20, to make it much less nice.

Most people are familiar with *nice* as a command you can use to make other commands happen slower or faster:

```
% nice -20 make vmunix
```

This would run *make vmunix* with a *nice* value of -20. This is generally the level of control desired and achieved by using *nice* (either the command form or the system call itself). Statistically, your *make* would go faster, but you really could not rely on exactly *when* the *make* would be scheduled relative to other processes in the system. Actual scheduling decisions are still in the hands of the time-sharing scheduler, and remember, that scheduler is not defined anywhere. The UNIX timesharing scheduler algorithms are just the way some of the current systems work, and other UNIX implementors will almost certainly be tinkering with those algorithms to make things even better for time-sharing users.

nice is ineffective for real-time programming, as all it really does is modify how the time-sharing scheduler operates on your process. *nice* is meant for other uses; don't expect consistent results if you try to use it for real-time process scheduling.

---

[*] These are described in two books on UNIX: Maurice Bach's *The Design of the UNIX Operating System,* (Prentice-Hall, 1986), and Leffler, McKusick, Karels, and Quarterman's book, *The Design and Implementation of the 4.3BSD UNIX Operating System* (Addison-Wesley, 1989).

SVR4 priocntl—Pretty Standard Real-Time Scheduling

System V's *priocntl*, while not part of POSIX, still can be used effectively to address the real-time scheduling issue, and so deserves some discussion. The good news is, System V Release 4 has done a better job at supporting real-time scheduling than it did at supporting inter-process communication. The bad news is, the interface is somewhat complicated.

priocntl[*] will probably achieve a measure of industry-standardness, at least as long as you're only programming on a UNIX system. Operating systems specifically targeted at real-time applications support will generally use simpler mechanisms than *priocntl*. Even given that, it still makes sense to at least know what *priocntl* is capable of.

There is a *priocntl* utility and a system call. The system call looks like this:

```
#include    <sys/types.h>
#include    <sys/procset.h>
#include    <sys/priocntl.h>
#include    <sys/rtpriocntl.h>
#include    <sys/tspriocntl.h>

long priocntl(idtype_t idtype, id_t id, int cmd, ...);
```

First, *idtype* and *id* together define whose priority is being modified. If *idtype* is P_PID, then *id* is a process ID;[†] that process's scheduling parameters are to be modified. If *idtype* is P_PPID, then this priority modification applies to all processes whose parent process ID is equal to *id*. The rest of the possibilities for *idtype* are rather less likely to be used, and are described below.

P_PGID   ID refers to every process with a process group ID equal to *id*.

P_SID   ID refers to every process with a session ID equal to *id*.

P_CID   ID refers to every process with a class ID equal to *id*. Scheduling algorithms are identified by class IDs (one class is "real-time," and another is "timesharing"); this call to *priocntl* would apply to every process running under a particular scheduler (for example, the real-time scheduler).

P_UID   ID refers to every process with a user ID equal to *id*.

P_GID   ID refers to every process with a group ID equal to *id*.

P_ALL   ID refers to every process in the system: *id* is ignored.

As you can see, you can change the scheduling attributes of just about anything you want, using *priocntl*. Realistically, a real-time application is probably going to use no more than P_PID, and possibly P_PGID and P_SID. A system administrator might be more inclined to use P_UID, P_GID, and P_ALL, but in the real-time applications I know, such an action would just screw up the application's scheduling and make it

---

* Pronounced "Pry-Oh-Control."

† Process, Process Group, and Session IDs are addressed in *POSIX Programmer's Guide*.

fail. My impression is that *priocntl* was designed so that it could be run by a system administrator, as opposed to a real-time applications programmer. Not that *priocntl* is useless. The stuff a real-time application needs is definitely in there, along with a lot of extras.

Well, now that we know who we can apply *priocntl* to, what can we use *priocntl* for? This is the *cmd* argument. It identifies various scheduling actions that can be taken. The values of the *cmd* argument, and the corresponding uses, are as follows:

PC_GETPARMS

> *priocntl* retrieves the scheduling "parmeters" for the indicated process, group, class, etc.[*]

PC_SETPARMS

> *priocntl* sets the scheduling parmeters for the indicated group, class, process, etc.

PC_GETCID

> *priocntl* retrieves the ID of a particular scheduling class. There are two useful scheduling classes defined in SVR4: realtime (RT) and timesharing (TS).[†] In order to make any process realtime, you must know the class ID of the program, so you are going to have to call *priocntl* with PC_GETCID at least once in your application.

PC_GETCLINFO

> *priocntl* retrieves information about a class, given the class ID. PC_GETCID does this too, and also retrieves the class ID; you can use this facility to get information if you've forgotten it.

Essentially, we have four functions in one. The fourth, PC_GETCLINFO, is not strictly necessary; we'll dispense with it for the moment. The important question is "how do I make a process real-time at a particular priority?" Here's an example which uses *priocntl* to run itself at a real-time priority of 10.

```
#include        <sys/types.h>              /* Needed for priocntl() */
#include        <sys/procset.h>            /* Needed for priocntl() */
#include        <sys/priocntl.h>           /* Needed for priocntl() */
#include        <sys/rtpriocntl.h>         /* Needed for priocntl() */
#include        <sys/tspriocntl.h>         /* Needed for priocntl() */

/* We'll run at a real-time priority of 10:  Real-time priorities range from
0 to a system-dependent number in System V. */

#define VIRTUAL_PRIORITY 10

main()
```

---

[*] I have no idea why this is, but UNIX culture forbids the use of the second "A" in any contraction of the word "parAmeter." Strange but true.

[†] A third class, *sys*, is used for scheduling "system processes." You can't put any process in the *sys* class, and you can't change the scheduling parameters of any process in the *sys* class. It's basically an indicator to keep your grubby hands off special processes needed to keep UNIX running.

```
{
        pcinfo_t        realtime_class_info;
        rtinfo_t        *rtinfo;
        pcparms_t       realtime_parameters_for_me;
        rtparms_t       *rtparms;

        /*
         * This is an example of how to use priocntl to set your
         * scheduling class to be real-time and your priority to a particular
         * value.
         */

        /* First we must figure out what the real-time scheduling class ID
         * is and what the maximum allowable priority value is. */
        strcpy(realtime_class_info.pc_clname, "RT");
        priocntl(0, 0, PC_GETCID, &realtime_class_info);
        rtinfo = (rtinfo_t *)realtime_class_info.pc_clinfo;
        if (rtinfo->rt_maxpri < VIRTUAL_PRIORITY) {
                /* Trouble, there are not enough real-time priorities to
                 * run our example. */
                fprintf(stderr, "Cannot run at RT prio %d: max is %d\n",
                        VIRTUAL_PRIORITY, rtinfo->rt_maxpri);
                exit(1);
        }

        /* The last thing we do is actually set the process class
         * and priority. */
        realtime_parameters_for_me.pc_cid = realtime_class_info.pc_cid;
        rtparms = (rtparms_t *)realtime_parameters_for_me.pc_clparms;
        rtparms->rt_pri = VIRTUAL_PRIORITY;
        rtparms->rt_tqnsecs = RT_TQINF; /* run free, run FIFO */
        rtparms->rt_tqsecs = 0; /* This value ignored for RT_TQINF quantum */

        priocntl(P_PID, getpid(), PC_SETPARMS, &realtime_parameters_for_me);
}
```

Two calls are required to use *priocntl* to set a process's scheduling attributes. First, you must call *priocntl(..PC_GETCID..)* to retrieve the class ID for the real-time scheduling class. Then, using the class ID, you'll call *priocntl(..PC_SETPARMS..)* to change the scheduling parameters of your process.

PC_GETCID

When you call *priocntl* with the *cmd* argument equal to PC_GETCID, it tells you the class ID for the class you describe in the fourth argument. This number is not, apparently, a constant (in contrast, the scheduling constants that POSIX.4 uses are true constants, so only one call is required to change scheduling classes). To find the class ID, you must partially initialize a structure of type *pcinfo_t*, with the name of the scheduling class whose ID you want, and pass this structure's address as the fourth argument to *priocntl*.

```
typedef struct {
        ...
        char    pc_clname[PC_CLNMSZ];
```

```
...
id_t    pc_cid;
...
long    pc_clinfo[PC_CLINFOSZ];
...
} pcinfo_t;
```

The two scheduling classes are named "RT" and "TS." Then, you pass in this structure as the fourth argument to *priocntl*. The third argument is PC_GETCID, and the first two arguments are ignored. The system will fill in the rest of the *pcinfo_t* structure with the attributes of the real-time scheduling class. There are two attributes. Most important is the class ID, which is stored in the *pc_cid* field of the *pcinfo_t* structure. Next most important is the *pc_clinfo* field of *pcinfo_t*. It contains class-specific information in a class-specific format. For the real-time scheduler, the data is in the form of a structure of type *rtinfo_t*. Unfortunately, System V did not see fit to define *pc_clinfo* as a union, so you must do your own casting:

```
pcinfo_t my_pcinfo;
rtinfo_t *my_rtinfo;
my_rtinfo = (rtinfo_t *)my_pcinfo->pc_clinfo;
```

You cannot define your own structure type to mimic *pcinfo_t*, because SVR4 hasn't defined the actual layout of the structure. All that's defined is that the three fields are in the structure, somewhere. If you define your own structure, you need to worry about rearrangement of the structure at some future date.

The structure *rtinfo_t* contains one field, *rt_maxpri*. This is the maximum scheduling priority available for real-time scheduling. The minimum scheduling priority is always zero, not a variable. If you try to set your priority higher than *rt_maxpri*, you'll get an error.

PC_SETPARMS

Once you know the realtime class ID and you've verified that your desired priority is within the allowable range, you can set your scheduling parameters. Call *priocntl* with an *idtype* of P_PID, *id* equal to your process *id* (use *getpid* for this), a *cmd* of PC_SETPARMS, and a structure of type *pcparms_t* in the fourth argument. Pcparms_t defines all your scheduling parameters.

```
typedef struct {
    ...
    id_t    pc_cid;
    ...
    long    pc_clparms[PC_CLPARMSZ];
    ...
} pcparms_t;
```

Set the *pc_cid* field to the realtime scheduling class ID returned from *priocntl(..PC_GETCID..)*. The *pc_clparms* field is like the *pc_clinfo* field of the *pcinfo_t* structure: you have to do your own casting.

```
pcparms_t my_pcparms;
rtparms_t *my_rtparms;
my_rtparms = (rtparms_t *)my_pcparms->pc_clparms;
```

There are three fields in the *rtparms_t* structure. Most important is the *rt_pri* field, which you set to your desired scheduling priority. Next most important are the two fields *rt_tqsecs* and *rt_tqnsecs*, which define your scheduling quantum (in seconds and nanoseconds, respectively). Your quantum is the maximum time interval you will be allowed to execute before the next process at the same priority level is given the CPU. Don't set *rt_tqnsecs* to one billion or greater, or the call will fail. *rt_tqnsecs* is meant to be less than 1 second. If you want to run in a true FIFO manner, where you run until you voluntarily give up the CPU, then set *rt_tqnsecs* to RT_TQINF. This sets your quantum value to infinity, and *rt_tqsecs* is ignored. If quanta are unimportant to you, you can set *rt_tqnsecs* to RT_TQDEF, and a default quantum for this priority will be assigned. You can also set *rt_tqnsecs* to RT_NOCHANGE if you are switching from one priority to another and wish your quantum to remain unchanged.

Even though you can specify a time quantum down to the nanoseconds, don't count on the system using exactly that number. In fact, you should count on the system *not* using that number unless it's an integral multiple of the clock tick on the machine. This is because, on many systems, scheduling decisions are made when the clock tick goes off. If you specify a time interval that is not equal to some number of ticks, these systems will round the interval up to the next number of ticks. The tick granularity is given by the constant HZ, in *<sys/param.h>*. Usually it's 60 or 100; the minimum value it'll generally take on is 50. Thus, if you use nanosecond values that are multiples of (1,000,000,000 / 50 = 20,000,000), you should be pretty much O.K. (although 60 Hz works out to a number of nanoseconds that doesn't quite fit).

Will *priocntl* work for our example? You bet. The problems with *priocntl* are twofold. One, the interface is complicated and error-prone. Second, *priocntl* is only going to be provided on System V UNIX boxes—not generally the right boxes for your real-time apps. If you want to run your application on a real live embedded or hard real-time system, you're probably going to go with an operating system other than SVR4 UNIX. For maximum portability, you need the POSIX interfaces.

Portable Real-Time Scheduling: the POSIX.4 Scheduling Interfaces

The POSIX real-time scheduling option (_POSIX_PRIORITY_SCHEDULING) is what you need. These interfaces are simple, sufficient, extensible, and portable. They smell good and they are always neatly groomed. Here's a synopsis of the interfaces POSIX.4 provides.

```
#include          <unistd.h>
#ifdef _POSIX_PRIORITY_SCHEDULING
#include          <sched.h>
int i, policy;
struct sched_param scheduling_parameters;
pid_t pid;

int sched_setscheduler(pid_t pid, int policy,
    struct sched_param *scheduling_parameters);
int sched_getscheduler(pid_t pid);
int sched_getparam(pid_t pid, struct sched_param *scheduling_parameters);
int sched_setparam(pid_t pid, struct sched_param *scheduling_parameters);
int sched_yield(void);
int sched_get_priority_min(int);
int sched_get_priority_max(int);
#endif _POSIX_PRIORITY_SCHEDULING
```

What's Your Policy?

In POSIX, processes run with a particular scheduling policy and associated scheduling attributes. Both the policy and the attributes can be changed independently. POSIX.4 defines three policies:

- **SCHED_FIFO**: Preemptive, priority-based scheduling.

- **SCHED_RR**: Preemptive, priority-based scheduling with quanta.

- **SCHED_OTHER**: An implementation-defined scheduler.

Under the SCHED_FIFO policy, a process has one scheduling attribute, its priority. Processes running under SCHED_FIFO run until they give up the processor, usually by blocking for I/O, waiting on a semaphore, or executing some other blocking system call. SCHED_FIFO is the equivalent of *priocntl*'s RT scheduling class with a time quantum of RT_TQINF. In fact, a System V box with POSIX.4 conformance probably has implemented the POSIX scheduling stuff as calls to *priocntl*. SCHED_RR operates just like SCHED_FIFO, except that processes run with a system-given quantum. This is equivalent to *priocntl*'s RT_TQDEF time quantum. POSIX.4 provides no means to change a particular process's time quantum. SCHED_OTHER is not *defined* by POSIX.4; its presence is merely mandated. It's kind of a back-door scheduler, meant as an exit from "real-time mode" back into "timesharing mode." Since implementors can do whatever they want with this scheduling algorithm, SCHED_OTHER can turn out to be more of a trap-door than a back-door.

Scheduling Parameters

The way the POSIX interfaces are defined, you can pass in any number and sort of scheduling parameters, depending on which policy you are running under. The way this is done is by passing a structure, *struct sched_param*, to each function that gets or sets the scheduling parameters. Right now this structure has only one member, but future scheduling policies—or non-standard schedulers provided as extensions by the operating system vendor—can add new members.*

The current commercial (as opposed to research and academic) state-of-the-art in process scheduling is pretty simple: priority scheduling. If there is a quantum associated with the priority scheduling, it's usually just a system parameter, not changeable by the individual process. The scheduling algorithms defined by POSIX, therefore, don't need a lot out of *struct sched_param*. There is only one field defined:

```
struct sched_param {
        ...
        int sched_priority;
        ...
};
```

and this field is used by both of the scheduling algorithms defined by POSIX.4

An example: scheduling in the future

Future scheduling algorithms will be permitted to extend this structure to accommodate their own requirements. For example, consider a deadline scheduler. The deadline scheduler is the current (circa 1993) darling of the academic circuit and will probably eventually find its way into common commercial use. This scheduling algorithm operates by stating the time by which a process must be done running. To successfully know when to schedule processes under the deadline scheduler, the operating system would need to know when the deadline is, and also how much time the process will need in order to complete its job. Thus, a future SCHED_DEADLINE might add two fields to the structure:

```
struct sched_param {
        ...
        int sched_priority;
        ...
        struct timespec sched_deadline;
        struct timespec sched_timerequired;
        ...
};
```

Notice that the *struct sched_param* is a structure, not a union. Thus, the *sched_priority* element will always be visible from the programmer's standpoint. However, SCHED_FIFO only cares about *sched_priority*; SCHED_DEADLINE would only care about *sched_deadline* and *sched_timerequired*.

Also, like all structures in POSIX, the exact contents and layout of the structure is not defined. That means that if you do any static initialization of *struct sched_param*, it will be non-portable.

---

* Each scheduling algorithm uses a certain subset of the members of this structure. So, if you're setting SCHED_FIFO, you only need to set the members that SCHED_FIFO cares about. The other, uninitialized members will be ignored.

Defined Policies in POSIX.4

As mentioned above, there are two (maybe three) scheduling policies defined by POSIX.4. These policies are SCHED_FIFO and SCHED_RR; the third pseudo-scheduler is called SCHED_OTHER. I'll describe each in turn.

SCHED_FIFO: First In, First Out

SCHED_FIFO is a simple, priority-based, preemptive scheduler. This is the most common scheduling algorithm found in real-time systems, and is the most generally useful. You'd use this algorithm in most cases, unless you had an explicit need to timeslice between multiple processes. For instance, our data collectors, data logging, and display processes would tend to all run under SCHED_FIFO. It's called FIFO because the First process In at a given priority level will be the First one at that priority level to go Out to run; that process runs until it voluntarily gives up the processor, or is preempted by a process of higher priority. This is really just simple preemptive priority scheduling, so calling it SCHED_FIFO may be a little confusing. The FIFO part of the algorithm only applies to what happens *within* each priority level, and is probably meant to differentiate this algorithm from SCHED_RR, which does something *else* (described in the next section) within each priority level.

To understand how SCHED_FIFO works, imagine an array of queues, one queue per priority level. Priority zero has a queue, priority five has a queue and so forth. Now, imagine that each process is on the queue for its particular scheduling priority. The system decides who to run by going to the highest-numbered non-empty queue, and running the process on the head of that queue. If that process wants to run forever, and no higher priority process becomes runnable, well, that's what the system does. A process gives up the CPU in one of two ways: either it becomes blocked (on I/O, a semaphore, or some other activity that requires it to wait), or it explicitly relinquishes the processor to another process of the same priority (by calling *sched_yield*, described later in this chapter). When the process finally gives up the CPU, the system goes back and examines the queues again to determine the highest-priority runnable process. Lather, rinse, and repeat.

Another handy property of the SCHED_FIFO scheduler is that, on a uniprocessor at least, you know that the processor is all yours if you are the highest priority runnable process. Sometimes, if you work it right, you can avoid explicit synchronization with other processes at the same priority level.

SCHED_RR: Round and round we go

SCHED_RR, the round-robin scheduler, is a simple enhancement of SCHED_FIFO which allows processes at the time priority to timeslice amongst each other. Add the concept of a quantum to the policy, and you have it. That is, processes running under SCHED_RR run just like those under SCHED_FIFO, except that SCHED_RR processes only get to run for the time quantum before being shuffled back to the end of the queue for their priority level. This gives another process with the same priority a chance to run. You'd use SCHED_RR if there's some need to forcibly kick a process off the CPU after an amount of time. For instance, background computations might run SCHED_RR. The goal of SCHED_RR is not to provide fair scheduling like the SVR4 TS scheduling class does—this algorithm is far too simple for that. Rather, SCHED_RR is supposed to give a weak approximation of timesharing for those real-time systems that need it. Unlike SVR4's *priocntl*, which lets you alter your quantum values, SCHED_RR uses a system-provided quantum value which you cannot alter. This value is not necessarily a constant. You can find out what it is, for a particular process, by calling *sched_rr_get_interval*. This call takes a process ID as an argument, so the quantum value can actually vary on a per-process basis. More likely, though, it will vary on a per-priority level basis: different priorities may have different quanta. Alternatively, the quantum (for a priority level, a particular process, or even for the entire system) may be changed by a system administrator. I find SCHED_RR useful at the lower priority ranges, where you may want to run several processes performing computations when nothing more important is running.

SCHED_OTHER: Curtain number three

Finally, a third scheduler, SCHED_OTHER, is defined, if you can call it that, by POSIX. The behavior of processes running under the SCHED_OTHER scheduler is defined by each implementation. This means that in the conformance document for POSIX.4 system X, there will be a paragraph stating exactly what SCHED_OTHER does, and how it interacts with the other scheduling algorithms. Beyond that, there are no real requirements on SCHED_OTHER. SCHED_OTHER is defined to "allow strictly conforming applications to...indicate that they no longer need a realtime scheduling policy in a portable way." [POSIX.4 Draft 13, page 149, lines 107-108] What SCHED_OTHER actually provides is a way of guaranteeing a non-portable scheduling item that will vary from one implementation to another. Here's an example.

Under a standard UNIX system, SVR4, SCHED_FIFO maps directly to the RT scheduling class with quantum RT_TQINF. SCHED_RR might map to the RT scheduling class with RT_TQDEF. Now, I am not privy to the plans for SVR4 POSIX.4 conformance, but it would be perfectly sensible and reasonable to map SCHED_OTHER onto the TS timesharing scheduler. That way, processes running under SCHED_OTHER get out of the way of the real-time processes. Great!

On the other hand, consider a dedicated real-time operating system. A hard real-time system doesn't usually *have* a time-sharing scheduler at all. Time-sharing is approximated by the use of a round-robin scheduler. Under such an operating system, SCHED_FIFO and SCHED_RR are directly supported by the operating system, and SCHED_OTHER maps to ...SCHED_RR! In other words, SCHED_OTHER processes are still real-time processes that contend with the SCHED_FIFO and SCHED_RR processes.

Now, imagine some poor soul implements a real-time POSIX.4 application on SVR4 using SCHED_OTHER to run some sort of background, unimportant tasks. On SVR4, this solution works fine. However, when the application is carted over to LynxOS (a representative hard real-time operating system), it breaks horribly because the SCHED_OTHER processes get in the way of the SCHED_FIFO processes!

Speaking standardese, the application above is not a "strictly conforming" application, because it relies on an implementation-defined facility (the behavior of SCHED_OTHER) for its correct operation. However, how many applications do you know of that require the person porting the application to look at the conformance document for the new operating system? How many applications have their own conformance statements? And, most importantly, how likely is someone porting a supposed "POSIX.4 application" to read all the conformance documents before trying to get the code running? These are all rhetorical questions. Here's what will probably happen: the application will be compiled and run; it will break, probably in some obscure way related to scheduling fringe conditions; hair will be torn, Jolt cola will be consumed, management will scream. Eventually someone will think to look at the conformance documents for SVR4 and the hard real-time system, and will say, "Oh . . . . "

Don't use SCHED_OTHER if you want a portable real-time application. Stay within the bounds of the defined real-time schedulers.

Like Father, Like Son

Where do a process's scheduling algorithm and parameters get set? By default, each process inherits this stuff from the parent process. Scheduling attributes are inherited across a fork or one of the *exec* family of calls. Consider the following pipeline:

```
% rt_data_acquire | rt_data_process | \
        tee rt_file | rt_data_output > /dev/output < /dev/input
```

All processes in the pipeline run with the scheduling attributes of the shell. This is probably what you expect to happen, but some surprises can occur. For instance, consider the program *atprio*,[*] which allows you to run a process under the FIFO scheduler at a particular priority. Say you wanted to run this whole pipeline at priority 127, and your shell was running under some other scheduler or at some other priority. You might be tempted to try:

```
% atprio 127 rt_data_acquire | rt_data_process | \
        tee rt_file | rt_data_output > /dev/output < /dev/input
```

This wouldn't work because the other processes in the pipeline are forked by the shell, not by *rt_data_acquire*. *rt_data_acquire* would run FIFO at 127, but the other processes in the pipe would run under the default scheduler of the shell. A workaround here is to use *sh –c*:

```
% atprio 127 sh -c "rt_data_acquire | rt_data_process | \
        tee rt_file | rt_data_output > /dev/output < /dev/input"
```

---

* See the "Exercises" at the end of the chapter for more detail on *atprio*.

Since the shell is run at priority 127, and it, in turn, runs the pipeline, all the elements of the pipeline will be set to the proper priority.

POSIX.4 introduced some exact definitions of when a child process runs after a *fork*. In POSIX.1 the execution time was indeterminate; all you knew was that the child would run *sometime*. Under POSIX.4, when *fork* is called, the child process inherits exactly the same scheduling parameters as the parent. If the parent was running under the SCHED_FIFO scheduler at priority 100, the child process will also be running under the SCHED_FIFO scheduler at priority 100. In this case the child process is not going to run until there is a free processor for it to run on. On the basic uniprocessor machine, the processor is occupied by the parent process until it blocks. It may be a while before the child runs. The parent process cannot rely on the child running before it returns from *fork*, or at some unspecified time "soon" after *fork* is called. The parent process will have to explicitly *let* the child process run. This is important to remember when you want the child process to do some sort of initialization task. You have to let it run before it can initialize!

A Change of Policy

Scheduling parameters are inherited at *fork/exec* time. In general, a process that is part of a real-time application will want to set its scheduler and priority explicitly. To do so, you use one call, *sched_setscheduler*. For instance, to set your process priority to 17 under the FIFO scheduling policy, you could do the following:

```
#include        <sched.h>

struct sched_param scheduling_parameters;
int scheduling_policy;
int i;

scheduling_parameters.sched_priority = 17;
i = sched_setscheduler(getpid(), SCHED_FIFO, &scheduling_parameters);
```

The call to *sched_setscheduler* does all the work. Its first argument is a process ID. This code calls *sched_setscheduler* with its own PID, as discovered by *getpid*, but in fact you can use *sched_setscheduler* to change the scheduling of any process. Of course, you must have the right permissions in order to make a successful call to *sched_setscheduler*, and POSIX.4 does not define what permissions are required, only that the implementation has to tell you. A reasonable set of permissions might be that root can do anything, others can only modify their own scheduling policy. Or, perhaps, root can do anything, and no one else can use real-time scheduling at all. Don't expect to be able to change the scheduling of any process you choose.

Here's another hint about the use of the process ID argument. A positive PID identifies a particular process. If the PID is zero, then the call refers to the calling process. Now, for some functions (e.g., POSIX.1 and UNIX *kill*), a negative process ID applies the function to an entire process group. That makes sense for *kill*, as it allows you to send a signal to a whole pipeline of processes. On the other hand, it usually doesn't make sense to set the scheduling parameters for a whole group of processes at once. Therefore, POSIX.4 left the interpretation of negative PIDs unspecified. Even though there are cases where you might want to set the scheduler for a bunch of processes at once, don't try to do it with these calls. They won't do that. This applies to *sched_setscheduler* as well as all the other scheduling functions in this interface.

Now, back to our example. It will work, but only sometimes. Why? Because 17 may not be a reasonable priority value for the FIFO scheduler on your particular machine. To explain this, I need to talk a little about how schedulers are implemented on many systems.

Every operating system has a scheduling data structure very much like the FIFO scheduler's: a set of queues, one per priority level. What differs is how the priorities are set and how often they are modified. In other words, even under a time-sharing scheduler, each process has a priority which the system uses to determine when it runs; the system alters that priority on a regular basis to achieve better time-sharing response.

Each operating system, then, has some underlying range of priorities that are used for scheduling ALL the processes on the system. Some scheduling algorithms may not be able to use all those underlying priorities. For instance, many systems relegate time-sharing processes to the lower half of the priority scale, and leave the highest priorities for the real-time processes. Say you had 256 underlying priorities in your system. In that case, the real-time FIFO scheduler might use priorities 128 to 255. Or, it might use all 256 priorities, from 0 to 255. The round robin scheduler, as a sort of simulated time-sharing, might use the lower half of that range, or it might also have access to all 256 priority ranges.

In order to determine what the minima and maxima are for the scheduling algorithms are on your system, you use the *sched_get_priority_min* and *sched_get_priority_max* calls, as in this example:

```
#include        <sched.h>

int sched_rr_min, sched_rr_max;
int sched_fifo_min, sched_fifo_max;

sched_rr_min = sched_get_priority_min(SCHED_RR);
sched_rr_max = sched_get_priority_max(SCHED_RR);
sched_fifo_min = sched_get_priority_min(SCHED_FIFO);
sched_fifo_max = sched_get_priority_max(SCHED_FIFO);
```

You probably want to do this as part of your application initialization, and adjust all your process priorities accordingly.

This may seem like a needless complication to you, and I find myself, as an application programmer, in agreement. However, as an implementor I can see where the decision to allow different, possibly-overlapping priority ranges came from (even if I think it's silly). Well, you're stuck with it. How do you deal with it? It's actually quite simple.

The trick is to use a virtual priority range for all my application processes. All application processes have a priority from 0 to whatever the maximum for the algorithm is. The maximum, using the code above, would simply be *(sched_fifo_max - sched_fifo_min + 1)* for SCHED_FIFO. POSIX.4 dictates that this difference has to be at least 32, and the art of modern process scheduling pretty much dictates that you should have 128 or more priority levels.

Now, just define a function as follows:

```
int my_sched_setscheduler(pid_t pid, int sched_policy,
        const struct sched_param *sched_param) {

    struct sched_param tmp;

    tmp = *sched_param;
    switch (sched_policy) {
    case SCHED_FIFO:
            tmp.sched_priority += sched_fifo_min;
            break;
    case SCHED_RR:
            tmp.sched_priority += sched_rr_min;
            break;
    default:
            break;   /* Do nothing */
    }
    return (sched_setscheduler(pid, sched_policy, &tmp));
}
```

This function maps your virtual priorities into the proper range for your system and allows you to ignore the differing priority ranges that may occur from one platform to the next.

There is still one problem that has no easy solution. What if you want SCHED_RR and SCHED_FIFO processes to be scheduled together correctly? In other words, you may have two processes, one SCHED_RR and one SCHED_FIFO, and you want to run them at the same underlying system priority. How do you make that happen on a system where the priority ranges may be different for the two algorithms? In this case, using virtual priorities would be a bad thing. You might mistakenly assume that virtual priority 0 for SCHED_FIFO was the same as virtual priority 0 for SCHED_RR. One possibility is for your virtual priority subsystem to detect this condition and report it. Another possibility is for you to determine the underlying priorities when your application is deployed and adjust your application administratively. This is only a problem, though, if you are running multiple processes under different schedulers.

This is a tough issue and you probably will need to solve it administratively. If you want to mix scheduling algorithms and have them play together correctly, you should probably prepare to do some system administration before deploying your application on the target. I imagine a scheme where the various processes pull their priorities out of a file, database, or from a network service like Sun's NIS. Then, the priorities are not wired into the code to be recompiled each time. Of course, in that case you need to do system administration, but don't kid yourself—you're going to have to do that anyway. Just because POSIX increases portability, does not mean that you can slap down any old application and have it just work right!

Setting Your Scheduler Up

Now that you understand the basic concepts of policy and parameters, and I've told you about the defined policies, the actual interfaces for setting the policies and parameters are really simple. *sched_setscheduler* is the major component of the POSIX.4 scheduling facilities: it sets the scheduling policies and parameters. Of course, there are more functions required to create a complete facility. First of all, you might want to know which scheduler you are running under. For that, the *sched_getscheduler* call is provided.

```
#include        <sched.h>

int scheduler;

scheduler = sched_getscheduler(0);
```

This simple call returns the identifier of the scheduling algorithm for the given process ID (0 is shorthand for the calling process's ID). This value is either SCHED_FIFO, SCHED_RR, or SCHED_OTHER. If your system supports additional schedulers, another value could be returned, for instance the SCHED_DEADLINE which we postulated above. In such a case, though, the implementation must do two things in order to maintain its claim of POSIX.4 conformance:

- Document the additional implementation-defined schedulers
- Provide an environment in which you can build your application so that the implementation-defined scheduler would never come up

Remember that the scheduler SCHED_OTHER has implementation-defined effects.

What was my priority again?

sched_getscheduler is interesting, but really, you're not going to use that function too much. More likely, you will be interested in seeing and changing your (or another process's) scheduling parameters: in the case of the two defined schedulers, you want to see and change your priority.

```
#include        <sched.h>

int i;
struct sched_param my_sched_params;

i = sched_getparam(getpid(), &my_sched_params);
```

This call will fill in *my_sched_params* with my current scheduling parameters. Remember that *struct sched_param* contains a number of fields, corresponding to the various scheduling algorithms supported on the system. In the case of SCHED_FIFO and

SCHED_RR, you would be interested in the *sched_priority* field of *my_sched_params*. At present there are no other standard schedulers, and so there are no other fields in the structure which you would be (portably) interested in.

Changing parameters

Finally, I want to be able to change my scheduling parameters. To do so, use *sched_setparam*:

```
#include         <sched.h>

int i;
struct sched_param my_sched_params;

/* Be the highest possible priority */
my_sched_params.sched_priority = sched_get_priority_max(SCHED_FIFO);
i = sched_setparam(getpid(), &my_sched_params);
```

sched_setparam has a cousin, like many other functions. *sched_getparam* is used to retrieve the scheduling parameters for a particular process:

```
#include         <sched.h>

int i;
struct sched_param his_sched_params;

/* What scheduling parameters is process 86 running with? */
i = sched_getparam(86, &his_sched_params);
```

This code sample would retrieve the scheduling parameters for process 86 (assuming there *is* a process 86) into *his_sched_params*.

Back of the line

Whenever you request a change to your scheduling policy or parameters the system automatically moves you to the end of the queue for your new scheduling state. For example, say you are running FIFO at priority 13, and there is another priority 13 process waiting to run. Well, that process cannot run because you're running. But say you set your scheduling priority to 13 again. This is not even a real change, as your priority was 13 to begin with. However, the standard requires that you become the waiting process, and the process waiting in line gets to run.

Another scheduling rule is called "immediate preemption." If you set another process's priority such that that process becomes the highest priority runnable process, then that process must run before you even return from your call! Here's a fairly evil example:

```
#include         <sys/types.h>
#include         <signal.h>
#include         <sched.h>

pid_t pid;
struct sched_param params;
```

```
/* Be FIFO */
params.sched_priority = sched_get_priority_min(SCHED_FIFO) + 16;
sched_setscheduler(0, SCHED_FIFO, &params);

pid = fork();    /* Split -- two processes running under the
                  * same scheduler */

/* Because we are running under the FIFO scheduler on a uniprocessor,
 * the parent process is still running and the child is waiting */
if (pid) {
        /* parent */
        params.sched_priority++;/* Child, be higher priority */
        sched_setparam(pid, &params);  /* THIS CALL NEVER RETURNS */
        kill(pid, SIGINT);       /* Immediately kill the child! */
} else {
        /* child:  execute an infinite loop! */
        while (1)
                ;
}
```

On any truly POSIX.4-conformant system, this example will not terminate,[*] because the child must be scheduled to run before the parent returns from its call to *sched_setparam*. If this code terminates, then your POSIX.4 implementation is broken.

Yield right-of-way

Setting your scheduling parameters identical to what they were is an interesting way to allow another process to run; as we said previously, any attempt to modify your scheduling parameters (even if you don't change them) schedules yourself off the processor. The ability to give up the processor is useful—so POSIX.4 defines a function for this purpose:

```
#include      <sched.h>

void sched_yield(void);
```

sched_yield is very simple. It moves the calling process to the back of the line for its priority, allowing any other processes at that priority to run. Note that *sched_yield*, when called by a priority 10 process, is not going to allow a priority 9 process to run. Only another priority 10 process would get a chance. If there were no priority 10 processes other than the one calling *sched_yield*, then that process would immediately resume its execution!

---

[*] Not totally true: it won't terminate on a uniprocessor. On a multiprocessor, it may terminate, since you may run the parent and the child at the same time if you have two or more processors.

Yielding while not yielding

sched_yield is a handy little function, but don't fall in love with it. I use *sched_yield* a lot in little test programs where I want to make sure that one thing runs before another, like this one:

```
pid = fork();   /* Create a child process.  Because we are running
                 * under the SCHED_FIFO scheduling policy, we
                 * "know" (see text below) that the child is not
                 * going to run immediately -- the parent is still
                 * running, but the child should be ready to go.
                 */
if (pid) {
        /* Parent -- yield to child so it can go */
        sched_yield();
        printf("Parent\n");
} else {
        printf("Child\n");
}
```

This code seems fairly self-explanatory. The problem with it is that it makes a couple of assumptions, such as:

- That we are running under SCHED_FIFO. The program can verify this, so it isn't a big assumption.

- That, upon return from *fork*, the child is in fact ready to run. This is true under LynxOS (I know from personal experience), but there is no guarantee of this under other POSIX systems. In particular, a swapping, paging system may need to reserve some system resources before a child process can be run, and this activity may happen after *fork* returns to the parent.

- That the example is run on a uniprocessor. On a multiprocessor, the system could simply run the parent on one brain, and the child on another, in parallel.

The point here is that *sched_yield* does something very simple. It merely moves a process to the end of the queue for its priority level. It does not guarantee that anything else is actually on that queue. It certainly does not guarantee *what* is on the queue. For example, some other process (unrelated to our sample program) might be waiting to run—in which case, neither the parent nor the child would be scheduled next. Therefore, don't use *sched_yield* to enforce a particular scheduling order. It's too simple for that. Use semaphores instead.

Making Things Happen On Time

Now that we know how to make the most important things happen before the least important things, we can move on. In particular: how do you make something happen at a particular time?

Consider the data collection example. There are two ways in which the input task could operate. In one way, it is driven sporadically by its input source(s). In this scenario, the task sits in a loop, waiting for the input, whenever it comes. The timing of the whole loop is directly driven by the hardware. If the hardware interrupts 100 times in a second, then the input task runs 100 times in a second.

```
while (1) {
        read(fd, buf, nbytes);          /* Wait for data */
        /* Process data */
}
```

This is an acceptable way to structure this part of a real-time application. You'd set the process priority at the right level so that it ran in a timely-enough fashion whenever data was available for it. If your input device interrupts sporadically (i.e., unevenly), you might want to adopt this model; it avoids running the input task more often than necessary.

However, the timing of the loop above relies on the I/O hardware to provide the proper timing base to keep your task running at the right rate. Maybe your hardware doesn't work that way. Maybe it interrupts sporadically, and you want your processing to go on at a 100 Hz drumbeat. Very often, for instance, devices you are controlling require a steady stream of output, even if the corresponding input is sporadic. Maybe, like in the case of a frame buffer, there is no interrupt you can use to drive your timing at all.

If you want a steady beat, the solution is to drive the timing by an external clock, called an interval timer. Such a timer does exactly what its name implies: it measures a time interval. When the time interval expires, the task that set the timer is awakened, usually by signal delivery.

You may also want facilities to set and tell the time. After all, when you're writing an application based on the time, it's reasonable to know what time it is. Therefore, we make a distinction between clocks (the things that contain the time) and timers (the alarms that go off and wake you up). Timers are generally based on particular clocks. In other words, you don't need to deal with a timer if all you care about is telling the time. But you need to know that a particular clock exists before you can successfully use a timer based on that clock.

Clocks and timers, unlike many features of POSIX.4, have been part of UNIX systems for a while. Standard UNIX has three clocks. One tells the time, while the others do strange things that don't really concern us. Timers come in two basic sorts: one-shot and repeating. A one-shot timer is like the buzzer I have on my oven. You set it, it counts down, it goes off. End of story. A repeating timer is like the alarm clock in my bedroom. It's set to go off at 6 every morning, and it repeats that behavior every day, day in and day out.[*]

---

[*] It can't help it—it's eight months old and wants to be fed!

Basic UNIX Clocks

First, let's talk about the standard UNIX and POSIX.1 facilities. In some cases, these may be sufficient for your needs. Even if they're not adequate, you may need some of these functions in addition to the POSIX.4 facilities, which we'll describe in the section after this.

There's only one real clock in a standard UNIX system, and so it doesn't really have a name. It's just the time-of-day clock. There are two standard ways of telling the time with this clock. The *time* call is standard in System V and POSIX.1. It returns a number of seconds, which are the number of seconds that have expired since the world was created. According to UNIX lore, the world was created in the dim, distant past, when monstrous beasts roamed the earth: 00:00 A.M., January 1, 1970. This time is called The Epoch, and in that time, there were no microwaves, compact discs, or ATM machines, and there was very little cable television. You can see why time doesn't go back any further than that.

time is a very simple function. It's usually called with a NULL argument:

```
#include        <time.h>

time_t time(time_t *what_time_it_is);
```

The value returned is the number of seconds since the epoch. You can pass in a parameter, a pointer to a *time_t*, where *time* will store the number of seconds for you. You can also just pass a NULL pointer if you don't need the value stored anywhere. *time* is the POSIX standard facility, so it will be available on your POSIX-conformant system. Unfortunately, *time* is pretty crude. You may require greater accuracy in telling what time it is; many real-time applications do.

Under Berkeley and SVR4 UNIX systems, the *gettimeofday* call is provided, which allows you to retrieve the time with a precision that may be measured in microseconds. *gettimeofday* stores the time in a timeval structure, which is defined as:

```
struct timeval {
        time_t tv_sec;          /* Seconds */
        time_t tv_usec;         /* and microseconds */
}
```

gettimeofday looks a lot like *time*, but since it uses a structure, it returns zero or –1 (for success or failure), rather than the time itself:

```
/*
 * This facility is only
 * predictably available in Berkeley and SVR4 UNIX.
 * As a standard UNIX facility, there is no compile-time
 * definition to indicate its presence or absence.
 */
#include        <sys/time.h>

int gettimeofday(struct timeval *what_time_it_is);
```

Notice that I said the time resolution *may* be measured in microseconds. Although the *struct timeval* supports such resolution, most operating systems don't (the overhead of that kind of accuracy is considered too great). Usually, time is measured in clock ticks, each clock tick being something like 10,000 microseconds (many machines run a 100 Hz clock tick). Do not expect a time granularity to come out finer than that. Even if it did, the overhead of calling *gettimeofday* itself might throw you off! *gettimeofday* is not completely standard. The totally standard, high-resolution time mechanism is *clock_gettime*, which I'll describe up ahead in the section, "The Real Real-Time Time."

The end of the world as we know it

It's worth remembering one more thing about UNIX time. Historically, the time of day was stored in a variable of type long; most *time_t* types today are, in fact, longs. Since most of the POSIX machines in use have a 32-bit long, that implies a certain limitation in how far into the future we can tell the time. On any machine with a 32-bit *time_t* structure, time will fail somewhere in the second half of February, 2038. Hopefully, by that time we'll all be either using bigger machines or retired. I know that I'm phrasing all *my* maintenance contracts to end in 2037... Actually, 2038 is 45 years from now (1993). If you look back 45 years, well heck! That was before the beginning of time! Seriously, in 1948, the computer state-of-the-art was programmed by rewiring and being used to crack the Enigma Machine. By 2038, I doubt anyone will even recognize a machine of today as a computer.

Time Intervals

So far, we've only discussed how to tell the time. What we really want, though, is to time a process's execution so that it goes off, for instance, 10 times a second. Standard UNIX and POSIX.1 provide a couple of potential solutions, but they don't generally provide the resolution we need.

The most well-known example of a one-shot interval timer is the *sleep* call:

```
unsigned int sleep(unsigned int nseconds);
```

sleep delays the task's execution for at least *nsec* seconds. It's simple, but not precise at all. You might try using *sleep* to provide a process with reasonable periodic timing. This would be a mistake. *sleep* is like the *nice* facility discussed in the "Being Nice—Or Not" section, earlier. It just wasn't meant for real-time applications. For one thing, the resolution the task can achieve is too low to be of use. A resolution of seconds is just too crude!

Another problem is that *sleep* might not actually *sleep* as long as you expect it to. Like other blocking system calls, *sleep* is interrupted by the delivery of a signal. In fact, that's how it's usually implemented: *sleep* sets a timer to go off, and then waits for the associated signal to be delivered. If a signal other than the timer signal arrives, the *sleep* call may terminate prematurely. In that case, the return value from *sleep* will be the number of seconds remaining to be slept.[*]

"Drift" is yet a third reason why *sleep* isn't particularly useful for real-time applications. Imagine that *sleep* actually could provide the resolution your application needed (it's possible). Then your application code would look like this:

```
while (1) {
        sleep(nsec);
        /* Do something */
}
```

Remember, the goal is to run every *nsec* seconds. Since it takes some amount of time to "Do something," whatever it is, this loop is not going to run every *nsec* seconds. It will run every *(nsec + s)* seconds, where *s* is the amount of time needed to "Do something." The timing will drift by *s* with every iteration of the loop.

You could try to compensate for drift by sleeping *s* fewer seconds each time:

```
while (1) {
        sleep(nsec - s);
        /* Do something */
}
```

This isn't likely to work. First, it requires that *s* be exactly some number of seconds: no overrun, no underrun. Chances are, your action takes far less than a second, or a second and 50 milliseconds, or some number other than an exact number of seconds. The second problem is that your action may take a variable number of seconds! How do you measure that?

These dilemmas are why interval timers were created. Using an interval timer, the timer regularly interrupts, no matter how long your loop takes.

Standard UNIX Interval Timers

The original interval timers came from Berkeley UNIX, and are now part of AT&T's System V Release 4. Here's how they are defined:

```
/*
 * This facility is only
 * predictably available in Berkeley and SVR4 UNIX.
 * As a standard UNIX facility, there is no compile-time
 * definition to indicate its presence or absence.
 */
#include         <sys/time.h>

int setitimer(int which_timer, const struct itimerval *new_itimer_value,
    struct itimerval *old_itimer_value);
int getitimer(int which_timer, struct itimerval *current_itimer_value);
```

---

[*] The return value of *sleep* is different in Berkeley-based and AT&T-based UNIX systems. AT&T systems (for instance, SVR4 and Solaris 2.0) return as I described above; Berkeley systems (for instance, BSD4.3 or SunOS 4.1) always return 0.

The standard UNIX interval timers support three different timers, which you specify in *which_timer*: ITIMER_REAL, ITIMER_VIRTUAL and ITIMER_PROF. Only one of these is useful in most cases: ITIMER_REAL. When each of these timers expires, it causes a signal to be delivered to the process that set up the interval timer. The ITIMER_REAL timer causes SIGALRM to be delivered; ITIMER_VIRTUAL sends SIGVTALRM, and ITIMER_PROF sends SIGPROF. Neither SIGVTALRM nor SIGPROF are defined by POSIX, although SIGALRM is.

The ITIMER_REAL timer operates in real time. If you set it to expire every second, then it will expire every second—regardless of how long your loop takes or how long your have to wait for that second to roll around.

Every process has its own set of timers. If one process sets its timers to expire every 10 seconds, and another process sets its timers to expire 100 times a second, that is fine. The different process's timers do not interact with each other.

The timer's interval is specified using a two-part structure, *struct itimerval*. It consists of two *timeval* structures, *it_value* and *it_interval*:

```
struct itimerval {
        struct timeval it_value;    /* Initial value, 0 to disable timer */
        struct timeval it_interval; /* Period value, 0 for one-shot timer */
}
```

it_value must be set to a non-zero value for the timer to work—setting *it_value* to zero turns the timer off (this is a useful capability, of course). *it_value*, when set, indicates the time to wait before the timer expires the first time. *it_interval*, if set, indicates the interval after which the timer should expire the second time, third time, and so on. If *it_interval* is zero, but *it_value* is not zero, then the timer will expire only that first time and will then be turned off.

These members together provide for time resolution down to the microsecond. Some calls require that the number of microseconds in *tv_usec* be less than 1,000,000 (the number of microseconds in a second); you should always take care to make sure this is the case in order for your programs to be fully portable.

Signal deliveries

Since each timer expiration causes a signal to be delivered, you can structure your tasks in a number of different ways depending on how you best like to wait for signal delivery. Most simply, you can just mask off SIGALRM during normal operation and wait for it using *sigsuspend*. This complete example shows how to combine a UNIX interval timer with *sigsuspend* to wait synchronously for your periodic timer to expire.

```
#include    <sys/types.h>
#include    <sys/time.h>
#include    <sys/signal.h>
#include    <sys/param.h>

#define DEFAULT_SECS 0
```

```
                                         /* Assure usecs is modulo HZ */
       #define DEFAULT_USECS (1000000 / HZ)   /* (HZ) times a second */

       extern void nullhandler(void);

       main(int argc, char **argv)
       {
           sigset_t block_these, pause_mask;
           struct sigaction s;
           struct itimerval interval;
           long secs, usecs;

           /* Block SIGALRM */
           sigemptyset(&block_these);
           sigaddset(&block_these, SIGALRM);
           sigprocmask(SIG_BLOCK, &block_these, &pause_mask);

           /* Set up handler for SIGALRM */
           sigemptyset(&s.sa_mask);
           sigaddset(&s.sa_mask, SIGINT);
           s.sa_flags = 0;
           s.sa_handler = nullhandler;
           if (sigaction(SIGALRM, &s, NULL) < 0) {
               perror("sigaction SIGALRM");
               exit(1);
           }

           interval.it_value.tv_sec = DEFAULT_SECS;
           interval.it_value.tv_usec = DEFAULT_USECS;
           interval.it_interval.tv_sec = DEFAULT_SECS;
           interval.it_interval.tv_usec = DEFAULT_USECS;

           setitimer(ITIMER_REAL, &interval, NULL);
           while (1) {
               sigsuspend(&pause_mask);
               /* Do something */
           }

       }

       void nullhandler()
       {
       }
```

Microsecond resolution, huh?

The alert reader will notice that we are making sure the time interval is 0 modulo
something called HZ. The *timeval* structure has the numeric resolution to support timings down to the microsecond; however, most operating systems, real-time and otherwise, do not support this resolution. In general, an operating system runs its time-
based services off a periodic timer interrupt that goes off at regular intervals. Under

most UNIX systems, this periodic timer goes off 60 or 100 times per second.* That is the best resolution you can get from the standard clock facilities on these machines. A 100 Hz clock interrupts every 10,000 microseconds (that's 1,000,000 / 100).

You're drifting off again

This behavior may lead to another sort of clock drift. If you set your interval timer to go off every 9000 microseconds, it will probably go off every 10,000 microseconds instead. Your application should be prepared for this possibility. Under UNIX, the constant HZ, in *<sys/param.h>*, defines the number of times per second the periodic system timer interrupts; dividing 1,000,000 by this number will tell you the maximum clock resolution you can expect from that system. You should code your interval timer to use numbers of microseconds that are multiples of (1,000,000 / HZ).

As I mentioned above, there are two other timers, ITIMER_VIRTUAL and ITIMER_PROF. ITIMER_VIRTUAL runs only when your process is running: it measures the time your application takes to run. Since our particular need is for a timer to wait for a time interval to pass, this timer will not be useful to us here. Likewise, ITIMER_PROF runs only when our task is running, or the operating system is running on behalf of your task. ITIMER_VIRTUAL and ITIMER_PROF are used for implementing profilers and other tools for program development; they're not generally useful for deployed applications. However, they *are* useful for determining the amount of time spent in a particular task, since they count task time only. One caution, though: on almost all systems, these timers are only incremented on a clock "tick." That is, if your application happens to be running when the system clock expires, then you get credit for the entire clock tick: all 1,000,000/HZ microseconds. Conversely, if your task wakes up, runs, and blocks again between two clock ticks, it will be credited with *no* CPU time. These measurements are statistical and can only be trusted when the process runs for at least several seconds at a time.

The discussion above has all been focused on periodically-interrupting timers, but you can also use interval timers as one-shot timers. If you set *it_interval* to 0, and *it_value* to a non-zero value, then the interval timer will expire at the time indicated by *it_value*, and then never again. This is useful for setting a timeout on something which may go over-long (like a *read* on a pipe or socket or a message queue receive operation, where you're not exactly sure there's anyone on the other end). For example:

```
/* Set alarm to go off in ten seconds */
interval.it_interval.tv_sec = interval.it_interval.tv_usec = 0;
interval.it_value.tv_sec = 10;
interval.it_value.tv_usec = 0;
setitimer(ITIMER_REAL, &interval, &old_settings);

/* Read from file descriptor, timing out after ten seconds */
```

---

* The clock *must* run at at least 50 Hz in order to conform to POSIX.4; a real-time operating system just isn't that useful without a clock of at least that resolution. Older UNIX systems used to run at 50 Hz, but just about everyone runs a bit higher than that now.

```
i = read(fd, buf, nbytes);
if (i != nbytes) {
    /* Something happened */
    if (errno == EINTR) {
        /* Timed out! */
    }
}
setitimer(ITIMER_REAL, &old_settings, NULL);    /* Turn alarm off */
```

However, if your one-shot time interval does not require microsecond resolution, you can use a simpler function. *alarm* takes an argument that is a number of seconds, and sets ITIMER_REAL to go off at that time. It's a handy way to make your code more clear, at least:

```
/* Set alarm to go off in ten seconds */
alarm(10);

/* Read from file descriptor, timing out after ten seconds */
i = read(fd, buf, nbytes);
if (i != nbytes) {
    /* Something happened */
    if (errno == EINTR) {
        /* Timed out! */
    }
}

/* Turn the alarm clock off */
alarm(0);
```

Now, isn't that a lot more clear? *alarm* is provided by POSIX.1. If you want to turn off an alarm before it goes off, set the number of seconds to 0, as in the last line of the previous example.

The Real Real-Time Time: POSIX Clocks and Timers

While the Berkeley timer functions are pretty good, they lack a couple of features that are either necessary or desirable in real-time operating systems.

- Support of additional clocks beyond ITIMER_REAL, ITIMER_VIRTUAL, and ITIMER_PROF

- Allowance for greater time resolution (modern timers are capable of nanosecond resolution; the hardware should support it)

- Ability to determine timer overruns: that's what happens when the timer goes off several times before you are able to handle the signal

- Ability to use something other than SIGALRM to indicate timer expiration (in particular, a POSIX.4 real-time extended signal would be nice)

As a result, POSIX.4 defined a new set of timer functions that, while very similar to Berkeley timers, meet the additional requirements of many real-time applications. The POSIX.4 timers are a lot like those of standard Berkeley and AT&T UNIX. However, the

POSIX facilities allow for greater time resolution, implementation-defined timers, and more flexibility in signal delivery. They are also a bit more complex. Here's a summary of the POSIX.4 offering.

```
#include        <unistd.h>
#ifdef _POSIX_TIMERS
#include        <signal.h>
#include        <time.h>

/* Getting and Setting Clocks */
int clock_settime(clockid_t clock_id,
        const struct timespec *current_time);
int clock_gettime(clockid_t clock_id, struct timespec *current_time);
int clock_getres(clockid_t clock_id, struct timespec *resolution);

/* One-Shot and Repeating Timers */
int timer_create(clockid_t clock_id,
        const struct sigevent *signal_specification,
        timer_t *timer_id);
int timer_settime(timer_t timer_id, int flags,
            const struct itimerspec *new_interval,
        struct itimerspec *old_interval);
int timer_gettime(timer_id, struct itimerspec *cur_interval);
int timer_getoverrun(timer_t timer_id);
int timer_delete(timer_t timer_id);

/* High-Resolution sleep */
int nanosleep(const struct timespec *requested_time_interval,
    struct timespec *time_remaining);

#endif  /* _POSIX_TIMERS */
```

It's very important to mention here that the POSIX.4 timers use *different* time structures than do the Berkeley interval timers. This is one instance where ANSI C function prototyping is really your friend. The POSIX.4 facilities use *struct timespec* and *struct itimerspec*, while Berkeley uses **val*.

The basic principles behind the Berkeley and the POSIX.4 timers are the same. I'll present the POSIX.4 functions immediately below; later in this chapter there's a complete example using the timers.

What time is it? It depends on what clock you look at

POSIX.4 provides a system wherein there may be a number of implementation-defined clocks. Different clocks are useful for different things: measuring the execution of other processes, measuring the time according to an external system, and so on. The various clocks in a POSIX.4 system are identified by identifiers that you get from *<time.h>*. Different clocks are going to give you different characteristics, useful for different things.

Of course, the most basic thing you can do with a clock is tell what time it is. This is going to vary depending on what clock you look at. POSIX.4's facility is extensible to new clocks, which are identified by the *clockid* argument to these functions. Each POSIX.4 system is required to support at least one clock, whose name is CLOCK_REALTIME. If you want to tell the time, the most portable way to do it is to look at CLOCK_REALTIME. (CLOCK_REALTIME is the only clock which *all* POSIX.4 systems must support, since most computer hardware setups do not include more than one hardware clock. Therefore, a totally portable application will be able to use only CLOCK_REALTIME.)

To get the time according to any clock, you call *clock_gettime*:

```
#include        <time.h>
struct timespec current_time;

(void) clock_gettime(CLOCK_REALTIME, &current_time);
```

POSIX.4 provides much higher clock resolution than the traditional UNIX time mechanisms. POSIX.4 time specifications are based on the *timespec* structure, which differs from the more familiar *timeval*. *timespec* has the following members:

```
struct timespec {
    time_t  tv_sec;        /* Seconds in interval, like struct timeval */
    long    tv_nsec;       /* NANOseconds in interval */
};
```

By using nanoseconds (10**9 per second), resolution 1000 times finer than the *struct timeval* is possible. Today, of course, very few vendors even provide a nanosecond-capable clock in their hardware, and even fewer software vendors support that sort of resolution in their operating systems. However, such fine granularity is becoming available,[*] and the *struct timespec* will be able to support that resolution.

What you do with the time is up to you, of course. One thing you could do is measure how long an operation took, by taking before and after snapshots of the clock. Another thing you might do is just print the time out. ANSI C provides several time functions that convert seconds into a human-readable time string. Since *timespec* has a seconds field, you can pass that off to *ctime*, *localtime*, or *gmtime*, and get back a string that tells you what time the clock says it is.[†]

Just how accurate is the clock?

Say you call *clock_gettime*, wait a nanosecond, then call *clock_gettime* again. Do you think you'll get back a timestamp that's one nanosecond bigger the second time? Not likely!

Although it is possible to support a clock with true nanosecond resolution, most hardware doesn't go that fine. Furthermore, most software supports a much coarser time

---

[*] The current generation of SPARC boxes, for instance, supports two timers, each of which can resolve time down to a granularity of 500 nanoseconds. That's pretty fine, but SGI's top-of-the-line offers a sporty 21-nanosecond resolution!

[†] Any good reference to ANSI C can describe these functions more completely than I intend to here. The *POSIX Programmer's Guide* does a reasonable job.

granularity than the underlying hardware provides. Otherwise, a system might spend all its time updating the nanoseconds hand of its clock! Clocks are generally implemented using a periodic clock interrupt that goes off, say, 100 times a second. (CLOCK_REALTIME probably expires every HZ seconds, while additional clocks will do something else). When the timer expires, the system updates its idea of the "current time." When you call *clock_gettime*, it's that software-maintained time that you get, not the time maintained in the hardware.* Clock resolution is obviously going to be important to you, so there had better be some way of figuring out what the resolution of any particular clock is. Of course, there *is* such a way.

POSIX.4 allows you to determine the resolution of the clock you are using, so that your code can compensate for drift and other quantization effects. Here's how:

```
#include        <time.h>

struct timespec realtime_res;
(void)clock_getres(CLOCK_REALTIME, &realtime_res);
```

The value returned in *realtime_res* will be the finest time interval that can be distinguished by using the indicated clock. How long can this interval be? Arbitrarily long, for any clock except CLOCK_REALTIME. POSIX.4 states that the resolution of CLOCK_REALTIME must be at least 50 Hz, or 20,000,000 nanoseconds.

clock_getres (and *clock_gettime*, for that matter) can also be used to check for the existence of a clock. Remember that, while all systems have to support CLOCK_REALTIME, additional clock support is up to the implementor. Say you have a clock called CLOCK_HIGHRES on a machine you're writing software for. Your first order of business should be to make sure the clock is really there. Either *clock_gettime* or *clock_getres* will return −1 and set *errno* to EINVAL if you pass an invalid clock ID. *clock_getres* is a better choice for existence checking because it also tells you some useful information about the clock.

Finally, you can set the time for your clock. Most applications don't need to do this; usually, you only need to read the current time. The system administrator usually sets the time, and it is maintained by hardware automatically. Nonetheless, there is a standard way of setting the time for a particular clock:

```
#include        <time.h>

struct timespec what_time_it_is;
what_time_it_is.tv_sec = 994039434;     /* Some time */
what_time_it_is.tv_nsec = 60000000;     /* Some time */
```

---

* Many systems provide a higher resolution timestamp by mapping the timer hardware into your application's address space. However, very few clocks actually allow you to schedule a clock interrupt at any given nanosecond (none that I know of). In fact, some clocks don't even have a readable version of the time: you just set them and they interrupt. You have to compute the time by counting the interrupts. Early versions of the IBM PC are the primary examples of this sort of system.

```
if (clock_settime(CLOCK_REALTIME, &what_time_it_is) < 0) {
        perror("clock_settime");
}
```

The indicated time is set, rounded down according to the resolution of the clock. There are obviously permissions associated with setting the clock; usually only a few users, privileged to perform system administration tasks, are allowed to set the clock. The permissions required will be detailed in the POSIX.4 conformance statement for your system.

Obviously, *clock_settime* isn't too useful as a general date-setting mechanism without some way of turning human-comprehensible times into the numbers of seconds used by *clock_settime*. Luckily, ANSI C provides the function *mktime*, which converts a date into a more understandable format. *mktime* is described below, in the discussion of absolute times.

Just a little nap

Moving along to the next most basic component of POSIX.4 timers, here's the POSIX.4 enhancement of *sleep*, *nanosleep*.

```
struct timespec a_little_nap, how_much_time_is_left;
int i;

i = nanosleep(&a_little_nap, &how_much_time_is_left);
```

nanosleep is essentially the same as *sleep*, except with much finer resolution.* Using *nanosleep*, an application can delay its execution for very small amounts of time. *nanosleep* is still subject, though, to the same drift problems as *sleep*; it still shouldn't be used for timing drift-sensitive tasks (at least, you shouldn't use it in such tasks when it may cause drift. Feel free to use it for other things.) It is useful when the timing requirements aren't particularly strict. For instance, sometimes hardware devices require small amounts of quiet time to respond after you poke them; *nanosleep*ing for a small time may be useful in this instance.

That explains the first argument to *nanosleep*, but what about the second one? Well, a delay in process execution, be it via *sleep* or *nanosleep*, may be prematurely interrupted by the arrival of a signal. In this case, *nanosleep* returns –1, and sets *errno* equal to EINTR. As in real life, when your *sleep* is interrupted prematurely, your first response (okay, maybe in real life it's your third or fourth response) is probably to figure out how long you slept. *nanosleep* sets its second argument (a pointer to a *timespec*) to the time that was remaining in the "sleep" interval when the process was awakened. That way, if the process is prematurely awakened, it knows how long it slept and how much more it would need to delay to make up the entire desired interval. You can set this second argument to NULL if you don't care to get this information; the call is defined to ignore a NULL pointer.

---

* *sleep* doesn't even use a *struct timeval*; it uses a number of seconds! Yicch!.

One important note regarding *sleep* and *nanosleep*. *sleep* may be implemented by using SIGALRM and an interval timer. Since that is the case, your application should not mix the use of interval timers and *sleep*, except with the utmost care. Trying to use one signal in two different ways, at the same time, can lead to confusing results. On the other hand, *nanosleep* is defined not to affect the disposition of any signals. This makes it a bit easier and cleaner to use from an application perspective.[*]

The POSIX Interval Timers: Fine Times

The POSIX Interval timer facilities are similar to the standard UNIX facilities in some ways, and different in others. I'd like to start from the familiar and work backwards to the unfamiliar. You use a POSIX.4 timer with the calls *timer_settime* and *timer_gettime*, which are very similar to *getitimer* and *setitimer*. However, there are a couple of differences in these two functions, and there are more differences in how you set up your clocks and timers using the POSIX.4 functions.

The first, and easiest difference is that the POSIX interval timers use a different structure that allows for nanosecond time resolution. The *struct timespec* has already been introduced; a new interval structure, *struct itimerspec*, simply incorporates two *timespecs* to form a high-resolution interval timer structure.

```
struct itimerspec {
        struct timespec it_value;
        struct timespec it_interval;
};
```

When you set your POSIX.4 interval timers, you use *struct itimerspec*, not *struct itimerval*.

The second difference is that POSIX timers are dynamically created. This is different from standard UNIX, which just provides you with three standard timers, no more and no less. You use the *timer_create* call to make a POSIX.4 timer, and when you're done with it, you get rid of it with *timer_delete*. Dynamically creating timers is an extra step you don't need to take with the standard UNIX timers; however, POSIX.4 compensates for this extra step by allowing you to use arbitrary system-supported clocks for your timers, rather than just the system clock. In addition, you can create at least 32 timers in any single process. That's a lot of distinct timers; certainly enough to completely confuse yourself.

Creating a timer for your application is simple. The function *timer_create* is used. Here's the simplest and most portable way to do it:

```
#include     <signal.h>
#include     <time.h>
```

---

[*] And it makes the function more of a pain to implement, for those of you in the business of writing operating systems. Oy!

```
int i;
timer_t created_timer;  /* Contains the ID of the created timer */

i = timer_create(CLOCK_REALTIME, NULL, &created_timer);
```

This code snippet creates a timer based upon the system clock called CLOCK_REALTIME. CLOCK_REALTIME exists on all POSIX.4-conformant systems, so you can count on it. A machine may define other clocks for you, corresponding perhaps to extra, dedicated hardware resources on your particular target machine. All you can count on for total portability, though, is CLOCK_REALTIME. If your application needs additional clocks, you should check for them in the conformance document for the system you're considering. Real-time systems often support extra timer hardware, and so long as you isolate use of extra clocks into separate, well-documented modules, you should have reasonably portable code (pay special attention to the resolution capabilities of different system clocks).

The second argument is supposed to define the signal delivery you want to have for this particular timer. The parameter is a pointer to a *struct sigevent*, which is used to define a signal, either POSIX.1 or POSIX.4. By setting this parameter to NULL, we tell the system we want the default delivery, which is defined to be SIGALRM on all POSIX.4-conformant systems. We could define a particular signal number and signal value by changing the example:

```
#include      <signal.h>
#include      <time.h>

#define A_DESCRIPTIVE_NAME 13
int i;
struct sigevent signal_specification;
timer_t created_timer;  /* Contains the ID of the created timer */

/* What signal should be generated when this timer expires? */
signal_specification.sigev_signo = SIGRTMIN;
signal_specification.sigev_value.sival_int = A_DESCRIPTIVE_NAME;
/* NOTIFY_SIGNALS stuff too */

i = timer_create(base_clock, &signal_specification, &created_timer);
```

This code defines a timer that delivers the signal SIGRTMIN, with the associated signal value equal to 13, whenever it expires. (This example would only work, of course, on a system where _POSIX_REALTIME_SIGNALS was supported.)

The third parameter is where the system stored the ID of the created timer. That's the POSIX.4 equivalent of ITIMER_REAL, etc. You'll need this ID in order to use the timer.

As I mentioned above, you can create more POSIX.4 timers than you may be used to having available. Each timer is a separate object, with its own signal notification setup and its own status in the operating system. You can use them totally separately from each other. The actual limit to the number of timers you can create is defined by

TIMER_MAX in *<limits.h>*. The least it can be is 32.* Because POSIX.4 timers are dynamically created, they dynamically use some system resources. In this sense, timers are analogous to open files. Each open file descriptor requires a little more memory from the operating system. In order to prevent the system from bloating up, you need to close files when you're finished with them. Similarly, when you're done with a timer, you should release the resources associated with it. More to the point, you are limited to a certain number of timers (defined by your implementation), so you do not want unused timers sitting around using resources that you could use elsewhere.

To remove a timer that you are no longer using, call *timer_delete*:

```
#include        <time.h>

i = timer_delete(created_timer);
```

This call will free up any system resources associated with the timer. If you delete a timer that is currently running (we discuss that below), it is automatically stopped before it is deleted, so you don't need to worry about the timer mysteriously expiring one last time after you've already deleted it. There might, however, still be a pending timer signal (from a previous expiration) that has yet to be delivered to your process if the process has blocked that signal with *sigprocmask*.

When your process calls *exit* or *exec*, its timers are automatically deleted, just as *exit* and *exec* automatically close your files (most of them, anyway).

Setting the alarm

Once you have a timer ID, you can set that timer, just like you can set ITIMER_REAL, ITIMER_PROF, and ITIMER_VIRTUAL. You use the POSIX.4 calls, of course, instead of *setitimer* and *getitimer*.

```
#include        <time.h>

struct itimerspec new_setting, old_setting;

new_setting.it_value.tv_sec = 1;
new_setting.it_value.tv_nsec = 0;
new_setting.it_interval.tv_sec = 0;
new_setting.it_interval.tv_nsec = 100000;
i = timer_settime(created_timer, 0, &new_setting, &old_setting);
```

This example sets the interval timer to expire in 1 second, and every 100,000 nanoseconds thereafter. The old timer setting is returned in the structure *old_setting*. Like *setitimer*, you can set the last parameter, the old setting, to NULL if you don't care about what the old setting was. The reason you can get the old setting returned to you is that, when you call *timer_settime*, you change the setting of the timer, overwriting and replacing the previous setting. If you want to restore this setting after you've used

---

* That's another little zinger that provides a lot of gratuitous joy for us OS vendors.

the timer (if this code may use the same interval timer as some other section of your application, for instance), then you need to keep track of the old setting.

The second argument to *timer_settime* (which, in the example, is rather undemonstratively set to zero) requires some special attention. This argument is a word of flags that modifies the way in which the interval timer is set. At present, there is only one flag you can set, but that one is pretty important.

So far, we have only discussed "relative" timers. These are timers that, when set, expire at a certain time relative to when they were set (when *timer_settime* was called). This sort of timer behavior is useful, of course, but there is often another sort of behavior desired. Many applications want to be able to set a timer to go off at an absolute time (for example, 6 A.M., Wednesday, March 1, 1995). This behavior is desirable if you want to set a timer to terminate some sort of computation, and you fear you may be preempted before setting the timer. I'll illustrate with an example.

Say you want a timer to go off at a particular date *d*, which you have in a *struct timespec*. Using a relative timer, you would have to figure out the current time, subtract it from your desired time, and then set your relative timer:

```
/* Time is NOW */
clock_gettime(CLOCK_REALTIME, &now);
expiration_time.it_value.tv_sec = d.tv_sec - now.tv_sec;
expiration_time.it_value.tv_nsec = d.tv_nsec - now.tv_nsec;
if (d.tv_nsec < now.tv_nsec) {
        expiration_time.it_value.tv_sec--;
        expiration_time.it_value.tv_nsec += 1000000000;
}
/* Time is NOW + i */
timer_settime(created_timer, 0, &expiration_time, NULL);
/* Time is NOW + i + j */
```

This approach works, in a kinda-pretty-much-you-can-almost-rely-on-it kind of way. If your calculation of the relative time value does not take too long, and if you are not preempted, then this approach will be OK. However, imagine you were preempted after determining the current time (NOW), but before you set the relative timer (NOW + i), as shown in Figure 5-2. Then you would set the timer to go off later than you wanted it to!

Furthermore, remember that clocks in most computer systems operate in units of ticks You might get the time right before the tick is about to increment. While you calculate your relative time, the system tick might go off. This alone will result in your missing your time by a tick. You really need to perform this entire sequence of events, while guaranteeing that no one preempts you and no clock interrupt expires. If you were the operating system, you could do that. But you're not. You're the application.

Luckily, POSIX.4 provides a way to do what you need. The solution is to set an interval timer to expire at an absolute time, rather than a relative time. By setting the *flags* parameter to *timer_settime* to TIMER_ABSTIME, you tell the system to interpret the

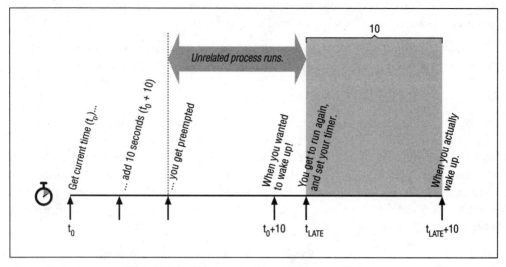

Figure 5-2. Race condition when setting an absolute timer by yourself

interval timer setting as an absolute, rather than a relative time.

```
/* Time is NOW */
timer_settime(created_timer, TIMER_ABSTIME, &d, NULL);
/* Time is NOW + i + j */
```

Does anybody really know what time it is?

There's one more little problem here. Where did that absolute time value come from? How was it created? We know how to get the current time, but so far, we haven't seen any way of getting a *timespec* structure for a future (or past) time.

Future times are generated in one of two ways. The future time you want may actually be relative to the current time, but you want to set it absolutely to avoid races. In that case, simply call *clock_gettime* and add the appropriate numbers to the timespec you get back.

To get a real, absolute, future time, use the *mktime* function. *mktime* is not part of POSIX.4. Its basic definition is part of ANSI C, and POSIX.1 extends it somewhat. *mktime* takes a structure, *struct tm*, which contains the date in a format like you might expect, and converts it to a *time_t* (number of seconds). You can use that *time_t* as the *tv_sec* field in a *struct timespec. Voilà*, instant absolute time! True, *mktime* only provides a resolution of one second, but if you *really* need to sleep until exactly November 17, 1995, at 2:05 PM and 3.178 seconds, you can add in the appropriate number of nanoseconds yourself. *struct tm* has the following members:

```
int tm_hour;    /* Hour of day, valid values 0..23      */
int tm_min;     /* Minute of hour, valid values 0..59   */
int tm_sec;     /* Second of minute, valid values 0..61 */
```

```
int tm_mon;      /* Month of year, valid values 0..11      */
int tm_mday;     /* Day of month, valid values 1..31 (or less) */

int tm_year;     /* Year, where 1900 is year 0.            */
int tm_isdst;    /* Whether Daylight Savings Time applies.  */
```

Many systems rearrange the members from the order I've given them in, and some systems have additional, implementation-defined members in them (which you can ignore if you're just using the POSIX.4/ANSI functions). These members correspond to a "user-friendly" representation of the time, like "12:30:07, September 6, 1997." However, there are a few interesting little points to be careful about.

- Note that the first day of the month is 1, whereas all the other fields start at 0.

- The value of *tm_sec* will generally be 0 through 59, but it can be 60 to deal with the possibility of leap seconds (those years when they adjust the atomic clocks).

- The value of *tm_isdst* sounds like it should be Boolean (true or false), but it's not. 0 means that DST does not apply, a positive value means DST does apply, and a negative value means you don't know.

The POSIX definition of *mktime* says that the environment variable TZ affects the interpretation of this structure, if you have it set. Otherwise, the system assumes a default time zone. Your timezone can be set with almost arbitrary complexity; generally, though, the value of TZ indicates the time zone in which the process is operating, and is used by the system to print the time values correctly. For instance, the value PST8PDT specifies the Pacific Time, in which daylight savings time is observed. (For a complete explanation of POSIX timezones and the TZ environment variable, go to section, "You're Entering . . . The Time Zone," at the end of this chapter.)

To set a *timespec* with an absolute date, here's what you'd do:

```
struct tm absolute;
struct timespec abs_time;

absolute.tm_hour = 23;      /* 12 (PM)                    */
absolute.tm_min = 30;       /*    :30                     */
absolute.tm_sec = 7;        /*        :07                 */
absolute.tm_mon = 8;        /*            September        */
absolute.tm_mday = 6;       /*                6 (NOT 7!)  */
absolute.tm_year = 97;      /*                   1997     */
absolute.tm_isdst = 0;

abs_time.tv_sec = mktime(&absolute);
abs_time.tv_nsec = 0;
```

There are two other members of the *struct tm*; *tm_wday* and *tm_yday*. These are redundant information: the day of the week (0..6) and the day of the year (0..365). When you call *mktime*, it fills in these two fields with the correct values for the time you've given. For this application of *mktime*, you probably don't care.

The "double" of *timer_settime* is *timer_gettime*, which (as you'd expect) reads the time left on the timer:

```
#include        <time.h>

struct itimerspec time_remaining;
i = timer_gettime(created_timer, &time_remaining);
```

This code sample initializes *time_remaining* with the time remaining until the timer expires, together with the interval setting for the timer.

The next function provides an important feature that's not available in standard UNIX. Applications frequently have to deal with the problem of signal loss. We addressed this problem when we talked about queued real-time signals, but the signal delivered on timer expiration is different. It's different because that signal can go off an arbitrary number of times before the process actually gets around to handling the signal. This means that the system may use more and more resources to queue up successive occurrences of the timer signal, eventually clogging up the system. Granted, you can solve the problem without using extra resources for additional queued timer signals, but that complicates the signal facility. Moreover, in the case of a timer, the application doesn't really need to get all those signals. The application really only needs to know how many of those signals there are.

Therefore, POSIX.4 doesn't queue up timer expiration signals if a timer overruns. Instead, it provides a function that allows the application to determine how many times the timer has overrun. If you want to use it, you can; meanwhile, the signal and timer implementation are not needlessly complicated by additional semantics.

```
#include        <time.h>

int n_overruns;

n_overruns = timer_getoverrun(created_timer);
```

The overrun count is reset each time you actually handle the timer signal. Thus, the count is the correct count *as of the time the signal was delivered to the process.* Subsequent overruns may (will) continue to occur as time goes by. If you take the timer signal on time, every time, without overruns, then the value returned by this function will always be zero. Obviously, the number of overruns may be very large, perhaps more than can be stored in a single int. Each implementation defines its own maximum number of overruns, DELAYTIMER_MAX. That is the largest value that *timer_getoverrun* will return. If you get more overruns than that, well, tough. Most implementations will probably set DELAYTIMER_MAX to MAXINT. For a 32-bit integer, for instance, the value is probably $2^{-331} - 1$ (assuming two's-complement integers).

POSIX.4 Timers: Notes and Hints

There are a lot of parts to the POSIX.4 clocks and timers facility, and it can be a little daunting. Below, there's a code example of the simplest, most common way in which you'd tend to use the POSIX.4 timer facilities.

```
#define _POSIX_C_SOURCE 199309
#include <unistd.h>
#include <signal.h>
#include <time.h>
#include <stdio.h>

#define OUR_CLOCK CLOCK_REALTIME

char *progname;

void timer_intr(int sig, siginfo_t *extra, void *cruft)
{
    int noverflow;
    if (noverflow = timer_getoverrun(*(timer_t *)
        extra->si_value.sival_ptr)) {
        /* Timer has overflowed -- error! */
    }
    return;
}

timer_t mytimer;

main(int argc, char **argv)
{
    int c;
    struct itimerspec i;
    struct timespec resolution;
    struct sigaction sa;
    sigset_t allsigs;
    struct sigevent timer_event;

    progname = argv[0];

    sigemptyset(&sa.sa_mask);
    sa.sa_flags = SA_SIGINFO;    /* Real-Time signal */
    sa.sa_sigaction = timer_intr;

    if (sigaction(SIGRTMIN, &sa, NULL) < 0) {
        perror("sigaction");
        exit(2);
    }

    /*
     * First, detemrine whether the desired clock exists (not necessary
     * with CLOCK_REALTIME, but a good idea in general
     */
    if (clock_getres(OUR_CLOCK, &resolution) < 0) {
        perror("clock_getres");
```

```
            exit(1);
        }
        printf("Clock resolution %d sec %d nsec\n",
            resolution.tv_sec, resolution.tv_nsec);
        /* Create a timer based upon the CLOCK_REALTIME clock */
        i.it_interval.tv_sec = 0;
        /* Set resolution to one-tenth the maximum allowable */
        i.it_interval.tv_nsec = resolution.tv_nsec * 10;
        i.it_value = i.it_interval;

        /*
         * This describes the asynchronous notification to be posted
         * upon this timer's expiration:
         * - use signals (not that there's any other alternative at present)
         * - send SIGRTMIN
         * - send extra data consisting of a pointer back to the timer ID.
         *   cannot pass the timer ID itself because we haven't created the
         *   timer yet!
         */
        timer_event.sigev_notify = SIGEV_SIGNAL;
        timer_event.sigev_signo = SIGRTMIN;
        timer_event.sigev_value.sival_ptr = (void *)&mytimer;

        if (timer_create(OUR_CLOCK, &timer_event, &mytimer) < 0) {
            perror("timer_create");
            exit(5);
        }

        /* Relative timer, go off at the end of the interval */
        if (timer_settime(mytimer, 0, &i, NULL) < 0) {
            perror("setitimer");
            exit(3);
        }

        sigemptyset(&allsigs);
        while (1) {
            sigsuspend(&allsigs);
        }
        exit(4);
    }
```

Some notes and hints on this example:

- We use a symbolic name for the clock, so that it's easy to switch to another clock when porting.

- We do a *clock_getres* to determine whether the desired clock exists.

- Not only does *clock_getres* tell us that the clock exists, it tells us how good the resolution is. We use that resolution in setting up the interval timer, so as to avoid timer drift.

- When creating the timer, you'd like to pass the ID of the timer to the signal handler. However, you don't *have* that ID yet, so you have to settle for passing the address of the ID of the timer.

- This example uses a single timer, interrupting on SIGRTMIN. To add multiple timers, you could easily set them up on multiple signals. Remember that the POSIX.4 signals are defined to be delivered highest-numbered signal first. So, you could set the higher-priority and higher-frequency timers to the higher signal numbers. You might want to consider using a more efficient signal pausing function, as well: *sigwaitinfo* is generally more efficient that *sigsuspend.*

Keeping Your Memory Handy: UNIX and POSIX Memory Locking

Everything we discuss in this chapter is targeted towards making your computations happen on time. That goal, in turn, depends on the operating system not putting some other obstacle in your way. Two such obstacles normally come up. One obstacle is the performance of your operating system, and your only recourse for a slow OS, if it's too slow, is to buy another OS (or a faster machine). We'll discuss performance issues in Chapter 7, *Performance, or How to Choose an Operating System.* The other obstacle you can program for, and we'll discuss it right now.

This obstacle, in two words, is virtual memory, or rather some of the facilities that go along with it. On the whole, virtual memory—mapping of virtual addresses to different physical locations—is helpful, both in normal timesharing and in real-time systems. Virtual memory mapping provides protection between distinct processes, and protects the operating system from a wayward program's wild memory writes or a malicious program's planned intervention. In addition, virtual memory eliminates most of the memory fragmentation problems that occur in physical memory machines.

The problem facilities are demand paging and swapping, which are generally bundled along with virtual memory mapping. Demand paging and swapping are two distinct varieties of the same thing, which we'll just call paging for conciseness. The idea is to run applications that require more physical memory than there is available on the machine. To do this, the operating system moves pages of application memory out to disk when they're not being used, and re-uses the physical memory for a process that needs the memory. Demand paging usually means stealing a page at a time from one process for another. Swapping is rather more drastic: the operating system dumps an entire process out to disk and re-uses all its physical memory. There's a whole literature devoted to paging; for more information, consult some of the references in the bibliography.

Paging is also a good thing in most situations. A 16-megabyte development box probably doesn't have enough physical memory to run your operating system, the X Window System, the window manager of your choice, your editor (especially if it's Emacs, the mother of all editors), *make*, and a slew of compiler, assembler, and loader processes. Then throw in profilers, debuggers, your window reading email, and news.

There is no way all that stuff is going to fit in the physical memory most machines come with. And say you want to run an Ada program? Never mind.

When is Virtual Virtual?

Lynx Real-Time Systems, where I used to work, provides an interesting and educational example of the distinction, and the confusion, between virtual memory and paging. Lynx supported virtual memory mapping, but not paging, until our 2.0 release. When the paging facility was implemented, it was conditionally compiled into the kernel using *#ifdef VM*—even though we already, technically, supported Virtual Memory! The other facet of this little tale is the reason we came out with paging—it's not really wanted in most real-time systems anyway. It turns out that two groups of customers were having problems with physical memory limits. One group wanted to use X and Emacs at the same time. The other group wanted to run Ada programs alone. Neither task set would fit in the 4 or 8 megabytes typically found on a 80386 machine! I understand the Ada runtimes are vastly improved since those days, and as for X and Emacs...sometimes you just have to page.

The problem is that paging takes time, lots of it, and you don't know when the operating system is going to decide to page your memory out to disk. That means, when your application demands responsiveness that may be measured in microseconds, you may find yourself waiting milliseconds or more while the operating system goes out to disk and fetches your memory. Your response times and scheduling guarantees go out to lunch. For example, let's say you get some input from a sensor which has to be handled within a millisecond, or else all Hell will break loose on your factory floor. The scenario goes like this: input comes into your sensor, which interrupts. Your interrupt routine pokes your Very Important Process in some system-specific way, causing it to be scheduled to run. The scheduler then tries to run your process, which has been blocked waiting for input; but, because the slob in the control room has been running Emacs, and hack, and compiling Ada programs on the system, your important process has been paged out to disk! It takes something like 8 milliseconds to get the data from the disk. Long before the data has arrived, the disk, and the control room, have been obliterated by a rain of 300-mph steel disks hurled across the room by an out-of-control robot lathe!

Well, we could have saved the factory if we'd thought to lock the Important Process's memory down so the operating system couldn't page it. SVR4 UNIX and POSIX both specify the same facilities for memory locking. SVR4 also provides a lower-level under-the-hood sort of facility that is overkill for most real-time applications. This facility goes by the name *memcntl*, just so you know what it is if you happen to stumble across it. Since the facility you really need is memory locking, and the POSIX.4 functions are in System V as well, there's no need to discuss *memcntl* any further here.

The more useful interfaces do two things. First, they allow you to lock down your entire process. That is generally what you want to do: just lock the whole thing down and be done with it. If you have a lot of big processes, though, you may not be able to lock them all down. In that case, you may want to try and lock down just the time-critical portions of those processes, if you can figure out what part of your memory contains time-critical code and data.

Locking It All

The facility for locking the entire process down is pretty simple, and defined unter the option _POSIX_MEMLOCK:

```
#include        <unistd.h>
#ifdef _POSIX_MEMLOCK
#include        <sys/mman.h>

int mlockall(int flags);
int munlockall(void);
#endif /* _POSIX_MEMLOCK */
```

mlockall, obviously enough, tries to lock all your memory down. This includes your program text, data, heap, and stack; it includes shared libraries you have mapped in and other shared memory areas you may be using. Depending on the flags you specify in the argument to *mlockall*, it will either lock all your current mappings (MCL_CURRENT), or your current mappings and any future mappings you may make (MCL_CURRENT|MCL_FUTURE). You can also specify just MCL_FUTURE (which would lock your future memory mappings, but not your present ones), although I can't for the life of me figure out why you would want to!

When you lock your future mappings down, you are assuming that your machine has enough memory to allow this. If your application grows without bounds, you will obviously run out of memory at some point. Assuring that you have enough memory is your problem; POSIX.4 does not specify any means by which the system will let you know if you can't lock any more memory. A nice system might cause a memory allocation attempt to fail if the memory couldn't be locked; a less nice system might send your process a signal, and a really nasty unusable system might just perform the allocation but not lock the memory down! All of these possibilities are allowed. What POSIX.4 does say is that the implementation shall define what mechanism it uses when it cannot honor MCL_FUTURE memory locking requests. That means that the implementation has to say, in its conformance statement, what it will do if you run out of memory. You should pay attention to that portion of the conformance statement.

munlockall unlocks your locked memory. When memory is unlocked, it does not necessarily mean that it will be paged; but it might be. *munlockall* really tells the system that it's okay to page this process's memory if the system must.

Locking Parts

If you cannot lock down your entire process, you may want to try locking down parts of it. The facility for locking down an address range is somewhat low-level, but it provides all the functionality you need. Notice that it is defined under a *different* POSIX.4 option, _POSIX_MEMLOCK_RANGE.

```
#include         <unistd.h>
#if defined(_POSIX_MEMLOCK_RANGE)
#include         <sys/mman.h>

int mlock(void *address, size_t length);
int munlock(void *address, size_t length);
#endif  /* _POSIX_MEMLOCK_RANGE */
```

mlock locks down the address range you specify, and *munlock* unlocks a range. The locking performed by *mlock* and the locking performed by *mlockall* are the same sort of thing. In other words, if you call *mlock* for a range of memory, and then call *munlockall*, the latter unlocks the memory you locked with *mlock*.

Locks do not stack. If you call *mlock* 10 times on a given page, how many times do you need to call *munlock* to unlock that page? Just one. This means that you cannot lock memory for a small section of code, then unlock it, expecting everything to go back to "the way it was." For example, look at the following code example:

```
/* Main routine of application. */
main()
{
    /* Lock down all memory in application */
    mlockall(MCL_CURRENT|MCL_FUTURE);
    ...                 /* Do application, whatever it is */
    munlockall();       /* Unlock memory. */
    exit(0);
}

/*
 * Routine supplied by third-party vendor to do highly specialized
 * function.
 */
char big_area[BIG_SIZE];
blah()
{
    /* Swapping any of the big area will seriously slow me down! */
    mlock(big_area, BIG_SIZE);
    ...     /* Compute */
    munlock(big_area, BIG_SIZE);    /* Unlock the big area */
}
```

When the application is first invoked, it locks itself down in memory. When *blah* is invoked, though, it does its own lock of the *big_area* array. And then—here's the problem—it *unlocks* the array. The unlock results in a "hole" in the locked memory space of the application, which may include other data structures than the *big_area* array, depending on whether BIG_SIZE is a multiple of PAGESIZE or not. (Remember that PAGESIZE is defined in *<limits.h>*.)

The conclusion is this: memory locking is a global issue that should *not* be performed by small, transient sections of code. Rather, these sections should document their requirements, so that the application writer can determine what memory in the application needs to be locked down, and when. You should not treat memory locking as something you do just for a small section of code, and then unlock the memory. You should plan on locking down your application and leaving it locked down until it is out of "real-time mode."

The choice of addresses and lengths to lock is bound to be non-portable, because different systems put different things in different places. For instance, say you want to lock down all your process's text (instructions). On a standard, statically-linked executable this is usually simple, if nonportable. For many machines, the text segment starts at a lower address than any other section, and extends up to a symbol, defined by the linker, called *etext*. You could reasonably lock down your memory between 0 and *etext*, and expect your application's text to then, in fact, be locked down:

```
i = mlock((void *) 0, (size_t)&etext);
```

Here are the things to watch out for. I won't call them problems because we know that this code is going to be non-portable anyway. First, text doesn't always start at 0. Solaris boxes, for instance, tend to start it at 16K. LynxOS starts text at 32 (no, not 32K, 32 *bytes*). Some machines put their text above their data and stack. Still other machines use completely separate address spaces for text and data. Unfortunately, *mlock* explodes if you pass it an address where there isn't any memory (like 0, on a Sun running Solaris). You really need to look at the start address for the executable in order to know where text starts. Luckily, you can get this information from a test compile of your application, using *nm* or any of a number of other object file inspectors (*nm* is provided under the User Portability Utilities and Software Development Utilities options of POSIX.2).

Second problem: POSIX is vague on what values the address parameter may take. Memory locking is performed in units of pages, though, and the system may require you to give it an address that is page aligned. I'd recommend you always align both the address and the length for increased portability, just as we did for *mmap*:

```
#include <limits.h>      /* For PAGESIZE definition */
#define ROUND_DOWNTO_PAGE(v)    ((unsigned long)(v) & ~(PAGESIZE-1))
#define ROUND_UPTO_PAGE(v)      \
        (((unsigned long)(v) + PAGESIZE - 1)
        & ~(PAGESIZE-1))

i = mlock(ROUND_DOWNTO_PAGE(address), ROUND_UPTO_PAGE(length));
```

The rounding macros are still not completely portable (casting a pointer to a long is an unsafe practice), but at least we've localized the non-portability into a header somewhere.

The third problem is a real killer. What if you want to use shared libraries? The discussion above was directed at a statically-linked executable. In contrast, many machines (almost all UNIX machines today) create dynamically-linked executables by default. These machines use shared libraries in an effort to conserve space. A shared library is mapped into the address space of a process when it first starts up, with the library text shared between all processes using the library. This can result in a big memory savings if many processes are using the same library (like, for example, the C library). However, shared libraries live in a totally different part of memory from static application text. On System V UNIX machines, they usually exist up above the process stack, in the zone between the stack and the beginning of the operating system. If you want to lock down a shared library, you need to determine where it is going to be mapped in and how big it is.

I may have frightened you away from the use of *mlock*. That's probably a good thing. Use *mlockall* when you can. If you must use *mlock*, localize all its use into a file or two, align the address and the length parameters, and flag the affected files as non-portable so you look at these files for each new machine you want to run your application on. Remember, portability is an attribute that can be maximized, not a binary value that's either true or false.

Locking a single function

Generally, you will want to lock down your application as a whole. The other common thing you might want to do, though, is to just lock down selected parts of your application. For instance, a high-priority interrupt handler[*] function may absolutely need to be present in memory, while the majority of the application can be swapped with no problem whatsoever. How would you lock down just that function?

Say this is our interrupt handler code:

```
void intr_handler()
{
    ...
}
```

First of all, you do *not* do it from within the function itself. The memory needs to be locked down *before* the interrupt handler gets called, right? So, you probably have another routine that initializes this whole subsystem of your application. Use *that* routine to do your locking:

---

[*] Usually, it's a signal handler in your application, because most operating systems don't allow your application code to handle interrupts directly. (Some systems, notably hard real-time embedded systems like QNX, do allow applications to handle interrupts directly.)

```
void intr_handler()
{
    ...
}

void intr_handler_init()
{
    ...
    i = mlock(addr, len);   /* Addr and len to be determined shortly */
}
```

Locking a single function requires you to know something about how your compiler and linker are going to rearrange your code. In the simplest situation, code is generated in the same order in which you wrote it. If function A follows function B follows function C in your code, then A will follow B will follow C in your executable. This is usually the case, and you can use this knowledge to lock down the area from the beginning of your function to the beginning of the next function:

```
void intr_handler()
{
    ...
}
void right_after_intr_handler()
{
}

void intr_handler_init()
{
    ...
    i = mlock(ROUND_DOWNTO_PAGE(intr_handler),
            ROUND_UPTO_PAGE(right_after_intr_handler));
}
```

This code will, on many machines, do the right thing: lock those pages containing the address range from *intr_handler* to *right_after_intr_handler*. However, you should still check into your linker's behavior on each system you port to. Optimizing compilers, like the Watcom C compiler under QNX, will seriously rearrange functions in a quest for efficient code. If code is not generated in a strict linear layout, your address calculations will be much more difficult, and definitely non-portable. You can usually do this just by looking at the symbol table of the generated executable, using something like *nm*. If *intr_handler* is immediately followed by *right_after_intr_handler*, you're okay. Otherwise, you've got problems!

So say you've figured out how to lock your interrupt-handler code in memory. You're set! except that you also need to lock down the data and stack memory *used* by that code...

Always lock

On many embedded real-time systems, there are no disks, and therefore no way the system can page or swap. On such a system, there would seem to be no reason to call *mlockall* and *munlockall.*

Wrong! There are two reasons. The most important reason is portability. If you are interested in portability, it means that you have an interest in seeing your application run on some other machine someday. That machine may have the ability to page, even if this one doesn't. Therefore, always lock down the memory of your real-time application, even in an embedded target.

The other reason is that memory locking may, on some systems, also lock MMU context.* However, certain memory management units (like those on the more archaic versions of the SPARCstation) are too small to keep all processes in the MMU at one time. On machines with smaller MMUs (and we're talking about embedded, read *smaller*, machines), there is some hardware context that is being swapped around for the purposes of running multiple processes. Managing that hardware context can add enormous overhead to your context switch times, and some systems will implement *mlock* and *mlockall* so as to lock the process into the hardware MMU context as well as physical memory. The standard does not require this behavior, but it's certainly possible that a vendor of embedded systems will implement memory locking in such a way that, in fact, your entire path to the memory is locked down, MMU context and all.

Brass Tacks

This next section discusses how to use the facilities I've just described, and helps you out with some "brass tacks" issues: how all these things can be appropriately used to help solve your real-world scheduling problems.

Assigning Priorities: Rate-Monotonic Analysis and POSIX Scheduling

Now that you know how to set priorities for different processes, you may be wondering how to decide what priorities to assign. Which processes should run at which priorities in order to make sure that your application meets its timing goals? Sometimes this decision is apparent. If there is one time-critical task, just run it at a higher priority than anything else that might want to run. If you can easily determine the response requirements of each task, make sure that the ones with the tighter requirements have the higher priorities. However, what if there are several tasks that are all time-critical?

---

* Often MMU context need not be locked. The Intel 80×86, the Motorola 68000 family, and the SPARC processors later than the SPARCstation 2, for instance, all provide enough MMU context that you do not need to lock MMU resources down explicitly. That's because their MMU tables use plain old physical memory to store MMU context in, instead of dedicated (and limited-size) memory resources. This seems to be the trend in memory management units, but many other MMUs use limited amounts of context.

How do you figure out which task should get the highest priority, and which should be lowest? Do you just figure out which task is "most important" and run that one at the highest priority? Do you need to alter priorities dynamically to meet the timing requirements of your application?

For hard real-time, periodic tasks, the answers are simple. Using *rate-monotonic analysis*, you can easily figure out what priorities you should assign to each process, and analyze whether those tasks can meet their timing goals.

Rate-monotonic analysis is a technique pioneered in 1972 by Drs. C.L. Liu and J.W. Layland. It was promptly buried in a deep, dark academic report[*] and forgotten until researchers at Carnegie Mellon University dug it up again in the 1980s.

Rate-monotonic priority assignment is simple. All you need to know is the frequency at which all your processes need to run. For sporadically-interrupting tasks, you can use the worst-case arrival rate as the frequency for the purposes of assigning priorities (this number is generally pessimistic—that's why they call it *worst* case!). The highest-frequency process gets the highest priority. The lowest frequency gets the lowest priority. And everyone in between gets a priority that is higher, or lower, depending on its frequency. Don't assign any two processes the same priority; and make sure that all your priorities are higher than anything else that may be running on the system. If two or more processes have identical frequencies, you can flip a coin to decide who gets the higher priority.

For example, say your application consists of five tasks, as shown in Table 5-1. A user-interface task, *U*, goes off 10 times a second. Two hard-real-time control tasks *A* and *B* run at 100 HZ; a data collection task, *C*, runs at 66 Hz, and a data logging task, *L*, runs at 50 Hz. You would run *A* and *B* at the highest priorities: say 90 and 100. *C* is the next-highest frequency, so run it at the next-highest priority: 80. *L* comes next; run it at priority 70. Finally, run *U* at a relatively low priority, 60. I use numbers that have room in between them so that the addition of new tasks will not require a total re-computation of the priorities.

---

[*] C.L. Liu and J.W. Layland, "Scheduling Algorithms for Multiprogramming in a Hard Real-Time Environment," *Journal of the ACM*, volume 10, number 1 (January 1973), pages 46 through 61. This is an academic paper. For those of us who are mathematically challenged (like me), I'd recommend skipping this paper and moving on to one of the easier introductions to rate-monotonic analysis. There was a particularly good introduction, I thought, in *IEEE Computer*, volume 23, number 4 (April 1990): "Real-Time Scheduling Theory and Ada," by Lui Sha and John B. Goodenough.

Table 5-1: Example rate-monotonic priority assignments

Task	Frequency	Rate-Monotonic Priority
A	100	90
B	100	100
C	66	80
L	50	70
U	10	60

Again, remember to avoid the use of actual numbers when using the POSIX real-time scheduling code; instead, use virtual scheduling numbers that are offsets from the minimum and maximum priorities for SCHED_FIFO.

Now that you've done rate-monotonic priority assignments, is it guaranteed that your application is always going to make all its deadlines? Of course not. It depends on how much time each task takes, as well as how those tasks interact, the resources they share, how long each task *holds* those resources, and so forth. The basic priority assignment remains the same, though.

Rate-monotonic analysis assumes a world in which tasks execute periodically with fixed frequencies, so it's mainly seen in the hard real-time and embedded control worlds. There are modifications to rate-monotonic scheduling that you can use to deal with changing frequencies and tasks that don't run on a static timeline. However, I'm not going to cover these here. The important rule to remember is that you assign the highest priority to the task with the tightest timing restriction.

Rate-monotonic analysis allows you to determine whether your task set is going to work by using one simple formula or ten.[*]

Determining Computation Times: ITIMER_VIRTUAL and ITIMER_PROF

You can use the other two Berkeley interval time I mentioned earlier in this chapter to determine how long your computations take. Recall that there are three interval timers provided by those, standard UNIX, timers: ITIMER_REAL, ITIMER_VIRTUAL, and ITIMER_PROF. While ITIMER_REAL measures actual, wall-clock time, ITIMER_VIRTUAL only measures time spent by your code, and ITIMER_PROF measures the time spent by your code or by the operating system on behalf of your code. For instance, say you have code that does nothing but perform system calls. Since it spends the vast majority of its time in the operating system, the time spent according to ITIMER_VIRTUAL would not be very great. However, according to ITIMER_PROF, the time spent by your process would be more substantial, since that time includes both user and system time.

---

[*] For the comprehensive deskside reference, I'd recommend *A Practitioner's Handbook for Real-Time Analysis: Guide to Rate-Monotonic Analysis for Real-Time Systems*, a book written by various people at the Software Engineering Institute (Klein, Ralya, Pollak, Obenza, Harbour) and published by Kluwer in 1993.

One way in which ITIMER_VIRTUAL and ITIMER_PROF are used is for profilers. These software tools interrupt your code every so often, and sample where the execution of the program is at that instant. By doing so, you can obtain a statistical picture of where your process is spending its time. ITIMER_VIRTUAL is especially useful in this instance, since it disregards system time and therefore tells you only what your application code is doing.

I'm considering another use of ITIMER_VIRTUAL and ITIMER_PROF here, though. If you can execute your code multiple times, in a loop, you can set up these timers to expire after a fixed amount of time: say, 60 seconds. Then, by counting iterations, you can determine how long one iteration of your computation will take. I suggest you use ITIMER_PROF for this purpose, since time spent in the operating system is still time spent by your computation. For rate-monotonic analysis, you need to know the total time required by each of your computations. For this purpose, ITIMER_VIRTUAL does not tell you the complete story.

ITIMER_PROF and ITIMER_VIRTUAL, as periodic timers, offer only a statistical measurement of your execution time. Just like ITIMER_REAL and CLOCK_REALTIME, these timers are probably driven off the system clock tick. Whenever a tick expires, the system checks which process is running, and where. If it happens to be your process, then you get the tick credited to your CPU bank account. Note that you get the *entire* tick, whether or not your process actually *ran* for that entire tick! In order to measure your computation time somewhat realistically, then, you need to make sure that your process, when being measured, occupies the CPU basically full-time.

In addition, running your computation multiple times will yield a different result than running your computation once. For example, when you run a computation once, it will not be able to take advantage of the cache on your machine. The second time you run the computation, though, cache lines will be filled up with data your application can access quickly. The result is that your application runs faster the second and subsequent times around the loop. When you run thousands of iterations, obviously this faster time is going to come out as the average time for the computation. There is no easy, portable solution to this problem. You simply need to be aware of cache characteristics on your machine, and take them into account when measuring your application's time. You may need to stoop so low as to count the cache lines used by your code, and project the result of an entirely empty cache on your code. You can do this, if you know certain things: cache line size, cache characteristics, and time to fill cache lines. However, the job is difficult, and, frankly, beyond the scope of this book!

Priority Inversion and System-Wide Scheduling

Priority inversion is an insidious and sometimes fatal disease that afflicts most real-time applications at one time or another. The idea behind priority inversion is that a high priority task can be blocked while a lower priority task runs, if the higher priority task is waiting for a semaphore or some other resource that is owned by a low-priority task. Assume that a high-priority task is at priority ten, and is waiting for a resource that is being used by a priority one task. A third task, at priority five, can preempt the priority one task, and therefore delay the priority ten task longer than it should have been delayed.

The problem of priority inversion comes up when a resource (any resource) is used by both a lower-priority task and a higher-priority task. How can it be avoided? You have two choices, neither of which is terribly attractive. One, you can analyze your application to determine where possible priority inversions occur, how long they can occur for, and whether the inversions matter to your application. The problem with this approach is that you don't always know all the shared resources being used by your application. The operating system has some resources inside of it which it shares for you without your knowledge. Consider two tasks opening files. Even if the files are unrelated, both tasks may need to look at the same directory blocks in order to look up their files. Those blocks must be shared. There's a prime opportunity for priority inversion that you don't know about.

The second way to avoid priority inversion is called "priority inheritance," and can be used in addition to the first. Unfortunately, it's only something you can be aware of, not something you can do anything about. If your operating system supports priority inheritance, then you have a solution to the problem of priority inversion.

Priority inheritance avoids priority inversion by temporarily elevating low-priority tasks to the priority of the highest task that is waiting for the resource. Thus, if priority ten is waiting for a directory block, and priority one owns it, priority one gets to run at priority ten until it releases the directory block. That way, no one at priority five can preempt the priority one task before the priority ten task gets its resource.

Priority inheritance is nothing that is really available to you, the programmer, as part of POSIX.4. You can really only know about it. If the operating system supports it, all the better for you. If the operating system does not support it, well, you just have to live with that. Or find another operating system.

Life During Real-Time

UNIX guys are not familiar, by and large, with how real-time scheduling policies impact one's day-to-day life. This section describes what you can expect when running processes under SCHED_FIFO or SCHED_RR: a couple of the gotchas together with a few other hints.

First, the most common comment I hear about SCHED_FIFO is a rhetorical question: "what if you write an infinite loop program and run it at the highest priority?" Well, the system goes away, as far as you're concerned. Don't do that. That is actually quite rare, but it does happen, especially if you're writing test programs to see how something works and you make a mistake. This is my preferred mode of programming. Some call it "rapid prototyping"; I call it "dorking around." The solution to this problem? Simple.

Run your shell under SCHED_FIFO, at the highest priority in the system. Then refrain from using the highest priority level in your test programs. That way you can usually regain control. Of course, you'll need some method for changing the priority of your shell. *Atprio*, introduced earlier in the chapter, will suit your needs nicely.* In the exercises, we extend *atprio* into a full-blown utility you can use for complete control over the priorities your processes run at. To wrestle the system back from the grips of an errant program, you either need to kill it with a signal, or alter its scheduling priority. If you run into a program that is unkillable via signals, a useful Plan B is to set the thing's priority as low as it'll go. That gets it out of your hair for a while. A simple addition to *atprio* allows it to set the priority of running processes; all you really need is the ability to pass a process ID in to *atprio*.

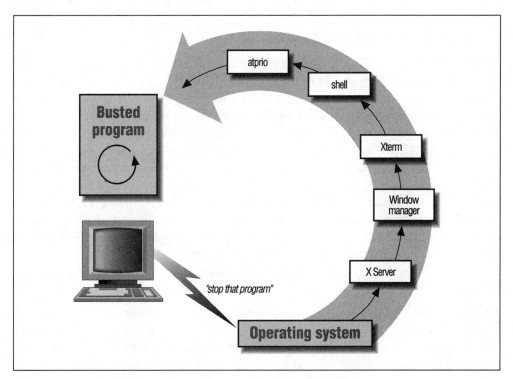

Figure 5-3. Layers of software between you and an errant program

kill, atprio and a high-priority shell are often all you need to regain control, but sometimes they are not sufficient. Layers of processes (see Figure 5-3) can intervene between an out-of-control real-time process and you, madly typing CTRL-Cs at the keyboard. If you are on a terminal connected directly to the machine, you are probably not talking to a lot of software in order to kill the process: there's your terminal, its interrupts, the operating system handling these, and your shell process getting the

---

* Some systems provide their own utilities that provide the same sort of functionality: QNX has *slay*, and LynxOS has *prio* and *setprio*, not to mention *q*.

input and executing programs to send the signals and/or change the priority. However, with a window system like X, the picture is different. If the window server is locked out by an errant program, it doesn't matter that your shell is at a high priority, because you can't get input to the shell! So, you need to run at least your X server, the window manager, and the client (*xterm, shelltool*, etc.) under the real-time scheduling discipline and at a high priority. Another problem might arise if your operating system is based on a microkernel (like Mach). In a standard, old-style operating system, when you ask to run a program, the operating system goes out and gets it directly, and runs it. In some newer systems, in which user-level processes may provide many system services, you must make sure that any separate processes you will need in order to run *kill* or *atprio* are *also* running at a high enough priority to do their jobs. In other microkernel operating systems, like QNX, priorities can be inherited by microkernel modules, avoiding priority inversions. This stuff can get a little complicated; it's easier to just run your possibly-errant program at a low priority.

What's it like living without a time-sharing scheduler? You'd be surprised at how easy it is. My development system runs only FIFO and round-robin scheduling, and I can effectively use it just like a standard UNIX workstation. Processes in day-to-day use generally block themselves rapidly enough that the CPU is available to you at any time. There are some differences, of course. Many programs have times when they do a lot of computing. When that happens, you may find your shell frozen for a second or two. For example, the linker I use for building programs has one compute-bound phase just before writing out the executables it has generated. During this phase, the disk light stops flashing and everything freezes while the linker thinks. It's actually sort of reassuring because I know, when everything momentarily freezes, that the linker is almost done. I take my hands off the keyboard, look at the disk light, and when it flashes again (a few seconds later), I continue with what I'm doing. Usually, of course, I'm waiting for the linker, so the fact that it monopolizes the CPU is fine by me. In the era of single-user workstations, a priority-based scheduler seems fine.

On a multi-user system, real-time scheduling can cause problems. For instance, my machine is also an NFS server for other developers who work with me. That means that my machine has to do some processing to get data to them from time to time. When I'm running the linker, their NFS requests tend to get choppy response for a couple of seconds. Taking it a little further, every now and then I'll run a high-priority benchmark that will essentially lock the system up for several minutes. Imagine the result of running a time computation, like I suggested for measuring time using ITIMER_PROF, where the application spins, at highest priority, for a minute or more—a good imitation of a crashed machine! In that case, my machine does what every good real-time system should do with asynchronous NFS requests. It sticks them in the queue and gets to them in priority order, usually several minutes later than expected!

A time-sharing system is probably a better choice for your day-to-day operations if you are engaging in mostly time-sharing activities, like software building. The advantages of building your software on the same machine you use for testing are enormous. However, if you're building software all the time, a timesharing machine may offer better performance, especially if you have multiple builds going on at the same time. After all, the time-sharing guys have gone to great lengths to make that sort of activity faster.

Nice but Not Necessary: How to Make the Time Readable

The time facilities we've discussed provide what's required for real-time applications, but there is a lot more to the time facilities than this. In particular, I have not discussed time zones or international Daylight Savings Times conventions, because they're not relevant to most real-time applications. In general, a real-time application, when it wants to know what time it is, just wants an absolute yardstick to measure against; Greenwich Mean Time (a.k.a. Coordinated Universal Time) works fine for this purpose. However, local time is desired often enough that we should probably talk about how to get it.

On your average machine, the hardware time is kept as the time in a particular time zone, usually Greenwich Mean Time. The system time is derived from this hardware-maintained time, so files transferred around the world have a consistent time base. Given this number of seconds, the conversion to a local time is done by a library routine, based on knowledge of what time zone the machine is operating in.

You're Entering . . . The Time Zone

How does the library know what time zone it is operating in? There is usually a system default that the library can fall back on, but that's implementation defined. The first place the library looks is in an environment variable called TZ. TZ contains a text string that describes completely the time zone in which the application is operating.

The format of TZ is a complicated matter, and more the province of the system administrator than the application writer. However, chances are you'll need to look at TZ once, or more, in your life, so here goes.

A fairly simple, common example of a TZ, or *timezone* string (for standard time in California, in this case) looks like this:

```
PST8PDT
```

The first three characters are the Standard Time Zone (*pst*); the final three characters are the Daylight Savings Time Zone (*pdt*). In between is a number, 8 here, which tells how much time to add to the local time to get back to Greenwich Mean Time. The time zone strings are used to determine which days daylight savings time begins on (it varies, of course, depending on which municipality you're in).

The assumption is that your daylight savings time is one hour ahead of standard time; that's usually the case. If it's not, you can specify that in the timezone string. For example, if your *dst* is seven hours and 15 minutes ahead of GMT (instead of the default seven), you could set TZ to:

```
PST8PDT7:15
```

In fact, you can set arbitrary offsets for your time zones, complete down to the second:

```
PST8:15:37PDT7:15:38
```

The fairly heinous example above uses the Pacific Standard and Pacific Daylight Savings Time Zones, but standard time is eight hours, 15 minutes and 37 seconds behind GMT; daylight savings time is seven hours, 15 minutes, and 38 seconds behind GMT. Implicit in this example is the fact that we're in a locale (California) that is west of the Prime Meridian. If we were east of it, we could indicate that fact by prepending a negative sign to our offsets.

The three-character time zone names are predefined for you and follow the rules defined for daylight savings scenarios around the world. If you are in a place where Daylight Savings Time is not practiced, you don't need to specify any *dst*:

```
PST8
```

This example would be for a locale where Pacific Standard Time applied, but there was no use of Daylight Savings Time (either PDT or otherwise).

Now, what if your system is in an area where the predefined zones do not apply? My first suggestion is a stiff drink. Okay, now that you've taken care of that, you can add more verbiage to TZ to set your own rules. The additional text is not too hard, actually. It looks like this: *date/time,date/time*. These two times tell when to switch from Standard to Daylight Savings time, and when to switch back. The times are specified just like the offsets above: *hh:mm:ss*. In fact, you don't even have to specify a time; the system will assume a default time of 2 A.M., when most people who are not system programmers are going to be asleep anyway.

The dates, on the other hand, come in a variety of shapes. First, you can specify a date based on day of the week of the month:

```
D4.3.1
```

This date means, reading backwards, day one (Monday; Sunday is zero) of week three of month four (April). If you want to specify the last Sunday in June, you'd say:

```
D6.5.0
```

The fifth week is kind of a flag value meaning "the last one, whenever it occurs."

Alternatively, you can specify a Julian date: a day between 1 and 365. In this scheme, April 1 is day 90 (31 + 28 + 31). So April 1 would be:

```
J90
```

Under this scheme, you cannot refer to February 29. If you really need to, leave off the "J" and count from 0 to 365:

```
92
```

April 1 is day 92 under this scheme (leap day is always counted).

We'll close with an example. The newly formed republic of Slobovia operates in SST and SDT (Slobovian Standard Time and Slobovian Daylight Time), where SST is four hours east of GMT, and SDT is five and a half hours east. SDT begins on the second Tuesday in May and ends November seventh at noon. The timezone string (since no one has been able to code up the proper standard tables for them yet) is:

```
SST-4SDT-5:30,M5.2.3,J280/12:00:00
```

My advice to budding Balkans is, consider the effects your actions will take on system administrators in your towns and cities! If you must secede, at least stick with California time. Or good Slobovian vodka.

Conclusion

Scheduling, timers, and memory access are all key to getting jobs done on time. The task of getting priorities right, timers set up correctly, and all necessary memory locked down is difficult, requiring you to go beyond the basics provided by POSIX.4, especially if your code is to perform portably across systems with differing priority ranges, clocks, and memory layouts.

We now have facilities for running multiple, cooperating processes in a high-performance, time-driven way. The next step is to interact with the outide world: perform I/O.

Exercises

Here are some exercises that will get you going on scheduling, timers, and memory locking. The solutions to problems that require programming can be found in the Appendix, in the section listed in parentheses after each such problem.

nice

Find, or write, a program which is compute-bound and will run for a long time, say 30 seconds. An infinite loop combined with a call to *alarm* will do nicely. *(cpubound.c)*

Now, write a program which continuously performs I/O. *(iobound.c)*

Time the execution of each program separately, and together.

Run the computation program by itself at various *nice* levels: 20, 10, –10, –20. Does the running time of the program change? Explain.

Running the computation program at various *nice* levels, also run the I/O program at the same time. How does the running time of each program compare to when the *nice* levels were not used?

Reverse the experiment: run the I/O program at various *nice* levels. What is the effect? How does it differ from the computation program?

priocntl

Write a program which will allow you to run other programs in realtime class at priorities given on the command line. In other words, write a primitive version of the *priocntl* utility.

POSIX.4 Scheduling

Modify the program you wrote for *priocntl* to do the same thing, only using the POSIX.4 functions. Which program is easier to understand? *(vsched.c, atprio.1.c)*

I mentioned that you generally want to run your shell at a higher priority than any program you might be prototyping, just in case that program goes nuts and tries to lock the machine up. Think of two modifications for the program above which would easily allow you to run programs at priorities lower than the priority of your shell. Implement the scheme that seems the most elegant to you. *(atprio.2.c)*

Implement a final modification that changes the priority of the process which invoked the program. Verify that it actually works to change the priority of your shell. Keep this program around—you may find it useful! *(atprio.3.c)*

UNIX Timers

Write a program that simply takes timer interrupts forever, using *setitimer* and a variable time interval (perhaps a command line argument). Run it at a high real-time priority. How is the responsiveness of your system affected as you vary the time interval? At what point do you begin to notice that your system is a bit more sluggish? Does your system *ever* become sluggish? Explain. *(periodic_timer.c)*

Quantify the "sluggishness" effect: find a throughput benchmark, like Dhrystone or Whetstone. Alternatively, write a simple program that you can use to measure how "fast" your CPU is running a computation. Run it without the periodic timer program, and with the periodic timer program running in the background. How are the numbers affected? How much of the machine is occupied by a timer running at 100 Hz? 1000

Hz? 5000 Hz? Explain your findings. *(cpubench.c)*

POSIX.4 Timers

Modify the program above so that it uses POSIX.4 interval timers. Note the differences in implementation. *(periodic_timer.p4.c)*

Timer overrun is when a timer expires several times before you get around to handling the signal generated by the timer expiration. POSIX.4 provides a special function, *timer_getoverrun*, to determine how many times a timer has expired since the last time you handled the signal. Since POSIX.4 signals are queued and not dropped, it would seem that this function is unnecessary. Explain why it is, in fact, necessary.

Devise a program which will hold off a timer expiration for several expirations, and will then allow the timer signal to come in. Use *timer_getoverrun* to determine the number of times the timer expired while you were busy doing something else. This is an interesting program in that you'll need two sources of time: one to expire periodically, and one other timer to delay a few expirations of the first timer. Maybe you can write this program without using two POSIX.4 timers, but try it using just the POSIX.4 real-time timers.

(Related to the exercise above) You *could* just set a timer, then spin in a loop for long enough that you knew the timer had expired several times—but that's gross. It's also nonportable, even though it will certainly compile on all POSIX.4 systems. Give an example of a system where this solution, initially written on your current machine and then ported to the new box, would fail.

Jitter is a measure of how steady your real-time system is. It is the amount your process drifts from the steady drumbeat of a periodic timer interrupt. Modify the POSIX.4 interval timer program to measure jitter. Run it for 24 hours. Do you have a steady or a jittery system? Try it with heavy disk, network, and/or computation traffic. *(jitter.p4.c)* (NFS service will fill the bill nicely if you want to load your system down.)

POSIX.4 Memory Locking

If your system seems jittery, based on the exercise above, two possible reasons are, you are not running the program at the highest priority in the system, or you have not locked down the process's memory and it is being paged. Modify your jitter program to lock itself down in memory. Does the jitteriness of the system improve at all? *(jitter.p4.c performs memory locking)*

CHAPTER

6

I/O for the Real World

I/O Is Everything

Previous chapters have covered essential mechanisms for setting up hierarchies of communicating, prioritized tasks; this chapter covers the key linkage between those tasks and the outside world.

Input and Output are the terms used to encompass all communication between a process and the outside world. Computer science theoreticians are fond of programs that don't perform I/O (except maybe at the end to print The Answer) because I/O is inherently messy. If a program doesn't have to deal with the outside world, it is generally easier to understand and less liable to break. Unfortunately, it is also much less likely to be useful.

When one is talking about real-time applications, I/O is everything. The program is tracking or controlling the real world in some way. Without the real world, there is no real-time.

I/O in Real-Time Systems

Examples of I/O in real-time include:

- **Data gathering from devices**. Here, a device means some weird piece of hardware associated with the real-world. Technically, disks, mice, and graphics tubes are devices, but that's not what I mean here.
- **Data output to devices.**
- **Data logging (usually to disk, perhaps over the network).**
- **Multimedia playback and recording (to/from disk or network).**

- **Database operations** (especially in the case of database systems!)
- **User I/O (keyboards, mice, bitmapped displays).**

Many times, I/O in the real world is just like normal UNIX I/O: standard *read* and *write* suffice. But sometimes when real-world applications perform I/O, they make a few extra demands of the I/O system. First, I/O should not block the task unnecessarily (the task probably has better things to do with its time then hang out). For instance, data collection and output should, when possible, be handled offline until the application absolutely needs to get involved, and both multimedia traffic and data logging benefit from a double-buffering approach that asynchronous I/O makes easy. Often, an application will want to know that data it's written is definitely safe on disk. This is a special concern in database systems. And finally, just about every real-time application wants fast, predictable performance out of its I/O subsystem.

UNIX Has a Problem with Real-Time I/O

I/O is a stumbling block for real-time UNIX systems. Why? Because the UNIX I/O model doesn't cater to the messiness of the real world. The UNIX I/O model is one of its most powerful features. It is simple, and yet it applies to everything. This makes UNIX programs much easier to write than programs for other operating systems: after learning five system calls, you can access the entire range of devices. Unfortunately, this abstraction comes at a price: lack of fine control. When you do an I/O call in UNIX, you don't really know what the operating system has done; you just know that what you've asked for was done, somehow.

For example, when you call *write* you have little or no control over whether your data actually goes out to the underlying hardware, or sits around in a buffer waiting for an opportune moment to be completed. You have no control over how long you are blocked in the operating system while the I/O request proceeds. You have no control over the "shape" of your file on the underlying media; you can't specify where the blocks comprising the file should be laid out on the disk.

We can list the deficiencies of the UNIX I/O model from a real-time standpoint:

1. **UNIX I/O is not synchronized.** Don't confuse synchron*OUS* with synchron*IZED*: the two words have different meanings. When I/O is synchronized with the underlying device, it is considered complete only when the underlying device is appropriately updated. As an example, a synchronized version of *write* would not return to the user until the I/O had actually gone down to the disk (or tape, or whatever).

   In contrast, most standard UNIX systems use a buffer cache to hold I/O for later flushing to disk. The flush operation is called *syncing*, after the *sync* system call. Buffering increases throughput for many applications (including many real-time applications) because data that is read or written is statistically likely to be read, or written, again. If that data hangs around in a buffer in memory, it will be much faster to get than if the data must be fetched from the slow device each time. But applications that live in hostile environments (e.g., factory floors, tanks) and applications with reliability constraints (e.g., transaction-processing and database systems) often require the knowledge that I/O is "safe" on disk, in case the machine crashes at an inopportune time. This is a service that standard UNIX does not provide.

2. **UNIX I/O is synchronous.** Synchronous means that the I/O takes place while you wait. The operative phrase here is "you wait." The *read* call blocks the calling process until the operating system has filled up the user buffer with the requested data, or an error occurs. When you call *write*, you do not return from that call until the operating system queues the data for writing. Many real-time applications (and other applications with high-performance I/O requirements) are written to perform I/O asynchronously: the system goes off and performs the requested I/O in parallel with the application, which is free to go about its business while the data is read in or written.

Using asynchronous I/O to good advantage is difficult, and relies heavily on the computer you are using and its support for parallel operation. However, it is a requirement of many existing applications, and therefore is something we need to consider.

3. **File geometry is hard or impossible to control.** Under UNIX, a file has no shape, only contents: a file is an unstructured stream of bytes. The file is laid out in some way on the underlying disk, but you don't (and can't) care *how* it is laid out. Typically, UNIX file system implementations attempt to provide performance that is uniformly "good enough." For example, the Berkeley Fast File System tries to lay out all blocks of a file close to each other on the disk, to minimize lengthy delays while the disk heads seek from one track to another; Sun recently published some results that improve this performance. However, there are no guarantees about disk file layout on disk, and certainly no way portable way to ensure that the file that is plenty fast on a SunOS machine will be plenty fast on an OSF/1 machine—or even that the file will be fast from one day to the next!

Real-time applications often desire two sorts of control over file geometry. First, the ability to allocate contiguous disk blocks is required, as shown in Figure 6-1. Allocating disk blocks that are next to each other eliminates seek times, allowing data to be read or written to the device at maximum speed. Second, a real-time application would like to preallocate a file of a certain size. This is because the software overhead of allocating blocks dynamically (as UNIX does) is unpredictable. When a real-time application needs to extend a file's size dynamically, it would like to allocate a large, preferably contiguous set of blocks, so the overhead doesn't occur often.

Aside from these common requirements, desires for control of disk file geometry are widely varied. What is common is the desire to have some say in how a disk file is laid out.

Figure 6–1. Normal UNIX disk layout and optimal layout for sequential access

Reads and writes are not the whole story. An application often wants to do something to a device that does not fall into either category (reading or writing data). UNIX provides a routine, *ioctl*, that is used to do assorted "other things" to files. There are various sets of *ioctl*s (one per UNIX variant, it seems) that can be applied to files in a file system and certain standard devices, like terminals. When the file refers to a strange device (e.g., */dev/robot-arm*), *ioctl* provides a magic interface to the device driver to do anything the driver happens to support.

There are three problems with *ioctl*:

- It's not standard. Each vendor's *ioctl* support is different. This makes portable programming difficult. However, each vendor supporting a weird piece of hardware is going to support the things most people need to do with that hardware. This means that all the necessary *ioctl*s should be there, somewhere; you can write your software at a slightly higher level using *#defines* for the *ioctl*s, and map your abstract *ioctl*s to each vendor's specific calls.

- *ioctl* only allows the application to do what the driver supports. If the driver allows three different sorts of *ioctl*, and you want to do something else, you have no choice but to hack driver code. Yum!

- *ioctl* is a kernel call, and as such, there is a great deal of overhead associated with it. For many devices, entering the kernel each time you want to do something is unacceptably slow. In many cases, a better solution is mapping the device's hardware registers into the application's memory, and allowing the application to drive the device directly. This ability is already supported in most modern UNIX systems, via *mmap*. Using *mmap* for direct device control is a dangerous game, and most applications will not have need to do this.[*]

---

[*] Direct hardware access usually requires a lot more than just *mmap*ing in the device registers. The application may need special permission to fully access the hardware (e.g., on 80386 systems, special processor permission bits must be set to perform the IN and OUT instructions that are used for a lot of CPU-supported I/O). If the device causes interrupts, then your application also needs some way of intercepting and handling the interrupt. At the moment, I know of no portable way for an application to achieve supervisor permission or directly handle interrupts. That's why we're not going to talk any more about this—there's no total solution. I could get you *into* trouble, but not back *out!*

Real-time applications use I/O heavily, making performance demands that far exceed the capabilities of the UNIX I/O model. Features in POSIX.1 and standard UNIX systems address a few of the problems that real-time applications face. First I'll go over those, since it's generally best to use the simplest, most standard facilities that you can find, and POSIX.1 is bound to be more standard than POSIX.4. For those cases where POSIX.1 doesn't cut it, the POSIX.4 facilities are necessary. These include synchronized I/O, asynchronous I/O, and direct device mapping.

Earlier versions of the POSIX.4 standard defined a facility for real-time file control, which would have allowed you to create and use contiguous and pre-allocated disk files. However, this chapter of the standard has fallen by the wayside. Later in this chapter, we'll spend a little bit of time bemoaning this fact and then seeing what you can do to live with it.

Standard UNIX Facilities for Real-World I/O

Many UNIX systems have some facilities that help solve some of the problems that real-time applications face. While these facilities are incomplete, they're more useful than UNIX's pre-POSIX offerings in the area of, say, interprocess communication. Let's briefly look at some of the more standard offerings.

Solutions for Synchronous I/O: select and poll

The *select* (BSD) and *poll* (System V) calls can be used to avoid unnecessary blocking for some *read*s and *write*s, especially when the file is a pipe, network socket, or special device (like a terminal). I/O to or from such devices depends on when someone puts data into the other end of the file.

For instance, harken back to our terminal and server example. In that example, when the terminals and server communicated via pipes, remember that the terminals took special pains not to block awaiting I/O on their pipe, because they might wait arbitrarily long for the server to get back to them. As another example, a networked multimedia recorder might have data streaming in on several network connections. It certainly cannot block waiting for data on one connection while dropping data on another! *select* and *poll* are useful for determining when data is available on pipes and network connections.

select and *poll* simply tell you whether there is data to be read or room to write. A timeout argument to either function limits how long the call will wait. Reading and writing data is still done via *read* and *write*, and is still potentially a blocking operation. Tellingly, *select* and *poll* always return "ready-to-go" for a disk file, even though you'll probably have to block waiting for your reads or writes to complete. It's only *really long, unbounded* blocking that these functions help you avoid. *select* and *poll* really just say, "yes, there's data there." For truly non-blocking I/O to *all* devices, we must look further.

Solutions for Synchronous I/O: O_NONBLOCK

An alternative solution is provided by the use of the O_NONBLOCK flag (provided in POSIX.1), which can be set on a per-file basis by *open* and *fcntl*. O_NONBLOCK causes *read*s, *write*s, and *open* itself to fail if the operation would have to block while waiting for data to become available. Again, though, the only blocking that O_NONBLOCK will avoid is the unbounded variety of blocking. A disk file *read* or *write* would never fail due to the need to block, even though *read*s and *write*s do generally block while the I/O proceeds.

select, *poll*, and O_NONBLOCK may be useful to people accessing data collection devices, although their utility is limited because the application has to go out and check the device repeatedly to tell whether it is ready. It would be much nicer if the *read* or *write* were able to proceed as soon as the device is ready, without having to wait for the application to *poll*. This was, in fact, the solution I adopted in the terminal/server example. By setting O_NONBLOCK on the pipe file descriptor, a *read* on the pipe would just return immediately if there were not data already in the pipe.

Solutions for Synchronized I/O: sync, fsync, O_SYNC

Standard UNIX systems provide decent solutions for synchronizing I/O with the underlying media. While there is no general way to assure that each I/O operation is individually synchronized, there are functions, called *sync* and *fsync*, that provide the equivalent of checkpoints. *sync* causes all the data in the operating system's internal buffers to be updated on disk, insofar as you can guarantee this at all with modern disks. Most disks today have caches on the disk itself, so transferring data *to the disk* means it's in the cache, but not necessarily on the platters of the disk yet. In general, you'll need to read the fine print on the disk drive itself to determine the behavior of the disk and its cache. *fsync* performs the same operation as *sync*, but for a single file, and so is more amenable to application use. In addition, some UNIX systems also provide a per-file flag, O_SYNC, that guarantees that each I/O operation is, in fact, synchronized with the underlying medium. POSIX.4 has standardized O_SYNC and *fsync*, described in more detail below; but *sync* is not part of POSIX as yet.

Solutions for Control over File Geometry: Ad Hoc

There are no real solutions provided in standard UNIX systems that allow for control over file shape (although several UNIX filesystems, like VxFS from Veritas Software, allow preallocated, extent-based files). I have heard it suggested quite seriously that a good way to make sure contiguous blocks are available is to back up a file system, wipe the disk clean, and then restore the file system using utilities that lay out the files as optimally as possible. Another common practice is to access the raw disk directly and implement a file system meeting the requirements at user level. Database systems often adopt this solution.

Achieving Greater Control over File Operations

As mentioned in the *POSIX Programmer's Guide*, one uses the lower-level I/O routines, like *read, write,* and the real-time extensions described here, to achieve greater control over I/O. I/O using *read* and *write* is much more predictable (if less convenient) than I/O using *fread* and *printf.* However, many applications need even more predictability.

How UNIX I/O Usually Happens

First, let's look at the typical model for I/O in a UNIX operating system. The system is designed to avoid touching the actual I/O device (disk, terminal, or what have you) whenever possible. If you use the stream I/O provided by *printf* and *fread*, you have a layer of buffering at the user level before you ever even make a call to the operating system. The operating system is called relatively infrequently: whenever a newline is encountered or the user buffer is overflowed, for instance.

Once the operating system is entered, there may be another layer of buffering to deal with. Some devices may have no buffering associated with them (like terminals, printers, and other devices with "character" interfaces). Other devices, in particular disks and other block devices that have file systems on them, are isolated from the *read* and *write* calls by a buffer cache that contains the most-recently read or written blocks of data. These data blocks are kept in memory, and are only flushed out to the disk occasionally. There are good reasons for this strategy. One, it is generally the case that data you looked at recently is data you will look at again. That's the principle of locality, which is what makes CPU caches, as well as I/O buffer caches, work. Second, going to disk is very slow. Disks are governed by gross mechanical realities like how fast you can move a head and how fast you can rotate the disk. So are processors, but electrons are much faster than disk arms. Going out to a processor's memory is like taking a short coffee break while your assistant runs down the hall for a printout. Going out to disk is like taking a short coffee break while your assistant takes a vacation in Bermuda! If you have work to do, you want to avoid the latter sort of delay.

So file I/O is done to buffer caches. These caches must eventually be flushed to the underlying disk so that the disk's version of reality matches the processor's. This generally happens at one of two times. First, when the buffer cache is full, blocks are flushed to disk to make room for new ones. Second, most UNIX systems support a method to flush the buffer cache entirely (the *sync* system call). Calling *sync* at regular intervals gives a statistical, probabilistic sort of assurance that your disk is pretty much in synch (hence the name of the call) with the rest of your system.

sync is not a part of the POSIX.1 standard, presumably because it is a system feature that just isn't required in many applications (this is another example, along with the lack of *select*, where useful UNIX functions are not present in POSIX). If you do a *ps* on your UNIX system, though, you may see a process called *update* or *syncer.* That is the process that sees to it that the buffer cache gets flushed on a regular basis. This process has the job of calling *sync* every ten seconds or so.

What's wrong with this picture? The typical UNIX I/O subsystem works pretty well for its intended applications. Avoiding the trip to disk improves the system's overall throughput. However, for most UNIX systems the intended applications are not real-time or database applications. These applications often require greater control: they want to know deterministically what is in the buffer cache and what is safely on disk. This is for reasons of fault tolerance and recovery. To support these applications, POSIX.4 provides two levels of file synchronization.

Data Synchronization

A file in the operating system is composed of two parts: the data in the file, and control information, or *metadata*, that allows you to get at the data and tells you more about it (modification times, owner ID, and so on). You may really want the file's data to be safe on disk, but you may not care so much about the metadata, which may rarely change. So POSIX.4 provides ways to synchronize just the data associated with a file. In the language of POSIX.4, this is called "data integrity."

Full File State Synchronization

In contrast, you might want to be sure that the whole file, control information and all, is safely out on disk at all times. POSIX.4 also supports this capability. This is called "file integrity." File integrity is what most people mean when they think about synchronized I/O: the entire file is safe out on disk. Data integrity might be slightly less expensive because a block of control information might not need to be written to disk.

You Do the Checkpointing . . .

POSIX.4 has two functions (defined in the _POSIX_SYNCHRONIZED_IO option of the standard) that allow you to flush the buffer cache for particular files. One function, *fsync*, provides file integrity by flushing the data and the control information as well. The other operation, *fdatasync*, just flushes the data out, possibly leaving the control information for the file in a slightly inconsistent (but presumably either recoverable or irrelevant, and definitely good enough to let you *access* all your data) state. You can use *fsync* or *fdatasync* to verify that your data is safe at regular intervals, or at some time of your choosing, when the system is otherwise quiescent. Here's a summary:

```
#include        <unistd.h>

#ifdef _POSIX_SYNCHRONIZED_IO
int fsync(int fd);
int fdatasync(int fd);
#endif _POSIX_SYNCHRONIZED_IO
```

These functions are simple to use: you call them, they synch the relevant file parts out, and you proceed. For instance, in a data logging application, you may be firing data off to disk via a storm of *writes*. At a relatively quiescent period in your application, you could choose to get this data out to disk, as follows:

```
int fd = open("file", O_RDWR);
  ...
/* Things are busy */
write(fd, buf, nbytes);
write(fd, another_buf, more_nbytes);
  ...
/* There's a lull in the action, so... */
fsync(fd);
```

The use of the checkpointing function might be even more incumbent upon you if you are using low-priority asynchronous I/O (described further on). You could fire off a bunch of asynchronous operations at a low priority, and then wait for them at a time of your choosing. (This example relies on _POSIX_ASYNCHRONOUS_IO, _POSIX_ SYNCHRONIZED_IO, _POSIX_PRIORITIZED_IO, *and* _POSIX_PRIORITY_SCHEDULING):

```
int fd = open("file", O_RDWR);
struct aiocb a1, a2, a3;
struct sched_param s;

/* Set AIO control blocks for low-priority execution */
sched_getparams(0, (&s);
a1.aio_reqprio = s.sched_priority;
a2.aio_reqprio = s.sched_priority;
a3.aio_reqprio = s.sched_priority;
  ...
a1.aio_fildes = a2.aio_fildes = a3.aio_fildes = fd;
  ...
aio_write(&a1);
aio_write(&a2);
aio_write(&a3);
  ...
fsync(fd);
```

... Or Leave It to the Operating System

fsync and *fdatasync* are well and good, but suppose you have an application where you *always* want your data to go out to disk immediately. You could do an *fsync* or *fdatasync* after every *read* and *write* operation. This is clumsy, however, and still leaves a small timing window where your file data is not necessarily out on disk, even if just for a small moment between calling *write* and calling *fsync*.

POSIX.4 lets you set three flags on a file descriptor that tell the operating system to bypass or write through the buffer cache for any file I/O. These flags offer successively more stringent control over I/O synchronization. In order, they are:

- O_DSYNC: This flag tells the operating system that when you write data to a file, that data should go directly to disk. File state information necessary for *accessing* that data must also be flushed immediately. For instance, if you extend a file with a write, the newly-expanded file size had better be permanently stored, along with the new bits! It is not necessary, however, to keep *all* the on-disk file control information (the inode) up to date. If your system crashes, the contents of your file will definitely be there, but the modification date of the file, for example, may be incorrect.

- O_SYNC: By setting O_SYNC, you tell the operating system to keep all the file's data and control information up to date when you perform writes. This is the same as the O_DSYNC flag, with the additional requirement to keep the inode up to date.

- O_RSYNC: O_DSYNC and O_SYNC apply only to calls that write data to the disk. When reading data, these flags make no additional requirement of the system. In particular, a *read* updates the access time for the file, but neither O_DSYNC nor O_SYNC require that the inode be updated when you read data. Is this important to you? I doubt it. However, if it is, you can set O_RSYNC. It means "whatever synchronization I've specified for my *writes*, apply that same synchronization to my *reads*." So, if you specify O_RSYNC|O_SYNC, you will cause the system to keep your inode information up to date on the disk whenever you do a *write or* a *read* (combining O_RSYNC and O_DSYNC has no additional effect).

You set these three flags using *fcntl*, in any of the following ways. Notice how you use *fcntl* to first get the current flags (F_GETFL), and then *or* in the new flags with F_SETFL.

```
#include        <sys/types.h>
#include        <unistd.h>
#include        <fcntl.h>

#ifdef _POSIX_SYNCHRONIZED_IO

int fd, return_val, previous_bits;

/* Get the old bits */
previous_bits = fcntl(fd, F_GETFL);

/* Synchronize the data written to the file */
return_val = fcntl(fd, F_SETFL, previous_bits | O_DSYNC);

/* Synchronize the data and file control information written to the file */
return_val = fcntl(fd, F_SETFL, previous_bits | O_SYNC);

/* Synchronize the data and file control information written or read */
return_val = fcntl(fd, F_SETFL, previous_bits | O_SYNC | O_RSYNC);

#endif _POSIX_SYNCHRONIZED_IO
```

Can You Really Do This?

The synchronized I/O facilities are available if, in *<unistd.h>*, _POSIX_SYNCHRONIZED_ IO is defined. However, the meaning of the word "available" might not be what you expect. Synchronized I/O may only be supported for certain file systems in a given implementation. For instance, there may be no reason to support synchronized I/O in a temporary or ramdisk-based filesystem. What you need to know is to look in *<unistd.h>* for _POSIX_SYNCHRONIZED_IO. If it is defined as –1, then synchronized I/O is not supported on your system. If it's defined as anything else, then *all* files in your system support synchronized I/O. And, finally, if _POSIX_SYNCHRONIZED_IO is not defined at all, then you need to go check, using *pathconf* or *fpathconf,* for whether the capability is there for a particular file. Call *pathconf* with the name of the file and the constant _PC_SYNC_IO (defined, again, in *<unistd.h>*), and it will tell you if synchronized I/O is supported for the given file name. The way it tells you may be somewhat strange: if _PC_SYNC_IO is supported, *pathconf* will return –1 and *not* set *errno* to any error value. That is what *pathconf* does, remember, when a particular variable (like _PC_SYNC_IO) has no limit for the given file. The ability to perform I/O is a Boolean quantity—you can either do it, or you can't—and there's no particular limit to it. My recommended way to use *pathconf,* then, would be like this:

```
#include <unistd.h>
#include <errno.h>

#ifdef _POSIX_SYNCHRONIZED_IO
#if _POSIX_SYNCHRONIZED_IO == -1
    /* No synchronized I/O at all */
#else
    /* Synchronized I/O available on all files */
#endif
#else
    /* Must dynamically check for synchronized I/O on my file */
    int i;

    errno = 0;
    i = pathconf("/file/i/want/to/do/sync/io/on", _PC_SYNC_IO);
    if (! errno) {
        /* Synchronized I/O is supported for my file */
    } else {
        /* Cannot do synchronized I/O here */
    }
#endif
```

You can also use *fpathconf,* which takes a file descriptor instead of a pathname.

Do You Really Need Synchronization?

You should think very carefully about whether your application really needs synchronized I/O before building it into your application. Buffer caches are generally a good thing: they improve the overall I/O performance. Bypassing the buffer cache will probably result in a big performance hit. If you need the determinism, then you need it. But if you can get by with periodic calls to *fsync* or *fdatasync,* that may achieve your application's goals with less overhead. After we discuss asynchronous I/O, I'll introduce a method that may, under some circumstances, be even lower-overhead than *fsync* and *fdatasync*—a way to call *fsync* or *fdatasync* without blocking the calling process.

Synchronized I/O is really a simple addition to normal POSIX.1 I/O. The fact that I/O is being performed through (or without) the buffer cache doesn't have a visible effect (except for performance) on any other system calls. You probably want to look over the use of *fcntl* and *open*, for setting the O_DSYNC and O_SYNC flags.

Asynchronous I/O: I/O While You Don't Wait

As I just mentioned, UNIX I/O is generally not synchronized with the disk. However, UNIX I/O is still synchronous. When you do a *read* or a *write* call, you block, waiting for the I/O to complete. In contrast, many non-UNIX and real-time operating systems support the ability to perform asynchronous I/O. In such a system, you just queue up a read or write request with the system, and then go about your other business while the system does the I/O. When the I/O completes, your application receives some kind of notification—for example, a signal. For instance, in a data logging application, the logging process might just periodically fire off asynchronous writes of log data, to be dribbled out to disk as the system sees fit. Meanwhile, it could continue to fill data up in a new log buffer. As another example, a multimedia player generally performs double-buffering to achieve smooth playback. That means that while one buffer is being used (displayed on the screen and played on the speakers), a second buffer is being filled up with the next chunk of data. When the player needs that next chunk, it is hopefully all ready to go; the system fires off the *next* asynchronous operation and proceeds.

POSIX 1003.4 asynchronous I/O (option _POSIX_ASYNCHRONOUS_IO) provides the ability to perform I/O in parallel with the other operations of an application. In essence, when you make an asynchronous *read* or *write* call, the operating system queues up the I/O and immediately returns control to you. The system performs the I/O while your application continues. When the I/O is complete, you can be informed (if you wish) by the delivery of a signal. The signal can be either a standard, plain old POSIX.1 signal, or it can be a POSIX.4 extended signal.

Although the functions look rather different from their synchronous brethren, the asynchronous calls are quite similar in their effects. Here's a summary of the POSIX.4 asynchronous I/O functions and data structures.

```
#include        <unistd.h>
#ifdef _POSIX_ASYNCHRONOUS_IO
#include        <aio.h>

int aio_read(struct aiocb *racbp);
int aio_write(struct aiocb *wacbp);
int lio_listio(int wait_or_not, struct aiocb * const lacb[],
    int num_acbs, struct sigevent *notification);
int aio_cancel(int fd, struct aiocb *acbp);
int aio_suspend(const struct aiocb *lacb[], int num_acbs,
```

```
          const struct timespec *timeout);
int aio_fsync(int mode, struct aiocb *acbp);

ssize_t aio_return(const struct aiocb *acbp);
int aio_error(const struct aiocb *acbp);
#endif _POSIX_ASYNCHRONOUS_IO
```

File Descriptors for Asynchronous I/O

Asynchronous I/O is very similar to standard I/O. The standard *open* and *close* functions are used; all the capabilities you can set with *open* and *fcntl* (setting parameters like the O_RSYNC, O_DSYNC, and O_SYNC flags for synchronized I/O) apply to asynchronous I/O.

The AIO control block

Asynchronous I/O operations are submitted using a structure called the AIO control block, or *aiocb*.[*] The *aiocb* groups all the parameters for a given AIO operation. It contains the normal parameters for a *read* or *write*: a buffer pointer, a number of bytes, and a file descriptor. As usual, one is reading or writing from or to the file descriptor, from or to the buffer, for the indicated number of bytes. Here's how the *aiocb* is defined:

```
struct aiocb {
        int     aio_fildes;     /* FD being used for the I/O */
        off_t   aio_offset;     /* Offset of the implied lseek */
        volatile void *aio_buf; /* Buffer to read to/write from */
        size_t  aio_nbytes;     /* Number of bytes to read/write */
        struct sigevent aio_sigevent;   /* Signal to deliver on completion. */
        int     aio_lio_opcode; /* Operation to be performed (lio_listio only) */
        int     aio_reqprio;    /* AIO priority (discussed later) */
};
```

The function *aio_read* is used to submit an asynchronous read; it's called like this:

```
aio_read(&a);
```

where a is an *aiocb*. This has roughly the same effect as the following code:

```
lseek(a.aio_fildes, a.aio_offset, SEEK_SET);    /* Seek to position */
read(a.aio_fildes, a.aio_buf, a.aio_nbytes);    /* Read data */
sigqueue(0, a.aio_sigevent.sigev_signo, a.aio_sigevent.sigev_value);
```

But that sequence of activities happens in parallel, while *aio_read* leaves your application free to go about its business, as shown in Figure 6-2.

---

[*] Pronounced "Ay-Eye-Oh-See-Bee," for those of you who wonder about such things.

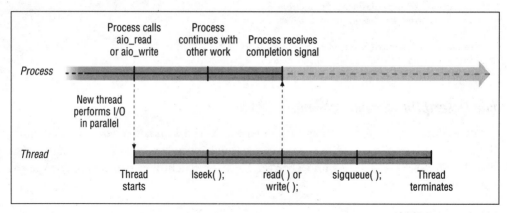

Figure 6–2. How AIO proceeds

A seek always occurs

The file offset element, *aio_offset*, indicates the offset in the file at which the I/O should occur. This implied seek ALWAYS occurs, unless the file descriptor has been explicitly set not to do the seek (via use of the O_APPEND flag, which appends all writes to the end of a file). Furthermore, any asynchronous I/O operation leaves the seek pointer in an undefined state, so that, to even perform a normal *read* or *write* to the file, you must first perform an *lseek* to reset the file pointer to a defined value! This is very important: if you are doing asynchronous I/O on a file, you must assume that the seek pointer is generally meaningless, and you must manage the seek pointer yourself!

Signal delivery

The AIO control block also contains structure elements (grouped together in *aio_sigevent*) that define a signal to be delivered when the asynchronous I/O is complete. The signal value can be any of the available signal values—either the POSIX.1 signals, or the POSIX.4 extended signals. If a POSIX.4 extended signal is used, a data value can also be passed to the signal handler. In most cases, you will want this data value to be the address of the AIO control block itself, so that your signal handler can identify which AIO operation caused the particular signal it is handling.

As an example, one might set up an asynchronous I/O signal delivery as follows:

```
a.aio_sigevent.sigev_notify = SIGEV_SIGNAL;
a.aio_sigevent.sigev_signo = SIGRTMIN;
a.aio_sigevent.sigev_value.sival_ptr = (void *)&a;
```

We used the address of the *aiocb* as the signal's data value because your signal handler will need to figure out which I/O requests caused the signal. Since different asynchronous I/O requests will have different *aiocb*s, looking at the control block is the easiest way to determine which request is responsible for the signal.

When the signal is delivered, the signal handler would be invoked as if you had called your function handler like this:

```
signo = SIGRTMIN;
info->si_signo = SIGRTMIN;
info->si_value.sival_ptr = (void *)&a;

signal_handler(signo, info, context);
```

This is not code you need to put in your application; the operating system dispatches out to your signal handler automatically. Note that your signal handler is passed the address of the *aiocb*, which allows it to figure out why the signal occurred.

AIO priority

There is one other element of the *aiocb* that I haven't talked about yet: *aio_reqprio*. This element allows you to indicate the priority of a particular AIO request relative to other AIO requests. *aio_reqprio* is an optional feature of POSIX.4 systems, and is a little bit complicated, so I'm going to discuss it after I've introduced the other, more familiar elements of asynchronous I/O. For now, all you really need to know is that setting *aio_reqprio* to 0 will have an innocuous effect on your asynchronous I/O.

For Example . . .

An example ties together the things I've discussed above. Here's a code module that would perform data logging for an application. It uses double-buffering, copying log data into an in-memory buffer while a second, filled buffer is being flushed to disk by use of asynchronous I/O.

```
#define _POSIX_C_SOURCE 199309L
#include <unistd.h>
#include <fcntl.h>
#include <sys/types.h>
#include <sys/stat.h>
#include <signal.h>
#include <string.h>
#include <errno.h>
#include <stdio.h>

#ifdef _POSIX_ASYNCHRONOUS_IO
#include <aio.h>
#else
ERROR: no asynchronous I/O!
#endif

#ifndef _POSIX_REALTIME_SIGNALS
ERROR: need queued signals!
#endif

#define SIG_AIO_BUFFER_WRITE (SIGRTMAX-10)

#define MIN(a,b) (((a) < (b)) ? (a) : (b))
```

```
#define BUFFER_FREE 1
#define BUFFER_FILLING 2
#define BUFFER_WRITING 3

#define BUFFERSIZE 4096
typedef struct {
    int state;          /* Free or not */
    int fillpt;         /* End of buffer */
    struct aiocb acb;        /* For flushing */
    char buffer[BUFFERSIZE];    /* Data buffer */
} buffer_t;

/* Double-buffer log output. */
#define NBUFFERS 2
static buffer_t buflist[NBUFFERS];

static buffer_t *curbuf;
static int log_fd;
static off_t seek_ptr;
static sigset_t aio_completion_signals;

buffer_t *  find_free_buf(void);
void        flush_filled_buf(buffer_t *);
void        aio_done(int, siginfo_t *, void *);
void        log_data(char *, int);
void        initlog(const char *);

buffer_t *find_free_buf(void)
{
    int i;
    sigset_t prevmask;

    sigprocmask(SIG_BLOCK, &aio_completion_signals, &prevmask);
    while (1) {
        for (i=0; i<NBUFFERS; i++) {
            if (buflist[i].state == BUFFER_FREE)
                break;
        }
        if (i == NBUFFERS) {
            /* found no buffer -- wait for something to complete */
            sigsuspend(&prevmask);
            /* And try again! */
        } else
            break;
    }
    buflist[i].state = BUFFER_FILLING;
    buflist[i].fillpt = 0;
    sigprocmask(SIG_SETMASK, &prevmask, NULL);
    return &buflist[i];
}

void flush_filled_buf(buffer_t *full_guy)
{
    /* Set up AIOCB */
    full_guy->acb.aio_fildes = log_fd;
```

```
        full_guy->acb.aio_offset = seek_ptr;
        seek_ptr += BUFFERSIZE;
        full_guy->acb.aio_buf = full_guy->buffer;
        full_guy->acb.aio_nbytes = BUFFERSIZE;
        full_guy->acb.aio_reqprio = 0;
        full_guy->acb.aio_sigevent.sigev_notify = SIGEV_SIGNAL;
        full_guy->acb.aio_sigevent.sigev_signo  = SIG_AIO_BUFFER_WRITE;
        full_guy->acb.aio_sigevent.sigev_value.sival_ptr =
            (void *)full_guy;

        /* Mark buffer as being written out */
        full_guy->state = BUFFER_WRITING;

        /* Fire off the asynchronous I/O! */
        if (aio_write(&full_guy->acb) < 0)
            perror("aio_write");

        return;
}

/* "AIO complete" signal handler */
void aio_done(int signo, siginfo_t *info, void *ignored)
{
        buffer_t *completed_buf;
        ssize_t rval;

        /* Sanity checking paranoia */
        if ((signo != SIG_AIO_BUFFER_WRITE) ||
            (info->si_code != SI_ASYNCIO)) {
                /* Not an AIO completion signal, handle error */
                return;
        }

        /*
         * Mark the buffer on which we performed I/O as being
         * available again
         */
        completed_buf = (buffer_t *)info->si_value.sival_ptr;
        if (aio_error(&completed_buf->acb) != EINPROGRESS) {
            if ((rval=aio_return(&completed_buf->acb)) != BUFFERSIZE) {
                /* Error, write failed for some reason! */
            }
        }
        completed_buf->state = BUFFER_FREE;

        return;
}

/* log some data */
void log_data(char *logdata, int nbytes)
{
        int nlogged = 0;
        int num_to_copy;

        while (nlogged < nbytes) {
```

```
            num_to_copy = MIN(BUFFERSIZE-curbuf->fillpt, nbytes-nlogged);
            memcpy(&curbuf->buffer[curbuf->fillpt],
                logdata + nlogged, num_to_copy);
            curbuf->fillpt += num_to_copy;
            if (curbuf->fillpt == BUFFERSIZE) {
                /* Buffer full, flush and get a new one */
                flush_filled_buf(curbuf);
                curbuf = find_free_buf();
            }
        }
        return;
    }

    void initlog(const char *log_file)
    {
        int i;
        struct sigaction sa;

        for (i=0; i<NBUFFERS; i++)
            buflist[i].state = BUFFER_FREE;

        curbuf = find_free_buf();

        log_fd = open(log_file, O_WRONLY|O_CREAT|O_TRUNC,
            S_IRUSR|S_IWUSR|S_IRGRP|S_IROTH);
        if (log_fd < 0)
            perror(log_file);
        seek_ptr = 0;

        sigemptyset(&aio_completion_signals);
        sigaddset(&aio_completion_signals, SIG_AIO_BUFFER_WRITE);
        sa.sa_flags = SA_SIGACTION;
        sigemptyset(&sa.sa_mask);
        sa.sa_sigaction = aio_done;
        sigaction(SIG_AIO_BUFFER_WRITE, &sa, NULL);

        return;
    }
```

The function *log_data* is the major external interface to the logging facility; in addition, one calls *initlog* to set up the buffers, the signal mask and signal handlers. Note the following features:

- The *struct aiocb* controlling each asynchronous operation is embedded within the *buffer_t* structure; we pass the address of the *buffer_t* itself to the AIO completion signal handler, which knows that the *aiocb* for the asynchronous operation is embedded in that structure.

- A seek offset is maintained in the software, since we need to explicitly provide an offset each time we submit an asynchronous I/O. The seek value is updated as soon as the AIO is submitted, so the next AIO operation will be submitted at the next appropriate offset.

- As usual, I've made up my own name for the signal I'm using, to centralize its definition in case I need to change it.

- Note that the AIO completion signal is masked while we look for a free buffer. This is to prevent the AIO completion signal handler from updating the data structures while we are examining them. If there is no free buffer, we await AIO completion by using *sigsuspend*.

- *aio_reqprio* is set to zero, so AIO is submitted at the priority of the calling process.

Error detection for asynchronous operations

You'll also notice that, in the signal handler for AIO completion, we checked for the AIO status using *aio_error* first, and then *aio_return*. For a synchronous (i.e., "normal") *read* or *write*, error detection is easy: you wait until the operation is done, and if it returned something unexpected, you look at *errno*. There are two values you are looking at: return value and error value. Error handling for synchronous I/O is simple and easy; unfortunately, it doesn't work for asynchronous I/O. What happens if you have a number (say, 10) of asynchronous I/Os going on all at once? How do you get a return value from an asynchronous read, since the call to *aio_read* returns before the operation has been completed? And how can you safely use *errno* if any one of the 10 outstanding asynchronous operations might update the value of *errno* at any moment?

The answer is that the system maintains a return value, and an *errno* value, for each asynchronous operation separately. This situation is described in Figure 6-3. You have to ask for these two values from the system when you want them, using the functions *aio_return* and *aio_error*.

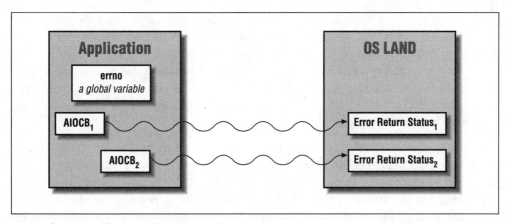

Figure 6-3. Asynchronous I/O error and return status

aio_return and *aio_error* both take the address of an *aiocb* structure that was used for submitting asynchronous I/O. Each function gives back the return value, or *errno* value, associated with the asynchronous operation at that moment.

The *errno* value for any asynchronous operation that is currently going on is EIN-PROGRESS. This is a new value for *errno*, meaning "not done yet! come back later!" After the asynchronous operation completes, the *errno* value will take on a more normal value—one of those you would expect for a normal, synchronous *read* or *write*. For instance, after submitting an asynchronous operation you could await its completion as follows:

```
aio_read(&acb);
while ((local_errno_value = aio_error(&acb)) == EINPROGRESS)
    ;
return_value = aio_return(&acb);
```

This code just loops, burning CPU cycles, until the I/O operation completes. It would be most useful in cases where you know the I/O operation has completed. If the I/O isn't completed, it just wastes time. On a real-time system, running under a priority scheduler, a possibly-infinite loop like the one given above is a no-no. You can conceivably hang your system by occupying the CPU forever!

In the example directly above and the data logger example, notice that we call *aio_error* first, to determine that the AIO is in fact completed, before we call *aio_return*. This is on purpose, and crucial.

The return value for an asynchronous operation is undefined until the operation is done. If you're not *absolutely sure* that an asynchronous operation has completed, call *aio_error* to find out. Furthermore, you can only call *aio_return* once. The return value and *errno* value for asynchronous operations may be maintained inside your operating system in an area of limited size. In order to avoid overflowing this area, the system has to remove error and return values from it. The system is supposed to take its cue from the *aio_return* function; when that function is called, the system can then free up the storage previously used for the return and error value, and use it for some other asynchronous operation. Lest you think this strange, the *wait* function does exactly the same thing with processes: you can only call it once for a given process ID that has terminated, and then the process "slot" is recycled for a new process. The moral of the story is: always call *aio_error* to verify that the *errno* value is *not* EIN-PROGRESS before you call *aio_return*.

There's one situation where you can avoid calling *aio_error*: in your signal handler for AIO completion, you don't have to check *aio_error* first, because you know that the operation is done. You still must call *aio_return*, of course, to find out what the return value of the asynchronous operation was. I just call *aio_error* and the *aio_return* in sequence always, out of paranoia, because it's easy to remember, and because it's probably a small overhead.

One final note on *aio_error* and *aio_return*. You may have been wondering why there are functions for *aio_error* and *aio_return*, when it would certainly be possible to have extra fields in the *aiocb* structure for the *errno* and the return value. There are functions because some operating systems have a hard time copying data from kernel space to user space, and would rather just maintain the information inside the operating system until the user calls for it. On other systems, copying data from kernel to user space is no problem. On those systems, it is perfectly acceptable for the operating system to have extra, added fields in the *aiocb* and update them asynchronously with *errno* and return value. On such systems, the *aio_return* and *aio_error* functions could be implemented as:

```
#define aio_error(a)   ((a)->hidden_special_errno)
#define aio_return(a)  ((a)->hidden_special_return_value)
```

POSIX doesn't say *where* these functions have to be implemented, after all—just that they have to be there when you compile your program. Just because a function is present, don't assume it's an expensive, slow system call.

Multiple I/O Operations at Once: lio_listio

Asynchronous I/O allows you to combine several *read* and *write* operations in a single system call, *lio_listio*. This function is useful for firing off large amounts of I/O all at once. For instance, if we wanted to fire off several log buffers at once, we might use *lio_listio* as follows:

```
#define SIG_LISTIO_DONE (SIGRTMAX-9)
struct aiocb *acb_list[AIO_LISTIO_MAX];
int num_in_listio;

void flush_several_bufs(buffer_t *bufs_to_flush, int nbufs)
{
    struct sigevent when_all_done;

    /* Set up AIOCBs */
    for (num_in_listio=0; num_in_listio<nbufs; num_in_listio++) {
        acb_list[num_in_listio] = &bufs_to_flush[num_in_listio].acb;
        acb_list[num_in_listio]->aio_lio_opcode = LIO_WRITE;
        /* Do remaining aiocb initialization exactly
         * as in flush_filled_buf above */
    }

    /* Set up signal to be delivered when ALL AIOs done */
    when_all_done.sigev_notify = SIGEV_SIGNAL;
    when_all_done.sigev_signo = SIG_LISTIO_DONE;
    when_all_done.sigev_value.sival_ptr = (void *)acb_list;

    /* Fire off the asynchronous I/Os! */
    if (lio_listio(LIO_NOWAIT, acb_list, num_in_listio,
        &when_all_done) < 0)
            perror("listio");

    return;
}
```

lio_listio takes an array of pointers to *aiocbs* (*not* an array of *aiocbs*!) as its second argument. The third argument tells the function how many elements are in the array—up to AIO_LISTIO_MAX. AIO_LISTIO_MAX is one of those limits that may be defined in *<limits.h>*. If it is defined, you can only count on being able to submit that many. If AIO_LISTIO_MAX is not defined, then the limit is generally either limited by your available memory, or it's a kernel-configurable option. To determine if it's a kernel configuration issue, call *sysconf(_SC_AIO_LISTIO_MAX)* to get dynamic system configuration information. Otherwise, the limit is indeterminate, and you can only tell how many *lio_listio*s you can do at once by trying it, or by asking the vendor.[*] Be aware that AIO_LISTIO_MAX can legally have a value as small as 2, so you can only submit 2-element *lio_listio* operations if you want to be portable to all possible implementations supporting asynchronous I/O!

Within the array, there are additional guidelines. First, a NULL pointer is allowed in the array; it's just skipped. NULL pointers let you add or remove *aiocb*s from your list from one operation to the next. Second, each *aiocb* indicates an asynchronous read, an asynchronous write, or a no-op. The *aio_lio_opcode* field of the *aiocb* determines the operation type; this field was ignored by *aio_read* and *aio_write*, because those operations already know what they're supposed to be doing! The *aio_lio_opcode* field can be initialized to either LIO_READ (do a read), LIO_WRITE (do a write), or LIO_NOP. The list entry is ignored if the opcode is LIO_NOP.

The operations in the array are not processed in any particular order. One system may go from 0 to the number of elements; another system may go backwards. A multiprocessor may process all the elements in parallel. Whatever. Do not count on any particular ordering of I/O in *lio_listio*.

The first parameter determines whether *lio_listio* operates asynchronously or synchronously. If the parameter is equal to LIO_NOWAIT, then all of the operations in the list are done asynchronously, like a bunch of *aio_read*s and *aio_write*s. In this case, the *sigevent* argument specifies a signal that will be sent to the process when *all* of the I/O operations on the list are completed. This means that you could conceivably receive N+1 signals for a *lio_listio* of N elements: one for each I/O, and one when they are all done.

If, on the other hand, the first parameter is LIO_WAIT, then all the operations on the list are done while the *lio_listio* function waits, just like a bunch of *read*s and *write*s. In this case, the final *sigevent* argument is ignored—no signal is delivered when all the operations are complete. However, you might still get signals from the individual asynchronous operations, each of which defines its own particular completion signal in the *aiocb*.

The synchronous mode is another present from the supercomputing community: they like to do a lot of different jobs at the same time. Synchronous use of *lio_listio* is not something you are likely to use every day. However, there is one really nice feature of

---

[*] Usually, an indeterminate limit means that the option is limited by the memory you have available to you, or that the option is somehow configurable in your kernel.

synchronous *lio_listio* that you should be aware of: the seek implied by the *aiocb*, and the read or write operation encoded in it, *still* happen atomically, just as if the I/O were being done asynchronously. In contrast, if you were to do a normal *lseek* and then a *read*, you have no way of ensuring that the file pointer for the file would be where you *lseek*ed: an asynchronous operation could jump in and muck up the seek pointer between the time of the call to *lseek* and the time of the call to *read*.

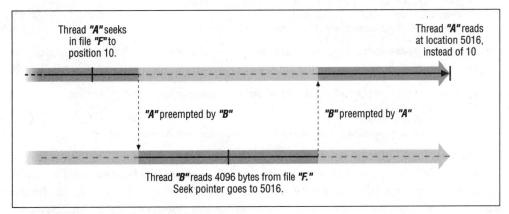

Thread *"A"* seeks in file *"F"* to position 10.

Thread *"A"* reads at location 5016, instead of 10

"A" preempted by *"B"*

"B" preempted by *"A"*

Thread *"B"* reads 4096 bytes from file *"F."* Seek pointer goes to 5016.

Figure 6–4. Race condition between seek and read/write

Thus, *lio_listio*, when called with LIO_WAIT and just a single *aiocb* on the list, provides a nice, atomic "seek-n-read" or "seek-n-write" facility that you can safely use for synchronous I/O even when asynchronous I/O is outstanding on the file descriptor.

Waiting for Asynchronous I/O: aio_suspend

Asynchronous I/O is usually used to allow I/O and processing to overlap. When all the processing has been done, the I/O itself may not be completed yet. If that I/O is a read, then data you are waiting for is not yet present; you have no choice but to wait for it. Or, in the case of asynchronous writes, if your application is in the form of an infinitely-repeating loop (and many real-time applications take this form), you will need some way to ensure that you do not soak the system with I/O requests by submitting them faster than they can be processed. In the data logger example, we used *sigsuspend* to wait for AIO to complete. However, *sigsuspend* tends to be a bit inefficient and imprecise. It's inefficient because it requires a signal to be delivered, the handler to be invoked, and for the handler to return before *sigsuspend* returns. It's imprecise because you cannot wait for a *particular* operation to complete: you are waiting for any occurrence of the signal.

This is why there is an operation called *aio_suspend*. This function allows you to wait for particular asynchronous I/O operations to complete. Here's how it's used:

```
int return_val, i;
struct aiocb *acb_list[XXX];
struct timespec timeout;
int nent;

/* Wait for one of a number of asynchronous operations to finish */
/* nent must be < XXX (see above)! */
return_val = aio_suspend(acb_list, nent, &timeout);
```

For instance, in the data logging example, we could wait for one of the buffers to complete by the following:

```
/* Wait for buflist[i] AIO to complete using aio_suspend */
struct aiocb *p[1];
p[0] = &buflist[i].acb;
return_val = aio_suspend(p, 1, NULL);    /* Wait forever if necessary */
```

aio_suspend takes a list of pointers to *aiocb* structures, like *lio_listio*. The second argument gives the number of elements in the list. *aio_suspend* blocks until one (or more) of the asynchronous I/Os on the list has completed. Obviously, the *aiocbs* on the list must have been used for submitting asynchronous I/O operations, either via *aio_read*, *aio_write*, or *lio_listio*. Elements in the array can be NULL; these elements are just skipped. Finally, a *timeout* argument is provided so that the operation will not wait indefinitely for I/O that may never finish.

aio_suspend does not tell you which I/O completed; it just returns 0 when it has determined that one of the asynchronous operations has finished. You must then go down the list with *aio_error* and *aio_return* to determine which request completed and whether it succeeded. In the data logger example, of course, that would be pretty easy.

If we call *sigsuspend* and there are no signals to be delivered, we're just going to hang. With *aio_suspend*, on the other hand, the system determines whether the particular AIO operations are still in progress. For instance, if *buflist[i]* had already been successfully written and the signal delivered, the *aio_suspend* would immediately return. The *sigsuspend*-based code, on the other hand, would have hung.

The final argument to *aio_suspend* is a pointer to a *struct timespec*. This argument, if you specify it, dictates a maximum time limit on how long the function should block awaiting I/O completion. If you suspect you may have a file that will not respond (one end of a pipe, or a network connection, for instance), it may be wise to set a timeout to catch errors. For disk writes, this is not generally necessary, so you can just pass a NULL.

There is an interesting facet of *aio_suspend* which you should be aware of. Like many blocking POSIX functions, *aio_suspend* can be interrupted by a signal. In that case, the *aio_suspend* function would return –1 and have *errno* set to EINTR. Remember, though, that each asynchronous operation may deliver a signal when it completes. Thus, the signal that interrupts *aio_suspend* may come from one of the awaited asynchronous I/Os completing!

Trying to Cancel Asynchronous I/O

aio_cancel is supposed to cancel asynchronous operations—that is, prevent the operation from taking place, if it isn't already too late. Let's be right up front about cancelling I/O. You should not use *aio_cancel* if you can avoid it, because it doesn't necessarily cancel I/O, even if it says it did! If you need to use it, here's how:

```
#include          <aio.h>
int rv;
struct aiocb acb;

/* Initialize aiocb */

/* Submit AIO */
rv = aio_read(&acb);     /* Or aio_write */
/* Change your mind--cancel the I/O if you can! */
rv = aio_cancel(acb.aio_fildes, &acb);
```

There may come a time when you decide that you should not have a certain asynchronous I/O going on, or that some I/O is no longer necessary. You may want to close a file and cancel all the outstanding requests pending against that file. Or you may start an asynchronous read on a network socket or a terminal where there is no one on the other end to reply. The *aio_cancel* function attempts to cancel such I/O. By specifying the number of an open file descriptor in *fd*, and leaving the *aiocb* pointer NULL, you can tell *aio_cancel* to try to cancel all outstanding I/O against that particular file descriptor. If the *aiocb* address is *not* NULL, then *aio_cancel* tries to cancel just that asynchronous operation. In that case, the *fd* argument to *aio_cancel* has to be the same as the file descriptor in the *aiocb* you've pointed to. Otherwise, unspecified things may happen: maybe an error, maybe it's okay, maybe the system crashes.

Successfully cancelled asynchronous I/O will have its error status set to ECANCELED. If *aio_cancel* successfully cancels all of the requested asynchronous operations, it returns AIO_CANCELED. Otherwise, it returns AIO_NOTCANCELED if it could not cancel one or more of the operations, and AIO_ALLDONE if all the operations specified were already done when *aio_cancel* got to them.

Why do I think *aio_cancel* is such an evil function? Two reasons. First, it is up to the vendor to decide which I/O is cancellable and which is not. It is a perfectly-valid implementation to never cancel any asynchronous I/O (i.e., only return AIO_ALLDONE or AIO_NOTCANCELED). Second, the meaning of "cancellation" may not be what you expect. Your first thought might be that a cancelled I/O operation does not do any I/O. But consider an I/O to or from a terminal or a pipe, an I/O that had half the data it wanted before being cancelled. What's it going to do with the data, put it back? Unlikely. In most cases, it'll probably just quit with the data it has already read or written. And it gets worse, because "cancelled" I/O has to have an error status of ECANCELED and a return value of –1, you cannot determine whether I/O you cancelled had any partial effects or not. All you really know about a cancelled I/O is that it's going to terminate. You don't know when, really, or how, or what the result of that termination will be. Given these possibilities (coupled with the fact that *aio_cancel* is really a vicious and bug-prone function to implement), it seems that there is little way to use *aio_cancel* in a portable fashion.

There are other places where AIO cancellation may occur, but these occasions are less noxious. If your process exits, or calls one of the *exec* functions, then any outstanding asynchronous I/O that is cancellable will be cancelled. Again, the vendor gets to say which asynchronous I/O is cancellable. However, it is less likely that your application will need to rely on this behavior.

More About Seeking

Why must you manage the seek pointer yourself? Why didn't the POSIX.4 group specify that the system must maintain the sanity of the seek pointer for you? An example will help make it more clear.

Pretend that AIO does nothing with the seek pointer. It merely uses the value that happens to be there with the file, and then it updates it, just like a normal I/O operation would.

Say you have an application, a database sort of application, where a single database file is written and read in fixed-size records at fixed places. Because your application is serving many users at the same time, you want to use asynchronous reads and writes to operate on the file. Because the AIO in this example does not do anything with the seek pointer, the application must first do a seek to the appropriate record, then perform the asynchronous operation, requiring two separate system calls. Now imagine two users, Pete and Dick. Pete wants to read record 17. Dick wants to write record 247. They both want to do it at the same time, so there are two asynchronous I/O operations in the system, one to read at offset 17, one to write at offset 247. As far as the application knows, both I/Os are proceeding at the same time. So where is the seek pointer? It really is rather indeterminate, depending on who got there first, Dick or Pete. After both operations, the file pointer will be at record 18 or at record 248, but the application has no idea which record it is at! Worse yet, the application could easily write incorrect data if one of the operations is interrupted midstream by the other. This possibility is illustrated by Figure 6-4, earlier.

In this scenario, Pete's file pointer value gets tromped on because the system context switched to Dick at an inopportune moment. To get around this possibility, we would have to perform file locking and unlocking. So, each operation our application made would look like Figure 6-5.

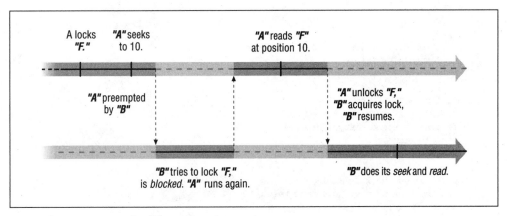

Figure 6–5. Preventing bad things from happening

This requires four system calls—an untoward number since all we really want to do is protect the atomicity of a seek and an I/O. And if all our I/O operations look like the example above, we are maintaining the seek pointer ourselves anyway! By passing in the file pointer at the time of the AIO submission, we can let the system perform the atomic seek-n-I/O much more quickly than we, as users, could hope to do it.

Gotchas

Asynchronous I/O is a different sort of creature in a UNIX system: it causes something to go off in parallel and do something. This "something," whatever it is, affects the state of the process *while the process is otherwise engaged,* and that is important to remember. Because of this parallelism, there are some gotchas you should be aware of when you use asynchronous I/O.

Mixing asynchronous and synchronous I/O

Using the "normal" *read* and *write* functions on a file descriptor is dangerous when you are also doing asynchronous I/O on that same file descriptor. If any asynchronous I/O is outstanding when you perform a normal *read* or *write,* you do not know where the seek pointer is going to be. If you absolutely have to mix asynchronous and synchronous I/O on the same descriptor, you must wait until all asynchronous I/O has completed before you submit a synchronous operation—and you must perform a seek to set the file pointer to a defined value before you do the *read*! Moreover, you must use SEEK_SET or SEEK_END to set the pointer. Doing a relative seek is meaningless because you do not know where the seek pointer already is; after moving it forward or ahead, you still won't know where it is. One safe way to combine synchronous and asynchronous I/O is to separate them clearly into different phases of an application:

```
/* Phase 1:  doing AIO */
/* AIO operations submitted */
aio_read(&a1);
```

```
aio_read(&a2);
aio_write(&a3);
aio_write(&a4);
/* Wait for all AIO operations to complete */
list_of_aios[0] = &a1;
list_of_aios[1] = &a2;
list_of_aios[2] = &a3;
list_of_aios[3] = &a4;
errno = 0;                    /* Yicch */
while ((aio_suspend(list_of_aios, 4) >= 0) &&
        (! errno))
            ;

/* Phase 2:  doing Regular I/O */
/* Set the seek pointer to a sane value */
lseek(fd, OFFSET, SEEK_SET);
/* Read synchronously */
read(fd, buf, nbytes);
```

Of course, doing things this way eliminates one possible advantage of asynchronous I/O. The asynchronous and synchronous I/O cannot be overlapped! If you really want to mix synchronous and asynchronous I/O to the same file, I suggest you use one file descriptor for asynchronous I/O, and an entirely separate descriptor (created using *dup* or *dup2*) for the normal *read*s and *write*s. This solution can be implemented like this:

```
fd_for_asynch_io = open(filename, flags, mode);
fd_for_synch_io = dup(fd_for_asynch_io);
/*
 * Both file descriptors access the same file, but
 * maintain different seek pointers.
 */
```

Each file descriptor is little more than a cache for a separate file descriptor. So long as you have enough file descriptors (and most systems today give you plenty), this is a fine solution to the problem of mixing synchronous and asynchronous I/O to the same file.

Re-use of the AIO control block

There is a simple line in the POSIX standards that you should be aware of: "Simultaneous asynchronous operations using the same *aiocb* produce undefined results". That translates to, "don't, don't, don't, don't even *think* about re-using an *aiocb* before the I/O it was last used for has completed." For instance, notice that our data logging example has a dedicated *aiocb* for each buffer that may be written, so there is *no way* we can use an *aiocb* twice.[*] This particular error can have devastating results because there are two quite divergent ways the operating system might use the *aiocb*. On one machine, the *aiocb* may be used only when asynchronous I/O is submitted. On that machine, *aiocb* reuse may be just fine. On other machines, though, the system may

---

[*] I know...never say never! The error would have to be *really stupid,* though.

use the *aiocb* for various reasons while the I/O progresses. For instance, we mentioned above that some systems will store the *errno* value and return value for asynchronous I/O inside the *aiocb*. If you reuse an *aiocb* on such a machine, what happens? Well, for one, your return and error values for *both* operations probably get messed up, along with your program logic that relied on them. Worse, if the pointers in the *aiocb* are re-initialized, your application might get killed; this is a common cause of bugs in applications on LynxOS, for instance. Remember. Don't don't don't don't don't even *think* about it.

AIO without the POSIX.4 extended signals

Asynchronous I/O is supported independently of the POSIX.4 extended signals. That means you can send yourself one of the normal POSIX signals if your system does not support the real-time signals. In that case, of course, you will not get the benefits of the signal being queued to you, and you will not get the additional data parameter that extended signals pass to the signal-handling function. In such a case, your signal handler will need some way to determine which asynchronous I/O, if any, completed. *aio_suspend* can be used for this purpose.

AIO without signals at all

You don't *need* to send a signal when your asynchronous I/O is complete. If your application doesn't need to be informed immediately when asynchronous I/O is done, you can simply set the *aio_sigevent.sigev_notify* field to SIGEV_NONE and no signal will be delivered when your asynchronous I/O operation is complete. You can always use *aio_suspend* to wait for such asynchronous operations. In fact, that might be a more efficient solution for our data logger above. It could perform *aio_suspend* for completed AIOs, and do the necessary cleanup in mainline code, without the hassle of calling a signal handler.

What do you really get out of it?

Finally, many people may perceive the use of asynchronous I/O as a definite performance win. After all, the I/O is going on in parallel, right? Not necessarily. You have to remember that on a uniprocessor machine there is only one CPU, and it is being timesliced. The kernel mechanism, whatever it is, that processes your asynchronous I/O will have to take CPU time to do it. Even where there is another processor available to take care of the I/O (either a multiprocessor machine, or a DMA engine that can be left to do its thing), you will have to contend with the effects of cycle stealing as the I/O accesses the application's memory. In many cases there may be no advantage to asynchronous I/O at all. If you are running on a machine with a buffer cache, your I/O may just be copied into this cache and queued up for later flushing to the device (see the synchronized I/O facilities for more on this). In that case, all you are doing asynchronously is copying data from user space to kernel space. And that is going to occupy as much real time, on a uniprocessor, as it would to just do it synchronously with *read* or *write*.

The same sort of thought sometimes leads people to consider the use of threads to achieve more throughput in their applications. It only works out if one of the threads of computation spends most of its time blocked, so the other can go at full speed.

AIO's Effect on Other POSIX Operations

The possibility of asynchronous I/O complicates the semantics of other POSIX.1 functions, most notably *fork*, the *exit* functions, and the *exec* family. Most of the complication has to do with what happens to outstanding asynchronous I/O when the process wants to terminate or transform itself. You should be aware that the I/O may be cancelled if you call _exit or an *exec* before the I/O is completed. Your vendor's conformance document should tell you which, if any, I/O may be cancelled on *exit* or *exec*. You should expect to wait for any I/O that is not cancelled. This can cause an unexpected delay in your *exits* or *execs*, especially if you are exiting because there's something wrong with the file. Say, for example, you're doing an asynchronous read from a terminal. That requires someone to type something, right? The asynchronous I/O will not complete until someone types something. What if your application tries to exit, and then the user goes into cardiac arrest? Well, it's tough for the user, all right, but what about the real question: how is your application ever going to exit with this asynchronous I/O outstanding? If this is the situation you find yourself in, you'd better hope your system cancels asynchronous I/O to terminals. Alternatively, you can hope that the paramedics have the presence of mind to hit the return key so you can get on with your processing.

In the case of a *fork*, asynchronous I/O just proceeds in the parent. The child process should not expect any outstanding asynchronous I/O to cause signals or fill up its buffers.

How Asynchronous I/O Is Queued

When you submit an asynchronous operation, it is queued up in line with all the other I/O going out to the disk, or whatever I/O device is underlying the file you're using. Where do your asynchronous requests end up in line? Do they go to the head of the line or the end? The typical UNIX method of queueing would dictate that the system would stick the requests at the end of the line. But what if your request is the most important thing in the system, and this particular *write* request is, say, going to keep a nuclear reactor from blowing up? You don't want that process to have to wait for umpteen other requests to be processed. So it would make sense to put the asynchronous request at the head of the queue. Or it might make sense to put the request somewhere in the middle.

To provide this flexibility, many real-time operating systems can prioritize I/O requests relative to one another. Prioritization is a global and all-pervading concern. Many real-time application and operating system writers maintain that every queue in a real-time system should be a priority queue.

There was no clean and politically acceptable way to provide I/O prioritization in POSIX.4 for all I/O. However, since the asynchronous I/O interface was brand new and perceived as a "tack-on" interface to existing non-real-time UNIX, we were able to provide the ability to prioritize asynchronous I/O. As a result, you can prioritize your asynchronous I/O, but not I/O you do through the normal *read/write* interface. One hopes, though, that the queue in the operating system is a priority queue and your I/O will be done before some unimportant process's. If you are really serious about prioritized I/O, you need to ask your system vendor how the I/O queues work within the operating system.

When prioritized I/O is being used, I/O requests of a higher priority are serviced before requests of lower priority. However, prioritized I/O doesn't mean that I/O is always *completed* in strict priority order. Because of buffer caches and other indeterminacies of device access, a lower priority request might still get finished before a high-priority request. And if you make a low priority request on a fast disk, it will probably finish before a high-priority request on a slow device. These intricacies (the timing interactions of every queue and every possible device that may be attached to your system) are not documented in the POSIX conformance statement.

As a small security measure, a process is not able to submit I/O requests at a priority higher than its scheduling priority at the time of the call to submit the I/O.[*] Processes that are not using one of the defined real-time schedulers cannot do prioritized I/O at all. This restriction is enforced by the interpretation of the *aio_reqprio* field in the AIO control block. *aio_reqprio* does not indicate the requested I/O priority directly. Instead, it indicates how much *less* than your scheduling priority the I/O request is. For example, if your scheduling priority is 10 when you call *aio_write*, and you submit an asynchronous I/O at *aio_reqprio* 0, then the asynchronous I/O's priority is 10. If you submit another asynchronous I/O with an *aio_reqprio* of 3, then that asynchronous I/O's priority will be 7. (You are not allowed to set your I/O's priority higher than yours by passing in a negative *aio_reqprio*.) *aio_reqprio* is similar to the *nice* value found in standard UNIX systems: it works backwards. Perhaps it should have been called *aio_nice*.

It is unfortunate that *aio_reqprio* works backwards. However, the good news is that you usually want "your I/O" to be at the same priority as "you." So, one generally just sets *aio_reqprio* to 0 and that's it.

Asynchronous, Synchronized I/O: aio_fsync

The concepts of POSIX synchronized I/O and asynchronous I/O are orthogonal and can easily be combined, assuming that both _POSIX_SYNCHRONIZED_IO and _POSIX_ASYNCHRONOUS_IO options are present on your system and supported for the files you're interested in. By setting the O_DSYNC, O_SYNC, and O_RSYNC flags on a

---

[*] POSIX.4 doesn't explicitly say it, but I/O priority probably doesn't track process priority. If you submit prioritized I/O and then up your process priority, don't expect the I/O priority to follow.

file, you can cause any asynchronous, as well as synchronous, reads and writes to go directly through to disk. If you set one of these flags, the asynchronous I/O isn't considered complete until it finds its way out safely to disk. Once the data has been synchronized on disk, then the error status of the asynchronous operation will be set to a value other than EINPROGRESS, the return value will be set appropriately, and the signal, if any, will be generated.

There is even a special function to asynchronously synchronize a file's data, *aio_fsync*:

```
#include        <aio.h>
int return_val;
struct aiocb fsacb;

fsacb.aio_fildes = /* FD of interest */;
/* initialize aio_sigevent structure as desired--other fields are ignored */

return_val = aio_fsync(O_SYNC, &fsacb);
```

The *aio_fsync* call performs either an asynchronous *fsync*, or an asynchronous *fdatasync*. If the first argument is O_DSYNC, an *fdatasync* is performed; if it is O_SYNC, then a full *fsync* is performed (O_RSYNC is not supported by *aio_fsync*, which may have been an oversight). For this function, only the *aio_fildes* and *aio_sigevent* fields of the AIO control block are used; the rest are ignored since no seeking, (specific) writing, or reading takes place in this operation. This asynchronous operation is pretty much like any other: you can use *aio_return* and *aio_error* to see how the operation did, *aio_suspend* to wait for it, and *aio_cancel* to try and cancel it.

One unexpected aspect of *aio_fsync* is that it is only required to synchronize I/O operations that were present when it was called. Subsequent I/Os made to the same file may not be synchronized.

An example will help here. Say you have 10 asynchronous writes to a particular file, and the results of those writes are now lying around in the buffer cache waiting to go out to disk. You call *aio_fsync(O_SYNC, ...)* to flush these operations out. What probably happens in the operating system is that a separate thread of control takes these 10 operations off the buffer queue, and then flushes each of them out to disk in turn. In the meantime, you may have submitted another asynchronous write to the same file. That I/O will go to the buffer cache and be flushed eventually. But the *aio_fsync* thread has already inspected the buffer cache and decided which I/O is to go immediately out to disk. It's not going to check again. And even if it did, you can have the same problem by just submitting a twelfth asynchronous write, right after the *aio_fsync* checks the buffer cache the second time. You see the problem?

Deterministic I/O

So far in this chapter we've covered two enhancements to standard UNIX I/O. Synchronized I/O lets you be sure that data is actually stored somewhere safe, a useful property for systems that live in dangerous environments where they may go down at any moment. Asynchronous I/O allows you, conceptually at least, to overlap I/O operations and application processing. Another important enhancement would be control over how long I/O is going to take. In many instances, the application wants the I/O to proceed as fast as possible (who doesn't?). In most instances, though, the application needs to know how long I/O is going to take. In other words, real-time applications often want I/O times to be *deterministic.*

Usually, the applications that want deterministic I/O times are multimedia and data-acquisition applications. In these, you presumably have a prodigious amount of data arriving or departing at all times. This data has to be shunted out the other end of the application to disk, tape, speakers, MPEG decompressor, or whatever, on a tight time schedule because there's tons more data right behind it. Now, your basic SCSI disk is theoretically capable of transferring at least a megabyte or two per second out to disk. However, when you try to write your data to a file and keep up with, say, half a megabyte per second of incoming data, you may find you can't do it. Why not?

File Systems Don't Come for Free

One answer may lie in the file system you're using. Most file systems today are laid out as series of blocks. Files' data are stored in these blocks. One of the most important characteristics of a file system is how these blocks are allocated. Most file systems support dynamic file growth (in fact, they *must* support dynamic file growth in order to be POSIX-conformant). That means you can't just lay out a files' blocks all next to each other. You need the ability to allocate a new block, somewhere off at the other end of the disk perhaps, to support this dynamic growth. So, it's possible, even probable, that a normal file on your system may consist of blocks that are scattered all over a disk. This scattering causes tremendous slowdown in accessing a file's data, because the seek times on disks are several orders of magnitude slower than the data transfer rates. In short: you seek, you lose. Another problem lies in the dynamic block allocation that comes along with dynamic file extension. Whenever you increase a file's size, you may need to allocate a whole new block from the file system. That's a pause the operating system has to take while you're trying to write your data out. All things being equal, you'd probably rather that the operating system have allocated all the blocks of your file ahead of time, and not have to go through the extra work of dynamic block allocation in the middle of real-time.

In summary, real-time data logging requires a guarantee of sustained data throughput from the underlying system. There are two basic ways to achieve this sort of guarantee: the low-level way, and the high-level way. Both ways have their pluses and minuses.

Low Level: Abusing the File System

In the abstract, a file system can be defined as a set of rules for how files should be laid out and accessed so as to maximally satisfy certain criteria: fairness, dynamic allocation, speed, lack of fragmentation, and so forth are all balanced in a particular file system. Some systems let you blow off these rules and tell the file system where you want your file, and how you want it laid out. In particular, most real-time operating systems provide the capability to create *contiguous files* in your file systems. These files are specially created so that all blocks of the file are laid one next to another. Implicit in this allocation scheme is that the file's blocks are pre-allocated when the file is created. When accessing such a file, you can then transfer data to or from the disk at the speed of the raw disk itself, at least theoretically. No seeking, no dynamic block allocation.

Advantages

Contiguous preallocation has a powerful advantage: it's simple. You know how much space you need, you allocate it.

Disadvantages

There are several disadvantages to this approach. First, it implies that your application will be the only one accessing this disk. If another process comes in and causes the data head to seek away from the blocks comprising your file, then you are still hit with a seek overhead.

Furthermore, contiguous layout may not be quite what you want. Contiguous layout is optimal if you are transferring data one file at a time, writing the whole file as fast as you possibly can. What if your application is only writing to the disk at *half* the speed of the underlying disk? In that case, you might want a file whose logical blocks were laid out every *other* physical disk block. Maybe what you want is the blocks of your file laid out every third block, or something like that. At the very best, you will need to tune your application to the underlying hardware. And remember that not all disks are created equal. If you replace the disk you've tuned your application to, your application may well fail because the new disk is either too fast or too slow!

Early drafts of the POSIX.4 standard contained a set of functions to create contiguous files. Because of the problems with using contiguous files, as well as disagreement on the characteristics of the interfaces themselves, these functions (the *real-time files* chapter of early drafts of POSIX.4) were removed, in favor of continuing work on another tack: using the file system rather than abusing it.

Using the File System

Another solution to this dilemma is to use the file system to your advantage. Most file systems come with tunable parameters you can either dynamically change or statically set when you create the file system. By varying these parameters, you may be able to achieve the sustained data rates you require.

Advantages

The file system is there for a reason: it's an abstraction mechanism that removes you a level from the hardware. In most cases, this is a good thing. You really do not want your application tied to the fact that you're operating on a particular sort of disk. Portability, remember? A more portable application will take advantage of the capabilities of the underlying systems it runs on to achieve its performance.

Disadvantages

Portability is a problem with this approach as well; there is no standard for file system parameters and file system tuning. Whether you use a file system or a raw disk, you still need to go through a non-portable configuration and tuning phase when getting your application up and running on a new system.

Even after tuning, you almost certainly cannot achieve a sustained data throughput close to the raw machine rates if you are using a file system, even a nice file system that really wants to be helpful to you. It's hard to ignore the fact that the underlying medium, the disk, has certain characteristics that affect how data transfer takes place. Usually a file system can provide only statistical guarantees of throughput. Such guarantees may or may not be sufficient for your application.

Abandoning the File System

A third approach is to abandon the file system altogether. Use a raw disk device and write your own, custom-tailored file handler for your application. Aim it at a disk that no one else is using, and file systems be damned! You're data-gatherin'.

Advantages

It's direct, I'll give it that! In fact, if you own up to the disadvantages in advance, this approach is a fairly good one. Think about it: no other users, no pesky operating system in the way, you tailor the I/O exactly as you want it. While you're at it, you can probably hack some device driver code to further optimize your data transfers if raw reads and writes are not sufficient to your purposes. Aside from driver hacking, your roll-your-own file system will be pretty portable, assuming that the underlying system gives you access to a raw device. Most systems do. This is the "Wild West" theory of application I/O handling, and it has its place.

Disadvantages

Complexity. File systems are hard. Before you try this approach, I'd exhaust the other two. Remember that this roll-your-own file system is another component of your application that will need to be debugged, documented, and maintained, not just designed and coded up.

Deterministic Drives?

Even with special application-specific file layouts, raw device access or sophisticated file systems, you may run into problems with the actual disks you're using. For instance, disk drives generally deal with bad sectors by pointing to a designated alternate sector. A read of block 10 may actually involve going to block 347, if physical block 10 happens to be bad on the disk! All drives have a small number of bad sectors which must be dealt with. Another problem that occurs regularly (every half hour or so in some drives) is that of thermal recalibration, which locks up the drive for several milliseconds while the drive adjusts itself to deal with the effects of thermal expansion. Some newer "multimedia" drives smooth out the thermal recalibration time by performing it on an on-going basis; however, multimedia drives are more expensive than standard hard drives. Finally, drives are often subject to "soft" errors which go away when the command is retried. This retry is automatic, but it takes more time than a normal operation that succeeds the first time through. Soft errors are known to be caused by neutrino bombardment and gremlins, neither of which you can do much about. No, but seriously: my own anecdotal experience suggests that a major cause of drive flakiness and poor performance is cable problems. Always check your drive cables, use high-quality cables, and don't use cables that are too long. Cables *matter*. Treat them as such.

Conclusion

Well! We now have the capabilities to write real-world applications performing I/O, time-based computations, coordinated with each other and nicely scheduled together. Is your operating system going to cut it, performance-wise? That's the subject of the final chapter.

Exercises

Here are some exercises to get you thinking about the various POSIX.4 real-time I/O facilities. The solutions to problems that require programming can be found in the Appendix, in the section listed in parentheses after each such problem.

Synchronized I/O

How much slower is a synchronized *write* than a non-synchronized *write*? Write a program that tells you. Use the POSIX real-time timer facilities (see Chapter 5, *On Time: Scheduling, Time, and Memory Locking*) to determine start and stop times. Alternatively, you could measure bytes written per second by using an interval timer (again, see Chapter 5). Check the time for data integrity completion (O_DSYNC), and for file integrity completion (O_SYNC). How different are they?

How much more predictable is synchronized *write* than non-synchronized *write*? You can determine this by running your program from up above numerous times. Or can you? Try it. Are the non-synchronized numbers varying? If not, why not? What can you do to make them vary?

It's pretty obvious what a synchronized *write* is: the data you write goes right out to disk, instead of sitting in the operating system's buffer cache. But what's involved in a synchronized *read*? Obviously, the data has to *be* there before the *read* call returns. Modify your benchmark program to do synchronized and non-synchronized reads for O_DSYNC|O_RSYNC and then for O_SYNC|O_RSYNC. What are the time differences?

Asynchronous I/O

Write two programs: one that uses *read* and *write* to copy its standard input to standard output, and one that copies its standard input to its standard output using asynchronous *read* and asynchronous *write*. By pointing these programs at various places on your machine, determine where asynchronous I/O offers a performance advantage. For each result, try to explain why there is, or is not, a performance advantage.

Modify your two programs to do synchronized I/O. How do your results change? Explain the change to your satisfaction. (*iopipe.c, aiopipe.c*)

What would you need to do to perform prioritized asynchronous I/O? Modify your asynchronous I/O program to accept "nice" values that you plug into *aio_reqprio*, so you can do asynchronous I/O at priorities other than your scheduling priority. By the way, what is your scheduling priority? What do you need to do to it to perform prioritized I/O? Run your modified program on devices that have a lot of I/O going on to them, by processes of priority equal to or less than your process. What is the difference in performance?

Disk Geometry

Say you wanted to lay out a file so you were absolutely sure it was contiguous, one block after another, on your disk. Come up with a few schemes for doing so. How do these schemes impact other users of your partition, disk, controller, data bus, or entire machine? Remember, the goal is to guarantee a certain level of I/O service at all times.

Say you wanted to pre-allocate a file so that there was no overhead for dynamic disk block allocation. How would you do so?

7

Performance, or How to Choose an Operating System

What I've covered in the last several chapters is only the functionality that is required for real-time applications. The other requirement is that all-consuming concern of real-time: performance.

Your application is going to require certain performance from the underlying system. Maybe you need a particularly fast piece of hardware: a big array processor or the latest RISC chip. Maybe, on the other hand, your hardware is already sufficient for your application, and all you need is software performance.

Those are *your* requirements. Now look at what your OS vendor has supplied. Maybe it performs, and maybe it doesn't. On the one hand, some companies have enough trouble getting software out the door that works at all. There's often no time or engineer bandwidth to pay attention to software performance. On the other hand, there are some companies that are able to spend the time tuning their software so it will give the performance you need. Given the differences between various software development efforts, you need to evaluate the performance of different software systems you may want to use for your application.

There are known, accepted metrics for hardware performance. There are few for software, and none, really, for real-time software.[*] The 1003.4 working group began work on a set of metrics that might have provided a standard measure of a system's real-time performance. These metrics were available in early drafts of POSIX.4, and can still be found in the Appendix of later drafts. Unfortunately, this effort was ruled to be out of bounds, beyond the charter of the 1003.4 working group. As a result, there are no standard performance metrics. I hope to make up for that lack in this chapter.

---

[*] One exception is the "Rhealstone" benchmark, which measures performance of certain common real-time facilities, like semaphores. However, Rhealstone is not a complete performance indicator, and seems to have fallen out of favor recently.

Unfortunately, this chapter points out that there is no standard way of measuring performance. You'll have to rely on your own wits to compare the performance of different operating systems. I hope that I've pointed out *what* the important measurements are; you'll have to make those measurements on your own. Performance measurement is a science unto itself, and many books have been written on the topic. I like Raj Jain's *The Art of Computer Systems Performance Analysis* (John Wiley and Sons, 1991).

Performance in Real-Time Systems

There are a couple of varieties of performance. The first, most commonly-used variety is throughput: how fast can I do operation X (alternatively, how many X's a second can I do)? This is the sort of performance that is most important for non-real-time systems. It is also important in real-time. However, there is a second variety of performance that is at least as important to real-time systems: the responsiveness of the system (how quickly the system responds to some input). Third, the determinism of the system is important. Determinism tells you how reliable your performance is; i.e., whether performance varies under heavy load. Finally, the space consumed by your system may be important to you. Bytes used by the operating system are not available to the application, and you may have a limited memory budget to contend with.

Throughput

Throughput is usually measured in number of operations per second: MIPS (Millions of Instructions Per Second), bytes per second, number of signals you can send in a second. Alternatively, you could talk in terms of the time taken for a single operation: 10 microseconds for a call to *getpid*. There's a subtle difference between the time taken for one operation and the time taken for many, though. If an operation requires several resources, then it may be possible to *pipeline* the operations together to obtain higher throughput. For instance, if an operation requires a computation followed by a disk write, then you can probably batch many disk operations together and perform them while yet more operations are busy computing. Furthermore, when you talk in terms of the number of operations per second, larger numbers imply better performance.

Responsiveness

Responsiveness means the speed with which the system responds to an event. An example from the timesharing world is the responsiveness of the system to your keystrokes. In real-time systems, we normally talk about response to interrupts, since all asynchronous events (disk I/O, device readiness, clock-based rescheduling, even keystrokes) in the system are implemented using interrupts.

The essence of performance measurement is deciding what you are going to measure. When it comes to responsiveness, different folks measure different things, usually according to which measurement presents their product in the best light. The most common measurements include:

- **Interrupt Latency**: The amount of time it takes your system to get to the first instruction of an interrupt routine in response to a particular interrupt.

- **Dispatch Latency**: The interval of time from the last instruction of your interrupt handler until the first instruction is executed in the process which this interrupt caused to become runnable.

- **Context Switch Time**: The time it takes the operating system to switch from one process to another.

There are a multitude of other measurements, and different people mean different things when they use a particular term—trying to compare different vendors' claims is a mess. A picture of what goes on during a response will help you understand what the various components of responsiveness are. Figure 7-1 outlines what happens when an interrupt occurs in a real-time system:

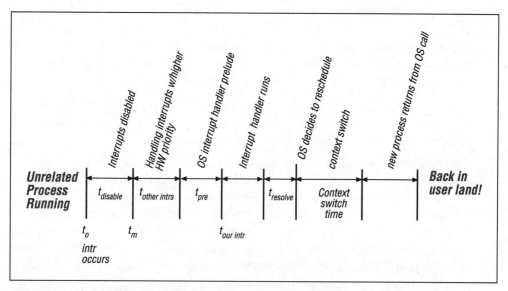

Figure 7–1. The computer responds

1. **The Interrupt Occurs.** At time t_0 an interrupt occurs. This causes the system to stop what it's doing and start running the operating system's interrupt-processing prelude code. This sequence eventually results in a call to the interrupt handler itself.

2. **Possible Delay for "Interrupts Disabled" Time.** Although interrupt processing usually begins immediately, the operating system sometimes blocks interrupts for (hopefully) short periods of time ($t_{disable}$). Interrupts are blocked when the operating system is modifying data structures that may be touched by interrupt routines

themselves. This *interrupts disabled time* will delay the handling of any interrupt that occurs during that time.

3. **Possible Delay for Other Interrupts**. A computer system normally fields several different sorts of interrupts. These are not allowed to arrive willy-nilly on top of one another; rather, the hardware will block out the delivery of other interrupts while one interrupt is being handled. Some systems block *all* further interrupts while handling any interrupt; others only block interrupts of equal or lower priority.[*] As a result, other interrupts can delay the servicing of your interrupt. Usually, any interrupt at a higher priority than yours will be able to delay your interrupt servicing. This time interval is denoted by $t_{other\ intrs}$.

4. **Operating System Interrupt Prelude**. Before an interrupt handler can run, the system must generally do some bookkeeping—among other things, saving the state of the processor at the time the interrupt arrived. This is identified by t_{pre}.

5. **The Interrupt Routine Is Called**. Finally, at time $t_{our\ intr}$ the operating system calls the interrupt handler itself.

6. **Your Interrupt Handler Runs**. This is the amount of time it takes your interrupt handler to run. Remember, if you're writing driver code as part of your application, your interrupts may delay the processing of other, lower-priority interrupts; for overall system performance, it's important for your handler to do what needs to be done and get out of the way as quickly as possible.

   For the purpose of this timeline, imagine that this interrupt not only causes your interrupt handler to run, but also results in your process becoming runnable. This assumption enables the rest of the timeline, below.

7. **The Operating System Decides to Reschedule**. After your interrupt has been successfully handled, the operating system takes some time to decide that it needs to reschedule your process. We are assuming that your process is the highest-priority runnable process; the time taken in this region is simply the amount of time for the operating system to perform the inevitable rescheduling. On a true real-time kernel, rescheduling will be nearly instantaneous; non-real-time systems may take milliseconds in here. This time is denoted by $t_{resolve}$.

8. **The Operating System Switches Contexts**. Once the OS has decided to reschedule, it goes through a small section of code where it switches context to the new process. This code merely sets up memory and registers for the new process.

9. **The New Process Returns from the Operating System**. Presumably, the process we've just switched to was blocked in a system call waiting for an interrupt to arrive. Now that the interrupt has arrived, the process must return out of the operating system to get back to user code.

---

[*] Interrupt Priority is a property of the hardware platform, and is not usually related to your application scheduling priorities. Hardware supports interrupts at different levels to provide timely response to the most urgent interrupts. Even if your hardware prioritizes interrupts, your operating system software may block all interrupts, just to make things simpler for itself.

10. **Back in User Mode**. Finally, our process is back in user application code!

As you can see, a great deal of processing goes on "under the hood" of a real-time operating system when interrupts come in. It's not surprising that few operating systems are really able to combine full POSIX conformance with real-time responsiveness.

When a vendor talks about interrupt latency, they are talking about the amount of time from t_0 to $t_{our\ intr}$. However, the vendor may be excluding the possibility of other interrupts, $t_{other\ intrs}$. Vendors often discuss their performance figures "in the absence of other devices," or some such nonsense—as if an application doing I/O will be able to dispense with interrupts! It is important that your performance evaluation include the specific machine configuration—both hardware *and* software—you'll be using. The particular device configuration makes a great difference in performance. Not all SCSI disks are created equally; nor are all motherboards or RAM chips. And interrupt handler times, of course, are dependent on the actual device driver you're using.

It is also possible that a vendor will not mention the interrupt disable time, $t_{disable}$. For instance, a vendor quoting average interrupt latency is implicitly discounting the interrupt disable time, which rarely gets in the way.

Similarly, vendors may discuss the average dispatch latency, which discounts the possibility of the operating system taking a long time to decide to reschedule. Depending on what the operating system was doing when your interrupt comes in, it may take longer to reschedule.

Take care with statements about context switch time. The biggest problem here is that you can find yourself comparing apples and oranges. Some vendors refer to the context switch time as the time interval I described above. However, an equal number call the *entire* interval, from one process stopping to handle an interrupt until the next process runs, as "context switch time." Obviously you cannot just compare the claims of vendors from both camps—you'll be comparing totally different measurements!

Context switch time numbers *can* give you a feel for the "heaviness" of the operating system. A long context switch time indicates a really heavy, slow operating system that may spend too much time in the mechanics of getting from one process to the next. This might be a problem if your application is composed of many processes that switch amongst each other a lot.

On the other hand, for *my* definition of context switch time, it is a small, almost meaningless component of responsiveness in all but the most trivial systems. So much software surrounds the context switch that its contribution to response is minimal.

Nevertheless, you'll hear figures for both sorts of context switching quoted all the time. That's because context switch time is easy to measure, and is usually a nice-sounding small number. I find that real measures of responsiveness are usually much more terrifying!

Lazy context switching

One fact about context switching needs to be mentioned. Today's processors feature more and more hardware context to be switched: huge numbers of registers, monstrous floating point and graphics pipelines, and so forth. Switching all that context generally takes much more time than a vendor is comfortable spending in context switch code. And honestly, many times you don't *need* to switch your floating point or graphics context, because only one process on your machine is *using* that particular, specialized part of the machine.

Modern software and hardware support so-called "lazy context switching." In a lazy context switch, the operating system simply marks a particular piece of context as "off limits," unavailable for use, when switching from the old to the new process. If the new process attempts to use the marked-off context, the system generally takes a trap, at which point that piece of context can be switched. The advantage, of course, is that you often never get that trap and never have to switch your extra context. Almost all processors support this sort of behavior, including the 80×86, SPARC, and MIPS chips.

From a software performance perspective, the problem with lazy context switching is that you normally don't see that part of the context switch in your performance numbers. For example, vendors can easily rig the benchmarks so that the floating point unit is not used. Watch out! Make sure your context switch time includes switching *all* the context you care about!

Caches

Lazy context switching is explicit: you're either switching the graphics pipeline context, or you're not. There is a more insidious detail of context switching that is very hard to identify and measure. Processor memory caches and MMU caches (Translation Lookaside Buffers, or TLBs) are supported directly by hardware, in most cases, and are lazily switched, their contents swapped around as memory accesses dictate.

The purpose of these hardware caches is to speed throughput of your computations, by caching frequently-used data. However, it takes time to fill the caches (*cache miss time*). When switching contexts, the new process generally needs to fault in several chunks of cache data, and that takes time. Code that just happens to access memory the wrong way can experience slowdowns of as much as three times.[*] So what can you do about this sort of performance degradation? Probably nothing, except pray and program your application to deal with the worst case. Some processors allow you to lock certain cache lines down, which can be useful *if* you can lay out your code so that the right code hits the locked cache lines, and *if* your operating system supports the cache-locking functionality. This is a very dicey proposition, though, and you're more than likely to mess it up. Remember, caches are there for a reason, and the vast

---

[*] I got the number "three" from a presentation by Phil Koopman at the October, 1993 Embedded Systems Conference, entitled "Hidden Horrors of Cached CPUs." He got his results on an Intel 80486. Mitch Bunnell at Lynx Real-Time Systems has found performance to suffer by as much as 10 times on machines with software-loaded TLBs, such as the MIPS R4000.

majority of the time they are going to make your code go faster. If you start telling the cache how to do its job, it may just quit on you!

Determinism

We've touched on determinism earlier, but it deserves its own discussion because it is so critical a topic. Determinism means how much you can *count* on your system to be responsive. In the discussion above, it's implicit that your process is the highest priority runnable process in the system, that its memory is locked down, and that in general, *all* it needs to run is that interrupt. However, that's not the real world: there are other processes, other demands on memory and I/O, etc. In a real real-time system, you should be able to count on a certain worst-case responsiveness for that process, *no matter what else is going on in the system!* That means that your application responds to changing conditions within a certain time, no matter how many other processes are running, what kernel code they're exercising, or how badly they're paging to and from disk.

It means that you get a certain level of responsiveness even when there are multiple, unrelated interrupting devices. You should be able to bang on a SCSI disk, on an Ethernet, and on a keyboard and *still* your highest-priority process should just keep on ticking without violating this worst case. In a true real-time system, all those other activities are done later, after the high-priority real-time job is finished.

Determinism is a hard quantity to measure, but there are mechanisms you can use to get a better feel for how deterministic your system is. You can set up a system where interrupts are periodically generated, and you have a process rigged to respond to that interrupt. By measuring the interval of time between interrupt occurrence and process response, you get an idea of the response time of the system. When you run the same experiment continuously, while bashing the system with other workloads, you will soon see whether the interrupt *always* provokes the same timely response. We'll talk some more about this sort of experiment below. It should be mentioned here, though, that such experiments are not foolproof. You're basically trying to hit the system with everything you've got to make it *not* respond well. Say the system never misses a beat, never responds late, seems fine. All you know is that the particular workload you've used does not slow the responsiveness down. Maybe some other workload does. What's really needed is a detailed analysis of the entire operating system to find the worst combinations of code sections, but you're not likely to get such an analysis. Pragmatically, an operating system is too complex to be analyzed in this sort of detail. On the other hand, you *are* going to run the system under particular workloads, which you *can* test.

Time versus Space

Throughput, responsiveness and determinism all refer to the time-performance of your system. Another axis of the performance graph is space-performance: how much memory your system occupies.

It's been said that you can decrease the time performance of any system by increasing its memory consumption, and vice versa. That's probably true, but only if you have the option of rewriting all the software, including the operating system. When it comes to space performance, your options really revolve around how easily you can tailor your operating system to your needs. If there's code you're not using, can you configure it out? If data structures are bigger than you need them, can you decrease their size?

Space-performance is not really something that the POSIX standards address at all. You want to look for configurability: the ability to remove unnecessary parts of your operating system. Some systems allow you to remove just about everything; others are much less flexible. A microkernel architecture generally allows for major parts of an operating system to be taken out if not necessary. So does a careful operating system code organization, even of a monolithic kernel. What's really required is that the operating system vendor have done the necessary work to allow major portions of the system to be removed. You might want to experiment with the smallest and largest operating system you can build for a given system, just to get a rough idea of how configurable the system is. System configuration and configurability is a topic unto itself, which I'm not going to discuss here.

Measuring the Right Thing

The most important aspect of determining the performance of a system is setting your own goals for performance. No single metric applies to all applications; the system that is speediest for one particular application (throughput-oriented supercomputer-level number crunching, say) may be utterly incompetent on some other application (hard real-time process control, for example). More importantly, you will evaluate the system differently depending on what you need the system to do. For the first, compute-bound application, you might look at Dhrystones and SPECmarks. Such metrics would be inappropriate for the second, real-time application because they don't measure the real-time aspects of performance that you care about! You might want to use them, on the other hand, to get a feel for the computation component of your real-time application.

Above, I've grouped performance considerations into four areas: throughput (or bandwidth), responsiveness (transaction rate), determinism (worst-case transaction rate), and space. In each area, you want to set out your requirements for the system. Once you have these goals written down, you'll probably find it easier to evaluate the performance of candidate real-time operating systems. Some sample applications you can run, and their performance requirements, will help you to evaluate systems.

The Important Factors for Hard Real-Time: Determinism and Responsiveness

In many systems, especially hard real-time systems, a process that is late may as well have never run at all. *Determinism* and *responsiveness* are the critical goals. This is not to say throughput is unimportant; it's very important, but the performance question is often binary. If the system is fast enough to meet all its deadlines *all the time*, then additional speed is irrelevant. But you'd better know how fast is "fast enough" because if the system misses a deadline, something very bad will happen. This requires knowledge of your task set, deadlines and periods for those tasks, amount of compute time allotted to each task, and so on. You need to perform detailed task analysis before you know what speed you need. Do the analysis before you evaluate the systems that may support your application.

Important Factors for Soft Real-Time: Throughput

In non-real-time and soft real-time applications, by contrast, *throughput* gains more visibility than in hard real-time. That's because better throughput means a better soft- or non-real-time application. The faster the application runs, the better.

When measuring throughput, keep in mind that some measurements are important, while others are not. The important operations are the ones that have to go fast. These are, in general, the operations that your application uses when it's running. If interprocess communication and data logging occur while your application is running, their speed will contribute directly to the overall throughput of your application; you'd like these operations to be as fast as possible. In contrast, start-up activities, like initializing all your processes and IPC, opening files, etc., are not time-critical, since they only happen once. Therefore, you'd test message *passing* speed very carefully, but you might not care about the time taken to *set up* a message queue.

Another Important Factor: Space

In either sort of application, there are probably space considerations. In standard paging, swapping UNIX environments, one tends to forget that physical memory is required for running processes. One tends to accept executables and operating systems that require multiple megabytes. Even if you're working with a real-time OS that supports paging and swapping, its performance will be crippled by these features, so you want to be sure the necessary parts of the OS and the application will fit into physical memory. If you're working on an embedded system, the requirements are even stricter: there probably isn't any virtual memory, so the entire OS and your application must all fit into a limited amount of real memory. This sort of metric is pretty easy once you know what your space budget is. You need to identify what functionality you need in the OS, how small an OS can supply that functionality, and then the decision is simple. A given OS is either small enough, or not.

Metrics for POSIX Systems

Below are a set of metrics you might ask for in order to get a picture of the performance characteristics of your operating system. Most of these measurements are throughput-oriented; however, the important metrics of interrupt and dispatch latency are also mentioned in the subsection on process scheduling. Responsiveness and determinism can't be measured in a portable way. You need to get down to the level of the hardware, because you're talking about interrupts and responses to them. We'll talk a little bit about measuring responsiveness and determinism at the end of this section.

Process Primitives

The basic POSIX process operations, *fork, exec, exit,* and *wait,* are called "process primitives." The speed with which you can create and terminate processes is not usually time-critical, since it's not something you generally do in the middle of real-time operations. The process primitives are usually used at the beginning or end of a real-time application, at start-up or tear-down of the application. As such, you're not usually concerned with the time taken to *fork, exec, exit,* or *wait.* You *are* concerned with context switch times, and the speed with which your multiple processes can communicate and coordinate. These facilities *will* need to be measured.

Signals

The performance of signals is very important—if your application uses signals (some applications don't). Obviously, the speed with which a signal can be delivered and handled is key; it is also important to be able to manipulate your signal masks quickly, since very often you'll find yourself disabling signals for small sections of code that are better left uninterrupted. Here are some critical parameters to look for:

sigprocmask(SIG_BLOCK)
The amount of time required to block signal delivery using *sigaction.*

sigprocmask(SIG_UNBLOCK)—no pending signal
The amount of time required to unblock signal delivery using *sigaction,* assuming that when you unblock the signal, there is no signal pending.

sigprocmask(SIG_UNBLOCK)—pending signal
This metric tells you the amount of time it takes you to get into your signal handler, assuming that a signal is pending when you unblock the signal. In this case, you should find yourself instantaneously in the signal handler.

sigaction

This is the amount of time it takes to modify a signal handler using *sigaction*. Usually, setting up handlers is an application start-up activity, and is therefore not time-critical. That's not always the case, however.

Signal delivery time

Here is the central metric for signals: how long does it take to get a signal sent from one process to another? You can use several subsidiary measurements to get a clearer picture of this time:

- **Signal Sent to Yourself.** Send yourself a signal and determine how long that takes. You can try two variants: First, send yourself the signal, but have it blocked. This gives you the time component without actually dispatching to handle the signal. Then, send yourself the signal without having it blocked, so you handle the signal each time it comes in. The difference between the former and latter measurement will give you a picture of how long it takes your system to set up a signal handler dispatch for your system. (You can find code for these two suggestions in the Appendix, *Exercise Code*, in *sending_sigs_self.c* and *sending_recving_sigs_self.c*.)

- **Signal Sent to Other Process.** Send a signal to another process and determine how long that takes. The difference between the first measurement and this one will be the extra overhead required to cross the boundary between one process and another. Be sure that the signal sender is lower-priority than the signal receiver, so the receiver runs immediately upon getting the signal. This time includes the time for the sender to send the signal, as well as for the receiver to receive it. Again, you can measure this time in two separate measurements, by sending the signal to a process that has the signal blocked, and then sending the signal to a process that is ready, willing, and high-enough priority to handle it immediately. (Code for this can be found in *sigs_sent_swtch.c*.)

- **kill/sigqueue, no delivery involved.** Send a signal to a process that is lower-priority, or that has signals blocked. This exercise measures how long it takes to send a signal. Because the receiving process is blocked or low-priority, the signal is never delivered. Having isolated the time required to send a signal, you can separate the previous measurements into the sending and receiving portions of time. (Code for this can be found in *sending_sigs.c*.)

sigwaitinfo, signal pending

If a process waits for a signal with *sigwaitinfo*, and there's already a signal there, how long will the call take?

sigsuspend, signal pending

If a process waits for a signal with *sigsuspend*, and there's already a signal there, how long will the call take? Remember that this time includes the invocation of a signal handler and return from that handler.

Real- and non-real-time signals

Run the tests above for both SIGUSR1 and real-time (queued) signals like SIGRTMIN. The queued signals probably take a bit longer to send. On the other hand, they carry more data and are more reliable.

I/O

Measuring I/O performance is difficult because it depends on the underlying disk media and the layout of the particular files you're using, as well as the operating system implementation. Figure 7-2 shows a typical set of layers.

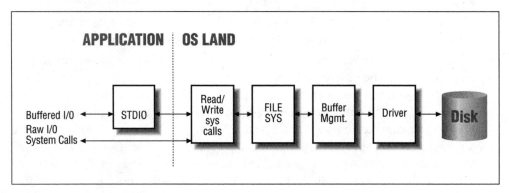

Figure 7–2. Layers of an I/O implementation

Depending on the test you run, you should be able to measure various components of the path data takes through the the operating system. When comparing I/O numbers, you must be sure to measure identical (or at least comparable) scenarios. This entails additional work beyond writing some portable POSIX code.

Before starting, you must know the characteristics of the disk media being used on each system. Determine the seek time, the transfer rate, the number of heads, cylinders, and sectors per track for each disk. You'll need to know whether the disk has a cache on it. If you're comparing systems that support SCSI disks, you should buy a reference disk that you can plug into the system you are measuring. That way, you know you're running your tests on the same disk.

Secondly, try to measure I/O performance without the file system, and with and without the buffer cache. For these tests, you'll need to access the disk directly (through the device files, if you're using a UNIX-like operating system).

Finally, to compare I/O through the file system (to normal disk files), you must be sure that the file systems start out in the same state of fragmentation. One way to ensure this is to run your tests on newly-created file systems. This isn't quite realistic, since fragmentation happens unavoidably over time; you'd be very puzzled if you built a real-time system that worked for a few months, but then started missing critical deadlines as disk performance degraded. If you're interested in the performance of the file system after time, you could take a new file system, abuse it in some reproducible way (by running a program that was known to create fragmentation, for instance), and then run your tests. Under no circumstances, though, can you point a file system benchmark at an existing, in-use file system and get meaningful results. You just don't know what the condition of that file system was before running your test.

Buffered and non-buffered I/O, no file system involvement

Using a block special file (these generally use the buffer cache of the system), test the performance of reads and writes for files for all values of the synchronized I/O flags: no flags, O_DSYNC, O_SYNC. Run the same test against the raw version of the same device.

File creation

On a clean file system, benchmark the performance of directory creation and file creation for files of various sizes. Test file creation with all the synchronized I/O flags: no flags, O_DSYNC, O_SYNC.

File read in synchronous, non-synchronous modes

After you have created all these files, sync the disks (most systems have a utility called *sync* which will do this, or you can use *fsync* on the files themselves) and then read the files with the synchronized I/O flags O_SYNC|O_RSYNC, and with no flags. This should give you a picture of the amount of time taken to update a disk node, since the O_RSYNC flag will cause the node to be updated. Non-synchronized *reads* will not be subject to this requirement.

File operations on contiguous files

If there is a way to do it, you might consider laying out a contiguous disk file and measuring the performance of reads and writes to that file. Compare these results to the performance of a normal, fragmented file. Be sure that the normal file is laid out similarly on all systems that you're comparing; you'll probably need to start with a clean file system and run a program that creates fragmentation in some reproducible way.

Asynchronous I/O

The synchronous or asynchronous nature of I/O has no bearing on the I/O performance itself. After all, you're using the same file system, buffer cache and device driver. Accordingly, the performance tests for asynchronous I/O stress the features of asynchronous I/O that are outside of the file system, buffer cache, and device code.

aio_suspend for completed operation

First, we want to determine what sort of overhead is involved in the *aio_suspend* call. To do this, you'll want to fire off some asynchronous I/O with the relevant signals blocked. Wait for the I/O to complete (by sleeping, or some other heuristic method), and then measure the time taken to call *aio_suspend* for the completed operation. This benchmark may be difficult because you can't fire off millions of asynchronous operations—the system generally imposes some sort of limitation.

aio_error and aio_return

You'll want to know how long these calls take as well. You can test *aio_error* by repeatedly calling it for a single *aiocb*. It's a little harder to test *aio_return* because it can only be called once for a given asynchronous operation. To test *aio_error*, you can simply perform an asynchronous read, *aio_suspend* until it completes, and then repeatedly do *aio_error* calls. For *aio_return*, you can get a feel for the amount of time taken by performing two experiments. In the first experiment, time an *aio_read* from some device that doesn't actually do I/O (*/dev/null*, for example), and *aio_suspend* for that I/O, and an *aio_return*. In the second experiment, time the same sequence, minus the *aio_return*. This may not work on those systems which actually *require* you to call *aio_return*. But at least you can try.

Memory Locking

There is very little to measure when it comes to locked memory. The implicit assumption is that locked memory is just like any other memory, except that it's immune from paging. If you're truly paranoid, you can measure access to locked memory versus access to non-locked memory. Another test you can do would be to determine whether locking really locks:

1. Lock the memory of an application down.
2. Measure the access time to that memory.
3. *Leave the application up* while you perform the following step.
4. Hammer the machine's physical memory and MMU. Run a large number of big processes, so that the machine's physical memory and MMU context are definitely overrun. (Overrunning physical memory is easy; just load in larger images than the machine has physical memory, and do memory reads or writes to every page. Overrunning MMU context takes a little more knowledge. You have to know how

many processes can store MMU context in the MMU at any given time. Then, run more processes than that, all at the same time. This will force MMU and memory contention, which should, in a good real-time system, not affect your memory-locked application at all.)

5. Now, measure the access time to your locked memory again. There should be no significant difference in access times.

Shared Memory

While shared memory is generally perceived as the fastest method of interprocess communication, there may still be a performance surprise waiting for you. You'd expect shared memory to be as speedy as non-shared memory. This may not be the case because of cache considerations; keeping the processor cache coherent when two different processes have access to the same memory can be a problem on some machines. It takes careful coding to work around the cache-coherency problem; alternatively, an OS developer can take the brute force approach and disable caching for shared memory. Performance suffers in this case. Some systems may support caching when the memory is mapped into certain areas, but not when it's mapped into other areas. Therefore, you'll want to determine how long memory accesses take to shared memory, and compared that to the time required for accessing non-shared memory.*

Semaphores

Semaphore performance is critical to the speed of cooperating processes. There are a few distinct ways in which semaphores are used. Each method has different performance characteristics. The following are some things to check for.

Semaphores as mutex: the no-contention case

Semaphores are often used as mutual exclusion devices: a process acquires a semaphore lock to protect its access to a shared object. When the process is done, it releases the lock. Unless the shared object is truly in demand, processes will very rarely block while acquiring the the semaphore. Each process is just going to do a quick *sem_wait*, do its thing, and release the lock with *sem_post*. The semaphore is just there for the rare case when two processes want to do their thing at the same time. The important performance measurement in this case is the speed with which a process can acquire and release a semaphore when no other processes are involved. This is the so-called no-contention case, as shown in Figure 7-3.

---

* Another surprise may be that shared memory isn't faster than message-passing at all! In QNX, for instance, the system is based on a message passing subsystem that's been tuned for the best possible performance. In this system, you may be better off doing message passing than trying to "roll your own" with shared memory and semaphores.

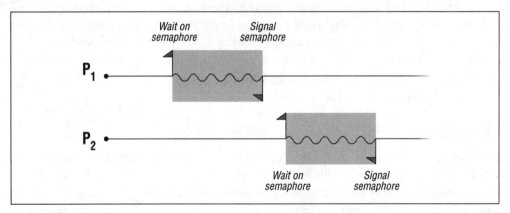

Figure 7–3. Non-contested use of semaphores

Semaphores for blocking

In the other mode of operation, a semaphore is to signal another process. In this case, a process will try to acquire a semaphore and block, waiting for a signal that tells the blocked process to proceed with whatever it's doing. The important performance measurement here is the speed with which a process can wake up other processes that are waiting on the semaphore. One way of measuring this time is to use two processes and two semaphores. Each process repeatedly signals one semaphore and then waits on the other. Figure 7-4 illustrates this.

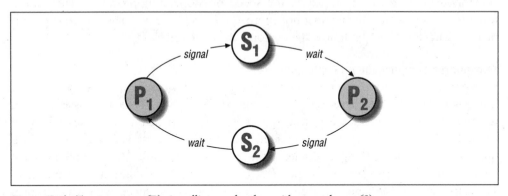

Figure 7–4. Two processes (P) signalling each other with semaphores (S)

Scheduling

Usually, scheduling is set up when an application starts, and doesn't change. However, there are a couple of cases in which a process may need to work with the scheduler while an application is running. Here are a few things to measure:

Setting scheduling parameters without rescheduling

First, you can determine how long it takes to set a process's scheduling parameters. For this, you'll want to change the scheduling parameters on a process so that the operation itself does not result in any rescheduling. For example, you might run your measurement program using the FIFO scheduler at a high priority, and then set some other process's scheduling parameters to FIFO scheduling at the lowest possible priority.

Sched_yield

The *sched_yield* call is used while an application is running; it gives the processor to another process of equal priority. This call can be used to benchmark the speed of a voluntary context switch (it's voluntary because the process is cooperating with its own preemption). Voluntary context switches are faster than involuntary ones, because there's no interrupt involved.

However, using *sched_yield* you can get a clear picture of the time taken in preemptive context switches (the context switch time from our earlier discussion). To measure this time, you'll first need to measure the time taken by the *sched_yield* call itself. Do this by yielding repeatedly when there are no other processes at the same priority. Since there will be no context switch, what you'll measure will be pure overhead. Then run the benchmark with two processes at the same priority, and determine how long each yield call takes when context switches are involved. The difference will be your in-operating-system context switch time. (Code for this experiment can be found in *noswitch.c* and *switch.c* in the Appendix.)

It can be interesting to run this test with many processes, all yielding to each other in a circular fashion. You would expect the context switch time to be unaffected by the number of active processes. However, this is often not the case.[*]

Finally, I should mention again that some people prefer to define context switch time as the time from the last instruction of one user-level process (the switched-from process) to the first instruction of the next (i.e., switched-to) user-level process. Take care that the numbers the vendor is giving you are measuring the time interval you *think* they're measuring!

Dispatch latency, average, worst

Finally, you want to measure the real meat of the scheduling question: how long does it take to get to your high-priority process when an interrupt wakes it up? This is the *dispatch latency* for the system. This is a complicated and non-portable measurement, which is described in more detail in the "Responsiveness and Determinism" section, later in this chapter.

---

[*] On machines with limited-size MMUs, in particular. An early generation of SPARCstations featured an MMU with a limit of 16 processes allowed in the MMU at once. These machines showed a very distinct performance difference between ten running processes and twenty—from microseconds to milliseconds!

Clocks and Timers

Access to the system time is critical. The resolution of the clock is not exactly a performance issue, but it is important for you to know. After that, the basic performance issue is the behavior of interval timers—how they're set, and how accurate they are.

Clock resolution

Calling *clock_getres* tells you the resolution supported by CLOCK_REALTIME on your system. This value will either be sufficient for your application, or not.

Getting the time

How long does it take to find out what time it is? This measurement impacts all your other performance measurements. The usual way of measuring performance is shown in Figure 7-5.

Figure 7-5. A generic performance measurement

Now, if your experiment takes long enough, the time taken in getting your two timestamps is inconsequential. However, if your experiment is very short, the time required to get the timestamp is more important. In any event, you should know this time and add it into your calculations for correctness.

Timer set and clear

In most cases, you will need to set a timer and then handle the signals generated by that timer, without resetting. It's possible, though, you may need to reset your timers during your application. As a result, the time taken to set and clear an interval timer may be important.

Drift

Drift is the propensity of a timer to move away from a steady clock tick over time. If you set a timer to go off every second, and run it 1 million times, then the final time it goes off should be a million seconds after the first time it went off, right? A timer that *drifts* will take a million-and-ten seconds, or something like that. You can measure drift by writing a program to perform the test I just described.

Jitter

We've mentioned jitter before. Jitter is a measure of how on-time your timer deliveries are. A very steady clock will deliver timer expirations every interval, on the interval—not a tick earlier, not a tick later. A jittery clock, in contrast, tends to deliver timer expiration signals *around* the time it's supposed to. Programs outlined in the exercises for timers allow you to measure your system's jitter.

Message Passing

Message passing speed is of prime importance for a running application. Throughput depends strongly on message size. For large messages, message passing time should grow linearly with the size of the message, since most of the time will be taken by copying the message in and out of system buffers. By measuring message passing performance at different message sizes, you can get a good feel for message passing overhead, and whether the performance scales appropriately with message size.

Pass zero bytes

This measurement tells you how efficient message queues can be as a means of synchronization. Zero bytes can be noticeably faster than one-byte message passing, given a few optimizations. Compare this number to the results you measure for semaphore-based synchronization—you may be surprised!

Pass one byte

Measure the performance of passing one-byte messages between two processes.

Pass the number of bytes you'll be using

Measure the performance of passing the messages *you* care about between two processes.

Responsiveness and Determinism

Responsiveness and determinism are tough to measure. You'll want to at least start with what your OS vendor tells you the relevant numbers are. However, you need to know the right questions to ask. Just as an executive summary, you want the average, worst-case, and best-case numbers for the following:

- What is the time from occurrence of an interrupt to the execution of the relevant interrupt handler?
- If I have a task waiting for that interrupt (via an *ioctl, read*, or whatever), and that task is the highest-priority process in the system, how long will it take for that task to run?
- What workload did you use to determine the average and worst-case numbers?
- How does my expected workload relate to the workload you used in determining these numbers?

- What hardware configuration did you measure these numbers on? (You need an absurd level of detail here: processor, architecture, manufacturer, amount and speed of memory, all attached peripherals and their configuration, OS version the vendor used, and so forth.)

- How can I apply numbers measured on *that* hardware to numbers I might expect to achieve on *my* hardware?

It's important to get at least two times for each measurement: average and worst case. The worst case measurement is the most important one, because you must program your application with this worst case time in mind. Average case is also important, because it tells you what you can in fact expect in day-to-day operation. The best case number is interesting, too, but worst and average case are critical.

The machine configuration used by the vendor is important, because machines vary considerably in their performance. My own experience is in the area of Intel 80×86-based PC machines, where every streetcorner seems to sport a new motherboard vendor. In such an environment, you can find supposedly "compatible" hardware that just doesn't cut the performance mustard! In the embedded area, as well, you'll generally be configuring your machine in a totally different manner than the setup in which performance numbers were measured. If your vendor provides you with the measurement tools they used to determine performance, then you can perform these experiments yourself on your target hardware of choice. The first issue, though, is to understand the numbers and what they mean.

So that you know what these questions mean, we'll talk a bit about them. The first two measurements are your interrupt and task response times. Imagine you're measuring them yourself. To measure the responsiveness and determinism of your system, you need to get machine-specific. You'll have to be able to trigger an interrupt at a particular time, determine when the interrupt handler runs in response to that interrupt, and then determine when a task awaiting that interrupt runs. The application structure you'll need is pretty simple, and is shown in Figure 7-6.

Obviously, the driver and machine-specific components of this application need to be redone for every target system. Likewise, the portion of the user-level application that deals with the hardware will need to be ported. However, the user-level application can probably be fairly portable, at least in its overall structure:

```
main()
{
        struct sched_params s;
        int nsamples = 0;

        /* lock all memory down */
        mlockall();
        /* run at the highest possible priority */
        s.sched_priority = sched_get_priority_max(SCHED_FIFO);
        sched_setscheduler(0, SCHED_FIFO, &s);
```

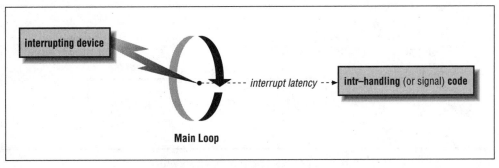

Figure 7–6. Responsiveness measurement application

```
/* Initialize device for performance measurement */
fd = open("/dev/rtperf_measurement", O_RDWR);        /* for example *
/

/* repeatedly measure performance */
while (1) {
        /*
         * wait to be awakened.  read or ioctl would work here.
         *
         * determine interrupt time, time interrupt service routine
         * ran, current time.
         *
         * log sample.
         */
        nsamples++;
}
}
```

There, I've made it simple. All you need to do is fill in the blanks! Seriously, this application can be made to work in two ways. Probably the most common is to have some sort of a timer card for your system, which generates a periodic interrupt. Your driver supports the ability to wait for that interrupt, determine the time at which the interrupt occurred, the time at which the interrupt routine itself runs, and the time at which the user task runs. Using these three time numbers, you can determine how long interrupt and task response take.

Alternatively, you could measure the time externally using a logic analyzer or some other large, scary piece of hardware. This solution requires a simpler driver that waits for a particular interrupt, and then toggles one or two special things that the logic analyzer is watching. The interrupt is generated externally; when they are called, the interrupt handler and the task toggle the bits the analyzer is watching for. The analyzer itself measures the time taken in interrupt and task response. Figure 7-7 shows the timeline.

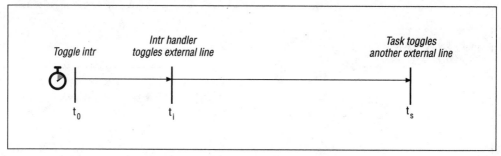

Figure 7–7. External measurement of interrupt and task response

Now you have a good idea how to measure the response of your system to an interrupt. Be careful, though. You only know how to measure one interrupt, probably under good conditions (not a lot else on the machine, etc.). That is probably the *best* response you will ever see from your system. Now, you need to determine how well the system is going to respond under the actual conditions you plan for your application. The determinism of your system is how well the system responds to your interrupt under arbitrarily heavy loads of processing. For instance, what if someone else is doing disk I/O? What if someone else is signalling another process? What if the network is busily interrupting?

Again, you need to determine what is important. OS vendors generally draw a line in the sand and talk about their performance under that particular workload. For instance, an OS may measure its responsiveness while there is heavy network, disk, and computational traffic. Another OS may measure its responsiveness only if there are no other interrupting devices (seriously)! You need to know what workload the vendor used in determining its numbers.

Finally, you need to determine what your own workload is going to be. If your application is going to use a lot of networking and disk I/O, then you should count on a heavy load of interrupt and driver processing going on. If your application has a strong computational component, that is part of your workload as well. You can probably simulate your own workload pretty easily, by banging on your disks and networks and processors with the appropriate numbers of tasks and I/O operations.

Conclusion

Performance measurement of real-time operating systems is not a cut-and-dried issue. POSIX has probably made two aspects of performance measurement easier: throughput and space measurement, because now there are standard facilities, of which you can measure the throughput and space consumption. You can compare apples and apples. In the area of responsiveness and determinism, POSIX hasn't helped much at all. You have to do the tests yourself, or trust the vendors to tell you the correct information. In either case, you need to know what numbers are important, and under what workloads those numbers were obtained.

The most important component of performance measurement, though, is to know what you're measuring ahead of time. Identify the areas that are important to you, and how important they are. Throughput, responsiveness, determinism, space: what performance do you need in each area? Measure the features that are important to you, and don't be distracted by numbers that are irrelevant.

Exercises

To a certain extent, most of this chapter is a big set of exercises; furthermore, much of it is so system-dependent that code samples would be useless or actually harmful. Code samples for several of the performance measurements are flagged throughout this chapter.

PART

II

Manpages

This section contains manual pages for the functionality of POSIX.4, with the goal of giving you a good, concise, function-by-function, header-by-header description of functions you may be using on a day-to-day basis.

I've contravened typical UNIX practice and tried to put more useful substance in the manpages. I've also added sections, willy-nilly, that describe POSIX-specific impacts (which header files may be included by other header files, for instance) and gotchas (such as reuse of the AIOCB). The manpages for your particular system should cover implementation specifics and details, but in general those systems won't be written from the standpoint of a pure POSIX system. These manpages are.

Being manpages, they're still terse and may be a bit opaque to the reader uninitiated in the wonders of POSIX.4. For additional information, you can always refer back to the body of the book.

Name

<aio.h> — Header file for POSIX 1003.4 asynchronous I/O.

Origin

<aio.h> is a header file that was created by and for POSIX.4. This header file contains nothing defined by standard UNIX or POSIX.1. Its POSIX.4 contents are structures and constants related to asynchronous I/O:

Conditionality

<aio.h> is only guaranteed to be present if _POSIX_ASYNCHRONOUS_IO is defined in *<unistd.h>*. Other than that, everything defined herein is unconditional. Prioritized I/O is conditional on _POSIX_PRIORITIZED_IO but the facility for it (*aiocb.aio_reqprio* field) is unconditional.

Namespace Reservation

The support of _POSIX_ASYNCHRONOUS_IO reserves the following symbol namespaces: names beginning with *aio_*, *AIO_*, *lio_*, and *LIO_*.

Contents: Constants

```
#define AIO_CANCELED    xx
#define AIO_NOTCANCELED xx
#define AIO_ALLDONE     xx
```

These are all values that may be returned by *aio_cancel*. AIO_CANCELED indicates that all the requested operations have been cancelled. AIO_NOTCANCELED indicates that at least one of the requested operations could not be cancelled (because it was in progress). In contrast, a return value of AIO_ALLDONE means that *none* of the requested asynchronous I/O could be cancelled because they are all already done. Remember that it is up to each vendor to decide which I/O is cancellable and which is not. Do not code your application to depend on AIO cancellation succeeding or failing.

```
#define LIO_WAIT    xx
#define LIO_NOWAIT  xx
```

These are values for the first parameter to *lio_listio*. These two constants indicate whether to wait synchronously for all the I/O to be done (if the parameter is

LIO_WAIT), or to return immediately and let all the I/O on the list proceed asynchronously (if the parameter is LIO_NOWAIT). Remember that if LIO_WAIT is specified, the *sig* argument to *lio_listio* is ignored.

```
#define LIO_READ       xx
#define LIO_WRITE      xx
#define LIO_NOP        xx
```

These are opcodes for the *aio_lio_opcode* field of the *aiocb*. They are *only* consulted by the *lio_listio* call.

Contents: Data Structures

All data structures are minimal contents, and members may not be in the order given. Vendors may add their own extensions.

```
struct aiocb {
    ...
    int      aio_fildes;     /* FD for asynchronous op */
    off_t    aio_offset;     /* Absolute offset to seek to */
    volatile void *aio_buf;  /* Buffer to read from/write to */
    size_t   aio_nbytes;     /* Number of bytes to read/write */
    struct   sigevent aio_sigevent;   /* Signal to deliver */
    int      aio_lio_opcode; /* lio_listio only: opcode */
    int      aio_reqprio;    /* AIO pr., IFF {_POSIX_PRIORITIZED_IO} */
    ...
};
```

This is the minimal structure of an asynchronous I/O control block. An implementation may define more members than are specified here. In particular, an implementation might choose to store the error number and return value of the asynchronous operation in this structure. Earlier versions of POSIX.4 asynchronous I/O actually had defined fields for this, called *aio_errno* and *aio_return*. Keep in mind that those fields, if they happen to be in your implementation, are *not* standard parts of POSIX.4—they will not be present on all POSIX.4 implementations!

aio_fildes, aio_buf, and *aio_nbytes:*

> These three fields describe an asynchronous read or write. The *aio_fildes* field is the file descriptor from which to read or to which to write; the *aio_buf* is the buffer, and *aio_nbytes* is the number of bytes to read or write. The only additional information required is the *aio_offset*, described below.

aio_offset:

> The *aio_offset* indicates an absolute offset within the file, at which the requested asynchronous read or write will take place. This offset is essentially used as the offset in a call to *lseek (aio_fildes, SEEK_SET, aio_offset)*. If the file descriptor is set for append-only mode (if

O_APPEND has been set for the file), then setting the offset will be meaningless.

aio_sigevent: The *aio_sigevent* field is consulted for *aio_read, aio_write,* and *lio_listio.* This element describes a signal to be delivered on completion of an asynchronous I/O request. The *aio_sigevent* structure has three fields, a notification flag (*sigev_notify*), a signal number (*sigev_signo*) and a value (*sigev_value*). *sigev_notify* dictates whether the signal is delivered or not, or whether some other asynchronous notification mechanism is invoked upon AIO completion (no other such mechanisms are defined at the moment). Set *sigev_notify* to SIGEV_NONE if you want no notification at all; set it to SIGEV_SIGNAL and a signal, described by the rest of the *struct sigevent,* will be delivered. If the signal number (*sigev_signo*) is one of the real-time extended signals (and if _POSIX_REALTIME_SIGNALS is supported), then *sigev_value* indicates the value to be passed as the third argument to the signal handler. Otherwise the value field is ignored.

aio_lio_opcode: Only consulted when the *aiocb* is part of the list passed to *lio_listio.* This field takes on one of the values LIO_WRITE, LIO_READ, or LIO_NOP, and allows the *lio_listio* call to know whether to treat this aiocb as an argument to *aio_write,* to *aio_read,* or whether to ignore the aiocb altogether.

aio_reqprio: Only consulted if _POSIX_PRIORITIZED_IO is supported. If so, indicates the priority of the I/O request relative to *other asynchronous I/O* requests on the same device.

This structure member is misnamed. Asynchronous I/O priority is calculated by taking the calling process's scheduling priority, and *subtracting* the *aio_reqprio.* Thus, *aio_reqprio* is actually something like a "nice" value. This allows you to lower your priority, but not to arbitrarily raise it and clog up the system.

Priority relative to synchronous writes (e.g., via normal *read* and *write*) is not defined and you shouldn't rely on it. However, priority applied to synchronous *lio_listio* requests will be enforced relative to prioritized asynchronous I/O, allowing you to fully prioritize device

I/O (assuming you have total control over what I/O goes to a particular device).

If you don't care about prioritized I/O, be sure to set this field to 0, because it is *always* consulted if _POSIX_PRIORITIZED_IO is supported; you don't want your asynchronous I/O requests to be rejected because of an uninitialized field that you don't care about!

POSIX.4 Contents: Declarations

```
#ifdef _POSIX_ASYNCHRONOUS_IO
int aio_read(struct aiocb *);
int aio_writes(struct aiocb *);
int lio_listio(int, struct aiocb **, int, struct sigevent *);
int aio_error(const struct aiocb *);
ssize_t aio_return(const struct aiocb *);
int aio_suspend(struct aiocb **, int, const struct timespec *);
int aio_cancel(int, struct aiocb *);
#ifdef _POSIX_SYNCHRONIZED_IO
int aio_fsync(int, struct aiocb *);
#endif /* _POSIX_SYNCHRONIZED_IO */
#endif /* _POSIX_ASYNCHRONOUS_IO */
```

Visibility

Inclusion of *<aio.h>* may make the following other header files visible:

<sys/types.h>   because *off_t* and *size_t* must be defined.

<signal.h>   because *struct aio_sigevent* must be defined.

<time.h>   because the *struct timespec* structure used in *aio_suspend* must be defined.

<fcntl.h>   For the definitions of O_SYNC, O_DSYNC, and O_RSYNC (for asynchronous synchronized I/O with *aio_fsync*).

Name

<fcntl.h> — Header file for file control (and POSIX 1003.4 synchronized I/O).

Origin

<fcntl.h> is a standard UNIX header file. Standard UNIX defines the O_SYNC flag, and POSIX.4 uses a compatible definition of this symbol. *<fcntl.h>* has been extended by POSIX.1 to contain definitions and structures related to the *fcntl* function of POSIX.1. POSIX.4 has added two new flags, relating to synchronized I/O, that can be set by the *fcntl* function of POSIX.1.

Conditionality

These additions to *<fcntl.h>* are unconditional. Now-current implementations of POSIX.1 (ISO 9945-1 (1990)) probably do not have these contents; however, they will be in POSIX conformant systems with a _POSIX_VERSION greater than or equal to 199309.

Namespace Reservation

The inclusion of *<fcntl.h>* reserves the following symbol namespaces: names beginning with *l_*, *F_*, *O_*, and *S_*.

Contents: Constants

```
#define O_SYNC      xx
#define O_DSYNC     xx
#define O_RSYNC     xx
```

O_SYNC, O_DSYNC, and O_RSYNC are file flags, like O_APPEND and O_NONBLOCK, which control how operations against this particular file are treated. O_DSYNC causes all writes to the file to be flushed right through the system's buffer cache and on out to the underlying medium (presumably a disk). O_SYNC requires even more—all data written to the file must be kept up-to-date on disk, and, in addition, other control information associated with the file (access times, permissions, and so forth), must also be kept up-to-date on each write. Both O_SYNC and O_DSYNC affect only writes to the file, not reads. If O_RSYNC is set on a file, then the synchronization behavior for the file is also required on read operations.

For instance, if O_SYNC and O_RSYNC are set for a file, then on each read, the access times for the file must be updated on the disk.

As another example, if O_DSYNC and O_RSYNC are both set for a file, then on any read, any pending writes to the file must be flushed to the underlying media for the file.

Synchronized I/O slows down file access. O_SYNC and O_DSYNC only slow down disk writes; however, if O_RSYNC is also set, then reads may be quite slow as well.

All three flags can be set on *open()* by *or*ing the values into the flags parameter to open. Alternatively, one can call *fcntl(fd, F_SETFL, flags)* with O_SYNC, O_DSYNC, or O_RSYNC *or*ed into the flags field to set synchronized mode behavior on a file that is already open.

Visibility

<fcntl.h> does not make anything else visible.

<limits.h>

Name

<limits.h> — Header file for POSIX numerical limits.

Origin

<limits.h> is part of POSIX.1.

Conditionality

Unconditional.

Namespace Reservation

Inclusion of *<limits.h>* reserves symbol namespaces ending with _MAX.

Determining Your System's Limits

<limits.h> defines the numeric parameters that go into a POSIX system. It is a counterpart to the standard header *<unistd.h>*, which defines what is present on a POSIX system; *<limits.h>* defines the size and shape of what is present.

The contents of *<limits.h>* fall into two categories: minimum values and actual values.

It would be simple if *<limits.h>* just had constants that gave you all the numeric limits for your system, but the real world is more complicated than that. For any given system, some limits will be constant and will never change with different machine configurations. Other limits will vary with different machine configurations, but for any given configuration, there will be a particular limit. Still other limits are totally indeterminate, depending on run-time characteristics of the system, such as the amount of free memory and the number of other processes running on the machine.

A constant, invariant limit is given in this file by the *actual limit* constants named below. If the constant is present in *<limits.h>*, then that is the actual limit, and it will not change no matter how you configure your system or how running conditions change on that system.

If, however, one of the actual limits is *not* defined in *<limits.h>*, it's because the actual limit is not constant. It is either a constant that depends on machine configuration, or it is not a constant at all.

For constants that vary with machine configuration, you need to determine the value of the limit at run time on the particular machine you are concerned with. You'll use *sysconf* and *pathconf* to query these values at runtime.

<limits.h> (continued)

For limits which are indeterminate, *sysconf* and *pathconf* will return to you a value of
−1, without setting *errno*. If this happens, then you know that the limit in question is
indeterminate. You are guaranteed, however, that the limit will be no *less* than the
"minimal maxima," the _POSIX_ values, listed below.

Contents: Minimum Values

Minimum values are distinguished by the prefix _POSIX_. These values all correspond
to another, *actual* limit. These numbers refer to the smallest the limit will ever be on
the system in question. Notice that all the values below are maxima. This table is the
smallest value any system may impose on that particular maximum.

Constant	Min. Value	Description	Related Function
		Required in All Implementations	
_POSIX_ARG_MAX	4096	The total length of the string arguments you pass to one of the *exec* functions.	*exec*
_POSIX_CHILD_MAX	6	The number of (child) processes one user ID can have active simultaneously.	*fork*
_POSIX_LINK_MAX	8	The number of links a single file can have.	
_POSIX_MAX_CANON	255	The number of bytes in the "canonical input queue" of a terminal.	
_POSIX_MAX_INPUT	255	The number of bytes which will fit into a terminal's "canonical input queue."	
_POSIX_NAME_MAX	14	The number of bytes in a file name or a pathname component.	*open, mkfifo*
_POSIX_NGROUPS_MAX	0	The number of supplementary group IDs a process can have at once.	
_POSIX_OPEN_MAX	16	The number of files a process can have open at once.	*open*
_POSIX_PATH_MAX	255	The number of bytes in a pathname.	*open*

_POSIX_PIPE_BUF	512	The number of bytes you're guaranteed to be able to write atomically (as a unit) to a *pipe*.	*pipe*
_POSIX_SSIZE_MAX	32767	The largest value you can reliably write to or read from a file at once. Also the largest value you can store in an *ssize_t*.	*write, read*
_POSIX_STREAM_MAX	8	The number of standard I/O "streams" a process can have open at once.	
_POSIX_TZNAME_MAX	3	The maximum number of bytes for a timezone name.	

The values that follow apply to the optional pieces of POSIX.4. As such, they'll only appear in *<limits.h>* if the corresponding functionality is supported by the system. You can determine this by looking at *<unistd.h>*.

Constant	Min. Value	Description	Related Function
Required for _POSIX_REALTIME_SIGNALS			
_POSIX_RTSIG_MAX	8	The difference between SIGRTMIN and SIGRTMAX.	*sigqueue*
_POSIX_SIGQUEUE_MAX	32	The maximum number of signals a process can queue to another process at one time (total number a process can have queued, but not yet handled, for its victim processes).	*sigqueue*

<limits.h> (continued)

Required for _POSIX_TIMERS

_POSIX_DELAYTIMER_MAX	32	The maximum number of timer overruns (after this number is exceeded for a particular timer, *timer_getoverrun* will just return DELAY-TIMER_MAX)	*timer_getoverrun*
_POSIX_TIMER_MAX	32	The maximum number of timers a single process is allowed to have.	*timer_create*
_POSIX_CLOCKRES_MIN	20,000,000	The *minimum* clock resolution, in nanoseconds.	*clock_getres*

Note: _POSIX_CLOCKRES_MIN is interpreted in a sense opposite to the other limits above. _POSIX_CLOCKRES_MIN is the *largest* (i.e., grossest) clock resolution allowed. If you take the inverse of _POSIX_CLOCKRES_MIN, and get a Hz value, you will see that larger values of _POSIX_CLOCKRES_MIN provide smaller values for Hz, and therefore worse and worse clock resolution. 20000000 nanoseconds corresponds to 50 Hz.

Actual clock resolutions are retrieved for a particular clock by calling *clock_getres*.

Constant	Min. Value	Description	Related Function
		Required for _POSIX_ASYNCHRONOUS_IO	
_POSIX_AIO_LISTIO_MAX	2	The maximum number of AIOs you can specify in a single *listio* call (the maximum length of the vector, NOPs not included).	*lio_listio*
_POSIX_AIO_MAX	1	The maximum number of outstanding simultaneous asynchronous I/O operations.	*lio_listio*, *aio_read*

Required for _POSIX_MESSAGE_PASSING

_POSIX_MQ_OPEN_MAX	8	The maximum number of message queues a particular process can have open.	*mq_open*
_POSIX_MQ_PRIO_MAX	32	The maximum message priority supported (maximum value for *msg_prio* in a call to *mq_send*).	*mq_send*

Required for _POSIX_SEMAPHORES

_POSIX_SEM_NSEMS_MAX	256	The maximum number of semaphores a particular process can have open.	*sem_open,* *sem_init*
_POSIX_SEM_VALUE_MAX	32,767	The maximum value a semaphore may have.	*sem_signal,* *sem_getvalue*

Contents: Actual Limits

The following actual limits refer to the actual values for the system being targeted. These values may, in fact, be increased at runtime or be indeterminate (subject to the amount of free memory, for instance). In this case, you would want to use *sysconf* or *pathconf* to determine the value of the limit at runtime.

Constant	Minimum Value	sysconf/pathconf Variable
Required in All Implementations		
NGROUPS_MAX	_POSIX_NGROUPS_MAX	_SC_NGROUPS_MAX
ARG_MAX	_POSIX_ARG_MAX	_SC_ARG_MAX
CHILD_MAX	_POSIX_CHILD_MAX	_SC_CHILD_MAX
OPEN_MAX	_POSIX_OPEN_MAX	_SC_OPEN_MAX
STREAM_MAX	_POSIX_STREAM_MAX	_SC_STREAM_MAX
TZNAME_MAX	_POSIX_TZNAME_MAX	_SC_TZNAME_MAX
LINK_MAX	_POSIX_LINK_MAX	_PC_LINK_MAX
MAX_CANON	_POSIX_MAX_CANON	_PC_MAX_CANON
MAX_INPUT	_POSIX_MAX_INPUT	_PC_MAX_INPUT

NAME_MAX	_POSIX_NAME_MAX	_PC_NAME_MAX
PATH_MAX	_POSIX_PATH_MAX	_PC_PATH_MAX
PIPE_BUF	_POSIX_PIPE_BUF	_PC_PIPE_BUF
SSIZE_MAX	_POSIX_SSIZE_MAX	(n/a)

There is no *sysconf* access to SSIZE_MAX because that value is not allowed to change with machine configuration.

The following actual limits are for parts of POSIX.4 and are present in *<limits.h>* only as required by *<unistd.h>*.

Constant	Minimum Value	sysconf/pathconf Variable
Required in Various POSIX.4 Options		
RTSIG_MAX	_POSIX_RTSIG_MAX	_SC_RTSIG_MAX
SIGQUEUE_MAX	_POSIX_SIGQUEUE_MAX	_SC_SIGQUEUE_MAX
DELAYTIMER_MAX	_POSIX_DELAYTIMER_MAX	_SC_DELAYTIMER_MAX
TIMER_MAX	_POSIX_TIMER_MAX	_SC_TIMER_MAX
AIO_LISTIO_MAX	_POSIX_AIO_LISTIO_MAX	_SC_AIO_LISTIO_MAX
AIO_MAX	_POSIX_AIO_MAX	_SC_AIO_MAX
MQ_OPEN_MAX	_POSIX_MQ_OPEN_MAX	_SC_MQ_OPEN_MAX
MQ_PRIO_MAX	_POSIX_MQ_PRIO_MAX	_SC_MQ_PRIO_MAX
SEM_NSEMS_MAX	_POSIX_SEM_NSEMS_MAX	_SC_SEM_NSEMS_MAX
SEM_VALUE_MAX	_POSIX_SEM_VALUE_MAX	_SC_SEM_VALUE_MAX

Visibility

Inclusion of *<limits.h>* doesn't make any other header files visible.

See Also

<unistd.h>
<aio.h>
<mqueue.h>
<semaphore.h>
<signal.h>
<time.h> (other headers related to this one)
open
fork

exec
kill
sigqueue
sem_open
sem_signal
lio_listio
aio_read
mq_open
mq_sendwrite
clock_getres
timer_create
timer_getoverrun

<mqueue.h>

Name

<mqueue.h> — Header file for POSIX 1003.4 message queues.

Origin

<mqueue.h> is a header file that was created by and for POSIX.4. This header file contains nothing defined by standard UNIX or POSIX.1. Its POSIX.4 contents are structures and constants related to POSIX.4 message queues.

Conditionality

<mqueue.h> is only guaranteed to be present if _POSIX_MESSAGE_PASSING is defined in *<unistd.h>*.

Namespace Reservation

The support of _POSIX_MESSAGE_PASSING reserves symbol namespaces beginning with *mq_* and *MQ_*.

Contents: Constants

```
#define MQ_NONBLOCK
```

This constant is a flag that, if set in the *mq_flags* field of an *mq_attr* structure, indicates that the process has the associated message queue open in non-blocking mode. This flag is only used by the *mq_getattr* and *mq_setattr* functions; although the flag can be passed to *mq_open* when a message queue is created, it is ignored in favor of the standard open flag, O_NONBLOCK.

Contents: Data Structures

All data structures are minimal contents, and members may not be in the order given. Vendors may add their own extensions.

```
typedef xx mqd_t;
```

The *mqd_t* type is a message queue descriptor. This is the return type from *mq_open*.

```
struct mq_attr {
    ...
    long    mq_maxmsg;    /* Max # messages in the queue at once */
    long    mq_msgsize;   /* Max size of a single message on queue */
```

```
    long    mq_flags;     /* Flags for message queue */
    long    mq_curmsgs;   /* # messages currently in the queue */
    ...
};
```

This structure is used when creating a message queue (with *mq_open*), and when querying and setting the attributes of a message queue (with *mq_getattr* and *mq_setattr*).

mq_maxmsg and mq_msgsize

These two fields describe the geometry of the message queue; how many messages can be in the queue at once, and how big a single message in the queue can be. These fields are used when the message queue is created, and are *not* consulted in a call to *mq_setattr*. You cannot dynamically change the geometry of a message queue.

mq_flags

This field contains flags that describe the behavior of the message queue. Only one flag, MQ_NONBLOCK, is defined. If it is set, then the message queue is open by this process in non-blocking mode. That is, an *mq_receive* will not block waiting for a message to arrive on an empty queue, and an *mq_send* will not block waiting for space to send a message to a full message queue. Instead, an error will be returned by these functions. *mq_flags* can be set by *mq_setattr*, but is ignored when you create the message queue. Instead of using MQ_NONBLOCK when creating the message queue, use the standard open flag O_NONBLOCK.

mq_curmsgs

This field is returned by the *mq_getattr* call and indicates how many messages are currently in the message queue (sent, but not yet received). You cannot set this read-only parameter either via *mq_open* or *mq_setattr*.

POSIX.4 Contents: Declarations

```
#ifdef _POSIX_MESSAGE_PASSING
int mq_open(const char *, int, ...);
int mq_close(mqd_t);
int mq_send(mqd_t, const char *, size_t, unsigned int);
int mq_receive(mqd_t, char *, size_t, unsigned int *);
int mq_notify(mqd_t, const struct sigevent *);
int mq_setattr(mqd_t, const struct mq_attr *, struct mq_attr *);
int mq_getattr(mqd_t, struct mq_attr *);
#endif /* _POSIX_MESSAGE_PASSING */
```

Visibility

Inclusion of *<mqueue.h>* may make the following other header files visible:

<sys/types.h>	For sundry type definitions
<fcntl.h>	For definitions of *oflags* values
<time.h>	For timer definitions
<signal.h>	For definition of the *struct sigevent*

See Also

mq_open
mq_close
mq_send
mq_receive
mq_notify
mq_getattr
mq_setattr (message-passing interfaces)
signal.h (definition of the *sigevent* structure)

Name

<sched.h> — Header file for the POSIX 1003.4 scheduling interface.

Origin

<sched.h> is a header file that was created by and for POSIX.4. This header file contains nothing defined by standard UNIX or POSIX.1. Its POSIX.4 contents are structures and constants related to process scheduling.

Conditionality

<sched.h> is only guaranteed to be present if _POSIX_PRIORITY_SCHEDULING is defined in *<unistd.h>*. Other than that, everything defined herein is unconditional.

Namespace Reservation

The inclusion of *<sched.h>* reserves symbol namespaces beginning with *sched_* or SCHED_.

POSIX.4 Contents: Constants

```
#define SCHED_FIFO xx    /* Preemptive, priority scheduling */
#define SCHED_RR xx      /* Preemptive priority with quantum */
#define SCHED_OTHER xx   /* Implementation-defined scheduler */
```

These constants name scheduling algorithms. Scheduling algorithms can be specified for each process independently of other processes. Each scheduling algorithm is identified by a symbolic constant, as defined above.

Implementations may define additional schedulers, but must provide a mechanism by which an application can be compiled with no extensions.

POSIX.4 Contents: Data Structures

All data structures are minimal contents, and members may not be in the order given. Vendors may add their own extensions.

```
struct sched_params {
    ...
    int     sched_priority; /* Used for SCHED_FIFO and SCHED_RR */
    ...
};
```

A single data structure definition contains all scheduling parameters that may be needed to describe a process's schedulability. Currently this structure only has a priority member defined, since POSIX.4 only defines strictly priority-driven schedulers.

POSIX.4 Contents: Declarations

```
#ifdef _POSIX_PRIORITY_SCHEDULING
int sched_setparam(pid_t, const struct sched_param *);
int sched_getparam(pid_t, struct sched_param *);
int sched_setscheduler(pid_t, int, const struct sched_param *);
int sched_getscheduler(pid_t);
int sched_yield(void);
int sched_get_priority_max(int);
int sched_get_priority_min(int);
int sched_rr_get_interval(pid_t, struct timespec *);
#endif /* _POSIX_PRIORITY_SCHEDULING */
int
```

Visibility

Inclusion of *<sched.h>* will make the following other header file visible:

<time.h>   Because *struct timespec* must be defined.

See Also

sched_get_priority_max
sched_get_priority_min
sched_getparam
sched_getscheduler
sched_rr_get_interval
sched_setparam
sched_setscheduler
sched_yield

<semaphore.h>

Name

<semaphore.h> — Header file for POSIX 1003.4 semaphores.

Origin

<semaphore.h> is a header file that was created by and for POSIX.4. This header file contains nothing defined by standard UNIX or POSIX.1. Its POSIX.4 contents are structures and constants related to POSIX.4 semaphores.

Conditionality

<semaphore.h> is only guaranteed to be present if _POSIX_SEMAPHORES is defined in *<unistd.h>*.

Namespace Reservation

The support of _POSIX_SEMAPHORES reserves symbol namespaces beginning with *sem_* and SEM_.

POSIX.4 Contents: Constants

There are no constants defined by POSIX.4 in *<semaphore.h>*.

POSIX.4 Contents: Types

```
typedef xx sem_t;
```

The *sem_t* is a semaphore. This structure is initialized in place by *sem_init*, or allocated and returned by a call to *sem_open*.

POSIX.4 Contents: Declarations

```
#ifdef _POSIX_SEMAPHORES
int sem_init(sem_t *, int, unsigned int);
int sem_destroy(sem_t *);
sem_t *sem_open(const char *, int, ...);
int sem_close(sem_t *);
int sem_unlink(const char *);
int sem_wait(sem_t *);
int sem_trywait(sem_t *);
int sem_post(sem_t *);
int sem_getvalue(sem_t *, int *);
#endif /* _POSIX_SEMAPHORES */
```

Visibility

Inclusion of *<semaphore.h>* may make the following headers available:

<sys/types.h> For sundry type definitions

<fcntl.h>   For definitions of the *oflags* values

See Also

sem_init
sem_destroy
sem_open
sem_close
sem_unlink
sem_wait
sem_post
sem_getvalue

Name

<signal.h> — Header file relating to POSIX signals.

Origin

<signal.h> exists in standard UNIX.

Conditionality

Mostly unconditional. The job control signals are conditional on POSIX_JOB_CONTROL being defined in *<unistd.h>*, and the real-time signals extensions are conditional on _POSIX_REALTIME_SIGNALS.

Namespace Reservation

The inclusion of *<signal.h>* reserves symbol namespaces beginning with *si_*, SI_, *sigev_*, or *sival_*.

Contents: Constants

POSIX Unconditional Signals (Supported on All Systems)	
Signal Name	*Used For*
SIGABRT	Abnormal termination, abort
SIGALRM	Alarm clock expired (real-time clocks)
SIGFPE	Floating point exception
SIGHUP	Controlling terminal hung up (probably a modem or network connection)
SIGILL	Illegal instruction exception
SIGINT	Interactive termination (usually CTRL-C at the keyboard)
SIGKILL	Unstoppable termination (signal 9 on most UNIX systems)
SIGPIPE	Writing to a pipe with no readers
SIGQUIT	Abnormal termination signal (interactive processes)
SIGSEGV	Memory access exception
SIGTERM	Terminate process
SIGUSR1	Application-defined uses
SIGUSR2	Application-defined uses

<signal.h> (continued)

The signals above are supported in *all* POSIX systems, regardless of POSIX.4 support level. You can count on these signals to be supported on all systems claiming conformance to any POSIX version.

POSIX Optional Signals

Signal Name	Default Action	Used For
Option: _POSIX_JOB_CONTROL		
SIGCHLD	Signal ignored	Child died or stopped
SIGSTOP	Stop the process	Stops process (uncatchable)
SIGTSTP	Stop the process	Stops process (from terminal)
SIGCONT	Continue process	Continues stopped process
SIGTTOU	Stop the process that tries to write to the terminal	Stop a background process
SIGTTIN	Stop the process that tries to read from the terminal	Stop a background process
Option: _POSIX_REALTIME_SIGNALS		
SIGRTMIN-SIGRTMAX	Termination	Application-defined uses

All the signal numbers given above must be *defined* by all conforming POSIX implementations (conforming to the 1993 standard, that is). However, the job control and realtime signals may not be *supported* by the system beyond that definition. You need to check for _POSIX_JOB_CONTROL and _POSIX_REALTIME_SIGNALS to be sure. The real-time signals, SIGRTMIN through SIGRTMAX, are defined for the real-time signals extension. These are the signals you can make queueable by setting SA_SIGINFO in a call to *sigaction.*

SIGBUS is unconditional, however, it only occurs in one instance in a POSIX system: when you try to access an unmapped region of memory. That would be either one you never mapped, or one you have unmapped (with *munmap*).

```
/* System-supplied signal actions (for sigaction) */
SIG_DFL         /* Do the default signal handling for this signal */
SIG_IGN         /* Ignore this signal */

/* Flags that can be set in sa_flags in a call to sigaction */
SA_NOCLDSTOP    /* sigaction(SIGCHLD) only: do not generate this
                 * signal for children that stop—only for those that die */
SA_SIGINFO      /* _POSIX_REALTIME_SIGNALS: queue this signal and call
                 * the handler as an extended handler
                 * (sa_sigaction, not sa_handler) */
```

SIG_DFL and SIG_IGN can be passed as *sa_handler* in a call to *sigaction*. They cause the relevant signal to be handled in the default manner or ignored, respectively. SA_NOCLDSTOP is set in *sa_flags* in a call to *sigaction* for the SIGCHLD signal; it tells the system not to generate the signal for stopped child processes, but only for those children that exit. SA_SIGINFO is used to specify real-time signal queueing behavior for the signal, and is supported under _POSIX_REALTIME_SIGNALS.

```
/* Actions for sigprocmask */
SIG_BLOCK          /* Block the given signals */
SIG_UNBLOCK        /* Unblock the given signals */
SIG_SETMASK        /* Set your signal mask to the current set
                    * (they'll be blocked) */
```

SIG_BLOCK, SIG_UNBLOCK, and SIGSETMASK are passed as the first argument to *sigprocmask*, and control whether the signals contained in the passed *sigset* are blocked, unblocked, or whether the passed set becomes the signal set, respectively.

```
/* Queued signals pass to their handlers an additional parameter that
 * defines the genesis of the particular signal. These codes are: */
SI_USER         /* signal was sent via kill, raise, or abort */
SI_QUEUE        /* signal was sent via sigqueue */
SI_TIMER        /* signal is the result of timer expiration */
SI_ASYNCIO      /* signal is the result of asynchronous I/O completion */
SI_MESGQ        /* signal is the result of mq_notify */
```

These codes are passed as the *si_code* field of the *siginfo_t* passed to a real-time signal handler. Each code indicates the general origin of the signal.

```
SIGEV_NONE          /* no notification desired */
SIGEV_SIGNAL        /* notify via signal */
```

SIGEV_SIGNAL and SIGEV_NONE are the only two values defined for the *sigevent* structure's *sigev_notify* field. This field dictates the sort of asynchronous notification that the *struct sigevent* defines: either a signal, or nothing at all. No other value for *sigev_notify* is currently defined.

Contents: Data Structures

All data structures are minimal contents, and members may not be in the order given. Vendors may add their own extensions.

```
/*
 * This opaque data structure contains a set of signal numbers. It is
 * usually implemented as an array of bits, one per each possible
 * signal number.
 */
typedef xx sigset_t;
```

The *sigset_t* defines a signal set, or mask, which is used for setting the signal mask of the process either through a call to *sigprocmask*, signal handling via *sigaction*, or one of the signal wait calls (*sigsuspend, sigwaitinfo,* or *sigtimedwait*).

```
/* Definition of a value that can be queued when using SA_SIGINFO */
union sigval {
    ...
    int             sival_int;      /* Integer interpretation */
    void *          sival_ptr;      /* Pointer interpretation */
    ...
};

/* This structure groups together the elements that define a
 * queued signal
 */
struct sigevent {
    ...
    int             sigev_notify;   /* Notification: SIGNAL or NONE */
    int             sigev_signo;    /* Generate this signal */
    union sigval    sigev_value;    /* Queue this value */
    ...
};
```

The *struct sigevent* is used in asynchronous I/O control blocks, POSIX.4 timer setup, and POSIX.4 message queue notification attachment to encapsulate the details of signal delivery to occur on each of these asynchronous events. The *sigev_notify* field takes on one of two currently-defined values: SIGEV_NONE indicates that no notification at all should occur, and SIGEV_SIGNAL says that a signal should be delivered. If a signal is to be delivered, then *sigev_signo* is the number of that signal. If the signal is one of the real-time variety (SIGRTMIN through SIGRTMAX), then the additional data value is given by *sigev_value*. This value can be either an integer or a pointer; the goal of the *union sigval* is to support "a pointer's worth of data."

```
/*
 * This structure defines the additional info passed to a SA_SIGINFO
 * handler (a sa_sigaction function, as defined below for struct
 * sigaction).
 */
typedef struct {
    ...
    int             si_signo;       /* Signal number (redundant) */
    int             si_code;        /* Cause of signal */
    union sigval    si_value;       /* Queued data value */
    ...
} siginfo_t;
```

The *siginfo_t* is passed as the second argument to a real-time signal handler (set up by *sigaction* when SA_SIGINFO is set in *sa_flags*). This structure passes additional information to the handler as to the cause of the signal. *si_signo* is the number of the signal being delivered, and will be identical to the first argument to the signal handler. *si_code* further classifies the signal's cause. Finally, *si_value* contains an application-specific value that is passed as part of AIO submission (*aio_read*, e.g.), timer setup (*timer_create*), message queue notification (*mq_notify*) or *sigqueue*.

```
/*
 * sigaction contains the elements that define a process's response to a
 * particular signal.
 */
struct sigaction {
        ...
        void (*)()      sa_handler(int);
        void (*)()      sa_sigaction(int, siginfo_t *, void *);
        sigset_t        sa_mask;
        int             sa_flags;
        ...
};
```

The *sigaction* structure is passed to the *sigaction* call, and defines how a particular signal should be handled upon delivery to the process.

The *sa_handler* field points to a function which is to be called upon receipt of the signal. Alternatively, if SA_SIGACTION is set in *sa_flags*, *sa_sigaction* is used to point to an extended real-time signal handler. This functionality is conditional on _POSIX_REALTIME_SIGNALS.

sa_mask specifies a set of signals to be blocked for the duration of the signal handler call. The signal mask of the process during this time is formed by taking the existing signal mask for the process, adding in the signals in *sa_mask*, and finally adding in the signal which is being handled (to prevent the signal coming in again on top of itself).

sa_flags contains flags that indicate miscellaneous behavior. Only two flags are defined by POSIX: SA_NOCLDSTOP and SA_SIGINFO. Both have been described above. SA_SIGINFO enables the real-time queueing signal behavior specified for _POSIX_ REALTIME_SIGNALS.

Contents: Declarations

```
extern int kill(pid_t, int);
extern int sigemptyset(sigset_t *);
extern int sigfillset(sigset_t *);
extern int sigaddset(sigset_t *, int);
extern int sigdelset(sigset_t *, int);
extern int sigismember(const sigset_t *, int);
extern int sigaction(int, struct sigaction *, struct sigaction *);
```

301

<signal.h> (continued)

```
extern int sigprocmask(int, const sigset_t *, sigset_t *);
extern int sigpending(const sigset_t *);
extern int sigsuspend(const sigset_t *);
#ifdef _POSIX_REALTIME_SIGNALS
extern int sigqueue(pid_t, int, const union sigval);
extern int sigwaitinfo(const sigset_t *, siginfo_t *);
extern int sigtimedwait(const sigset_t *, siginfo_t *, const struct timespec *);
#endif /*  _POSIX_REALTIME_SIGNALS */
```

Visibility

Including *<signal.h>* does not make any other POSIX headers visible.

See Also

kill

sigqueue

sigaction (for definition of *pid_t*)

<sys/mman.h>

Name

<sys/mman.h> — Header file relating to memory management.

Origin

<sys/mman.h> exists in standard UNIX and contains various facilities related to memory management. No contents of *<sys/mman.h>* are defined by POSIX.1. POSIX.4 requires that *<sys/mman.h>* contain structures and constants related to memory locking and file mapping

Conditionality

Support for POSIX.4 memory locking operations is predicated on support for _POSIX_MEMLOCK in *<unistd.h>*. Memory mapping is conditional on _POSIX_MAPPED_FILES. Shared memory is conditional on _POSIX_SHARED_MEMORY_OBJECTS. Memory protection relies on _POSIX_MEMORY_PROTECTION. Flags for the *msync* operation are defined only if both _POSIX_MAPPED_FILES and POSIX_SYNCHRONIZED_IO are supported.

Namespace Reservation

The inclusion of *<sys/mman.h>* reserves symbol namespaces beginning with *shm_*, MAP_, MCL_, MS_, or PROT_.

Contents: Constants

```
#ifdef _POSIX_MEMLOCK
#define MCL_CURRENT      xx
#define MCL_FUTURE       xx
#endif _POSIX_MEMLOCK
```

These are two flag values that are specified by the application in a call to *mlockall*. MCL_CURRENT tells *mlockall* to lock down all the process's currently-present pages of memory; however, pages allocated in the future might not be locked. MCL_FUTURE tells the system that pages allocated in the future should be automatically locked down. You *or* these two flags together and pass the combined flag to *mlockall*. Thus, you can specify just current mappings, just future mappings (which would be pretty strange), or both present and future mappings.

```
#if defined(_POSIX_MAPPED_FILES) \
        || defined(_POSIX_SHARED_MEMORY_OBJECTS)
#define PROT_NONE xx
#define PROT_READ xx
#define PROT_WRITE xx
#define PROT_EXEC xx
```

```
#define MAP_SHARED xx
#define MAP_PRIVATE xx
#define MAP_FIXED xx
#endif
```

These flags are used by the *mmap* function to specify memory protection possibilities and mapping options. The PROT flags are also used by *mprotect*.

```
#if defined(_POSIX_MAPPED_FILES) && defined(_POSIX_SYNCHRONIZED_IO)
#define MS_SYNC xx
#define MS_ASYNC xx
#define MS_INVALIDATE
#endif
```

These flags are used by the *msync* function to affect the way in which mappings are synchronized with the underlying object.

Contents: Declarations

```
#ifdef _POSIX_MEMLOCK
int mlockall(int);
int munlockall(void);
#endif /* _POSIX_MEMLOCK */
#ifdef _POSIX_MEMLOCK_RANGE
int mlock(const void *, size_t);
int munlock(const void *, size_t);
#endif /* _POSIX_MEMLOCK_RANGE */
#if defined(_POSIX_MAPPED_FILES) \
        || defined(_POSIX_SHARED_MEMORY_OBJECTS)
void *mmap(void *, size_t, int, int, int, off_t);
int munmap(void *, size_t);
#endif /* _POSIX_MAPPED_FILES or _POSIX_SHARED_MEMORY_OBJECTS */
#ifdef _POSIX_SHARED_MEMORY_OBJECTS
int shm_open(const char *, int, mode_t);
int shm_unlink(const char *);
#ifdef _POSIX_MEMORY_PROTECTION
int mprotect(const void *, size_t, int);
#endif /* _POSIX_MEMORY_PROTECTION
#if defined(_POSIX_MAPPED_FILES) && defined(_POSIX_SYNCHRONIZED_IO)
int msync(void *, size_t, len);
#endif /* _POSIX_MAPPED_FILES and _POSIX_SYNCHRONIZED_IO */
```

Visibility

Inclusion of *<sys/mman.h>* does not make any other header files visible.

See Also

mlock
mlockall
munlock
munlockall

\<sys/wait.h\>

Name

\<sys/wait.h\> — Header file relating to the wait functions.

Origin

\<sys/wait.h\> exists in standard UNIX and contains various facilities related to the *wait* and *waitpid* facilities. *\<sys/wait.h\>* has contents defined by POSIX.1.

Conditionality

Unconditional.

Namespace Reservation

The inclusion of *\<sys/wait.h\>* doesn't reserve any namespaces. However, the macros it defines all start with W, so you might want to avoid those names for your own stuff.

Contents: Macros

```
#define         WIFEXITED(s)       xx
#define         WEXITSTATUS(s)     xx
#define         WIFSIGNALED(s)     xx
#define         WTERMSIG(s)        xx
#define         WIFSTOPPED(s)      xx
#define         WSTOPSIG(s)        xx
```

These macros interrogate the process status returned by *wait* and *waitpid*.

Contents: Declarations

```
extern pid_t    wait(int *status_location);
extern pid_t    waitpid(pid_t who, int *status_location, int options);
```

Visibility

Inclusion of *\<sys/wait.h\>* makes no other headers visible.

See Also

wait
waitpid
\<sys/types.h\> (for definition of *pid_t*)

Name

<time.h> — Header file relating to time management.

Origin

<time.h> exists in standard UNIX and defines facilities used for time-based computing under standard UNIX. This is where *struct timeval* is defined. *struct itimerval*, on the other hand, is defined elsewhere, in *<itimer.h>*.

In POSIX.1, most of the stuff that is commonly found in *<time.h>* is standardized. The most useful and common of these definitions are:

time_t   A type used to hold a time value. (ANSI C says *time_t* is defined here; it may also be in *<sys/types.h>*)

CLK_TCK   The clock tick of the system (== *sysconf*(_SC_CLK_TCK) (obsolescent))

struct tm   Used by *mktime*, among others, to contain a human-comprehensible time value.

*extern char *tzname[]*
                Contains time-zone name strings.

POSIX.4 adds the definitions of structures and constants related to timers and clocks.

Conditionality

<time.h> is guaranteed to be present in a POSIX system. However, the POSIX.4 extensions, described below, are only guaranteed to be present if _POSIX_TIMERS is defined in *<unistd.h>*.

Namespace Reservation

The support of _POSIX_TIMERS reserves symbol namespaces beginning with *clock_*, *timer_*, *it_*, *tv_*, CLOCK_, and TIMER_.

POSIX.4 Contents: Constants

All POSIX.4 contents depend on _POSIX_TIMERS.

```
#define CLOCK_REALTIME xx /* the clock required by POSIX.4 */
```

A machine running under POSIX.4 is presumed to have one or more system clocks which may be used as the basis for interval timers. These clocks are identified by clock IDs of type *clockid_t*. One clock ID is required on all systems: CLOCK_REALTIME. An operating system may define additional clocks if it wishes.

```
#define TIMER_ABSTIME xx /* Absolute time flag for timer_settime */
```

This is a flag value used to indicate that an interval timer value is an absolute time value, not a value relative to the current time. This flag value has meaning when specified in a call to *timer_settime.*

POSIX.4 Contents: Data Structures

All data structures are minimal contents, and members may not be in the order given. Vendors may add their own extensions. All POSIX.4 contents depend on _POSIX_TIMERS.

```
struct timespec {
        ...
        time_t  tv_sec;  /* Number of seconds */
        long    tv_nsec; /* Number of nanoseconds (< 1,000,000,000) */
        ...
};
```

This structure contains a high-resolution indication of time. Accuracy down to the nanosecond is supported by the use of a number of nanoseconds in the structure, even though most operating systems do not support such accuracy today.

The number of nanoseconds is meant to indicate a fraction of a second. You should be careful to specify less than 1,000,000,000 nanoseconds in the *tv_nsec* field of this structure. Negative numbers of nanoseconds are not allowed.

```
struct itimerspec {
        ...
        struct timespec it_value;     /* First time */
        struct timespec it_interval;  /* and thereafter */
        ...
};
```

The *struct itimerspec* is used to define the settings for an interval timer. It consists of two timespecs. The *it_value* indicates the amount of time until the interval timer expires the first time; the *it_interval* indicates the interval at which the timer will interrupt thereafter.

POSIX.4 Contents: Data Types

All POSIX.4 contents depend on _POSIX_TIMERS.

```
typedef xx clockid_t;
typedef xx timer_t;
```

The type *clockid_t* is used in identifying different clocks used as timing bases under POSIX.4. *timer_t* identifies a particular timer, based on a clock. An application creates a timer by calling *timer_create*; Values of type *clockid_t*, on the other hand, are supplied by the operating system to identify the various clocks which are available to the application. The clock defined by POSIX.4 is called CLOCK_REALTIME (see above).

POSIX.4 Contents: Declarations

```
#ifdef _POSIX_TIMERS
int clock_gettime(clockid_t, const struct timespec *);
int clock_settime(clockid_t, struct timespec *);
int clock_getres(clockid_t, struct timespec *);
int timer_create(clockid_t, struct sigevent *, timer_t *);
int timer_delete(timer_t);
int timer_settime(timer_t, int,
                const struct itimerspec *, struct itimerspec *);
int timer_gettime(timer_t, struct itimerspec *);
int timer_getoverrun(timer_t);
#endif /* _POSIX_TIMERS */
```

Visibility

Inclusion of *<time.h>* does not make any other header files visible.

Notes

The current revision of the standard does not state that *<time.h>* may make *<signal.h>* visible, even though the *struct sigevent*, described in *<signal.h>*, is required for the *timer_create* call. That means that your application has to make sure itself that *<signal.h>* is included.

See Also

clock_getres
clock_gettime
clock_settime

\<time.h\> <small>(continued)</small>

nanosleep
timer_create
timer_delete
timer_getoverrun
timer_gettime
timer_settime

Name

<unistd.h> — Header file for POSIX conformance.

Origin

<unistd.h> is part of POSIX.1.

Conditionality

Unconditional.

Namespace Reservation

Inclusion of *<unistd.h>* reserves no namespaces. However, the inclusion of *any* POSIX header reserves the space of all names beginning with "_" (underscore).

Function Declarations

<unistd.h> is defined to contain function declarations for any POSIX functions which are not explicitly declared elsewhere. You should include *<unistd.h>* in any source module that uses POSIX functions, as a safety net of declarations and definitions.

Miscellany

NULL is defined in *<unistd.h>*, as is the symbol *cuserid* and the constants used by the *access* function:

F_OK	File existence
R_OK	Read permission
W_OK	Write permission
X_OK	Execute permission

The constants used for *lseek* are declared in *unistd.h*:

SEEK_SET	Set the seek pointer to the given offset
SEEK_CUR	Set the seek pointer to the current plus the given offset
SEEK_END	Set the seek pointer to EOF plus the given offset

<unistd.h> (continued)

Feature Test Macros

<unistd.h> defines the optional components that comprise a POSIX system. By examining constants found in *<unistd.h>*, you can determine which options are or are not available on your particular system. The following symbols are constant, and you should therefore be able to test for them using *#ifdefs*, with some confidence that the associated functionality will be present at run-time as well.

Constant	Description
POSIX_VERSION	Contains a constant indicating the year and month of POSIX supported by this system. A system supporting just the basic POSIX.1 functionality will set this constant to 199009. A system supporting POSIX.4 will set the constant to 199309.
Symbols defined by POSIX.1 (_POSIX_VERSION == 199009)	
_POSIX_SAVED_IDS	Support for saved set-user and set-group IDs.
_POSIX_JOB_CONTROL	Support for job control groups.
Symbols defined by POSIX.4 (_POSIX_VERSION >= 199309)	
_POSIX_REALTIME_SIGNALS	Real-time (queued) signals
_POSIX_MESSAGE_PASSING	Message queues (*mq_open, et. al.*)
_POSIX_MAPPED_FILES	Memory mapped files (*mmap*)
_POSIX_SHARED_MEMORY_OBJECTS	Shared memory (*shm_open, et. al.*)
_POSIX_SEMAPHORES	Semaphores (*sem_open, et. al.*)
_POSIX_PRIORITY_SCHEDULING	Real-time process scheduling (*sched_**)
_POSIX_TIMERS	POSIX.4 clocks and timers (*clock_*, timer_**)
_POSIX_MEMLOCK	Process memory locking (*mlockall*)
_POSIX_MEMLOCK_RANGE	Memory Range locking (*mlock*)
_POSIX_MEMORY_PROTECTION	*mprotect*
_POSIX_FSYNC	*fsync*
_POSIX_SYNCHRONIZED_IO	POSIX.4 synchronized I/O (O_SYNC, *et. al.*)
_POSIX_ASYNCHRONOUS_IO	POSIX.4 asynchronous I/O (*aio_**)
_POSIX_PRIORITIZED_IO	POSIX.4 prioritized I/O (*aio_reqprio*)

All the constants above may also be queried at runtime using *sysconf,* in case you wish to be sure that the functionality is present at runtime.

The following symbols may not necessarily be constant, most likely because the functionality they reflect varies with the file against which the functionality is directed. Therefore, you should be prepared to test for the following functionality at runtime, rather than compile-time. In fact, since these values may all have a per-file value, you should probably use *pathconf* and the associated _PC_-constant to determine the runtime behavior.

Constant	Description
POSIX.1 Execution-Time Constants	
_POSIX_CHOWN_RESTRICTED	Restrictions on *chown*: you cannot "give away" file permissions to another user or group.
_POSIX_NO_TRUNC	File names longer than NAME_MAX will not be silently truncated; rather, an error will be returned.
_POSIX_VDISABLE	Disabling of terminal special characters is supported using this character value.
POSIX.4 Execution-Time Constants	
_POSIX_SYNC_IO	Synchronized I/O may be performed.
_POSIX_ASYNC_IO	Asynchronous I/O may be performed.
_POSIX_PRIO_IO	Prioritized Asynchronous I/O may be performed.

Feature Test Macro Values

The constants named above are either defined or not, depending on whether the associated behavior is supported or not. That's simple.

Things are more complex for the execution-time constants. If the symbol is defined as −1, then the behavior is not supported anywhere on the system. If the symbol is defined with a value other than −1, then the associated behavior is supported for all files on the system. Finally, if the symbol is not defined in *<unistd.h>* at all, then the behavior is variable on a per-file basis; use *fpathconf* to determine the behavior at runtime.

All the optional POSIX functions return −1, with *errno* set to ENOSYS, if you call such a function and it is not supported on the operating system under which you are currently running. I've not duplicated this fact in every manual page, in the interest of preserving our precious natural heritage of printer's ink.

Visibility

Inclusion of *<unistd.h>* doesn't make any other header files visible.

See Also

<limits.h>
<aio.h>
<mqueue.h>
<semaphore.h>
<signal.h>
<time.h> (other headers related to this one)
fpathconf
pathconf
sysconf

Name

aio_cancel — Try to cancel an asynchronous operation.

Synopsis

```
#include      <aio.h>
int           aio_cancel(int fildes, struct aiocb *aiocbp);
```

Conditionality

```
#ifdef _POSIX_ASYNCHRONOUS_IO
```

Description

aio_cancel can be used to try to cancel one or more asynchronous I/O operations that are pending in the given file descriptor. If *aiocbp* is not NULL, then it is assumed to refer to an asynchronous operation on the file descriptor (*aiocbp->aio_fildes* must match *fildes*), and *aio_cancel* will only try to cancel that single operation. If *aiocbp* is NULL, then *aio_cancel* attempts to cancel all asynchronous I/O that is pending on the file descriptor.

For every asynchronous operation that *aio_cancel* successfully cancels, the I/O operation shall terminate in the normal way, sending its signal as it was supposed to based on the *aiocb*. However, the error status for a cancelled operation is ECANCELED, and the return status is –1. If *aio_cancel* cannot cancel a particular asynchronous operation, that operation is not affected in any visible way.

Return Values

aio_cancel returns AIO_CANCELED if all of the requested operations were successfully cancelled. If all of the operations were finished before *aio_cancel* got to them, then AIO_ALLDONE is returned. If one or more of the requested operations could not be cancelled, then AIO_NOTCANCELED is returned. In this case, some of the operations may have been cancelled and others not cancelled. It is up to you to determine which are which.

Under erroneous conditions, *aio_cancel* returns –1.

Errors

If *aio_cancel* fails, it returns −1 and sets *errno* to the following value:

EBADF   *fildes* is not a file descriptor.

Notes

Each operating system must document which asynchronous operations are cancellable. However, a valid implementation might simply state that no asynchronous I/O is cancellable. You should be aware of the possibility that the I/O you can cancel on system X will not be cancellable on system Y.

Current UNIX Practice

SVR4:   No asynchronous I/O operations are specified in SVR4.

BSD: No asynchronous I/O operations are specified in BSD UNIX (as of 4.3).

SunOS: SunOS has an asynchronous I/O facility similar to the POSIX facility, but it is not identical.

See Also

aio_read, aio_write (these functions submit asynchronous I/Os)
lio_listio (this function allows many AIOs to be done at once)
aio_error (this function retrieves the error status of an AIO)
aio_return (this function retrieves the return status of an AIO)
close (may perform an implicit *aio_cancel*)
_exit (may perform an implicit *aio_cancel* on all file descriptors)
exec (may perform an implicit *aio_cancel* on all file descriptors)

Name

aio_error — Retrieve the error status for an asynchronous operation.

Synopsis

```
#include        <aio.h>
int             aio_error(struct aiocb *aiocbp);
```

Conditionality

```
#ifdef _POSIX_ASYNCHRONOUS_IO
```

Description

The *errno* value from *aio_read*, *aio_write*, and *lio_listio* generally only indicates the success or failure to queue up an asynchronous operation. The error status of the actual I/O is what is returned by the *aio_error* call.

The error status of an asynchronous operation is, in general, the same as the error status (*errno* value) would be if the operation were synchronous (the error status for an *aio_read* is generally the same as the *errno* value for the equivalent read, for example). However, there are some additional possible error values related to the asynchronous nature of the operation and to the implied *lseek* that occurs before an asynchronous read or write. These values are described in the manual pages for *aio_read* and *aio_write*.

If an asynchronous operation has not yet completed when *aio_error* is called, it will return EINPROGRESS.

Returns

aio_error retrieves the error status of the asynchronous operation that was submitted using *aiocbp*. That error status is passed back as the return value of the call. Notice that the return value is not the 1 return you might expect from a system call—it is an *errno* value such as 0, EINPROGRESS, EINVAL, or EAGAIN. *aio_error* may return −1, as well, if it is called erroneously (with a bad *aiocbp*, for example). I am not aware of any systems that use −1 as a value for *errno*, so you should be able to determine when *aio_error* itself has failed, as opposed to the asynchronous operation failing.

aio_error has undefined results when called for an asynchronous operation that has already been "completed" by a call to *aio_return*. Do not use *aio_error* once *aio_return* has been called for a given asynchronous operation.

Errors

aio_error returns −1 in only one possible case, and, in this case, it only returns the error if the system detects the error.

EINVAL   The *aiocb* address passed to *aio_error* does not represent a valid asynchronous operation whose return status has not yet been retrieved. Either you have passed in a bogus *aiocb*, or that *aiocb* has not yet been used for submitting asynchronous I/O, or you have already called *aio_return* with this *aiocb* address.

Notes

aio_error may be called as many times as you wish for a given asynchronous operation, but may not be called after *aio_return* has been called for the operation.

See Also

read (the return values for *aio_read* are based on those of read)
write (the return values for *aio_write* are based on those of write)
lseek (possible errors related to the implied seek are explained here)
aio_read, aio_write, lio_listio (used to submit asynchronous I/O)
aio_return (this function retrieves the return status of an AIO)

Name

aio_read — Asynchronously read from a file.

Synopsis

```
#include        <aio.h>
int             aio_read(struct aiocb *aiocbp);
```

Conditionality

```
#ifdef _POSIX_ASYNCHRONOUS_IO
    /* Asynchronous I/O is supported */
#ifdef _POSIX_PRIORITIZED_IO
    /* Asynchronous I/O is prioritized relative to other AIO. */
#endif
#endif
```

Description

aio_read submits a single asynchronous read operation to the system. The call returns immediately after submitting the operation, leaving the system to perform the read concurrently with the execution of other processes. The read operation behaves roughly as if it were the following code snippet:

```
lseek(aiocbp->aio_fildes, aiocbp->aio_offset, SEEK_SET);
rv = read(aiocbp->aio_fildes, aiocbp->aio_buf, aiocbp->aio_nbytes);
/* If a signal is desired, then deliver it */
if (aiocbp->sigevent.sigev_notify == SIGEV_SIGNAL) {
        sigqueue(pid, aiocbp->aio_sigevent.sigev_signo,
        aiocbp->aio_sigevent.sigev_value);
        /* When the signal handler is invoked, its
         * info->si_code field will be set to SI_ASYNCIO
         * to indicate that the signal was the result of
         * asynchronous I/O completion. */
}
```

The seek and the read are performed atomically with respect to other outstanding I/O in the system. In other words, you definitely will read data from the offset you specified. On devices that are not capable of seeking, and on files which are set to append-only mode (via the O_APPEND flag), the seek offset is ignored.

The concurrent read operation behaves just like the synchronous read operation, and all the flags and behaviors defined for *read* can be expected to apply to the concurrent read operation as well.

If _POSIX_PRIORITIZED_IO and _POSIX_PRIORITY_SCHEDULING are both supported, and the process is running under either SCHED_FIFO or SCHED_RR, then the asynchronous

aio_read (continued)

operation is submitted at a priority equal to the process's scheduling priority, *aio_reqprio*. Requests of higher priority to a given file are processed by the system before requests of lower priority.

Return Values

aio_read returns successfully if the asynchronous read operation was successfully queued into the system. In this case, 0 is returned. The actual success or failure of the read operation itself cannot be readily determined at this point; *aio_read* generally only returns an indication of the success of the submission of the operation. You use *aio_error* and *aio_return* to determine the status and return value of a particular asynchronous I/O operation. The return and error status of an asynchronous read operation are the same as for the corresponding synchronous read operation, with a few additional errors possible, as described below.

aio_read returns –1 on error.

Errors

If *aio_read* returns –1, it sets *errno* to one of the following values:

EAGAIN   *aio_read* could not queue up the asynchronous request due to system resource limitations (out of queueing elements in the operating system, for instance).

The system may check for these error conditions when the I/O request is submitted. In that case, *aio_read* might also return these values:

EBADF   The file descriptor passed in *aiocbp->aio_fildes* is not a valid file descriptor open for reading.

EINVAL   Some other element in the *aiocb* is invalid: *aio_nbytes* is not a valid value, the offset *aio_offset* is bad for the given file, or *aio_reqprio* is not a valid value.

If *aio_read* returns 0, then the I/O operation is successfully queued up and will proceed. In that case, the return and error values are as for the equivalent call to read. In addition, one of the following error conditions may occur:

ECANCELED   The AIO operation was cancelled by *aio_cancel.*

EINVAL   The offset implied by *aio_offset* is bad for the file.

Notes

aio_return must be called once and only once for every asynchronous operation, or your system may run out of resources for asynchronous I/O. The *aiocb* used for an *aio_read* (or *aio_write* or *lio_listio* or *aio_fsync*, for that matter) should be considered to be owned by the operating system for the duration of the asynchronous I/O operation. That means you should not modify any of the contents of the *aiocb*. You should not use the *aiocb* in submitting another asynchronous operation. You should not declare your *aiocb* as a local variable unless there is *no way* the local variable can disappear (through function return) before the end of the asynchronous operation. Lastly, you should not deallocate the memory containing the *aiocb* (either via *free* or via automatic stack shrinkage) until the asynchronous operation has finished.

With a normal *read*, there is no way to deallocate the buffer while the *read* is progressing because the process is blocked awaiting completion of the *read*. With asynchronous I/O, it is possible to deallocate the buffer being used for a concurrent read or write.

On systems that support prioritized I/O, the *aio_reqprio* field is always used. If you do not desire prioritized I/O, then you should be sure to set this field to 0.

Current UNIX Practice

SVR4:   No asynchronous I/O operations are specified in SVR4.

BSD: No asynchronous I/O operations are specified in BSD UNIX (as of 4.3).

SunOS: SunOS has an asynchronous I/O facility similar to the POSIX facility, but it is not identical.

See Also

read (the asynchronous operation of *aio_read* is based on *read*)
lseek (the behavior of the implied seek is explained here)
sigqueue (the behavior of signal delivery is explained here)
aio_write (this is the write analogue to this read call)
lio_listio (this function allows many AIOs to be done at once as well as allowing for a synchronous seek-n-read)
aio_error (this function retrieves the error status of an AIO)
aio_return (this function retrieves the return status of an AIO)
aio_suspend (this function is used to wait for an AIO to complete)
aio_cancel (this function tries to cancel an AIO that has not completed yet)

aio_return

Name

aio_return — Retrieve the return status for an asynchronous operation.

Synopsis

```
#include       <aio.h>
ssize_t        aio_return(struct aiocb *aiocbp);
```

Conditionality

```
#ifdef _POSIX_ASYNCHRONOUS_IO
```

Description

aio_return is used to determine the return status of an asynchronous operation. The return status of an asynchronous operation is the same as it would be if the operation were synchronous (the return status for an *aio_read* is generally the same as the *return* value for the equivalent *lseek* and *read*, for example).

In addition, the *aio_return* has the side effect of retiring this asynchronous I/O control block from the system.

Returns

aio_return retrieves the return status of the asynchronous operation that was submitted using *aiocbp*. That status is passed back as the return value of the call. *aio_return* may return –1, as well, if it is called erroneously (with a bad *aiocbp*, for example). In this case, *aio_return* will also set *errno*.

Errors

aio_return returns –1 in only one possible case, and in this case, it only returns the error if the system detects the error.

EINVAL   The *aiocb* address passed to *aio_return* does not represent a valid asynchronous operation whose return status has not yet been retrieved (either you have passed in a bogus *aiocb*, or that *aiocb* has not yet been used for submitting asynchronous I/O, or you have already called *aio_return* with this *aiocb* address).

Notes

aio_return must be called once and only once for every asynchronous operation, or your system may run out of resources for asynchronous I/O.

aio_return must only be called once an asynchronous operation is complete. In order to determine whether an asynchronous operation is complete, you can call *aio_error* and verify that the error status for the asynchronous operation is something other than EINPROGRESS.

The operating system may maintain error and return status for an asynchronous operation within the operating system. For this reason, the operating system needs an indication of when an application is "done" with a particular asynchronous operation, so that any resources can be freed. A call to *aio_return* serves this purpose. Therefore, once *aio_return* has been called for a particular asynchronous operation, neither *aio_return* nor *aio_error* may be called again for that asynchronous operation.

See Also

read (the return values for *aio_read* are based on those of *read*)
write (the return values for *aio_write* are based on those of *write*)
lseek (possible errors related to the implied seek are explained here)
aio_read, aio_write, lio_listio (used to submit asynchronous I/O)
aio_error (this function retrieves the error status of an AIO)

aio_suspend

Name

aio_suspend — Wait for asynchronous operations to complete.

Synopsis

```
#include        <aio.h>
int             aio_suspend(struct aiocb *lacb[],
                int nent,
                const struct timespec *timeout);
```

Conditionality

```
#ifdef _POSIX_ASYNCHRONOUS_IO
```

Description

aio_suspend allows you to wait for any of a set of asynchronous I/O operations to complete. The set is indicated by the list *lacb* of pointers to asynchronous I/O control blocks that have been used for submitting asynchronous I/O. The list is of size *nent* elements, and NULL elements are allowed on the list (these are ignored, but count as one of the *nent* elements). A timeout argument, if not NULL, specifies a maximum time to wait for I/O to complete. If the time specified elapses, then *aio_suspend* will return −1 with *errno* set to EAGAIN.

Return Values

aio_suspend returns 0 if one or more of the awaited asynchronous operations completes; otherwise it returns −1. *aio_suspend* does not tell you which asynchronous operation completed; you can scan the array using *aio_error* and *aio_return* to determine which of the I/Os has finished when you return from *aio_suspend*.

Errors

aio_suspend returns −1 and sets *errno* to the following values under the following conditions:

EAGAIN   The time specified by the timeout argument has elapsed with none of the asynchronous I/O on the list completing.

EINTR   A signal interrupted this function.

Notes

There is no maximum number of elements specified for the array that is passed to *aio_suspend*.

aio_suspend may be interrupted by a signal, returning −1 with *errno* == EINTR. The signal may be one of those signals that was supposed to be delivered upon completion of an asynchronous I/O operation. If your asynchronous I/Os do send signals, then you should be aware of the possibility of *aio_suspend* returning −1 and EINTR even though an I/O has completed.

Current UNIX Practice

SVR4:   No asynchronous I/O operations are specified in SVR4

BSD: No asynchronous I/O operations are specified in BSD UNIX (as of 4.3)

SunOS: SunOS has an asynchronous I/O facility similar to the POSIX facility, but it is not identical

See Also

aio_read, *aio_write* (these functions submit asynchronous I/Os)
lio_listio (this function allows many AIOs to be done at once)
aio_error (this function retrieves the error status of an AIO)
aio_return (this function retrieves the return status of an AIO)

aio_write

Name

aio_write — Asynchronously write to a file.

Synopsis

```
#include        <aio.h>
int             aio_write(struct aiocb *aiocbp);
```

Conditionality

```
#ifdef _POSIX_ASYNCHRONOUS_IO
        /* Asynchronous I/O is supported */
#ifdef _POSIX_PRIORITIZED_IO
        /* Asynchronous I/O is prioritized relative to other AIO. */
#endif
#endif
```

Description

aio_write submits a single asynchronous write operation to the system. The call returns immediately after submitting the operation, leaving the system to perform the write concurrently with the execution of other processes. The write operation behaves roughly as if it were the following code snippet:

```
lseek(aiocbp->aio_fildes, aiocbp->aio_offset, SEEK_SET);
rv = write(aiocbp->aio_fildes, aiocbp->aio_buf, aiocbp->aio_nbytes);
/* If a signal is desired, then deliver it */
if (aiocbp->aio_sigevent.sigev_notify == SIGEV_SIGNAL) {
        sigqueue(pid, aiocbp->aio_sigevent.sigev_signo,
                aiocbp->aio_sigevent.sigev_value);
        /* When the signal handler is invoked, its
         * info->si_code field will be set to SI_ASYNCIO
         * to indicate that the signal was the result of
         * asynchronous I/O completion. */
}
```

The seek and the write are performed atomically with respect to other outstanding I/O in the system. In other words, you definitely will write data to the file offset you specified. On devices that are not capable of seeking, and on files which are set to append-only mode (via the O_APPEND flag), the seek offset is ignored.

The concurrent write operation behaves just like the synchronous write operation, and all the flags and behaviors defined for *write* can be expected to apply to the concurrent write operation as well.

If _POSIX_PRIORITIZED_IO and _POSIX_PRIORITY_SCHEDULING are both supported, and the process is running under either SCHED_FIFO or SCHED_RR, then the asynchronous operation is submitted at a priority equal to the process's scheduling priority, *aio_reqprio*. Requests of higher priority to a given file are processed by the system before requests of lower priority.

Return Values

aio_write returns successfully if the asynchronous write operation was successfully queued into the system. In this case, 0 is returned. The actual success or failure of the write operation itself cannot be readily determined at this point; *aio_write* generally only returns an indication of the success of the submission of the operation. You use *aio_error* and *aio_return* to determine the status and return value of a particular asynchronous I/O operation. The return and error status of an asynchronous write operation are the same as for the corresponding synchronous write operation, with a few additional errors possible, as described below.

aio_write returns –1 on error.

Errors

If *aio_write* returns –1, it sets *errno* to one of the following values:

EAGAIN   *aio_write* could not queue up the asynchronous request due to system resource limitations (out of queueing elements in the operating system, for instance).

The system may check for these error conditions when the I/O request is submitted. In that case, *aio_write* might also return these values:

EBADF   The file descriptor passed in *aiocbp->aio_fildes* is not a valid file descriptor open for writing.

EINVAL   Some other element in the *aiocb* is invalid: *aio_nbytes* is not a valid value, the offset *aio_offset* is bad for the given file, or *aio_reqprio* is not a valid value.

If *aio_write* returns 0, then the I/O operation is successfully queued up and will proceed. In that case, the return and error values are as for the equivalent call to write. In addition, one of the following error conditions may occur:

ECANCELED   The AIO operation was cancelled by *aio_cancel*.

EINVAL   The offset implied by *aio_offset* is bad for the file.

aio_write (continued)

Notes

aio_return must be called once and only once for every asynchronous operation, or your system may run out of resources for asynchronous I/O.

The *aiocb* used for an *aio_write* (or *aio_read*, *lio_listio*, or *aio_fsync*, for that matter) should be considered to be owned by the operating system for the duration of the asynchronous I/O operation. That means you should not modify any of the contents of the *aiocb*. You should not use the *aiocb* in submitting another asynchronous operation. You should not declare your *aiocb* as a local variable unless there is *no way* the local variable can disappear (through function return) before the end of the asynchronous operation. Lastly, you should not deallocate the memory containing the *aiocb* (either via *free* or via automatic stack shrinkage) until the asynchronous operation has finished.

By setting the O_APPEND flag on the file descriptor (using either *open* or *fcntl*), you can cause asynchronous writes to always append to the file, for an asynchronous logging facility. In this case, the seek offset is ignored.

On systems that support prioritized I/O, the *aio_reqprio* field is always used. If you do not desire prioritized I/O, then you should be sure to set this field to 0.

Current UNIX Practice

SVR4:   No asynchronous I/O operations are specified in SVR4.

BSD: No asynchronous I/O operations are specified in BSD UNIX (as of 4.3).

SunOS: SunOS has an asynchronous I/O facility similar to the POSIX facility, but it is not identical.

See Also

write (the asynchronous operation of *aio_write* is based on *write*)
lseek (the behavior of the implied seek is explained here)
sigqueue (the behavior of signal delivery is explained here)
aio_read (this is the read analogue to this write call)
lio_listio (this function allows many AIOs to be done at once as well as allowing for a synchronous seek-n-write)
aio_error (this function retrieves the error status of an AIO)
aio_return (this function retrieves the return status of an AIO)
aio_suspend (this function is used to wait for an AIO to complete)
aio_cancel (this function tries to cancel an AIO that has not completed yet)

Name

clock_getres — Get resolution of a POSIX.4 clock.

Synopsis

```
#include        <time.h>
int             clock_getres(clockid_t which_system_clock,
                        struct timespec *resolution);
```

Conditionality

```
#ifdef _POSIX_TIMERS
```

Description

clock_getres returns the resolution of the clock identified by *which_system_clock*. Every POSIX.4 conformant system must support at least one clock, identified as CLOCK_REALTIME. Other clocks provided by your machine are described in the POSIX.4 conformance statement.

Every clock has a particular resolution which is probably coarser than a nanosecond. CLOCK_REALTIME must support a resolution at least as fine as 50 Hz, or 20,000,000 nanoseconds. The clock resolution affects the accuracy of the time you set using *clock_settime*. This setting is rounded down to the clock resolution. The resolution also affects your interval timer settings: they are rounded up to the clock resolution. The same goes for *nanosleep*.

To set a clock's time, or tell what time it is, use *clock_settime* and *clock_gettime*, respectively. Interval timers may be created based on particular clocks, using *timer_create*.

Return Values

When *clock_getres* is successful, it returns 0 and sets resolution with the resolution of the indicated system clock. *clock_getres* returns –1 on error.

Errors

If *clock_getres* fails, it returns –1 and sets *errno* to the following:

EINVAL   The clock ID specified is not one that exists on this system.

Notes

Clock resolution is generally a hard-wired feature of the system clock. You cannot change it.

Current UNIX Practice

On standard UNIX systems (BSD and System V), which support only one standard clock, one looks at the constant HZ in *<sys/param.h>*.

See Also

clock_settime, clock_gettime (to set and get the time)
timer_create, timer_settime, timer_gettime (to create and use interval timers)

Name

clock_gettime — Get the time according to a particular POSIX.4 clock.

Synopsis

```
#include        <time.h>
int             clock_gettime(clockid_t which_system_clock,
                        struct timespec *current_time);
```

Conditionality

```
#ifdef _POSIX_TIMERS
```

Description

clock_gettime retrieves the time, as indicated by the clock identified by *which_system_clock*. Every POSIX.4 conformant system must support at least one clock, identified as CLOCK_REALTIME. Other clocks provided by your machine are described in the POSIX.4 conformance statement.

The time value you get for the clock is only correct to a certain resolution, and represents a snapshot of the time when the system looked at it. Remember that it takes some (hopefully small) amount of time to get back to the process.

To determine the resolution of a clock, use *clock_getres*.

POSIX.4 clock values have nothing to do with time zones, and POSIX.4 does not define anything in particular to deal with time zones. You must manage time zones yourself if you care about them. The ANSI standard functions (*ctime, localtime, gmtime, mktime*), which take time as a number of seconds since the Epoch, will function with the *tv_sec* field of a *struct timespec*.

Return Values

When *clock_gettime* is successful, it returns 0 and sets *current_time* with the time according to the indicated system clock. *clock_gettime* returns –1 on error.

Errors

If *clock_gettime* fails, it returns –1 and sets *errno* to the following:

EINVAL   The clock ID specified is not one that exists on this system.

Current UNIX Practice

BSD systems use the *gettimeofday* system call to get the time according to the one defined clock on those systems.

See Also

clock_settime (to set the time)
clock_getres (to determine the resolution of a clock)
timer_create, timer_settime, timer_gettime (to create and use interval timers)

Name

clock_settime — Set the time on a particular POSIX.4 clock.

Synopsis

```
#include      <time.h>
int           clock_settime(clockid_t which_system_clock,
                    const struct timespec *setting);
```

Conditionality

```
#ifdef _POSIX_TIMERS
```

Description

clock_settime sets the clock identified by *which_system_clock*. The clock is set to the absolute time indicated by setting. Every POSIX.4 conformant system must support at least one clock, identified as CLOCK_REALTIME. Other clocks provided by your machine are described in the POSIX.4 conformance statement.

Every clock has a particular resolution which is probably coarser than a nanosecond. Therefore, the setting you pass in for the clock may need to be rounded. The system rounds this value down to the resolution of the clock.

To determine the resolution of a clock, use *clock_getres*.

The settings of POSIX.4 clocks has nothing to do with time zones, and POSIX.4 does not define anything in particular to deal with time zones. You must manage time zones yourself if you care about them. The ANSI standard functions (*ctime*, *localtime*, *gmtime*, *mktime*), which take time as a number of seconds since the Epoch, will function with the *tv_sec* field of a *struct timespec*.

Return Values

When *clock_settime* is successful, it returns 0 and sets the indicated clock to the requested time, possibly with rounding. If *clock_settime* fails, it returns –1 and does not disturb the setting of the clock.

Errors

If *clock_settime* fails, it returns −1 and sets *errno* to one of the following:

EINVAL   The clock ID specified is not one that exists on this system. Alternatively, the time setting you specified contains a number of nanoseconds that is less than zero, or greater than or equal to 1,000,000,000. Nanoseconds are meant to be a fraction of a second.

EPERM   The calling process does not have the right to set the indicated clock. Appropriate privilege for setting a clock varies from system to system, and is described in the POSIX.4 conformance statement for the system.

Current UNIX Practice

Typically, a clock is set as part of the system administration activities for a system, and applications use the existing clock setting.

BSD systems use the *settimeofday* system call to set the one defined clock on those systems.

See Also

clock_gettime (to tell the time)
clock_getres (to determine the resolution of a clock)
timer_create, *timer_settime*, *timer_gettime* (to create and use interval timers)

Name

close — Close a file or a shared memory object.

Synopsis

```
int         close(int fd);
```

Conditionality

Unconditional.

Description

The *close* function severs the connection between the file descriptor *fd* and the underlying object which was opened with *open*. Normally, these objects are disk files.

close also closes shared memory objects which were opened with *shm_open*.

After a file descriptor has been closed, you cannot use it for anything. The file descriptor number is recycled and may come up again on a subsequent *open* (or *shm_open*) by this process.

Return Values

close returns 0 if it successfully closes the file descriptor. It will in general be able to do this unless you pass in a bad file descriptor number. *close* returns −1 if it fails.

Errors

If *close* returns −1, it sets *errno* to one of the following:

EBADF   *fd* is not a valid open file descriptor for this process.

EINTR   The operation was interrupted by a signal. This is not generally likely, although it can happen, for instance, if the process has to wait for asynchronous I/O to complete on the file descriptor. Usually a *close* operation is nonblocking, and therefore cannot be interrupted by a signal.

Current UNIX Practice

close is standard in all UNIX systems.

close (continued)

See Also

open (to open a file)
shm_open (to open a shared memory object)
exit, exec (effects on open file descriptors)

Name

exec family of functions — Transform the calling process into another image.

Synopsis

```
int         execl(const char *path, const char *arg, ...);
int         execle(const char *path, const char *arg, ..., NULL,
                const char *envp[]);
int         execlp(const char *path, const char *arg, ...);

int         execv(const char *path, const char *argv[]);
int         execve(const char *path, const char *argv[],
                const char *envp[]);
int         execvp(const char *path, const char *argv[]);
```

Conditionality

Unconditional.

Description

The *exec* family of calls each transform the calling process into a new process. It's actually still the same *process*: the process ID and probably most of the operating system state are the same before and after the call to *exec*. However, after *exec* the process begins executing a new program, named by the argument *path*.

The different flavors of *exec* are merely different ways of passing arguments to the new program. The versions of *exec* with an argument *arg* pass arguments as separate parameters to the call: *execl("/bin/ls", "ls", "/tmp", NULL)*. The other versions, with an array of strings, pass the arguments in that array, with the last argument a NULL pointer.

execve takes a third argument which becomes the environment for the new program. *execle*, likewise, takes an array of strings for its environment for the new program; however, this argument follows all the other arguments to the program.

All other versions of the *exec* call inherit the environment from the calling process.

execlp and *execvp* use the environment variable PATH to locate the executable file to run. If */bin* were in your PATH, for instance, you could run */bin/ls* by calling *execlp("ls", ...)*. All other versions of the *exec* call require you to give the full pathname of the executable file, e.g., *execl("/bin/ls", ...)*.

POSIX.1 Semantics

Calls to *exec* do not return *per se*; instead, execution begins in the new program. Thus, *exec* is sort of a yin to *fork*'s yang; where *fork* creates a process that is mostly the same, *exec* creates one that is almost entirely different from the caller. However, certain OS state is retained across an *exec*, as described in the following table:

Object	Effect in Exec-ed Process
Process ID	Inherited
Parent process	Inherited
Process group ID	Inherited
Session membership	Inherited
Real user and group IDs	Inherited
Supplementary group IDs	Inherited
Current working directory	Inherited
Root directory	Inherited
Accounting time	Inherited
Umask	Inherited
Signal mask	Inherited
Signal handlers	SIG_DFL and SIG_IGN inherited, others set to SIG_DFL
Pending signals	Cleared
Alarms	Left pending
Files	Inherited, unless FD_CLOEXEC set for file (then closed)

Much of the operating system state for the *exec*ed process remains the same, although the process memory image is almost completely altered.

POSIX.4 Semantics

As POSIX.4 adds more context to each process, the effect of *exec* on this context is explained in the following table:

Object	Effect in New process image
Semaphores	Closed
Message queues	Closed
Shared memory	Unmapped
File mappings	Unmapped
Pending real-time signals	Retained in new process image

Asynch I/O	May be cancelled; if not, process may block awaiting completion (new process memory is not affected by pre-*exec* AIO)
Memory locks	Released
Scheduling attributes	SCHED_FIFO and SCHED_RR attributes inherited
Timers	Deleted

Pending real-time signals are retained, as are other signals. Real-time signal handlers are modified as described for POSIX.1 signals above.

Scheduling attributes for the defined schedulers are inherited. If your operating system provides other scheduling disciplines, it must document whether those attributes are inherited.

Asynchronous I/O presents an odd conundrum if you call *exec* while AIO is going on for your process. The basic fact is that AIO in the process before *exec* is not allowed to affect the post-*exec* process image. The I/O may be cancelled, if your system supports that; otherwise, the I/O must proceed *as if the process had waited for it to complete.* That means that the systems need to keep around whatever memory in your process is necessary for the I/O until that I/O no longer needs it. If you are going to call *exec*, do yourself a favor and cancel or wait for all your outstanding asynchronous I/O first.

All other POSIX.4 process state is reset, cleared, and freed when *exec* is called.

Return Values

exec doesn't return if it is successful. Instead, it begins execution of the new process. If *exec* fails, then the process image is retained as it was before the call, and –1 is returned.

Errors

If *exec* returns –1, it sets *errno* to one of the following values:

E2BIG
: You passed too many arguments/environment variables, overrunning the system limit ARG_MAX.

EACCES
: Either permission was denied to execute the named file, or the named file was not executable.

ENAMETOOLONG
: The name of the file to execute violated POSIX naming constraints by being too long, either in a path component or in total.

ENOENT   The pathname to the executable contains elements that do not exist
                (*/bun/ls* instead of */bin/ls*, e.g.).

ENOTDIR   The pathname contained elements that are not directories.

Current UNIX Practice

exec is standard in all UNIX systems; POSIX.4 semantics are new to POSIX.4.

See Also

fork (often performed before *exec*)
aio_suspend, aio_cancel (how to wait for or cancel asynchronous I/O)

Name

exit, _exit — Terminate the calling process.

Synopsis

```
void            _exit(int status);
void            exit(int status);
```

Conditionality

Unconditional.

Description

The *_exit* function, mandated by POSIX, and its cousin *exit*, perform basically the same action: they terminate the calling process. *exit* is a requirement of ANSI C, and cleans up more ANSI C constructs than *_exit* does. It is assumed that *exit* is a library call which calls *_exit* to actually terminate the process. You should generally use *exit* in your programs, assuming that your system supports ANSI C. Further references to *exit* should be read as, "*exit* or *_exit.*"

When *exit* is called, all process state is cleared out, except for a data structure related to the recently-departed process. This data structure contains one interesting field, the *exit* status of the process, as passed in the call to *exit*. This status may be retrieved by the parent process of the caller, by using *wait* or *waitpid*. The *wait* calls have the side effect of cleaning up the corpse, and therefore can only be called once for a given process.

POSIX.1 Semantics

Calls to *exit* do not return, but rather tear down all process state as shown in the following table:

Object	Effect of Exit
All IDs	Retired
Accounting time	Stopped
Pending signals	Cleared
Alarms	Cleared
Files	Closed

This table can be summed up in the following sentence: Everything goes away.

exit (continued)

POSIX.4 Semantics

The same basic semantic applies to POSIX.4 objects:

Object	Effect in New Process Image
Semaphores	Closed
Message queues	Closed
Shared memory	Unmapped
File mappings	Unmapped
Pending real-time signals	Cleared
Asynch I/O	May be cancelled; if not, process may block awaiting completion (new process memory is not affected by pre-*exec* AIO)
Memory locks	Released
Timers	Deleted

Asynchronous I/O can be strange if you call *exit* while AIO is going on for your process. Such I/O may be cancelled, if your system supports that; otherwise, the I/O must proceed *as if the process had waited for it to complete*. That means that whatever memory in your process is necessary for the I/O, the system needs to keep it around until that I/O no longer needs it. If you are going to call *exit*, do yourself a favor and cancel/wait for all your outstanding asynchronous I/O first.

All other POSIX.4 process state is reset, cleared, and freed when *exit* is called.

Return Values

exit never returns, either successfully or not.

Errors

exit is infallible.

Current UNIX Practice

exit is standard in all UNIX systems; POSIX.4 semantics are new to POSIX.4.

See Also

fork, *exec* (fellow POSIX.1 process primitives)
aio_suspend, *aio_cancel* (how to wait for or cancel asynchronous I/O)

Name

fdatasync — Synchronize at least the data part of a file with the underlying media.

Synopsis

```
#include        <unistd.h>
int             fdatasync(int fildes);
```

Conditionality

```
#ifdef _POSIX_SYNCHRONIZED_IO
```

Description

fdatasync causes the system to flush out all the buffered contents associated with *fildes* to the underlying media. The call doesn't return until all data has been successfully transferred to the disk (or whatever other hardware device the file may reside on).

fdatasync, in contrast to *fsync*, causes the system to flush out the actual bytes comprising the file's data, but not necessarily to control information about the file, like access and modification times, or permission bits. When *fsync* is called, for comparison, *all* data relevant to the file is flushed from the system's internal buffers.

fdatasync may be slightly faster than *fsync*. Of course, *fdatasync* only updates part of your file, so you should be aware of what you're doing when you use it.

fdatasync may also be implemented as a call to *fsync*, in which case *fdatasync* will be no faster than *fsync*.

POSIX.4 declines to state exactly what it means for something to be "successfully transferred." Instead, it just says that each vendor has to provide enough documentation for you, the application writer, to determine what the vendor does for an *fdatasync* call. Usually, one assumes that after you've called *fdatasync*, you can crash the machine and be pretty much assured of getting your data back. Of course, if some *other* file is sufficiently screwed up, your disk may just be hosed entirely. In any event, this is something to check in the vendor's conformance document.

Return Values

fdatasync returns 0 if it successfully flushed all buffered data to disk. Otherwise, it returns –1 and sets *errno* accordingly.

Errors

If *fdatasync* returns −1, it sets *errno* to one of the following values:

EBADF   *fildes* is not a valid file descriptor.

EINVAL   The file descriptor is valid, but the system doesn't support *fdatasync* on this particular file.

Notes

fdatasync is provided under the _POSIX_SYNCHRONIZED_IO option. *fsync*, in contrast, is provided loosely under _POSIX_FSYNC, with some additional rigor applied if _POSIX_SYNCHRONIZED_IO is also defined. That's because *fsync* is a more useful function, and non-real-time people also want to support it. This means that a system may support *fsync*, but not *fdatasync*. You can easily check this using a system configuration check program that looks for the proper options.

Current UNIX Practice

SVR4:   *fdatasync* is not part of SVR4

BSD: *fdatasync* is not part of BSD

SunOS: *fdatasync* is not part of SunOS

See Also

write (that which is written is pretty much what you're going to be interested in flushing via *fdatasync*)
read (read modifies the access bits for a file, which may or may not be flushed by *fdatasync*)
fsync (the more rigorous, slower cousin of *fdatasync*)
aio_fsync (a way to asynchronously synchronize your files)

Name

fork — Duplicate the calling process.

Synopsis

```
int          fork();
```

Conditionality

Unconditional.

Description

fork is the call used to duplicate a process under POSIX. This function is mandated by the base POSIX standard and is present on all POSIX systems.

POSIX.1 Semantics

When a process calls *fork*, it returns as two processes. The original process gets returned the process ID of the newly-created, or child process. The child process is returned a 0. Other than that difference, the two processes are very close copies of one another. The processes have the same memory context and mostly the same operating system context. Exceptions to this operating system context are noted below.

Object	Effect in Child
Open files	Inherited
File locks	Cleared in child
Pending alarms	Cleared in child
Signal handlers	Inherited
Signal mask	Inherited
Pending signals	None in child

Files that are open in the parent process will be open in the child as well. File locks which the parent had are not duplicated for the child process.

If the parent had called *alarm* to cause an alarm signal to be delivered at some time in the future, that alarm is cancelled in the child.

Signal handlers and signal mask are inherited by the child process; however, the child process will have no signals pending even if several were pending in the parent.

POSIX.4 Semantics

As POSIX.4 adds more context to each process, the effect of *fork* on this context is explained in the following table:

Object	Effect in Child
Semaphores	Inherited
Message queues	Inherited
Shared memory	Inherited
File mappings	Inherited
Pending real-time signals	None in child
Asynch I/O	Buffers, seek pointers in indeterminate state; no notification received
Memory locks	Released in child
Scheduling attributes	SCHED_FIFO and SCHED_RR attributes inherited
Timers	Not inherited

POSIX.4 semaphores that are created or accessible in the parent, either named semaphores or unnamed semaphores, will be inherited and available for use in the child process.

POSIX.4 message queues that are accessible in the parent process will be accessible in the child process.

POSIX.4 mappings, either for shared memory or for files, will be maintained in the child. Mappings which are mapped with the flag MAP_PRIVATE will retain that semantic as follows: changes that the parent made before calling *fork* will be visible to the child, but changes made after *fork* will remain private.

Real-time extended signals that are pending in the parent process will be cleared from the child process. The child returns from *fork* with no pending signals.

There are no clear statements about the effect of *fork* on asynchronous I/O in a child process. The implication is that any buffer being used in the parent may be in a corrupt state in the child, depending on how far the I/O proceeded before the call to *fork*. Likewise, the seek pointer for a file being used for asynchronous I/O is left in an indeterminate state, for both the parent and the child (this fact is independent of *fork*).

A child process has no locked memory, even if the parent explicitly locked memory by calling *mlock* or *mlockall*.

POSIX.4 timers created in the parent are not inherited in the child. The child begins life with no timers.

Scheduling attributes for the defined schedulers are inherited. If your operating system provides other scheduling disciplines, it must document whether those attributes are inherited.

Return Values

fork returns 0 in the child, and the process ID of the child to the parent. If *fork* fails, then no child process is created, and *fork* returns –1 to the parent.

Errors

If *fork* returns –1, it sets *errno* to one of the following values:

EAGAIN   The system ran out of some resource necessary for duplicating the process. This may be memory, process slots, files, semaphores, signal vector state, message queues, space for mappings, or whatever.

ENOMEM   The system ran out of memory. This error may or may not be returned.

Current UNIX Practice

fork is standard in all UNIX systems; POSIX.4 semantics are new to POSIX.4.

See Also

exec (often performed after *fork*)

fsync

Name

fsync — Synchronize a file with the underlying media.

Synopsis

```
#include         <unistd.h>
int              fsync(int fildes);
```

Conditionality

```
#ifdef _POSIX_FSYNC
        /* Function is present and synchronizes data to an
        implementation-defined stage (documented in the conformance
        document) */
#ifdef _POSIX_SYNCHRONIZED_IO
        /* Function forces all I/O to the stage of synchronized
        I/O file integrity completion. */
#endif
#endif
```

Description

fsync causes the system to flush out all the data associated with *fildes* to the underlying media. The call doesn't return until all data has been successfully transferred to the disk (or whatever other hardware device the file may reside on).

fsync causes all data relevant to the file to be flushed from the system's internal buffers. In contrast, there is also a function, called *fdatasync*, which is only guaranteed to flush out the actual bytes comprising the file's data (but not necessarily control information about the file, like access and modification times, or permission bits). *fdatasync* may be slightly faster than *fsync*. Of course, *fdatasync* only updates part of your file, so you should be aware of what you're doing when you use it.

POSIX.4 declines to state exactly what it means for something to be "successfully transferred." Instead, it just says that each vendor has to provide enough documentation for you, the application writer, to determine what the vendor does for an *fsync* call. Usually, one assumes that after you've called *fsync* you can crash the machine and be pretty much assured of getting your data back. Of course, if some *other* file is sufficiently screwed up, your disk may just be hosed entirely. In any event, this is something to check in the vendor's conformance document.

Return Values

fsync returns 0 if it successfully flushed all buffered data to disk. Otherwise, it returns −1 and sets *errno* accordingly.

Errors

If *fsync* returns −1, it sets *errno* to one of the following values:

EBADF   *fildes* is not a valid file descriptor.

EINVAL   The file descriptor is valid, but the system doesn't support *fsync* on this particular file.

Notes

fsync is provided under the _POSIX_FSYNC option, so that systems that don't really want to do real time can still support *fsync* in a somewhat well-defined manner. However, if the underlying implementation does not support POSIX.4 synchronized I/O as well (i.e., _POSIX_SYNCHRONIZED_IO is not supported), then it is rather unclear exactly what you are doing when you call *fsync*. POSIX.4 supplies at least some rudimentary definitions of what is required from *fsync*. You should look for both _POSIX_FSYNC and _POSIX_SYNCHRONIZED_IO to determine how well-supported *fsync* is on your target system.

If *fsync* ever returns an error of EINVAL, it's because the underlying file doesn't support the semantics required for POSIX.4 synchronized I/O. The *fsync* call may still have done something, but it is not able to satisfy the requirements of POSIX.4 file integrity I/O completion.

Current UNIX Practice

SVR4:   *fsync* is part of SVR4

BSD: *fsync* is part of BSD

SunOS: *fsync* is part of SunOS

fsync (continued)

See Also

write (that which is written is pretty much what you're going to be interested in flushing via *fsync*)
fdatasync (the less-rigorous, maybe faster cousin of *fsync*)
aio_fsync (a way to asynchronously synchronize your files)

Name

kill, sigqueue — Send signals to a process.

Synopsis

```
#include        <unistd.h>
#include        <signal.h>

int             kill(pid_t pid, int sig);
#ifdef _POSIX_REALTIME_SIGNALS
int             sigqueue(pid_t pid, int sig, const union sigval val);
#endif _POSIX_REALTIME_SIGNALS
```

Conditionality

The *kill* function is present in all POSIX systems; *sigqueue* is conditional on
_POSIX_REALTIME_SIGNALS.

Description

The *kill* and *sigqueue* functions send the signal whose number is *sig* to the process
whose ID is *pid*. Either function can send any of the defined signals, including the
real-time extended signals SIGRTMIN through SIGRTMAX. However, *kill* has no provi-
sion to include the extra data value that these signals carry along with them. In order
to pass the extra data, you must use *sigqueue* and its third parameter, *val*.

For either function, the process must have appropriate privileges to send the signal to
the named process, and the process must, of course, exist. If you specify a signal number of 0, then these checks for permission and process ID validity will be performed,
but no signal sill be sent. This can be handy for verifying process existence.

Normal Signal Delivery

The signals other than SIGRTMIN through SIGRTMAX are delivered via a simple handler
function which takes a single argument, the signal number.

```
void    signal_handler(int signo)
{
}
```

This handler function is installed in the target process by *sigaction*, by specifying the
handler address in the *sa_handler* field of the *struct sigaction*.

Real-Time Extended Signal Delivery

The real-time signals SIGRTMIN through SIGRTMAX can be delivered either as normal signals above, or as extended, queued signals. To specify the extended, queueing behavior for these signals, you set SA_SIGINFO in *sa_flags* of the *struct sigaction* when you call *sigaction*; you set the handler function address in *sa_sigaction*. Note that this is a different field from *sa_handler*. A queued signal handler is invoked as follows:

```
void    signal_handler(int signo, siginfo_t *info, void *extra)
{
}
```

The parameter *info* points to a *siginfo_t*. This structure contains several fields:

```
typedef struct {
        int             si_signo;
        int             si_code;
        union sigval    si_value;
} siginfo_t;
```

si_signo will be set to the number of the signal delivered (the same as the *signo* parameter). *si_code*, which indicates the cause of the signal, is set to the constant SI_USER in the case of a real-time signal sent by *kill*, and is set to SI_QUEUE if the signal was sent by *sigqueue*. The field *si_value* will contain the value that was sent as the *val* parameter to *sigqueue*. If this signal was sent by *kill* rather than *sigqueue*, then the contents of this field are undefined.

The third parameter (**extra*) is not defined by POSIX; however, other UNIX systems sometimes pass a third parameter to their signal handlers.

Return Values

These functions return successfully when they deliver a signal to the indicated process. That process, in turn, may handle the signal immediately, or it may be blocking the signal or ignoring it. A successful return from *kill* or *sigqueue* merely means that the signal has been delivered to the target process. What that process *does* with the signal is another matter. These functions return 0 when they succeed. In the case of error, −1 will be returned.

Errors

If these functions return –1, they set *errno* to one of the following values:

EINVAL   The signal number is invalid, not one the system supports.

EPERM   You do not have the right to send this signal to the specified target process.

ESRCH   No such process exists.

EAGAIN   The system ran out of resources to queue the signal and its associated data value (*sigqueue* only).

Current UNIX Practice

kill is standard UNIX functionality, but *sigqueue* is new for POSIX.4.

See Also

sigaction (information on handling signals)
sigprocmask (information on blocking signals)

lio_listio

Name

lio_listio — Perform a list of I/O operations, synchronously or asynchronously.

Synopsis

```
#include      <aio.h>
int           lio_listio(int mode, struct aiocb *acb_list[],
              int nent, struct sigevent *sig);
```

Conditionality

```
#ifdef _POSIX_ASYNCHRONOUS_IO
       /* Function is present */
#ifdef _POSIX_PRIORITIZED_IO
       /* Prioritized I/O is performed. */
#endif
#endif
```

Description

lio_listio submits a list of read and write operations to the system. The call can run in synchronous or asynchronous mode.

If the mode parameter is equal to LIO_NOWAIT, then *lio_listio* operates in asynchronous mode. In this case, all the operations on the *acb_list* are submitted as if by corresponding calls to *aio_read* and *aio_write*, and then the *lio_listio* call returns immediately. In this case, the normal asynchronous operation takes place, and, in addition, when all the asynchronous operations are complete, a signal, specified by the *sig* argument, is sent (if the *sigev_notify* field is equal to SIGEV_SIGNAL).

If the mode parameter is equal to LIO_WAIT, then *lio_listio* operates in synchronous mode, submitting all the read and write operations and then waiting for them all to complete before returning. In synchronous mode, the last parameter, *sig*, is ignored.

The *acb_list* argument contains a list of AIO control blocks that specify operations to be done (either synchronously or asynchronously). The length of the list is *nent* elements; the maximum list size is AIO_LISTIO_MAX. NULL elements on the list are ignored. In the AIO control block, there is an opcode field, *aio_lio_opcode*, which is used only by *lio_listio*. If an AIO control block's *aio_lio_opcode* field is LIO_READ, then the operation is an asynchronous read. If the opcode is LIO_WRITE, then the operation is an asynchronous write. If the opcode is LIO_NOP, then the AIO control block is skipped.

The asynchronous operations are submitted in an unspecified order. You should not count on the operations being submitted in any particular order.

For more detail on the semantics of the individual asynchronous read and write operations, take a look at the man pages for *aio_read* and *aio_write*.

Return Values

In asynchronous mode, *lio_listio* returns 0 if all the functions were successfully queued up to be done; otherwise it returns –1 and sets *errno* to indicate the error.

In synchronous mode, *lio_listio* waits for all the asynchronous operations to complete, and then returns 0. Otherwise, *lio_listio* returns –1. In either case, you should use *aio_error* and *aio_return* to determine the success or failure of individual operations. The return and error status of asynchronous operations are the same as for the corresponding synchronous operation, with a few additional errors possible, as described for *aio_read* and *aio_write*. These additional errors relate to the possibility of the asynchronous I/O being cancelled or the seek offset being invalid on the file.

Errors

If *lio_listio* returns –1, it sets *errno* to one of the following values:

EAGAIN   *lio_listio* could not queue up the asynchronous request due to system resource limitations (out of queueing elements in the operating system, for instance, or because there would be too many outstanding asynchronous operations in the system). This error can occur in either synchronous or asynchronous mode, even though, in synchronous mode, the system waits for all the asynchronous operations.

EINVAL   *mode* was not LIO_WAIT or LIO_NOWAIT, or *nent* was greater than AIO_LISTIO_MAX.

EIO   One or more of the asynchronous operations failed for some reason. This error is possible in both the synchronous and asynchronous cases.

EINTR   (Synchronous mode only.) A signal delivery interrupted the *lio_listio* call while it was waiting for all the I/O operations to complete. Note that, since each individual asynchronous I/O operation may cause a signal to be delivered, the signal that causes EINTR to be returned may be because of one of the asynchronous operations completing. In that case, you should probably use *aio_suspend* to wait for the other operations.

The individual asynchronous operations will each have their own error and return status, which can be retrieved using *aio_error* and *aio_return*. These values are the same as for the corresponding synchronous read or write operation, with a few additional possibilities:

EINVAL   The value specified by *aio_offset* is invalid for the file.

ECANCELED   The operation was cancelled (by *aio_cancel*, presumably).

EAGAIN   The asynchronous operation could not be queued for reasons similar to those given above. This error can be delivered either synchronously at the time of the call to *lio_listio*, or asynchronously, when the system actually gets around to trying to queue up the operation. It really depends on how asynchronous the *lio_listio* call is on a particular operating system. Different implementations will behave differently; you should be prepared for either possibility.

EINPROGRESS   The error status for any operation that has not completed is EIN-PROGRESS.

Notes

aio_return must be called once and only once for every asynchronous operation, or your system may run out of resources for asynchronous I/O.

If *lio_listio* fails due to resource limitations (EAGAIN), interruption in synchronous mode (EINTR), or failure of a particular I/O operation (EIO), then you should be aware that other operations on the list may actually have been successfully submitted and may well be in progress. In that case, you should use *aio_error* to determine which operations are in progress and deal with them appropriately.

The *aiocbs* used for asynchronous operations should be considered to be owned by the operating system for the duration of the asynchronous I/O operation. That means you should not modify any of the contents of the *aiocbs*. You should not use the *aiocbs* in submitting other asynchronous operations. You should not declare your *aiocbs* as local variables unless there is *no way* the local variables can disappear (through function return) before the end of the asynchronous operations. Lastly, you should not deallocate the memory containing the *aiocbs* (either via **free** or via automatic stack shrinkage) until the asynchronous operations have finished.

On systems that support prioritized I/O, the *aio_reqprio* field is always used. If you do not desire prioritized I/O, then you should be sure to set this field to 0.

Current UNIX Practice

SVR4:   No list-directed I/O operations are specified in SVR4.

BSD: No list-directed I/O operations are specified in BSD UNIX (as of 4.3).

SunOS: SunOS has an asynchronous I/O facility similar to the POSIX facility, but it is not identical. In particular, no list-directed I/O operations are specified in SunOS.

The *listio* facility is modeled on the current practice of Cray computer and other vendors in the supercomputing field.

See Also

aio_write
aio_read
sigqueue
aio_error (this function retrieves the error status of an AIO)
aio_return (this function retrieves the return status of an AIO)
aio_suspend (this function is used to wait for an AIO to complete)
aio_cancel (this function tries to cancel an AIO that has not completed yet)

mkfifo

Name

mkfifo — Create a named *pipe* for interprocess communication.

Synopsis

```
#include          <sys/types.h>
#include          <sys/stat.h>
int               mkfifo(char *fifo_name, mode_t mode);
```

Conditionality

Unconditional.

Description

mkfifo creates a special file, called *fifo_name*, and with permissions given by *mode*. This special file is, once you open it, a *pipe*, as described by the *pipe* manual page.

Pipes created by *pipe* are unnamed, and therefore only visible to the process calling *pipe* and child processes of that process. *mkfifo*, in contrast, puts the *pipe* in the file system, where any process can access it.

To access the *read* end of a named *pipe*, open the *pipe* for reading. To access the *write* end, open the *pipe* for writing.

Notes

This creation call is modeled on *open(path, O_CREAT, mode)*. However, unlike *open*, *mkfifo* does not return a file descriptor for the newly-opened file. In fact, it does not open the *pipe* at all—it just creates it. You'll have to call *open* yourself after creating the *pipe*.

Return Values

mkfifo returns 0 if it successfully created the *pipe*. If *mkfifo* fails, then no pipe is created, and *mkfifo* returns –1.

Errors

If *mkfifo* returns –1, it sets *errno* to one of the following values:

EACCES   Permission is denied on some component of the *fifo_name*.

EEXIST   A file named *fifo_name* already exists.

ENAMETOOLONG

      Either *fifo_name* is too long (longer than PATH_MAX), or a component
      of *fifo_name* is too long (longer than NAME_MAX) and
      _POSIX_NO_TRUNC is in effect.

ENOENT   Either *fifo_name* is an empty string, or some component of *fifo_name*
      (an intervening directory) does not exist.

ENOTDIR   Some component of *fifo_name* (some part you thought was a direc-
      tory) is not a directory.

ENOSPC   No space is available on the file system to create the *pipe*.

EROFS   The file system is a read-only file system.

Current UNIX Practice

mkfifo is defined by POSIX.1.

See Also

pipe (for the full discussion of pipes)
read, write (to use the pipe)

mlock

Name

mlock — Lock a range of memory.

Synopsis

```
#include       <sys/mman.h>
int            mlock(const void *addr, size_t len);
```

Conditionality

```
#ifdef _POSIX_MEMLOCK_RANGE
```

Description

mlock locks down the memory range between the addresses *addr* and *addr+len*. Because locking is performed on a page basis, entire pages containing the specified range will be locked down. Furthermore, some operating systems may require that the address be a multiple of the page size. *mlock* locks a process address space into physical memory, rendering the memory immune from being paged or swapped to disk. Processes that require fast, deterministic response to events must lock their memory, or there is a possibility that memory needed for a response will be paged to disk.

Because some implementations may require that the address to be locked be aligned on a page boundary, you should probably assure that your calls to *mlock* pass page-aligned parameters, both address and size. That means one less portability consideration for you, and it's especially innocuous since memory is locked by the page even if you don't specify a page-aligned address. PAGESIZE is defined in *<limits.b>*.

The determination of which memory ranges should be locked for optimum performance is going to vary from system to system. Any use of *mlock* is, therefore, a flag of non-portability in your application. Be careful.

munlock removes locks that were placed with *mlock*. *munlock* unlocks a memory range, just as *mlock* locks a range. In addition, *munlockall* will remove locks placed with *mlock*. *munlockall* unlocks a process's entire memory range. Memory locks do not stack: if *mlock* is called three times for a particular range, a single call to *munlock* or *munlockall* will still unlock the memory.

Return Values

mlock returns successfully if it was able to lock the requested memory for the process. If *mlock* fails, it fails cleanly. It will not fail and leave some memory locked and other memory unlocked.

If *mlock* is successful, it returns 0. Otherwise, it returns –1 and sets *errno* accordingly.

Errors

If *mlock* returns –1, it sets *errno* to one of the following values:

EAGAIN   Some of the memory requested to be locked could not be locked. Usually, this means that the system has, at least temporarily, run out of lockable physical memory.

EINVAL   The address to be locked is not aligned to a page boundary.

ENOMEM   The address range specified by the call is not all valid memory.

ENOMEM   Locking all the requested memory would exceed an implementation-defined limit on the amount of memory the process can lock. Note that this is more a permission/quota-related error than EAGAIN up above. Not all systems must implement ENOMEM; it is there for systems that enforce a quota on locked memory. The POSIX.4 conformance statement must tell you what this limit is, if there is any.

EPERM   The process does not have the appropriate privilege to lock its memory. The POSIX.4 conformance statement will define what sort of privileges are required for locking memory.

Notes

mlock and *munlock* are separate from *mlockall* and *munlockall*. *mlock* is provided if _POSIX_MEMLOCK_RANGE is defined; *mlockall* is conditional on _POSIX_MEMLOCK.

Specification of addresses and lengths to be locked is a risky and non-portable business; you should use *mlockall* whenever possible instead.

Your individual platform may not perform paging or swapping, but for portability reasons, your real-time processes should always lock themselves down. Otherwise, they may fail when ported to platforms that perform swapping or paging.

Memory locks are released in a child process created by *fork*, and abandoned when *exit* or one of the *exec* functions are called.

mlock (continued)

Current UNIX Practice

SVR4:   *mlock* is provided in SVR4.

BSD: No memory locking operations are specified in BSD UNIX (as of 4.3).

See Also

munlock (to release your locked memory)
mlockall, munlockall (to try and lock your entire address space)
fork (for the definition of memory locks across a fork)
exec (for the definition of memory locks across an exec)
exit (for the definition of memory locks upon an exit)
<limits.h> (PAGESIZE is defined in this header)

Name

mlockall — Lock your entire memory space down.

Synopsis

```
#include        <sys/mman.h>
int             mlockall(int how);
```

Conditionality

```
#ifdef _POSIX_MEMLOCK
```

Description

mlockall locks a process address space into physical memory, rendering the memory immune from being paged or swapped to disk. Processes that require fast, deterministic response to events must lock their memory, or there is a possibility that memory needed for a response will be paged to disk.

The entire process memory image is locked down according to the flag word *how*. *how* contains two flags, MCL_CURRENT and MCL_FUTURE. If MCL_CURRENT is set, then all currently-mapped memory is locked down. If MCL_FUTURE is set, then all future mappings (stack growth, additional memory allocation, use of additional shared memory areas) will also be locked down when they are made. It is possible to specify either flag independently of the other.

munlockall is called to remove the locks placed by *mlockall*. Locks do not stack: if *mlockall* is called ten times, a single call to *munlockall* will still unlock the memory.

Return Values

mlockall returns successfully if it was able to lock the requested memory for the process. In the case of MCL_FUTURE being specified, it is possible that future memory allocation will cause the system to run out of lockable physical memory. In that case, the operating system will inform the process in an implementation-defined way. This notification method must be specified in the system's POSIX.4 conformance statement.

The operating system may require that the process calling *mlockall* be privileged. The definition of appropriate privilege to successfully call *mlockall* is defined in the system's POSIX.4 conformance statement.

If *mlockall* is successful, it returns 0. Otherwise, it returns −1 and sets *errno* accordingly.

Errors

If *mlockall* returns –1, it sets *errno* to one of the following values:

EAGAIN Some of the memory requested to be locked could not be locked. Usually, this means that the system has, at least temporarily, run out of lockable physical memory.

EINVAL The value of the flag word *how* was bogus. Either the value was 0, or some extra flag value was set.

ENOMEM Locking all the requested memory would exceed an implementation-defined limit on the amount of memory the process may lock. Note that this is more a permission/quota-related error than EAGAIN is. Systems are not required to implement ENOMEM; it is there for systems that enforce a quota on locked memory. The POSIX.4 conformance statement must tell you what this limit is, if there is any.

EPERM The process does not have the appropriate privilege to lock its memory. The POSIX.4 conformance statement will define what sort of privileges are required for locking memory.

Notes

Your individual platform may not perform paging or swapping, but for portability reasons, your real-time processes should always lock themselves down. Otherwise, they may fail when ported to platforms that perform swapping or paging.

Memory locks are not inherited in a child created by *fork*, and are also abandoned when *exit* or one of the *exec* functions are called.

Current UNIX Practice

SVR4: *mlockall* is provided in SVR4.

BSD: No memory locking operations are specified in BSD UNIX (as of 4.3).

See Also

munlockall (to release your locked memory)
mlock, munlock (to try and lock less than your entire address space)
fork (for the definition of memory locks across a fork)
exec (for the definition of memory locks across an exec)
exit (for the definition of memory locks upon an exit)

Name

mmap — Map a shared memory object (or possibly another file) into process's address space.

Synopsis

```
#include      <sys/mman.h>
void          *mmaps(void *desired_addr, size_t length,
                  int memory_protections, int mapping_flags,
                  int fd, off_t offset_within_file);
```

Conditionality

```
#if defined(_POSIX_SHARED_MEMORY_OBJECTS) \
       || defined(_POSIX_MAPPED_FILES)
```
The MAP_PRIVATE mapping flag is only supported if _POSIX_MAPPED_FILES is defined. MAP_FIXED is entirely optional. Memory protections are only guaranteed to be enforced if _POSIX_MEMORY_PROTECTION is also defined; even if this option is defined, memory protection is not supported in all its possibilities.

Description

The *mmap* function creates a virtual memory mapping for a region of the file *fd*. This mapping allows you to refer to the contents of the file as if it were memory.

The area of the file from offset *offset_within_file*, and with length *length*, will be mapped into the virtual address space of the process. The address at which the mapping is performed is the return value from *mmap*.

Sorts of Files You Can Map

POSIX does not state which sorts of files you can and cannot map. Since most operating system objects in UNIX are accessed as files, the question becomes pertinent.

Most obviously, you can use *mmap* with a shared memory object opened via *shm_open*. You can also probably map a regular disk file opened with *open*. As far as other sorts of files, you are probably into the realm of implementation details. Can you map a pipe? Probably not. A terminal? Doubtful. Some random device, for instance a frame buffer, special-purpose array processor or address space on a particular bus? Quite possibly. The *mmap* function returns an error and sets *errno* to ENODEV for an attempt to map a device "for which *mmap* is meaningless." In the case of special devices, this probably means that the device driver code has no entry point to service an *mmap* request. This is more an issue of device support than operating system POSIX conformance.

Mapping Flags

The *mapping_flags* parameter influences the manner in which your mapping is performed. Three bits are defined for *mapping_flags*:

Constant	Meaning
MAP_SHARED	Create a mapping shared by all shared mappers
MAP_PRIVATE	Create a private (copy-on-write) mapping
MAP_FIXED	Map at *desired_addr*, or else fail

MAP_SHARED and MAP_PRIVATE are mutually exclusive. You must set one or the other, but you cannot set both.

The MAP_FIXED flag indicates that the system should use *desired_addr* as the address at which to perform the mapping, and if it cannot map at exactly that address, to fail. MAP_FIXED is optional in implementations, so you should not use it in portable programs.

Memory Protections

Memory generally has some protections associated with it. For instance, you can read and write your process's data space and stack, but if you try to write in the text (instructions) of your program, you will cause a machine exception and probably get a signal. Most memory protections are implicit in the intended use of the area. However, with mapped regions, there is no implicit memory protection. You might be using the area only to read from, or only to write to. You might, in fact, be executing code in the mapped area (most shared library facilities today are implemented using *mmap* to map in the shared library text and data).

When you map in a file, you set the desired protections in the *memory_protections* parameter. There are three bits you can set, and an alternative value you can set instead of any of the three bits:

Constant	Meaning
PROT_READ	Read permission for the memory area
PROT_WRITE	Write permission for the memory area
PROT_EXEC	Execute permission for the memory area
PROT_NONE	No permissions for the memory area

I'm not sure why you would ever establish a mapping with PROT_NONE, since in that case you cannot use the memory at all. The other three bits, though, indicate the permission to read, write, and execute code in the shared memory area, respectively. (Obviously, if you want to execute code in the shared memory area, it had better be full of compiled, executable code!)

You cannot request more permissions in the mapping than you requested in the original *open* or *shm_open* of the file. For instance, if you want to map the file with PROT_WRITE, you must have opened the file with O_WRONLY or O_RDWR permissions.

Desired Address

The *desired_addr* parameter tells the system where you want the mapped object to reside in your shared memory area. If this parameter is NULL, you give the system free license to map the region wherever it sees fit. Otherwise, the system will use your desired address as a hint as to where to place the mapped area.

Notes

Page Alignment: Implementations may require you to pass an offset that is a multiple of the system memory page size, PAGESIZE. Implementations will also, in general, map a region that is an integral multiple of PAGESIZE in length, regardless of what you specify as the desired *length*. For maximal portability, use lengths, offsets, and addresses that are integral multiples of PAGESIZE. You can find PAGESIZE in *<limits.h>* or by using *sysconf*(_SC_PAGESIZE).

Pointers into Shared Memory: If you have multiple processes with a shared memory area, it is possible that they will each have the area mapped at a different address. Thus, they cannot share pointers into the shared memory area without adjusting those pointers to take into account the mapping each process has. I recommend that you use offsets into the shared memory area, rather than plain old pointers, to access memory in a shared region. Alternatively, your process can simply modify the pointers it uses to take shared memory mapping address into account.

Zero-Fill at the End of the File: Say you have a file (or shared memory region) that is 10 bytes long, and you map it into your space. Since mappings are done in units of PAGE-SIZE, your mapping will consist of PAGESIZE bytes, where PAGESIZE is certainly greater than 10 (4096 is a common value). The bytes beyond the 10 that comprise the file are initialized by the system to 0. Furthermore, those bytes are not part of the file, even though they are part of the mapping. You should not use those bytes. If you have some need for them, then you should probably expand the file you're mapping, eh?

mmap and Shared Memory: Shared memory objects are opened/created using *shm_open*, rather than *open*, and are sized using *ftruncate*. While *shm_open* returns a file descriptor, the shared memory object is most emphatically not a file in the normal sense. You cannot *read* or *write* it. In fact, all you can really do is *mmap* it and *close* it.

Shared memory is persistent so long as the system remains up. That means you can create and map in a shared memory region, store data in the memory, *close* and unmap it, go away for a few days, then come back and find the same data you stored.

The memory mapping of the underlying object may not always reflect the underlying object exactly. For instance, if you map a disk file, you are probably not writing to disk each time you modify the mapped memory. The performance penalty of such disk writes would be enormous. The system generally keeps the mappings and the underlying object pretty much consistent. However, if the system were to crash, the underlying object might not reflect all your modifications to the mapping. To synch up the underlying object with the mappings, you use the *msync* function.

Return Values

mmap returns the address at which the mapping was performed, or MAP_FAILED if the call failed. Each operating system chooses the value of MAP_FAILED so that is a value that cannot possibly be a valid address for mapping.

Errors

If *mmap* returns MAP_FAILED, it sets *errno* to one of the following values:

EACCES   The permissions on the file do not allow the mapping permissions you requested. A file mapped for writing must be opened for writing; and *all* files must be opened for reading before being mapped.

EBADF   The file descriptor *fd* is bogus.

EINVAL   The flags you specified in *mapping_flags* are bogus. For instance, you specified neither MAP_PRIVATE nor MAP_SHARED.

ENODEV   The file you are trying to map cannot be mapped; such a mapping would be meaningless (for instance, mapping a pipe or a terminal).

ENOTSUP   You asked for MAP_FIXED or MAP_PRIVATE in *mapping_flags*, and this system does not support those operations. Alternatively, you requested permissions in *memory_protections* which the system does not support.

ENXIO   The area you specified (from *offset* for *length* bytes) is invalid in the file. Perhaps you specified a region off the end of the file. This is also the error returned if MAP_FIXED is supported, you asked for MAP_FIXED, and your *desired_addr*, *offset*, and *length* do not work together. Check to make sure that all the aforementioned quantities are page-aligned.

EAGAIN   If you have locked down your future mapping with *mlock-all(MCL_FUTURE)*, you will get back this error if you are not able to lock this mapping into memory due to a lack of system resources (other than physical memory; see below).

ENOMEM   You can also get this error back for trying to map when you have locked your mappings down. This error is returned for only one sort of resource shortage: not enough physical memory to lock down the mapping. You can also get this error if you specified a MAP_FIXED mapping and *desired_addr* is outside the allowed address space for your process. Finally, you can get this error even if you have *not* locked your memory *or* asked for a MAP_FIXED mapping, if your address space is simply too full for another mapping.

Current UNIX Practice

mmap is part of System V release 4.

See Also

munmap (to release a mapping established by *mmap*)
msync (to make mapped regions consistent with the underlying object)
shm_open (to open a shared memory object)
close (to finish using a file or shared memory object descriptor)
ftruncate (to set the size of a shared memory object)

mprotect

Name

mprotect — Change memory protections on a mapped area..

Synopsis

```
#include        <sys/mman.h>
int             mprotect(const void *addr, size_t length, int prot);
```

Conditionality

```
#if defined(_POSIX_MEMORY_PROTECTION)
```
Even if _POSIX_MEMORY_PROTECTION is defined, memory protection is not supported in all its possibilities.

Description

The *mprotect* function allows you to change the memory protections of the mapped region starting at *addr* and proceeding for the given *length*. This region must have been mapped using *mmap*, or the effects of this function are undefined. The protection modification is done in units of PAGESIZE, to include the area specified. Some systems may require you to pass in an *addr* that is an integral multiple of PAGESIZE.

The protections applied by this function mimic those applied by *mmap* and its *mapping_protections* parameter. There are three bits you can set, and an alternative value you can set instead of any of the three bits:

Constant	Meaning
PROT_READ	Read permission for the memory area
PROT_WRITE	Write permission for the memory area
PROT_EXEC	Execute permission for the memory area
PROT_NONE	No permissions for the memory area

I'm not sure why you would ever establish a PROT_NONE protection, since in that case you cannot use the memory at all. The other three bits, though, indicate the permission to read, write, and execute code in the shared memory area, respectively. (Obviously, if you want to execute code in the shared memory area, it had better be full of compiled, executable code!)

Even when _POSIX_MEMORY_PROTECTION is specified, these protection facilities are not airtight in the POSIX specification. The permissions, for instance, may not be interpreted exactly: all that's required is that a write to read-only memory not succeed. Reads from write-only memory may be allowed! As another example, PROT_EXEC need not be supported on your machine. In fact, the only protection combinations that an implementation *has* to support are PROT_NONE, PROT_READ, PROT_WRITE, and PROT_READ | PROT_WRITE. If your application has a strong need for some other protection combination, though, you've got a very unique application!

Finally, you cannot request more permissions in a MAP_SHARED mapping than you requested in the original *open* or *shm_open* of the file. For instance, if you want to map the file with PROT_WRITE, you must have opened the file with O_WRONLY or O_RDWR permissions. (The MAP_SHARED flag is set when you call *mmap*). If this mapping is a private mapping (established with the MAP_PRIVATE flag set in the call to *mmap*), then you can basically set any permissions you want because you're just modifying your own private copy anyway.

Return Values

mprotect returns 0 if it successfully changed permissions on the mapped region. It returns –1 if it fails. If it fails and *errno* is set to a value other than EINVAL, then this function may have changed *some* of the protections in the mapped area.

Errors

If *mprotect* returns –1, it sets *errno* to one of the following values:

EINVAL   The address *addr* is not a multiple of PAGESIZE.

EACCES   You asked for more permissions than were granted for the underlying file. For instance, you opened the shared memory area with O_RDONLY, and are now trying to add PROT_WRITE permission to the mapping you established. This error only occurs for shared (MAP_SHARED) mappings.

ENOTSUP   You requested permissions which the system does not support.

EAGAIN   If you have locked down your future mapping with *mlockall(MCL_FUTURE)*, you will get back this error on a MAP_PRIVATE mapping when you attempt to change permissions to permit writing (in this case, the system needs to make new copies of your memory area and lock the new copies down; there may not be enough of some system resources for this operation).

ENOMEM   You can also get this error back for trying to make a locked, MAP_PRIVATE mapping writable. This error is returned only if there is not enough physical memory to lock down the mapping. You can also get this error if the range of addresses you specified are not in your address space or if the range includes some unmapped pages.

Current UNIX Practice

mprotect is part of System V release 4.

See Also

mmap (to establish a mapping)
munmap (to release a mapping established by *mmap*)
shm_open (to open a shared memory object)
close (to finish using a file or shared memory object descriptor)
ftruncate (to set the size of a shared memory object)

Name

mq_close — Terminate access to a POSIX.4 message queue.

Synopsis

```
#include        <mqueue.h>
int             mq_close(mqd_t mq);
```

Conditionality

```
#ifdef _POSIX_MESSAGE_PASSING
```

Description

Use *mq_close* to sever the connection to a message queue which you made with *mq_open*.

Message queues are *persistent*, that is, the messages sent to a message queue remain in the queue even if no one has the queue open.

A message queue only ceases to exist when either the system goes down (and all bets are off in that case), or when the queue is removed with *mq_unlink*. Once a message queue has been removed with *mq_unlink*, and all processes that have the queue open *close* it, then all traces of the message queue disappear. Until that time, though, processes that have the queue open may continue to use it—even though other processes can no longer access the "removed" queue.

Notes

Message queues do not reside in the file system namespace. The name must obey construction rules as for a normal file pathname, but the message queue may or may not actually appear in the file system namespace. That is, when you do an *ls*, message queues may or may not appear. Therefore, your application must be careful to clean up its message queues, since there is no (POSIX-standard) equivalent of the *rm* command for message queues.

Return Values

mq_close returns 0 if the named message queue is successfully closed. After such time, the process will no longer be able to access the message queue through that descriptor. If *mq_close* fails, then it returns –1.

mq_close (continued)

Errors

If *mq_close* returns −1, it sets *errno* to the following value:

EINVAL   The descriptor passed does not describe an open message queue.

Current UNIX Practice

POSIX message queues are brand new to POSIX.4.

See Also

mq_open (to begin using a message queue)
close (similarities to this call)
mq_unlink (to remove a message queue from the system entirely)
mq_receive (to receive messages on a queue you've accessed)
mq_send (to send messages to a queue you've accessed)

Name

mq_getattr — Get POSIX.4 message queue attributes.

Synopsis

```
#include        <mqueue.h>
int             mq_getattr(mqd_t mq, struct mq_attr *attrbuf);
```

Conditionality

```
#ifdef _POSIX_MESSAGE_PASSING
```

Description

mq_getattr is used to retrieve the message queue attributes for the message queue named by *mq*. The attributes are stored in the location referenced by *attrbuf*. With one exception, all these attributes are set when the message queue is created (with *mq_open* with the O_CREAT flag set). The exception is *mq_flags*, which can be dynamically set using *mq_setattr* to change the blocking/nonblocking behavior of the message queue.

The *mq_attr* structure contains two fields in particular which dictate the sizing of the queue. *mq_msgsize* dictates the maximum size of a single message on the queue. Messages larger than this sent to the queue will generate an error. *mq_maxmsg* dictates the largest number of messages which may be in the queue at one time.

mq_attr.mq_flags includes flags affecting the message queue's behavior. Only one such flag is defined, MQ_NONBLOCK. If this flag is set, then the message queue is nonblocking, and requests to send or receive messages will never block awaiting resources. Otherwise, message sending and message receipt may involve waiting for empty queue space or a message to arrive on the queue, respectively.

mq_attr.mq_curmsgs indicates how many messages are in the queue (sent, but not yet received) at the time *mq_getattr* is called.

Return Values

mq_getattr returns 0 if it successfully retrieves the message queue's attributes. If *mq_getattr* fails, then it returns −1.

mq_getattr (continued)

Errors

If *mq_getattr* returns −1, it sets *errno* to the following value:

EBADF   The message queue descriptor *mq* does not refer to a valid, open message queue.

Current UNIX Practice

POSIX message queues are brand new to POSIX.4.

See Also

mq_open (which sets message queue attributes)
mq_setattr (which can set the *mq_flags* attributes)
mq_receive (to receive messages on a queue you've accessed)
mq_send (to send messages to a queue you've accessed)

Name

mq_notify — Register a request to be notified when a message arrives on an empty
message queue.

Synopsis

```
#include        <mqueue.h>
int             mq_notify(mqd_t mq, const struct sigevent *notification);
```

Conditionality

```
#ifdef _POSIX_MESSAGE_PASSING
```

Description

mq_notify tells the system to notify the process if a message arrives on the otherwise-
empty message queue *mq*. This functionality can be useful for asynchronous notification of message arrival on a message queue, to avoid polling or blocking with
mq_receive.

A message queue can register only one such request from *all* processes. Once one
process has successfully attached a notification request, subsequent attempts by that or
any other process to attach a notification request will fail. One exception to this rule is
that the process which originally attached the notification request can remove it by
passing a NULL pointer for the *notification* parameter.

Notification works as follows. If the message queue is empty, and there are no processes blocked in *mq_receive* waiting for a message on the queue, and a message
arrives, *then* the signal indicated by *notification* will be sent to the process which originally attached the notification request. The *struct sigevent* is defined in *<signal.h>*.
Notification will not be performed if the queue was not empty before the message
arrived, nor will it be performed if there are any processes waiting for a message with
mq_receive. The idea is to let the notified process know that it can grab a message off
the queue, where before it could not.

Notes

It is possible that, after notification is delivered, another process will jump in with a
mq_receive and pull the message off the queue before the notified process has a
chance to. Notified processes should be prepared for this possibility.

mq_notify (continued)

Return Values

mq_notify returns 0 if the notification was successfully attached (or, if *notification* was NULL, successfully removed). If *mq_notify* fails, then it returns –1, and the message queue's notification request is not modified.

Errors

If *mq_notify* returns –1, it sets *errno* to one of the following values:

EBADF   The descriptor *mq* does not refer to a valid message queue.

EBUSY   A notification request is already attached to this queue (*notification*, in this case, was not NULL).

Current UNIX Practice

POSIX message queues are brand new to POSIX.4.

See Also

mq_open (to begin using a message queue)
mq_send (to send messages on a queue you've accessed)
mq_receive (to send messages on a queue you've accessed)
sigaction (to establish a signal handler for the notification signal)

Name

mq_open — Create/access a POSIX.4 message queue.

Synopsis

```
#include        <mqueue.h>
mqd_t           mq_open(char *mq_name, int oflags,
                        mode_t mode, struct mq_attr *mq_attr);
```

Conditionality

```
#ifdef _POSIX_MESSAGE_PASSING
```

Description

mq_open is used to create or open a message queue. The function call is modeled on *open*, and the interpretation of *oflags* and *mode* are especially reminiscent of *open*. Significant differences emerge in the sort of object returned—it's a message queue, not a file—and in the interpretation of the first and final arguments.

Name Resolution

First, the message queue name. The name must obey construction rules as for a normal file pathname, but the message queue may or may not actually appear in the file system namespace. That is, when you do an *ls*, message queues may or may not appear. Therefore, your application must be careful to clean up its message queues, since there is no (POSIX-standard) equivalent of the *rm* command for message queues.

To ensure portability, you must obey two more rules. First, the message queue name must begin with a "/"; relative message queue names are interpreted differently by different systems. A portable application must use a fully-rooted name, therefore, to achieve utmost portability of message queue names. Second, the name may not contain additional "/" characters. Again, different systems will interpret the name in different ways, some treating it as a pathname and applying all the standard pathname semantics, and others treating the name as a simple string.

Other Parameters

The *oflags* argument controls the way in which the message queue is opened. You must specify one of O_RDONLY, O_WRONLY, or O_RDWR, depending on whether you wish to only receive, only send, or send and receive messages on the message queue.

Message queues can have multiple senders and receivers. In addition, you can specify the following flags in *oflags*:

O_NONBLOCK   If you set this flag, you tell the system that you should not block waiting to send or receive a message on a full or an empty message queue, respectively. By default, message send and receipt are blocking operations, which wait until the resources necessary for their successful operation are available.

O_CREAT   This flag is set to indicate that this call to *mq_open* is to create the message queue, not just access a queue that already exists. It is only in this case that the third and fourth arguments to *mq_open* are used. The message queue is created with a mode as specified in *mode*, just as for file creation. All three triplets of permissions are set for the message queue: read and write (receive and send) permission creator, group, and others. There is no meaning for execute permission on a message queue. Portable symbols for constructing a mode are found in *<sys/stat.h>*: S_IWUSR, S_IROTH and so forth. The uid and gid of the message queue are set to the effective IDs of the calling process.

The geometry of the created queue is dictated by the *mq_attr* argument. This structure contains two fields which dictate the sizing of the queue. *mq_msgsize* dictates the maximum size of a single message on the queue. Messages larger than this sent to the queue will generate an error. *mq_maxmsg* dictates the largest number of messages which may be in the queue at one time. If the *mq_attr* argument is NULL, then the system creates a message queue with implementation-defined default attributes. You should definitely provide some values for *mq_attr*.

The *mq_flags* field is not consulted on *mq_open*. The O_NONBLOCK flag, described above, is used instead. *mq_flags* is only used to determine and change the blocking behavior of the message queue (using *mq_getattr* and *mq_setattr*).

O_EXCL   This flag modifies the behavior of O_CREAT and is consulted only if O_CREAT is also set. If O_CREAT is set and O_EXCL is *not* set, then *mq_open* will silently fail to create the message queue, and instead just attach to the existing queue. If both flags are set, though, and a message queue already exists, then *mq_open* will return an error. It is meaningless and undefined to set O_EXCL without O_CREAT.

Notes

The *mq_flags* field of the *mq_attr* structure is not consulted when creating the message queue. The O_NONBLOCK flag to *mq_open* is used instead. The field is used only for *mq_getattr* and *mq_setattr*.

Message queues are persistent so long as the system remains up. That means you can create a message queue, send a couple of messages into it, *close* it, go away for a few days, then come back and receive the messages you sent.

It is possible that vendors will implement message queues atop files. In this case, a set of file-like error returns, documented below, are possible.

Return Values

mq_open returns the descriptor for the created or accessed message queue as its return value. This value is an integral type, but is definitely not a file descriptor. Do not attempt file operations on a message queue descriptor. The effects are unknown. If *mq_open* fails, then it returns (mqd_t)-1.

Errors

If *mq_open* returns −1, it sets *errno* to one of the following values:

EACCES
: Either the message queue exists and the permissions you request in *oflags* are denied, or you're trying to create a non-existing message queue and permission to do so is denied.

EEXIST
: You specified O_CREAT and O_EXCL in *oflags*, and the message queue already exists.

EINVAL
: You passed in an inappropriate name, one which broke one or more of the rules given above. Each implementation must describe the set of names it will accept for message queues; you can use this documentation to determine exactly what the problem was. Alternatively, you can stick to the rules quoted above.

 You can also get EINVAL if you are creating the message queue, and the values you specified for *mq_maxmsg* or *mq_msgsize* are less than or equal to 0.

ENOENT   The message queue does not exist, and you did not specify O_CREAT.

EINTR   The call was interrupted by a signal. This is not likely to happen unless the call blocks waiting for some resource which is in short supply.

EMFILE   The process is using too many file or message queue descriptors. Note that in an implementation that supports message queues atop files, the limit applies to the total of open files *and* open message queues.

ENFILE   The system has run out of system resources to support more open message queues. Note that this error is a *system* error, while EMFILE is more of a process-limit error.

ENAMETOOLONG

                mq_name is too long, greater than PATH_MAX, or, if you used multiple "/" characters and the system supports that, a component of the pathname exceeded NAME_MAX while _POSIX_NO_TRUNC is in effect.

Current UNIX Practice

POSIX message queues are brand new to POSIX.4.

See Also

open (similarities to this call)
pipe (another means to create a channel between processes)
mq_close (to finish using a message queue)
mq_unlink (to remove a message queue from the system entirely)
mq_receive (to receive messages on a queue you've accessed)
mq_send (to send messages to a queue you've accessed)

Name

mq_receive — Receive a message from a POSIX.4 message queue.

Synopsis

```
#include      <mqueue.h>
int           mq_receive(mqd_t mq, char *msg_buffer,
                 size_t buflen, unsigned int *msgprio);
```

Conditionality

```
#ifdef _POSIX_MESSAGE_PASSING
```

Description

mq_receive receives a message from the queue *mq*.

The received message is removed from the message queue and stored in the area pointed to by *msg_buffer*, whose length is *buflen*. The *buflen* must be less than or equal to the *mq_msgsize* attribute with which the message queue was created, otherwise the call will fail.

Messages are retrieved from the queue in FIFO order within priorities. Greater values of *msgprio* indicate higher priority, and are received before messages of lower priority. The received message's priority is stored in the location referenced by *msgprio*. If *msgprio* is a NULL pointer, then the message priority will be discarded by the system.

Empty Message Queues

If there is a message waiting on the queue for you, you will immediately receive it. If, however, the message queue is empty, your process will behave in one of two ways. If you *mq_open* the queue with the O_NONBLOCK flag set, then you will be immediately returned an error, with *errno* set to EAGAIN. If you do *not* set O_NONBLOCK, then you will block until either a message is sent to the queue, or you are interrupted by a signal.

Notes

Message queues are persistent so long as the system remains up. That means you can create a message queue, send a couple of messages into it, *close* it, go away for a few days, then come back and receive the messages you sent. You may be able to use this persistence to your advantage, if you are careful. However, watch out for persistence in the case where the system may go down. A careful application should always include a startup phase where the status and general sanity of all required objects, including message queues, is assured.

Return Values

mq_receive returns 0 if a message was successfully received. The message is stored in the buffer at *msg_buffer*, and its priority is stored in *msgprio*. If *mq_receive* fails, then it returns (mqd_t)-1, and no message is removed from the queue.

Errors

If *mq_receive* returns –1, it sets *errno* to one of the following values:

EBADF	The descriptor *mq* does not refer to a valid message queue, or the queue is valid but you did not *mq_open* it for reading (O_RDONLY or O_RDWR in *oflags*).
EMSGSIZE	The *buflen* was less than the *mq_msgsize* attribute of the message queue.
EAGAIN	The message queue is non-blocking, and the queue is empty.
EINTR	The message queue is a blocking queue, you were waiting for a message to arrive, and a signal arrived, interrupting your wait.

Current UNIX Practice

POSIX message queues are brand new to POSIX.4.

See Also

pipe (another means to create a channel between processes)
mq_open (to begin using a message queue)
mq_send (to send messages on a queue you've accessed)

Name

mq_send — Send a message on a POSIX.4 message queue.

Synopsis

```
#include    <mqueue.h>
int         mq_send(mqd_t mq, const char *msg,
                    size_t msglen, unsigned int msgprio);
```

Conditionality

```
#ifdef _POSIX_MESSAGE_PASSING
```

Description

mq_send sends the indicated message on the message queue referenced by *mq*.

The message is stored in the area pointed to by *msg*, and is of length *msglen*. The *msglen* must be less than or equal to the *mq_msgsize* attribute with which the message queue was created, otherwise the call will fail.

Messages are stored on the queue in FIFO order within priorities. The message's priority is given by *msgprio*. Greater values of *msgprio* indicate higher priority. The value of *msgprio* must be less than or equal to MQ_PRIO_MAX (see *<limits.h>*), or the call will fail.

Full Message Queues

A limited number of messages may be stored in the message queue before being received by processes. This number is the *mq_maxmsg* attribute with which the message queue was created. If this many messages have been sent to the queue and not yet received, then the message queue is said to be *full*.

If you try to send a message to a full message queue, your process will behave in one of two ways. If you *mq_open* the queue with the O_NONBLOCK flag set, then you will be immediately returned an error, with *errno* set to EAGAIN. If you do *not* set O_NONBLOCK, then you will block until either a space opens up for your message, or you are interrupted by a signal.

Notes

Message queues are persistent so long as the system remains up. That means you can create a message queue, send a couple of messages into it, *close* it, go away for a few days, then come back and receive the messages you sent. You may be able to use this

mq_send (continued)

persistence to your advantage, if you are careful. However, watch out for persistence in the case where the system may go down. A careful application should always include a startup phase where the status and general sanity of all required objects, including message queues, is assured.

Return Values

mq_send returns 0 if the message was successfully enqueued. If *mq_send* fails, then it returns (mqd_t)-1, and no message is inserted on the queue.

Errors

If *mq_send* returns –1, it sets *errno* to one of the following values:

EBADF	The descriptor *mq* does not refer to a valid message queue, or the queue is valid but you did not *mq_open* it for writing (O_WRONLY or O_RDWR in *oflags*).
EINVAL	The value of *msgprio* was greater than MQ_PRIO_MAX.
EMSGSIZE	The *msglen* exceeded the *mq_msgsize* attribute of the message queue.
EAGAIN	The message queue is non-blocking, and there is no room on the queue for the message.
EINTR	The message queue is a blocking queue, you were waiting for space to free up on the queue, and a signal arrived, interrupting your wait.

Current UNIX Practice

POSIX message queues are brand new to POSIX.4.

See Also

pipe (another means to create a channel between processes)
mq_open (to begin using a message queue)
mq_receive (to receive messages on a queue you've accessed)

Name

mq_setattr — Set a subset of POSIX.4 message queue attributes.

Synopsis

```
#include          <mqueue.h>
int               mq_setattr(mqd_t mq, const struct mq_attr *new_attrs,
                             struct mq_attr *old_attrs);
```

Conditionality

```
#ifdef _POSIX_MESSAGE_PASSING
```

Description

mq_setattr is used to set some of the attributes associated with the message queue named by *mq*. New attributes are set from the values given in the structure referenced by *new_attrs*. The previous attributes are stored in the location referenced by *old_attrs*, if that pointer is not NULL. A NULL pointer is ignored.

Only one of the attributes of a message queue can be set with this call: *mq_attr.mq_flags*. This field includes flags affecting the message queue's behavior. Only one such flag is defined, MQ_NONBLOCK. If this flag is set, then the message queue is non-blocking, and requests to send or receive messages will never block awaiting resources. Otherwise, message send and message receipt may involve waiting for empty queue space or a message to arrive on the queue, respectively.

All other fields in *new_attrs* are ignored by the call. Set them to whatever you want.

When a message queue is created, a *mq_attr* structure is passed to define the geometry of the message queue. However, the *mq_flags* field of this structure is not consulted in message queue creation. Instead, the O_NONBLOCK flag to *mq_open* is used.

Return Values

mq_setattr returns 0 if it successfully sets the message queue's attributes. If *mq_setattr* fails, then it returns −1.

mq_setattr (continued)

Errors

If *mq_setattr* returns −1, it sets *errno* to one of the following values:

EBADF   The message queue descriptor *mq* does not refer to a valid, open message queue.

EINVAL   The value in *new_attrs->mq_flags* is invalid.

Current UNIX Practice

POSIX message queues are brand new to POSIX.4.

See Also

mq_open (which sets message queue attributes)
mq_getattr (retrieve the attributes)
mq_receive (to receive messages on a queue you've accessed)
mq_send (to send messages to a queue you've accessed)

Name

msync — Make a mapping consistent with the underlying object..

Synopsis

```
#include      <sys/mman.h>
int           msync(const void *addr, size_t length, int flags);
```

Conditionality

```
#if defined(_POSIX_MAPPED_FILES) && defined(_POSIX_SYNCHRONIZED_IO)
```

Description

When you map a file into an address space, the resulting memory mapping may not always reflect the underlying object exactly. For instance, if you map a disk file, you are probably not writing to disk each time you modify the mapped memory. The performance penalty of such disk writes would be enormous. The system generally keeps the mappings and the underlying object pretty much consistent. However, if the system were to crash, the underlying object might not reflect all your modifications to the mapping. To synch up the underlying object with the mappings, you use the *msync* function.

The *msync* function synchs the mapped region starting at *addr* and proceeding for the given *length* out to the underlying object (presumably a disk file) which you originally mapped. This region must have been mapped using *mmap*, or the effects of this function are undefined. The synch operation is done in units of PAGESIZE, to include the area specified. Some systems may require you to pass in an *addr* that is an integral multiple of PAGESIZE.

The synchronization operation is performed in a number of ways, depending on the value set in *flags*.

Constant	Meaning
MS_SYNC	Synch the data out *now* and don't return until it's done.
MS_ASYNC	Start the synch operation and immediately return.
MS_INVALIDATE	Invalidate cached copies of the data that are inconsistent with the synched data.

You must specify either MS_SYNC or MS_ASYNC, but you cannot specify both. If you set MS_SYNC, then the data is stored out to the underlying object before the *msync* call returns. In this case, you know that the data is safe.

If you set MS_ASYNC, then the system will queue the data to be flushed out to the underlying object, and immediately return to you. In this case, you know that you have started the synch operation and it should finish at some point in the future.

The MS_INVALIDATE flag can be set to invalidate other mappings to the underlying object if those mappings do not match the data you have just updated the object with, for instance, if you had several processes with mappings to a single file, and your process modified its mapping. Then, by calling *msync* with MS_INVALIDATE, you would cause all the other processes to update their mappings to reflect the new data just updated on disk. MS_INVALIDATE is useful for maintaining the consistency of multiple mappings to the same object. The other processes would not see any effect of this action, other than the fact that their mappings were updated with the new contents of the mapped memory.

This function may not do anything if the underlying object has no underlying storage. For instance, if you *msync* a shared memory object, there's nothing to synch to, so the operation will just return. Likewise, MAP_PRIVATE mappings probably have no underlying physical storage, and calls to *msync* will do nothing in this case either.

Return Values

msync returns 0 if it successfully performed the desired synchronization with the underlying object. It returns −1 if it fails.

Errors

If *msync* returns −1, it sets *errno* to one of the following values:

EINVAL   The address *addr* is not a multiple of PAGESIZE. Alternatively, the value in *flags* is bogus.

ENOMEM   The range of addresses you specified is not in your address space, or includes some unmapped pages.

EBUSY   You specified MS_INVALIDATE and some of the mappings to be invalidated have been locked down. You cannot invalidate such mappings if it would require a page fault to retrieve the new data, because that would violate the requirements of memory locking.

Current UNIX Practice

msync is part of System V release 4.

See Also

mmap (to establish a mapping)
munmap (to release a mapping established by *mmap*)
shm_open (to open a shared memory object)
close (to finish using a file or shared memory object descriptor)
ftruncate (to set the size of a shared memory object)

munlock

Name

munlock — Unlock a range of memory.

Synopsis

```
#include          <sys/mman.h>
int               munlock(const void *address, size_t length);
```

Conditionality

```
#ifdef _POSIX_MEMLOCK_RANGE
```

Description

munlock removes memory locks made by either *mlockall* or *mlock*. It unlocks all memory in the range specified by address and length. After a call to *munlock*, that range of a process's memory may be paged or swapped. This does not mean that the memory *must* be paged or swapped; the operating system is allowed to keep the memory locked down if it wishes.

Address and length may need to be page-aligned. It's recommended practice to round both parameters to the appropriate page boundary before calling either *munlock* or *mlock*. PAGESIZE is defined in *<limits.h>*.

Return Values

munlock generally succeeds unless you mess up the parameters. Even if you have not locked the memory you are trying to unlock, *munlock* will still return successfully. After all, the memory is unlocked.

munlock returns 0 on success and –1 when it fails.

Errors

If *munlock* returns –1, it sets *errno* to one of the following values:

EINVAL   The addresses to be unlocked are not aligned to a page boundary.

ENOMEM   The address range specified by address and length is not all valid memory.

Notes

mlock and *munlock* are separate from *mlockall* and *munlockall*. *mlock* is provided if _POSIX_MEMLOCK_RANGE is defined; *mlockall* is conditional on _POSIX_MEMLOCK.

Specification of addresses and lengths to be locked is a risky and non-portable business; you should use *mlockall* whenever possible instead.

Memory locks are not inherited in children created by *fork*, and are also abandoned when *exit* or one of the *exec* functions are called.

Memory locks do not stack: if *mlock* is called seven times, a single call to *munlock* will still unlock the memory.

Current UNIX Practice

SVR4:   *munlock* is provided in SVR4.

BSD: No memory locking operations are specified in BSD UNIX (as of 4.3).

See Also

mlock (to lock a range of memory down)
mlockall, *munlockall* (to try and lock less than your entire address space)
fork (for the definition of memory locks across a fork)
exec (for the definition of memory locks across an exec)
exit (for the definition of memory locks upon an exit)
<limits.h> (PAGESIZE definition)

munlockall

Name

munlockall — Unlock your entire address space.

Synopsis

```
#include      <sys/mman.h>
int           munlockall();
```

Conditionality

```
#ifdef _POSIX_MEMLOCK
```

Description

munlockall unlocks all currently mapped memory for the calling process, and causes any future mappings to not be locked into physical memory. After a call to *munlockall*, a process's memory may be paged or swapped. This does not mean that the memory *must* be paged or swapped; the operating system is allowed to keep the memory locked down if it wishes.

Memory locks do not stack: if *mlockall* or *mlock* are called ten times, a single call to *munlockall* will still unlock the memory.

munlockall removes locks made by either *mlockall* or *mlock*.

Return Values

munlockall always succeeds, unless the operating system does not support _POSIX_MEMLOCK.

Errors

There are no error returns for *munlockall*, other than the possible ENOSYS if _POSIX_MEMLOCK is not specified.

Notes

Memory locks are not inherited by children created by *fork*, and are also abandoned when *exit* or one of the *exec* functions are called.

Current UNIX Practice

SVR4:   *munlockall* is provided in SVR4.

BSD: No memory locking operations are specified in BSD UNIX (as of 4.3).

See Also

mlockall (to lock your memory down)
mlock, munlock (to try and lock less than your entire address space)
fork (for the definition of memory locks across a fork)
exec (for the definition of memory locks across an exec)
exit (for the definition of memory locks upon an exit)

munmap

Name

munmap — Undo a mapping established by *mmap*.

Synopsis

```
#include        <sys/mman.h>
int             munmap(void *addr, size_t length);
```

Conditionality

```
#if defined(_POSIX_SHARED_MEMORY_OBJECTS) \
        || defined(_POSIX_MAPPED_FILES)
```

Description

This function removes a mapping established by *mmap*. The region starting at *addr*, for *length* bytes, is unmapped. The unmapping is done in units of PAGESIZE, to include the area specified. Some systems may require you to pass in an *addr* that is an integral multiple of PAGESIZE.

If the mapping was of the MAP_PRIVATE sort, it disappears entirely. MAP_SHARED mappings, on the other hand, are reflected in the underlying object.

If the memory region was locked (by *mlock* or *mlockall*), such locks are removed. You'd expect this, since there's no longer anything to *be* locked.

You can only *munmap* an area you mapped using *mmap*.

Notes

Shared memory is persistent so long as the system remains up. You can create and map a shared memory region, store data, *close* and unmap the region, go away, then come back and find the same data you stored. Persistence is more likely to be a problem than a feature; be careful.

For maximal portability, use addresses and offsets that are integral multiples of PAGESIZE. You can find PAGESIZE in *<limits.h>* or by using *sysconf(_SC_PAGESIZE)*.

The standard dictates that further references to an unmapped area result in SIGSEGV being delivered to the offending process. This specification is fine on a machine with an MMU, but cannot be implemented on MMU-less (read "embedded") machines. I would not rely on this particular semantic, since embedded systems are going to support POSIX even if the underlying hardware can't quite meet the dictates of the standard in all respects.

Return Values

munmap returns 0 if it successfully performed the unmapping, and −1 if it could not. If a mapping is successfully unmapped, then subsequent references to the unmapped area will result in the SIGSEGV signal being delivered to the process (but see caveat above).

Errors

If *munmap* returns −1, it sets *errno* to the following value:

EINVAL   The specified address range was wrong, somehow. Either *addr* was not a multiple of PAGESIZE, or the specified region was outside the address space of the process.

Note that there is no error defined for the case where you attempt to *munmap* a region that was not mapped using *mmap*. The effects of such an action are not defined by POSIX.

Current UNIX Practice

munmap is part of System V release 4.

See Also

mmap (to establish a mapping)
shm_open (to open a shared memory object)
close (to finish using a file or shared memory object descriptor)
ftruncate (to set the size of a shared memory object)

nanosleep

Name

nanosleep — Pause execution for a number of nanoseconds.

Synopsis

```
#include        <time.h>
int             nanosleep(const struct timespec *requested_time,
                    struct timespec *remaining);
```

Conditionality

```
#ifdef _POSIX_TIMERS
```

Description

nanosleep is a higher-resolution version of the sleep call that is available in standard UNIX and POSIX.1 systems. *nanosleep* causes the calling process to block for the amount of time indicated by *requested_time*. Since the *struct timespec* measures time down to the nanosecond, much finer intervals may be passed to *nanosleep* than to sleep (which takes a number of seconds).

Since few if any systems actually support nanosecond timings, the value passed to *requested_time* may be rounded up to the resolution of the system clock. A usual clock resolution on many systems is 100 Hz, or 10,000,000 nanoseconds. Because of this rounding, *nanosleep* may cause a process to sleep a bit longer than requested. The operating system is not allowed to round the nanosleep interval down, so the calling process will always sleep for at least the requested amount of time, assuming no signals arrive (see below).

nanosleep, like *sleep*, is interruptible by the delivery of signals to the process. If a signal arrives at the process, and it is not blocked or ignored, then the process will handle the signal, and then return from *nanosleep* prematurely. In this case, *nanosleep* will return –1, with *errno* set to EINTR, and the time remaining to be slept will be stored in the result parameter remaining.

Return Values

nanosleep returns 0 when the process sleeps the entire interval without being interrupted by a signal. If *nanosleep* fails, the call returns –1 and sets *errno* to indicate the error.

Errors

If *nanosleep* fails, it returns –1 and sets *errno* to one of the following:

EINVAL   A nanosecond value greater than or equal to 1,000,000,000, or less than 0. Nanoseconds are supposed to indicate a fraction of a second.

EINTR   A signal interrupted the sleeping process.

Notes

Sleep is often implemented using interval timers and SIGALRM; thus, if you mix interval timers and sleep, you are taking a chance that something will break. Not so *nanosleep*. *nanosleep* is defined to not alter the status or action of any signal.

Be careful when coding *nanosleep* calls: it takes *struct timespec*, not *struct timeval*.

Current UNIX Practice

Standard UNIX supports *sleep*, but not *nanosleep*.

See Also

sleep (POSIX.1/UNIX coarsely-timed pause)
sigaction (how to handle a signal)

pathconf, fpathconf

Name

pathconf, fpathconf — Query filename-variable system options at run-time.

Synopsis

```
#include        <unistd.h>

long            pathconf(char *pathname, int option);
long            fpathconf(int fd, int option);
```

Conditionality

Unconditional.

Description

The *pathconf* and *fpathconf* functions allow your application to determine information about the run-time system under which the application is running. Unlike *sysconf*, these functions query system options that may vary on a per-file or per-pathname basis. Hence, these functions take a *pathname* (*pathconf*) or an already-opened file descriptor *fd* (*fpathconf*), and return to you the value of the named *option* for that file. This is to support the ability to reconfigure operating systems with or without various POSIX options, and with differently-sized data structures.

The *option* argument to *pathconf* and *fpathconf* indicates a POSIX option or limit you wish to query. The following table shows available options from POSIX.1 and POSIX.4:

pathconf Option Name	System Value Returned	Standard
_PC_CHOWN_RESTRICTED	_POSIX_CHOWN_RESTRICTED (binary)	POSIX.1
_PC_NO_TRUNC	_POSIX_NO_TRUNC (binary)	POSIX.1
_PC_VDISABLE	_POSIX_VDISABLE	POSIX.1
_PC_LINK_MAX	LINK_MAX	POSIX.1
_PC_MAX_CANON	MAX_CANON	POSIX.1
_PC_MAX_INPUT	MAX_INPUT	POSIX.1
_PC_NAME_MAX	NAME_MAX	POSIX.1
_PC_PATH_MAX	PATH_MAX	POSIX.1
_PC_PIPE_BUF	PIPE_BUF	POSIX.1
_PC_ASYNC_IO	_POSIX_ASYNC_IO (binary)	POSIX.4
_PC_PRIO_IO	_POSIX_PRIO_IO (binary)	POSIX.4
_PC_SYNC_IO	_POSIX_SYNC_IO (binary)	POSIX.4

Return Values

pathconf and *fpathconf* return the value of the given option or limit for the named file on the currently running system. Some systems do not support particular limits for these facilities. In this case, these functions will return −1 *without* setting *errno*. Therefore, you should initialize *errno* before calling *pathconf* or *fpathconf* if it is possible that an option may have an indeterminate limit.

Note

The *pathconf* and *fpathconf* functions return −1 without setting *errno* for a different reason than *sysconf*. If an option is not supported for a given file, these functions will set *errno* to EINVAL. If the option is not supported *anywhere* on the system, you can probably determine that information by an appropriate call to *ssysconf*. Be careful when programming using these three functions!

Errors

pathconf and *fpathconf* return −1 when an option is supported with no explicit limit. In this case they will not set *errno*. If they fail for another reason, they will return −1 and set *errno* as follows:

EINVAL The option number you passed was not a reasonable option number, or the named option is not supported for the given file or pathname.

EACCES Permission denied in looking up the given *pathname* (*pathconf* only).

ENAMETOOLONG
Either the overall *pathname* length exceeded PATH_MAX, or a component of the *pathname* exceeded NAME_MAX and the _POSIX_NO_TRUNC option is in effect (*pathconf* only).

ENOENT Either the named *pathname* is a non-existent file, or you passed in an empty string (*pathconf* only).

ENOTDIR A component of *pathname* (other than the final component) was not a directory (*pathconf* only).

EBADF The *fd* you passed was not a valid file descriptor (*fpathconf* only).

Current UNIX Practice

These functions are new for POSIX.

See Also

sysconf (overall run-time system configuration)
<unistd.h>
<limits.h> (limit and option definitions)

Name

pipe — Create a pipe for interprocess communication.

Synopsis

```
int             pipe(int pipe_ends[2]);
```

Conditionality

Unconditional.

Description

pipe creates a special sort of file known as a *pipe*. A *pipe* is used to communicate between processes. It has two ends: a *read* end and a *write* end. Data you write into the *write* end can be read from the *read* end. Data flows through a *pipe* in FIFO order—first data written in is the first data to be read out.

The *pipe* is accessed as a file, using *write* and *read*. The *pipe* call returns two file descriptors in the parameter *pipe_ends*. *pipe_ends[0]* is the file descriptor from which you *read*. *pipe_ends[1]* is the file descriptor to which you *write*.

The call to *pipe* creates a new *pipe*. This pipe is not visible to calls like *open* and *unlink*; the *pipe* file descriptors are only available to processes which are created by this process as it *forks* and *execs*. (You can also create pipes that are visible in the file system namespace by using the *mkfifo* function.)

Notes

Pipes are created with neither O_NONBLOCK nor FD_CLOEXEC set for the file descriptors. Thus, the default *pipe* performs blocking reads and writes, and will not be closed if the process calls one of the *exec* functions. You can change this behavior using *fcntl*.

Multiple writers to a *pipe* generally write in atomic chunks, without having to worry about their data being interleaved with one another. However, if a process *writes* a particularly large amount of data to a *pipe*, this guarantee may break down. The constant PIPE_BUF, defined in *<limits.h>*, is the largest amount of data you can write to a *pipe* without having to worry about your writes being interleaved with other writes to the *pipe*. PIPE_BUF is at least 512 on all POSIX systems.

pipe (continued)

If PIPE_BUF is not present in *<limits.h>*, it's because the system limit varies depending on the file you apply it to. In that case, you can use *pathconf(fd,_PC_PIPE_BUF)* to determine the limit for that particular *pipe*.

Return Values

pipe returns 0, initializing *pipe_ends* with the two file descriptors for the read and write ends of the *pipe*. If *pipe* fails, then no pipe is created, and *pipe* returns –1.

Errors

If *pipe* returns –1, it sets *errno* to one of the following values:

EMFILE   The calling process is already using more than OPEN_MAX – 2 file descriptors.

ENFILE   The system has run out of system resources to support more open files. Note that this error is a *system* error, while EMFILE is more of a process-limit error.

Current UNIX Practice

pipe is standard in all UNIX systems.

See Also

fork (creates other processes that can access the pipe)
exec (often performed after *fork*)
<limits.h> (for definitions of PIPE_BUF and OPEN_MAX)
pathconf (in case PIPE_BUF is not defined)
read, write (to use the pipe)
mkfifo (to make a named pipe)

Name

sched_get_priority_max — Get maximum priority value for a scheduler.

Synopsis

```
#include       <sched.h>
int            sched_get_priority_max(int alg);
```

Conditionality

```
#ifdef _POSIX_PRIORITY_SCHEDULING
```

Description

sched_get_priority_max returns the maximum priority value of the scheduling algorithm identified by *alg*. *alg* should be one of the SCHED_ constants defined in *<sched.h>*.

Processes with numerically higher priority values are scheduled before processes with lower priority. Thus, the maximum value returned by this function will be greater than the maximum value returned by *sched_get_priority_min*. For SCHED_FIFO and SCHED_RR, there is required to be a spread of at least 32 between minimum and maximum priority.

Scheduling priority ranges for the various algorithms are not alterable by an application. Generally, they are not alterable at all.

Return Values

sched_get_priority_max returns the maximum priority value for the named scheduler. If it encounters an error, it returns −1.

Errors

If *sched_get_priority_max* returns −1, it sets *errno* to the following value:

EINVAL   *alg* does not name a defined scheduling algorithm.

Notes

Since the range of scheduling priorities varies from system to system, applications should refrain from calling the POSIX.4 scheduling algorithms with straight priority numbers. Rather, a virtual priority range should be used; then it should be shifted appropriately based on the values returned from *sched_get_priority_min* and *sched_get_priority_max*.

Current UNIX Practice

SVR4:   None. SVR4 uses *priocntl*, a different mechanism for controlling scheduling parameters which has roughly the same functionality as the POSIX.4 mechanisms.

BSD: No priority scheduling operations are specified in BSD UNIX (as of 4.3).

See Also

sched_get_priority_min (sibling function)
sched_setscheduler
sched_getscheduler
sched_setparam
sched_getparam
fork (for the definition of scheduling across a *fork*)
exec (for the definition of scheduling across an *exec*)

Name

sched_get_priority_min — Get minimum priority value for a scheduler.

Synopsis

```
#include      <sched.h>
int           sched_get_priority_min(int alg);
```

Conditionality

```
#ifdef _POSIX_PRIORITY_SCHEDULING
```

Description

sched_get_priority_min returns the minimum priority value of the scheduling algorithm identified by *alg*. *alg* should be one of the SCHED_ constants defined in *<sched.h>*.

Processes with numerically higher priority values are scheduled before processes with lower priority. Thus, the minimum value returned by this function will be less than the maximum value returned by *sched_get_priority_max*. For SCHED_FIFO and SCHED_RR, there is required to be a spread of at least 32 between minimum and maximum priority.

Scheduling priority ranges for the various algorithms are not alterable by an application. Generally, they are not alterable at all.

Return Values

sched_get_priority_min returns the minimum priority value for the named scheduler. If it encounters an error, it returns −1.

Errors

If *sched_get_priority_min* returns −1, it sets *errno* to the following value:

EINVAL   *alg* does not name a defined scheduling algorithm.

Notes

Since the range of scheduling priorities varies from system to system, applications should refrain from calling the POSIX.4 scheduling algorithms with straight priority numbers. Rather, a virtual priority range should be used; then it should be shifted appropriately based on the values returned from *sched_get_priority_min* and *sched_get_priority_max.*

Current UNIX Practice

SVR4:   None. SVR4 uses *priocntl,* a different mechanism for controlling scheduling parameters which has roughly the same functionality as the POSIX.4 mechanisms.

BSD: No priority scheduling operations are specified in BSD UNIX (as of 4.3).

See Also

sched_get_priority_max (sibling function)
sched_setscheduler
sched_getscheduler
sched_setparam
sched_getparam
fork (for the definition of scheduling across a *fork*)
exec (for the definition of scheduling across an *exec*)

Name

sched_getparam — Retrieve scheduling parameters for a particular process.

Synopsis

```
#include        <sched.h>
int             sched_getparam(pid_t pid, struct sched_param *p);
```

Conditionality

```
#ifdef _POSIX_PRIORITY_SCHEDULING
```

Description

sched_getparam retrieves the scheduling parameters for the process, identified by *pid*, into the structure referenced by *p*. Depending on the scheduling policy under which the process is running, different members of *p* will be set. Currently-defined scheduling policies use the following members:

SCHED_FIFO   *sched_priority*

SCHED_RR   *sched_priority*

SCHED_OTHER   *<implementation-defined>*

If the process ID given is 0, then the call to *sched_getparam* is applied to the calling process.

An implementation may require that a process have special privileges to get the scheduling parameters of various processes. The implementation must define the privileges required in its POSIX.4 conformance document.

Return Values

sched_getparam returns successfully if it was able to retrieve the scheduling parameters of the named process into *p*. Upon success, *sched_getparam* returns 0. Otherwise, it returns –1 and sets *errno* accordingly.

Errors

If *sched_getparam* returns –1, it sets *errno* to one of the following values:

ESRCH   The process whose ID is *pid* could not be found.

EPERM   The caller does not have the appropriate privilege to set the process's scheduling parameters to those specified by *p*.

Current UNIX Practice

SVR4:   None. SVR4 uses *priocntl*, a different mechanism for controlling scheduling parameters which has roughly the same functionality as the POSIX.4 mechanisms.

BSD: No priority scheduling operations are specified in BSD UNIX (as of 4.3).

See Also

sched_setscheduler, *sched_getscheduler*, *sched_setparam* (sibling functions)
fork (for the definition of scheduling across a *fork*)
exec (for the definition of scheduling across an *exec*)

Name

sched_getscheduler — Retrieve scheduling algorithm for a particular purpose.

Synopsis

```
#include      <sched.h>
int           sched_getscheduler(pid_t pid);
```

Conditionality

```
#ifdef _POSIX_PRIORITY_SCHEDULING
```

Description

sched_getscheduler retrieves the identifier for the scheduling policy under which the process *pid* is running. If *pid* is zero, then the scheduler of the calling process is returned. Negative values of *pid* should not be used, as their effect is not specified by POSIX.4.

The defined schedulers which may be returned under POSIX.4 are SCHED_FIFO, SCHED_RR, and SCHED_OTHER. Each of these constants must have a unique value. A particular system may provide additional schedulers, but if it does, it has to identify in its conformance statement what the effects of the additional algorithms are, and how you can compile an application without getting these extensions.

Return Values

sched_getscheduler returns successfully if it was able to find out the scheduling policy of the named process. In that case, it returns the identifier for that scheduling algorithm. Otherwise, *sched_getscheduler* will return –1.

Errors

If *sched_getscheduler* returns –1, it sets *errno* to one of the following values:

ESRCH   The process whose ID is *pid* could not be found.

EPERM   The caller does not have the appropriate privilege to set the process's scheduling policy and parameters to those specified by *p*.

Notes

An implementation may require that a process have special privileges to inquire as to the scheduling policies of various processes. The implementation must define the privileges required in its POSIX.4 conformance document.

Current UNIX Practice

SVR4:   None. SVR4 uses *priocntl*, a different mechanism for controlling scheduling parameters which has roughly the same functionality as the POSIX.4 mechanisms.

BSD: No priority scheduling operations are specified in BSD UNIX (as of 4.3).

See Also

sched_setscheduler, sched_setparam, sched_getparam (sibling functions)
sched_get_priority_min
sched_get_priority_max (to determine the maxima and minima for a given scheduling algorithm)
sched_rr_get_interval (to determine the quantum under which processes run, when using the SCHED_RR policy)
fork (for the definition of scheduling across a *fork*)
exec (for the definition of scheduling across an *exec*)

Name

sched_rr_get_interval — Get the SCHED_RR interval for the named process.

Synopsis

```
#include        <sched.h>
int             sched_rr_get_interval(pid_t pid, struct timespec *t);
```

Conditionality

```
#ifdef _POSIX_PRIORITY_SCHEDULING
```

Description

sched_rr_get_interval fills in the structure referenced by *t* with the time quantum for the process identified by *pid*. If *pid* is 0, the time quantum for the calling process is set in *t*. The process should be running under the SCHED_RR scheduler.

The time quantum value is not alterable under POSIX.4. This function returns information about the implementation under which the process is running. *sched_rr_get_interval* fills in *t* with the quantum for the named process and returns 0 upon success. If it encounters an error, it returns −1.

Errors

If *sched_rr_get_interval* returns −1, it sets *errno* to the following value:

ESRCH   The process identified by *pid* could not be found.

Notes

It is not currently stated whether the process identified by *pid* must be currently running under the SCHED_RR scheduler. Just to be sure, you had best assure that the process identified by *pid* is, in fact, running under SCHED_RR.

Current UNIX Practice

SVR4:   None. SVR4 uses *priocntl*, a different mechanism for controlling scheduling parameters which has roughly the same functionality as the POSIX.4 mechanisms.

BSD: No priority scheduling operations are specified in BSD UNIX (as of 4.3).

sched_rr_get_interval (continued)

See Also

sched_get_priority_min, sched_get_priority_max (sibling functions)
sched_setscheduler
sched_getscheduler
sched_setparam
sched_getparam

Name

sched_setparam — Set scheduling parameters for a process.

Synopsis

```
#include        <sched.h>
int             sched_setparam(pid_t pid, const struct sched_param *p);
```

Conditionality

```
#ifdef _POSIX_PRIORITY_SCHEDULING
```

Description

sched_setparam sets the scheduling parameters for the process, identified by *pid*, to those parameters specified in *p*. Depending on the scheduling policy under which the process is running, different members of *p* may be used. Currently-defined scheduling policies use the members as defined below.

SCHED_FIFO   *sched_priority*

SCHED_RR   *sched_priority*

SCHED_OTHER   *<implementation-defined>*

If the process ID given is 0, then the call to *sched_setparam* is applied to the calling process.

An implementation may require that a process have special privileges to set the scheduling parameters of various processes in different ways. The implementation must define the privileges required in its POSIX.4 conformance document.

Depending on the scheduling policy under which the process is running, the members of *p* will also be checked for validity vis-a-vis that particular scheduling policy. Under both SCHED_FIFO and SCHED_RR, the scheduling priority must lie within the range of values given by *sched_get_priority_min* and *sched_get_priority_max* for that scheduling algorithm. Processes with numerically higher scheduling priorities are scheduled before processes with lower priority.

Return Values

sched_setparam returns successfully if it was able to set the scheduling parameters of the named process to the values indicated in *p*. Upon success, *sched_setparam* returns 0. Otherwise, it returns −1 and sets *errno* accordingly.

Errors

If *sched_setparam* returns –1, it sets *errno* to one of the following values:

EINVAL   The scheduling parameters specified in *p* do not make sense for the scheduling policy under which the process is running.

ESRCH   The process whose ID is *pid* could not be found.

EPERM   The caller does not have the appropriate privilege to set the process's scheduling parameters to those specified by *p*.

Notes

The POSIX.4-defined schedulers, SCHED_FIFO and SCHED_RR, both specify that a call to either *sched_setscheduler* or *sched_setparam* will result in the specified process being moved to the end of the queue for its priority level, even if there is no actual change in scheduling parameters.

Current UNIX Practice

SVR4:   None. SVR4 uses *priocntl*, a different mechanism for controlling scheduling parameters which has roughly the same functionality as the POSIX.4 mechanisms.

BSD: No priority scheduling operations are specified in BSD UNIX (as of 4.3).

See Also

sched_setscheduler, sched_getscheduler, sched_getparam (sibling functions)
sched_get_priority_min, sched_get_priority_max (to determine the maxima and minima for a given scheduling algorithm)
fork (for the definition of scheduling across a *fork*)
exec (for the definition of scheduling across an *exec*)

Name

sched_setscheduler — Set scheduling algorithm/parameters for a process.

Synopsis

```
#include        <sched.h>
int             sched_setscheduler(pid_t pid, int policy,
                        const struct sched_param *p);
```

Conditionality

```
#ifdef _POSIX_PRIORITY_SCHEDULING
```

Description

sched_setscheduler sets both the scheduling policy and the associated parameters for the process identified by *pid*. Depending on the scheduling policy (policy) which is set for the process, different members of *p* are used. Currently-defined scheduling policies use the members as defined in the table below.

SCHED_FIFO	sched_priority
SCHED_RR	sched_priority
SCHED_OTHER	<implementation-defined>

If the process ID given is 0, then the call to *sched_setscheduler* is applied to the calling process.

An implementation may require that a process have special privileges to set the scheduling policy and parameters of various processes in different ways. The implementation must define the privileges required in its POSIX.4 conformance document.

Depending on the scheduling policy specified in the call to *sched_setscheduler*, the members of *p* will also be checked for validity vis-a-vis that particular scheduling policy. Under both SCHED_FIFO and SCHED_RR, the scheduling priority must lie within the range of values given by sched_get_priority_min and *sched_get_priority_max* for that scheduling algorithm. Processes with numerically higher scheduling priorities are scheduled before processes with lower priority.

Return Values

sched_setscheduler returns successfully if it was able to set the scheduling policy of the named process to policy, and to set the scheduling parameters of the named process to the values indicated in *p*. Upon success, *sched_setscheduler* returns 0. Otherwise, it returns −1 and sets *errno* accordingly.

Errors

If *sched_setscheduler* returns −1, it sets *errno* to one of the following values:

EINVAL   The scheduling policy, policy, is not one of the recognized scheduling policies of POSIX.4, or the parameters specified in p do not make sense for that scheduling policy.

ESRCH   The process whose ID is *pid* could not be found.

EPERM   The caller does not have the appropriate privilege to set the process's scheduling policy and parameters to those specified by p.

Notes

The currently-specified scheduling policies, SCHED_FIFO and SCHED_RR, are both pre-emptive. This means that if a process changes the policy/priority of another process to be higher than its own priority, the calling process had better be prepared to be immediately preempted before even returning from the call to *sched_setscheduler*.

SCHED_FIFO and SCHED_RR both specify that a call to either *sched_setscheduler* or *sched_setparam* will result in the specified process being moved to the end of the queue for its priority level, even if there is no actual change in scheduling parameters.

Current UNIX Practice

SVR4:   None. SVR4 uses *priocntl*, a different mechanism for controlling scheduling parameters which has roughly the same functionality as the POSIX.4 mechanisms.

BSD: No priority scheduling operations are specified in BSD UNIX (as of 4.3).

See Also

sched_getscheduler, sched_setparam, sched_getparam (siblings)
sched_get_priority_min, sched_get_priority_max (to determine the maxima and minima for a given scheduling algorithm)
sched_rr_get_interval (to determine the quantum under which processes run, when using the SCHED_RR policy)

fork (for the definition of scheduling across a *fork*)
exec (for the definition of scheduling across an *exec*)

sched_yield

Name

sched_yield — Yield the processor.

Synopsis

```
#include       <sched.h>
int            sched_yield();
```

Conditionality

```
#ifdef _POSIX_PRIORITY_SCHEDULING
```

Description

sched_yield, when called, causes the calling process to give up its processor, and move to the back of the queue for its priority. A scheduling decision is then made and a new process gets to run. Note that if the calling process is the single, highest priority runnable process in the system at that time, then that process will get to keep on running.

The effect of *sched_yield* is simple for the defined schedulers of POSIX.4, SCHED_FIFO and SCHED_RR. In the case of SCHED_OTHER and additional, implementation-defined schedulers, the operating system's conformance statement must say what effect *sched_yield* has.

Return Values

sched_yield can only fail if it's not supported: i.e., if _POSIX_PRIORITY_SCHEDULING is not defined. On successful return, *sched_yield* returns 0; when it fails it returns −1 and sets *errno*. In the case of SCHED_OTHER or new, implementation-defined schedulers, it is theoretically possible that *sched_yield* may fail for some reason or another. Again, the conformance document will describe under what conditions *sched_yield* may fail.

Current UNIX Practice

SVR4:   None. SVR4 uses *priocntl*, a different mechanism for controlling scheduling parameters which has roughly the same functionality as the POSIX.4 mechanisms. By setting a process's RT-class scheduling parameters to be the same as they were before the call (no change), a scheduling decision can be forced, to imitate the effect of *sched_yield*.

BSD: No priority scheduling operations are specified in BSD UNIX (as of 4.3).

See Also

sched_getscheduler, sched_setscheduler, sched_getparam, sched_setparam
(sibling functions)

sem_close

Name

sem_close — Terminate access to a POSIX.4 named semaphore.

Synopsis

```
#include        <mqueue.h>
int             sem_close(sem_t *sem);
```

Conditionality

```
#ifdef _POSIX_SEMAPHORES
```

Description

Use *sem_close* to sever the connection to a named semaphore which you made with *sem_open*. Only named semaphores should be closed with *sem_close*. Unnamed semaphores are destroyed using *sem_destroy*.

Named semaphores are persistent; that is, the state of a semaphore persists even if no one has the semaphore open.

A semaphore only ceases to exist when either the system goes down (and all bets are off in that case), or until the semaphore is removed with *sem_unlink*. Once a semaphore has been removed with *sem_unlink*, and all processes that have the semaphore open *close* it, then all traces of the semaphore disappear. Until that time, though, processes that have the semaphore open may continue to use it—even though other processes can no longer access the "removed" semaphore.

Notes

Named semaphores do not reside in the file system namespace. The name must obey construction rules as for a normal file pathname, but the named semaphore may or may not actually appear in the file system namespace. That is, when you do an *ls*, named semaphores may or may not appear. Therefore, your application must be careful to clean up its semaphores, since there is no (POSIX-standard) equivalent of the *rm* command for semaphores.

Return Values

sem_close returns 0 if the named semaphore is successfully closed. After such time, the process will no longer be able to access the semaphore through that descriptor. If *sem_close* fails, then it returns –1.

Errors

If *sem_close* returns –1, it sets *errno* to the following value:

EINVAL   The descriptor passed does not describe an open semaphore.

Current UNIX Practice

POSIX semaphores are brand new to POSIX.4.

See Also

sem_open (to begin using a message queue)
close (similarities to this call)
sem_wait, sem_trywait (wait and nonblocking wait on a semaphore)
sem_post (signal a semaphore)

sem_destroy

Name

sem_destroy — Deinitialize a POSIX.4 unnamed semaphore.

Synopsis

```
#include        <semaphore.h>
int             sem_destroy(sem_t *sem_location);
```

Conditionality

```
#ifdef _POSIX_SEMAPHORES
```

Description

sem_destroy deinitializes an unnamed semaphore in the location pointed to by *sem_location*. The semaphore, it is assumed, was previously initialized by *sem_init*. Unnamed semaphores are usable until they are *sem_destroy*ed, or until the memory in which the semaphore resides is deallocated by the system.

Notes

Unnamed semaphores are a parallel to named semaphores. Both types of semaphores are used with the *sem_wait*, *sem_trywait*, and *sem_post* calls. However, they are created and destroyed in totally separate ways. Named semaphores are accessed by their name, through the *sem_open* call, and closed with *sem_close*. Names are removed using *sem_unlink*. Unnamed semaphores, in contrast, are simply initialized (with this function), and destroyed by *sem_destroy* (or implicitly when the memory containing the semaphore is deallocated). Do not try and mix use of the interfaces on a single semaphore. In particular, don't *sem_close* an unnamed semaphore, and don't *sem_destroy* a named semaphore.

A semaphore need only be deinitialized once. Only one of your cooperating processes needs to call this routine; alternatively, you can simply unmap, *close*, and unlink the shared memory area in which the semaphore is presumed to reside (unnamed semaphores in non-shared memory are not very useful between multiple processes, although they *are* useful if you have multiple threads).

Shared memory, and therefore unnamed semaphores, are persistent so long as the system remains up. That means you can create a shared memory area, put an unnamed semaphore in it, signal it a few times, *close* and unmap the shared memory area, go away for a few days, then come back and the semaphore would have the same value as when you left it. You may be able to use this persistence to your advantage, if you are careful. However, watch out for persistence in the case where the system may go down. A careful application should always include a startup phase where the status and general sanity of all required objects, including shared memory and unnamed semaphores, is assured.

The EBUSY error value may not be detected on all systems. You shold not count on it being returned. A better approach is to be sure that your processes are done with the semaphore by some other means before you destroy the semaphore.

Return Values

sem_destroy returns 0 and destroys the semaphore. If *sem_destroy* fails, then it returns −1 and the semaphore is not destroyed.

Errors

If *sem_destroy* returns −1, it sets *errno* to one of the following values:

EINVAL   The location passed does not correspond to a valid unnamed semaphore.

EBUSY   The system has detected that there are processes currently using the semaphore. This error may or may not be detected by the system. Don't count on it.

Current UNIX Practice

POSIX semaphores are brand new to POSIX.4.

See Also

sem_init (to initialize an unnamed semaphore)
sem_open, sem_close, sem_unlink (parallel interface to named semaphores)
sem_wait (to wait on a semaphore)
sem_trywait (to not wait on a semaphore)
sem_post (to signal a semaphore)
shm_open, mmap (to open and map a shared memory area)

sem_getvalue

Name

sem_getvalue — Get the value of a POSIX.4 semaphore (named or unnamed).

Synopsis

```
#include         <semaphore.h>
int              sem_getvalue(sem_t *sem, int *value);
```

Conditionality

```
#ifdef _POSIX_SEMAPHORES
```

Description

sem_getvalue takes a snapshot of the value of the semaphore referenced by *sem*, and stores it in the location referenced by *value*. Obviously, this value is subject to change, and represents a value the semaphore had at one point during the call to *sem_getvalue*. This function is provided for use in debugging semaphore code.

Notes

Positive semaphore values indicate an unlocked semaphore, and zero indicates a locked semaphore. Some, not all, implementations will also return a negative value. In these implementations, the absolute value of a negative semaphore value indicates the number of blocked processes. In other implementations, the semaphore value may simply go to zero and then stay there until all blocked processes are unblocked. Both implementations have their merits.

Return Values

sem_getvalue returns 0 and stores the semaphore value in *value*. If it fails, it returns –1.

Errors

If this function returns –1, it sets *errno* to the following value:

EINVAL   The location passed does not correspond to a valid semaphore.

Current UNIX Practice

POSIX semaphores are brand new to POSIX.4.

See Also

sem_init, sem_destroy (interface to unnamed semaphores)

sem_open, sem_close, sem_unlink (parallel interface to named semaphores)

sem_wait (to wait on a semaphore)

sem_trywait (to not wait on a semaphore)

sem_post (to signal a semaphore)

sem_init

Name

sem_init — Initialize a POSIX.4 unnamed semaphore.

Synopsis

```
#include        <semaphore.h>
int             sem_init(sem_t *sem_location, int pshared,
                unsigned int value);
```

Conditionality

```
#ifdef _POSIX_SEMAPHORES
```

Description

sem_init initializes an unnamed semaphore in the location pointed to by *sem_location*. Any process that can access that location will be able to use the resulting semaphore in calls to *sem_wait*, *sem_trywait*, and *sem_post* by passing the appropriate pointer. The assumption is that such a semaphore will be placed in an area of shared memory in order to be used. The semaphore will be usable until either it is destroyed with *sem_destroy*, or the memory in which the semaphore resides is deallocated by the system.

The *pshared* argument describes whether the semaphore is to be usable between multiple processes, or merely within the calling process. Unless you have a system with *threads*, you will always set this parameter to 1. If you set *pshared* to 0, then multiple processes may not be able to use the resulting semaphore, even if it *is* located in a shared memory area. (The *pshared* attribute is there because it will be used when POSIX threads (pthreads) are finalized.)

The semaphore is initialized with an initial value given by *value*. The initial value cannot be negative. Negative values indicate a locked semaphore with processes blocked on the semaphore. This is not possible for a newly-created semaphore.

Notes

Unnamed semaphores are a parallel to named semaphores. Both types of semaphores are used with the *sem_wait*, *sem_trywait*, and *sem_post* calls. However, they are created and destroyed in totally separate ways. Named semaphores are accessed by their name, through the *sem_open* call, and closed with *sem_close*. Names are removed using *sem_unlink*. Unnamed semaphores, in contrast, are simply initialized (with this function), and destroyed by *sem_destroy* (or implicitly when the memory containing the semaphore is deallocated). Do not try and mix use of the interfaces on a single semaphore. In particular, don't *sem_close* an unnamed semaphore, and don't *sem_destroy* a named semaphore.

A semaphore need only be initialized once. Be careful that only one of your cooperating processes initializes the semaphore, and be especially careful that the semaphore is not initialized while it is in use.

The unnamed semaphore is linked to its memory location in an operating system dependent (read, "magical and mysterious") way. You cannot take a copy of the created semaphore and use it as a semaphore.

Shared memory, and therefore unnamed semaphores, are persistent so long as the system remains up. That means you can create a shared memory area, put an unnamed semaphore in it, signal it a few times, *close* and unmap the shared memory area, go away for a few days, then come back and the semaphore would have the same value as when you left it. Persistence is more likely to be a problem than a feature; be careful.

Return Values

sem_init returns 0 and initializes the semaphore in the location passed in *sem_location*. If *sem_init* fails, then it returns –1 and the semaphore is not initialized.

Errors

If *sem_init* returns –1, it sets *errno* to one of the following values:

EPERM
: The process does not have permission to initialize the semaphore. Maybe the shared memory in which the semaphore resides was mapped in read-only mode.

EINVAL
: The initial *value* you specified is greater than SEM_VALUE_MAX.

ENOSPC
: The system has run out of system resources to support more semaphores. Alternatively, the process has reached the limit on the number of semaphores it may have open (SEM_NSEMS_MAX). Note that this error is both a *system* error and a process-limit error.

Current UNIX Practice

POSIX semaphores are brand new to POSIX.4.

sem_init (continued)

See Also

sem_destroy (to deinitialize an unnamed semaphore)

sem_open, sem_close, sem_unlink (parallel interface to named semaphores)

sem_wait (to wait on a semaphore)

sem_trywait (to not wait on a semaphore)

sem_post (to signal a semaphore)

shm_open, mmap (to open and map a shared memory area)

Name

sem_open — Create/access a POSIX.4 named semaphore.

Synopsis

```
#include      <semaphore.h>
sem_t         * sem_open(char *sem_name, int oflags,
              mode_t mode, unsigned int value);
```

Conditionality

```
#ifdef _POSIX_SEMAPHORES
```

Description

sem_open is used to create or open a named semaphore. The function call is modeled on *open*, and the interpretation of *oflags* and *mode* are especially reminiscent of *open*. Significant differences emerge in the sort of object returned—it's a pointer to a semaphore, not a file—and in the interpretation of the arguments.

Name Resolution

First, the semaphore name. The name must obey construction rules as for a normal file pathname, but the semaphore may or may not actually appear in the file system namespace. That is, when you do an *ls*, semaphores may or may not appear. Therefore, your application must be careful to clean up its semaphores, since there is no (POSIX-standard) equivalent of the *rm* command for them.

For maximum portability you must follow two more rules. First, the semaphore name must begin with a "/". Relative names are interpreted differently by different systems. A portable application must use a fully-rooted name, therefore, to achieve utmost portability of semaphore names.

Second, the name may not contain additional "/" characters. Again, different systems will interpret the name in different ways, some treating it as a pathname and applying all the standard pathname semantics, and others treating the name as a simple string.

Other Parameters

Unlike *open*, the *oflags* parameter to *sem_open* only relates to semaphore creation. It is not used in opening a semaphore that already exists; you do not have to set O_RDONLY, O_RDWR, or O_WRONLY. In fact, the effect of setting those flags is *undefined*, meaning you shouldn't do it. The reason for this is that semaphores are always used in the same way—you wait on them, you signal them—so there is no reason to signal your intentions through the *oflags* parameter.

The *oflags* argument is used, however, if you want to *create* a named semaphore. The following two flags can be set in *oflags*:

O_CREAT   This flag is set to indicate that this call to *sem_open* is to create the named semaphore, not just access a semaphore that already exists. It is only in this case that the third and fourth arguments to *sem_open* are used. The semaphore is created with a mode as specified in *mode*, just as for file creation. All three triplets of permissions are set for the semaphore: read and write (wait/signal?) permission for creator, group, and others (but see following note). Portable symbols for constructing a mode are found in *<sys/stat.h>*: S_IWUSR, S_IROTH and so forth. The *uid* and *gid* of the semaphore are set to the effective IDs of the calling process.

Note that a hole in the standard exists. Since one does not specify O_RDONLY, O_WRONLY, or O_RDWR on *sem_open* calls, it's not quite clear which permissions are checked when you try to *sem_open* a semaphore. Is it read permission? Write permission? Execute permission? The standard does not say. This is an annoyance, but you can easily deal with it by specifying *all* permissions for user, or group, or others, depending on who you want to be able to access the semaphore. You can specify S_IRWXG for group access, S_IRWXO for other's access, and S_IRWXU for your own access.

The initial value of the created semaphore is set from the *value* argument. Since the value is an unsigned quantity, you cannot specify a negative value. Positive values indicate an unlocked semaphore, and zero indicates a locked semaphore with no waiters.

O_EXCL   This flag modifies the behavior of O_CREAT and is consulted only if O_CREAT is also set. If O_CREAT is set and O_EXCL is *not* set, then *sem_open* will silently fail to create the semaphore, and instead just attach to the existing semaphore. If both flags are set, though, and a semaphore already exists, then *sem_open* will return an error. It is meaningless and undefined to set O_EXCL without O_CREAT. Don't do it.

Notes

Do not mix named semaphore operations (sem_open, sem_close, sem_unlink) with unnamed semaphore operations (*sem_init, sem_destroy*) on the same semaphore. Named and unnamed semaphores are two parallel methods for creating and accessing semaphores. In particular, do not *sem_destroy* a named semaphore, and do not *sem_close* an unnamed semaphore. Undefined (but probably bad) results will occur.

Semaphores are persistent so long as the system remains up. That means you can create a semaphore, signal it a few times, close it, go away for a few days, then come back and the semaphore would have the same value as when you left it. You may be able to use this persistence to your advantage, if you are careful. However, watch out for persistence in the case where the system may go down. A careful application should always include a startup phase where the status and general sanity of all required objects, including semaphores, is assured.

It is possible that vendors will implement named semaphores atop files. In this case, a set of file-like error returns, documented below, are possible.

Return Values

sem_open returns a pointer to the created or accessed semaphore as its return value. This value is not a file descriptor. Do not attempt file operations on a semaphore pointer. The effects will probably be disastrous. If *sem_open* fails, then it returns (sem_t *)-1.

Errors

If *sem_open* returns (sem_t *)-1, it sets *errno* to one of the following values:

EACCES   Either the named semaphore exists and you do not have permission to access it, or you're trying to create a non-existing semaphore and permission to do so is denied.

EEXIST   You specified O_CREAT and O_EXCL in *oflags*, and the semaphore already exists.

EINVAL   You passed in an inappropriate name, one which broke one or more of the rules given above. Each implementation must describe the set of names it will accept for semaphores; you can use this documentation to determine exactly what the problem was. Alternatively, you can stick to the rules quoted above.

           You can also get EINVAL if you are creating the semaphore, and the initial *value* you specified is greater than SEM_VALUE_MAX.

ENOENT   The semaphore does not exist, and you did not specify O_CREAT.

EINTR   The call was interrupted by a signal. This is not likely to happen unless the call blocks waiting for some resource which is in short supply.

EMFILE   The process is using too many files or semaphores. Note that in an implementation that supports semaphores atop files, the limit applies to the total of open files *and* open semaphores.

ENFILE   The system has run out of system resources to support more open semaphores. Note that this error is a *system* error, while EMFILE is more of a process-limit error.

ENAMETOOLONG

sem_name is too long, greater than PATH_MAX, or, if you used multiple "/" characters and the system supports that, a component of the pathname exceeded NAME_MAX while _POSIX_NO_TRUNC is in effect.

Current UNIX Practice

POSIX semaphores are brand new to POSIX.4.

See Also

open (similarities to this call)
sem_close (to finish using a named semaphore)
sem_unlink (to remove a named semaphore from the system entirely)
sem_wait (to wait on a semaphore)
sem_trywait (to not wait on a semaphore)
sem_post (to signal a semaphore)
sem_init
sem_destroy (alternate unnamed interface to semaphores)

Name

sem_post — Post (signal) a POSIX.4 semaphore (named or unnamed).

Synopsis

```
#include      <semaphore.h>
int           sem_post(sem_t *sem);
```

Conditionality

```
#ifdef _POSIX_SEMAPHORES
```

Description

sem_post performs the semaphore unlock operation on the given semaphore. This is also called posting, or signalling, the semaphore. If the semaphore value is positive, it is simply incremented. If the semaphore value is not positive, then the semaphore is said to be *locked* and there may be processes *blocked* on the semaphore. If there are such processes, then one is chosen and unblocked. If there are no such processes, then the semaphore value is just incremented (to 1).

If there are blocked processes, they are blocked in an order dictated by their scheduling algorithms. In particular, processes running under SCHED_FIFO or SCHED_RR are blocked in priority order, highest priority at the head of the queue. Within a single priority, processes are queued First-In-First-Out.

Notes

There are no fancy errors defined for fringe conditions like deallocation of a semaphore while there are waiters, and so forth. That's because such error detection might slow down the operation of semaphores. Semaphores must have a fast implementation for optimum usability. The result is, this interface is a loaded weapon. Don't point it at yourself.

Return Values

sem_post returns 0 if it successfully signals the semaphore. If it fails, then it returns –1 and the operation is not performed. The unlock operation, when performed, is performed as a single, uninterruptible unit. You don't need to worry about races between processes.

Errors

If this function returns −1, it sets *errno* to the following value:

EINVAL   The location passed does not correspond to a valid semaphore.

Current UNIX Practice

POSIX semaphores are brand new to POSIX.4.

See Also

sem_init
sem_destroy (interface to unnamed semaphores)
sem_open
sem_close
sem_unlink (parallel interface to named semaphores)
sem_wait
sem_trywait (to lock a semaphore)

Name

sem_unlink — Destroy a POSIX.4 named semaphore.

Synopsis

```
#include      <semaphore.h>
int           sem_unlink(char *sem_name);
```

Conditionality

```
#ifdef _POSIX_SEMAPHORES
```

Description

sem_unlink destroys the named semaphore *sem_name*. The function call is modeled on *unlink*, and the way we handle deletion of semaphores in use is similar to the way open files are unlinked. That is, those processes which have the semaphore open will still be able to use it, but as soon as the last such process closes the semaphore (via *sem_close*), all vestiges of the named semaphore will be removed from the system. Moreover, when the semaphore is unlinked, processes will no longer be able to *sem_open* it.

Notes

Unnamed semaphores (those initialized with *sem_init*) are not unlinked, because there is no name to be removed from a system. Unnamed semaphores are destroyed either by *sem_destroy*, or implicitly when the memory containing the semaphores is deallocated.

Semaphores are persistent so long as the system remains up. That means you can create a semaphore, signal it a few times, *close* it, go away for a few days, then come back and the semaphore will have the same value you left it with.

Return Values

sem_unlink returns 0 when it successfully deletes the named semaphore. If *sem_unlink* fails, then it returns –1.

sem_unlink (continued)

Errors

If *sem_unlink* returns −1, it sets *errno* to one of the following values:

EACCES   Permission to unlink the named semaphore is denied.

ENOENT   No semaphore by that name exists.

ENAMETOOLONG

        sem_name is too long, greater than PATH_MAX, or, if you used multiple "/" characters and the system supports that, a component of the pathname exceeded NAME_MAX while _POSIX_NO_TRUNC is in effect.

Current UNIX Practice

POSIX named semaphores are brand new to POSIX.4.

See Also

unlink (similarities to this call)
sem_open (to open/create a message queue)
sem_close (to finish using a message queue)
sem_wait (wait on a semaphore)
sem_trywait (don't wait on a semaphore)
sem_post (signal a semaphore)

sem_wait, sem_trywait

Name

sem_wait, sem_trywait — Wait on a POSIX.4 semaphore (named or unnamed).

Synopsis

```
#include        <semaphore.h>
int             sem_wait(sem_t *sem);
int             sem_trywait(sem_t *sem);
```

Conditionality

```
#ifdef _POSIX_SEMAPHORES
```

Description

sem_wait and *sem_trywait* perform the semaphore lock operation on the given semaphore. If the semaphore value is positive, it is simply decremented and the process continues without any blocking whatsoever. If the semaphore value is not positive, then the semaphore is said to be *locked* and the process is *blocked* until another process comes along and signals the semaphore (with *sem_post*).

The *sem_trywait* function never blocks; that is, it only does the semaphore lock operation if it can do so without blocking (if the semaphore value is positive).

Notes

When I say *blocking* above, all I'm really saying is that the process does not return from the call to *sem_wait* until it is signalled by another process. The blocking itself may be implemented by actual blocking (removal of the process from the running state by the operating system), or by another mechanism, such as spinning. Spinning uses a processor, and is also known as busy-waiting. Such an implementation is sometimes used on multiprocessors. This is a decision that the implementor is free to make. Generally, you're not going to care about this detail.

There are no fancy errors defined for fringe conditions like deallocation of a semaphore while there are waiters, and so forth. That's because such error detection might slow down the operation of semaphores. Semaphores must have a fast implementation for optimum usability. The result is, this interface is a loaded weapon. Don't point it at yourself.

Return Values

sem_wait and *sem_trywait* return 0 if they successfully perform the lock operation on the semaphore. If they fail, then they return −1 and the lock operation is not performed. The lock operation, when performed, is performed as a single, uninterruptible unit. You don't need to worry about races between processes.

Errors

If these functions return −1, they set *errno* to one of the following values:

EINVAL   The location passed does not correspond to a valid semaphore.

EINTR   The process was blocked on the semaphore, and it received a signal. (This error can only occur for *sem_wait*).

EAGAIN   The semaphore could not be locked without blocking (This error is only returned by *sem_trywait*, because *sem_wait* will just go ahead and block).

EDEADLK   The system detected a situation in which a deadlock is going to occur. Most systems will not perform deadlock detection, because it is costly; therefore this error will not be returned on most systems. Don't count on it.

Current UNIX Practice

POSIX semaphores are brand new to POSIX.4.

See Also

sem_init
sem_destroy (interface to unnamed semaphores)
sem_open
sem_close
sem_unlink (parallel interface to named semaphores)
sem_post (to signal a semaphore)

Name

shm_open — Create/access a POSIX.4 shared memory object.

Synopsis

```
#include      <sys/mman.h>
int           shm_open(char *shm_name, int oflags, mode_t mode);
```

Conditionality

```
#ifdef _POSIX_SHARED_MEMORY_OBJECTS
```

Description

shm_open is used to create or open a POSIX.4 shared memory object. This object is then mapped into the process's address space with *mmap*, and unmapped with *munmap*. The object itself is of little use other than for establishing the memory mapping; at that time, the object can be closed using *close*.

The function call is modeled on *open*, and the interpretation of *oflags* and *mode* are very similar to *open*. In addition, unlike *sem_open* and *mq_open*, *shm_open* returns a file descriptor, which may be used in calls to *mmap*, *ftruncate* and *close*. (All the other "file" calls have undefined results when applied to this particular descriptor. You wouldn't want to *read* or *lseek* in this file anyway. It's *memory*.) Shared memory naming, however, is interpreted as for semaphore names and message queue names.

Name Resolution

The name must obey construction rules as for a normal file pathname, but the shared memory object may or may not actually appear in the file system namespace. That is, when you do an *ls*, shared memory objects may or may not appear. Therefore, your application must be careful to clean up its shared memory objects, since there is no (POSIX-standard) equivalent of the *rm* command for shared memory objects.

For completely portable memory, you must follow two more rules. First, the name must begin with a "/". Relative shared memory object names are interpreted differently by different systems. A portable application must use a fully-rooted name to achieve portability (the same rule applies to semaphore and message queue names).

Second, the name may not contain additional "/" characters. Again, different systems will interpret the name in different ways.

Other Parameters

The *oflags* argument controls the way in which the shared memory object is opened. You must specify one of O_RDONLY or O_RDWR, depending on whether you wish to only read, or read and write in the shared memory. Unlike files and message queues, you do not have the option of opening a shared memory object in "write-only" mode (O_WRONLY); the effect of that flag is not defined for shared memory objects. In addition, you can specify the following flags in *oflags*:

O_CREAT This flag is set to indicate that this call to *shm_open* is to create the shared memory object, not just access an object that already exists. It is only in this case that the *mode* argument to *shm_open* is used. The shared memory object is created with a mode as specified in *mode*, just as for file creation. All three triplets of permissions are set for the object: read and write permission for the creator, its group, and others. There is no meaning for execute permission on shared memory. Portable symbols for constructing a mode are found in *<sys/stat.h>*: S_IWUSR, S_IROTH and so forth. The *uid* and *gid* of the shared memory object are set to the effective IDs of the calling process.

O_EXCL This flag modifies the behavior of O_CREAT and is consulted only if O_CREAT is also set. If O_CREAT is set and O_EXCL is *not* set, then *shm_open* will silently fail to create the shared memory object, and instead just return a descriptor for the existing object. If both flags are set, though, and a shared memory object by that *name* already exists, then *shm_open* will return an error. It is meaningless and undefined to set O_EXCL without O_CREAT.

O_TRUNC If you set O_TRUNC, then the shared memory object's size is truncated down to zero. This flag can only be used if you are opening the shared memory object for writing (O_RDWR); this flag is superfluous if you create the shared memory object with this call (shared memory creation *always* creates a zero-size object).

Notes

Shared memory objects are created with a size of zero. They are sized using *ftruncate* and mapped in using *mmap*. The descriptor returned by this call is only useful for those functions (and, obviously, *close*).

Shared memory is persistent so long as the system remains up. You can create and map a shared memory region, store data, *close* and unmap the region, go away, then come back and find the same data you stored. Persistence is more likely to be a problem than a feature; be careful.

Return Values

shm_open returns the descriptor for the created or accessed shared memory object as its return value. This value is a restricted-use file descriptor. Do not attempt file operations, other than *ftruncate*, *mmap*, and *close*, on a shared memory object descriptor. The effects are unknown. If *shm_open* fails, then it returns –1.

Errors

If *shm_open* returns –1, it sets *errno* to one of the following values:

EACCES   Either the shared memory object exists and the permissions you request in *oflags* are denied, or you're trying to create a non-existing shared memory object and permission to do so is denied.

EEXIST   You specified O_CREAT and O_EXCL in *oflags*, and the shared memory object already exists.

EINVAL   You passed in an inappropriate name, one which broke one or more of the rules given above. Each implementation must describe the set of names it will accept for shared memory objects; you can use this documentation to determine exactly what the problem was. Alternatively, you can stick to the rules quoted above.

ENOENT   The shared memory object does not exist, and you did not specify O_CREAT.

EINTR   The call was interrupted by a signal. This is not likely to happen unless the call blocks waiting for some resource which is in short supply.

EMFILE   The process is using too many file descriptors. Note that the limit applies to the total of open files *and* open shared memory objects.

ENFILE   The system has run out of system resources to support more open shared memory objects. Note that this error is a *system* error, while EMFILE is more of a process-limit error.

ENOSPC   There is not enough space to create this shared memory object.

ENAMETOOLONG

> *shm_name* is too long, greater than PATH_MAX, or, if you used multiple "/" characters and the system supports that, a component of the pathname exceeded NAME_MAX while _POSIX_NO_TRUNC is in effect.

Current UNIX Practice

POSIX shared memory objects are brand new to POSIX.4. The *mmap* function itself is present in many UNIX systems, including System V Release 4 and SunOS. System V supports a completely different mechanism.

See Also

open (similarities to this call)
close (to finish using a shared memory object descriptor)
mmap (to establish a memory mapping for this object and your memory space)
ftruncate (to set the size of a shared memory object)

Name

shm_unlink — Destroy a POSIX.4 shared memory object.

Synopsis

```
#include        <sys/mman.h>
int             shm_unlink(char *shm_name);
```

Conditionality

```
#ifdef _POSIX_SHARED_MEMORY
```

Description

shm_unlink destroys the shared memory object named *shm_name*. The function call is modeled on *unlink*, and the way we handle deletion of mapped or opened shared memory objects is similar to the way open files are unlinked. That is, those processes which have *shm_open*ed or *mmap*ed the object will still be able to use it, until all such processes *close* the shared memory object and *munmap* it as well (since *shm_open* returns a file descriptor, standard *close* is used to *close* it). When all open descriptors are closed, and all extant mappings are unmapped, then all vestiges of the shared memory object will be removed from the system. Moreover, when the shared memory is unlinked, processes will no longer be able to *shm_open* it.

Notes

Shared memory is persistent so long as the system remains up. That means you can create and map a shared memory region, store some data into it, *close* and unmap it, go away for a few days, then come back and still see the data you stored, assuming no one unlinks the shared memory object in the meantime. You may be able to use this persistence to your advantage, if you are careful. However, watch out for persistence in the case where the system may go down. A careful application should always include a startup phase where the status and general sanity of all required objects, including shared memory, is assured. Such a phase might consist of just *shm_unlinking* all needed shared memory objects before anyone opens them up—just to be sure that the memory, when created and mapped, is empty.

Return Values

shm_unlink returns 0 when it successfully deletes the named shared memory object. If *shm_unlink* fails, then it returns –1.

Errors

If *shm_unlink* returns –1, it sets *errno* to one of the following values:

EACCES   Permission to unlink the named shared memory object is denied.

ENOENT   No shared memory object by that name exists.

ENAMETOOLONG

shm_name is too long, greater than PATH_MAX, or, if you used multiple "/" characters and the system supports that, a component of the pathname exceeded NAME_MAX while _POSIX_NO_TRUNC is in effect.

Current UNIX Practice

POSIX shared memory is brand new to POSIX.4.

See Also

unlink (similarities to this call)
shm_open (to open/create a shared memory object)
shm_close (to finish using a shared memory object)
mmap (to map an opened shared memory object)
munmap (to dis-establish a mapping made by *mmap*)

Name

sigaction — Establish a process's reaction to a signal.

Synopsis

```
#include        <signal.h>

int             sigaction(int sig, const struct sigaction *reaction,
                    struct sigaction *old_reaction);
```

Conditionality

sigaction itself is an unconditional part of POSIX. The functionality of the SA_SIGINFO flag is conditional on _POSIX_REALTIME_SIGNALS.

Description

The *sigaction* function establishes a process's reaction to a signal.

When a process receives a signal, a number of things can happen. If the process has not indicated any special handling for the signal, it can be handled in the normal, system-wide default way. Usually this means the process will be terminated. The process can choose to ignore the signal, in which case the signal will disappear. Finally, the process may choose to *handle* the signal by invoking a *signal-handler* function. Each of these options are dealt with by *sigaction*.

The first argument to *sigaction, sig*, indicates which signal we are establishing the handler for. The second argument dictates the desired signal handling action. The third argument is a result parameter, into which the system will store the previous signal handler. This parameter can be used to store a signal's previous handler state, to be restored at a later time. Either *reaction* or *old_reaction* may be NULL, in which case the portion of *sigaction*'s functionality related to these parameters will be skipped. If both are NULL, *sigaction* becomes a rather boring function.

The handler itself is completely encapsulated in the *struct sigaction*, which has the following required members:

```
struct sigaction {
        void (*)()                              sa_handler;
        void (*)(int, siginfo_t *, void *)      sa_sigaction;
        sigset_t                                sa_mask;
        int                                     sa_flags;
};
```

sa_handler is a pointer to a function, and is used to indicate the handler function for all signals except the queued real-time signals SIGRTMIN through SIGRTMAX (when SA_SIGINFO is set in *sa_flags*). If, on the other hand, you are setting up a handler for a queued real-time signal, you will use *sa_sigaction* rather than *sa_handler*. In no case will you ever need to set both *sa_handler* and *sa_sigaction*. In fact, most vendors will probably use the same storage space for both fields, by using some sort of a union.

The *sa_mask* field tells the system which signals should be blocked from delivery when you handle this signal. The system will automatically block *sig* while it is being handled; this field tells the system which *additional* signals you want blocked. In most cases, you'll just empty out this set using *sigemptyset*.

Finally, *sa_flags* provides some miscellaneous control over signal handling. There are two bits which can be set in *sa_flags*. SA_NOCLDSTOP, the first bit, is used only when the signal is SIGCHLD. This bit tells the system not to deliver a SIGCHLD signal for children who stop, but only for children who terminate. This bit is probably not going to come into play unless _POSIX_JOB_CONTROL is supported.

The other bit is SA_SIGINFO. If *sig* is between SIGRTMIN and SIGRTMAX, inclusive, then SA_SIGINFO tells the system that this signal is to be queued to the process rather than just registered. In addition, the signal handler for this signal is to take three arguments instead of the normal one. This allows extra data parameters to be passed to these signal handlers. When you set SA_SIGINFO, you indicate your choice of a handler function in *sa_sigaction*, not *sa_handler*.

You can ignore a signal by setting *sa_handler* to the constant SIG_IGN. You can set the handling of a signal to its system default by making *sa_handler* the constant SIG_DFL.

Real-Time Signals are Queued Rather Than Registered

Normally, signals are delivered to a process by setting a bit that corresponds to that signal for the process. This leads to the possibility of signal loss. If more than one signal is delivered before you handle that signal, then those subsequent deliveries are lost, because the bit used to register signal delivery only contains the information "this signal occurred." By queueing signals rather than registering them, signals are not lost. Of course, extra storage is required to support signal queueing, so this option is more expensive in storage.

Handler Differences

A non-real-time signal is handled via a handler function which takes a single argument, the number of the signal received:

```
int     signal_handler(int sig_num)
{
}
```

In contrast, a real-time queued signal (one between SIGRTMIN and SIGRTMAX, for which SA_SIGINFO has been set in *sa_flags*) is handled with a function that takes three arguments:

```
int    rt_signal_handler(int sig_num, siginfo_t *extra, void *v)
{
}
```

The first parameter is the same in either case. The second parameter, a pointer to a *siginfo_t*, contains additional information about the signal received. This structure contains several fields:

```
typedef struct {
        int             si_signo;
        int             si_code;
        union sigval    si_value;
} siginfo_t;
```

si_signo will be set to the number of the signal delivered (the same as the *sig_num* parameter). *si_code*, which indicates the cause of the signal, is set to the constant SI_USER in the case of a real-time signal sent by *kill*, and is set to SI_QUEUE if the signal was sent by *sigqueue*. If the signal is delivered as a result of asynchronous I/O completion, *si_code* will be set to SI_ASYNCIO, it will be set to SI_MESGQ if the signal is the result of an *mq_notify* call, and it will be set to SI_TIMER if the signal is delivered as a result of a POSIX.4 timer expiration. The field *si_value* will contain the value that was sent as the *val* parameter to *sigqueue*, or as the *sigev_value* component of a *struct sigevent* used for timers, asynchronous I/O or message queues. If this signal was sent by *kill*, then the contents of this field are undefined.

The third argument to a real-time signal handler has no standard meaning; it is there because several existing UNIX implementations pass three arguments to their signal handlers already. On these systems, argument three usually contains the process's machine context at the time it was interrupted by the signal. This sort of information can be very useful when the signal is delivered as a result of a machine exception (an illegal instruction generating a SIGILL or an invalid memory access generating a SIGBUS, for instance). In the case of an asynchronous interrupt, like timer expiration, such information is rather less useful because it has very little to do with the signal.

Return Values

The *sigaction* returns successfully if it establishes the signal action as desired, and returns the previous signal handler as desired. In that case, 0 is returned. In the case of error, −1 will be returned.

Errors

If *sigaction* returns −1, it sets *errno* to one of the following values:

EINVAL   The signal number is invalid, not one the system supports.

EINVAL   You attempted to set a handler (either SIG_IGN or your own function) for a signal that cannot be caught or handled. These signals are SIGKILL and SIGSTOP. Not all systems will return an error in this case. Some will simply ignore your attempt to change the handler.

Current UNIX Practice

sigaction is standard UNIX functionality; SA_SIGINFO is new for POSIX.4. Some versions of UNIX require you to reset a handler function after each individual signal is received. POSIX does not suffer from this deficiency.

See Also

kill
sigqueue (sending signals)
sigprocmask (information on blocking signals)
mq_notify (signal delivery on message arrival)
aio_read
aio_write
lio_listio (signal delivery for asynchronous I/O)
timer_create (signal delivery on timer expiration)

Name

sigprocmask — Block/unblock signal deliveries.

Synopsis

```
#include        <signal.h>
int             sigprocmask(int op, const sigset_t *set, sigset_t *oset);
```

Conditionality

Unconditional.

Description

Each process maintains a signal mask which controls which signals are immediately delivered to the process and which have their delivery deferred. If a signal is in this set, then it is said to be *blocked* from immediate delivery. The *sigprocmask* function manipulates and interrogates this signal mask.

The first argument, *op*, controls how the next argument, *set*, is applied to the process's signal mask. If *op* is SIG_BLOCK, then the set will be added in to the process's current signal mask. If *op* is SIG_UNBLOCK, then the set will be subtracted out of the process's mask. Finally, if *op* is SIG_SETMASK, the given *set* becomes the process's signal mask.

set is a set of signal numbers, set up by the *sigset* functions.

oset, if specified, is a pointer to a *sigset_t*. The system will store the process's previous signal mask into this set. This supports the ability to restore a signal state at a later time.

Either *set* or *oset* can be NULL. In such a case, the functionality related to each parameter is just skipped.

A process's signal mask is initially empty; any signal can be delivered. Some signals cannot be blocked: SIGKILL and SIGSTOP. However, if you try to block these signals you will not get an error back from *sigprocmask*; it will merely ignore your request to block those particular signals, and do all the rest you requested.

Notes

Blocking a signal is merely a temporary deferral of signal delivery. It should not be confused with ignoring a signal, as done by calling *sigaction* with a *sa_handler* field of

sigprocmask (continued)

SIG_IGN. In that case, you are telling the system to discard deliveries of a particular signal.

Return Values

The *sigprocmask* function returns successfully if it establishes the signal mask as desired. In that case, 0 is returned. In the case of error, −1 will be returned.

Errors

If *sigprocmask* returns −1, it sets *errno* to the following value:

EINVAL   The op-code *op* was not one of the three possible values.

Current UNIX Practice

sigrocmask is standard UNIX functionality.

See Also

kill
sigqueue (sending signals)
sigaction (handling/ignoring signals)
sigemptyset
sigfillset
sigaddset
sigdelset
sigismember (manipulation of signal sets)

Name

sigemptyset, sigfillset, sigaddset, sigdelset, sigismember — Manipulation of signal sets.

Synopsis

```
#include         <signal.h>

int              sigemptyset(sigset_t *set);
int              sigfillset(sigset_t *set);
int              sigaddset(sigset_t *set, ing sig_num);
int              sigdelset(sigset_t *set, ing sig_num);
int              sigismember(sigset_t *set, ing sig_num);
```

Conditionality

Unconditional.

Description

These functions allow you to initialize an empty signal set, a full signal set, add a signal to a set, remove a signal from a set, and determine if a signal is a member of a set, respectively.

Signal sets are used to manipulate a process's signal mask (*sigaction* and *sigprocmask*), and to await signal arrival (*sigsuspend* and *sigwaitinfo*). A signal set is merely a collection of signal numbers. Signal sets are usually implemented as bit vectors, and these operations resolve to little functions that set, clear, and test bits in said vectors.

A signal set must first be initialized to a starting state with either *sigemptyset* or *sigfillset* before it can be meaningfully operated on by one of the other functions, or passed to any other signal-using function.

Return Values

These functions return 0 on success and −1 on failure.

Errors

sigemptyset and *sigfillset* have no defined failure modes; the three functions which take a signal number may fail if the signal number is bad and if the system happens to notice. In that case, *errno* will be set to the following:

EINVAL   The signal number was not one of the known signals.

sigset (continued)

Current UNIX Practice

All these functions are from standard UNIX.

See Also

sigprocmask (blocking signals)
sigaction (handling/ignoring signals)
sigwaitinfo
sigsuspend (awaiting signals)

Name

sigsuspend — Await signal arrival; handlers called.

Synopsis

```
#include      <signal.h>
int           sigsuspend(const sigset_t *new_mask);
```

Conditionality

Unconditional.

Description

The *sigsuspend* function provides the ability to synchronously await a signal's arrival. *sigsuspend* installs the signal mask given, and then blocks the calling process until an unblocked, un-ignored signal arrives. That signal is *handled* in the normal way, by calling the signal handler for the function. Then, the original signal mask is restored, and *sigsuspend* returns –1 with *errno* set to EINTR.

This function and *sigwaitinfo* are duals. This function pauses execution until a signal arrives, but goes through the normal signal delivery mechanism of calling the handler function. *sigwaitinfo*, on the other hand, also pauses execution, but bypasses normal handler invocation, instead returning the number of the signal received.

Another difference is in the interpretation of the signal mask passed to the two functions. The mask passed to *sigsuspend* is installed as the process's signal mask. Signals which are in this set are signals that will be blocked from delivery. In contrast, you pass *sigwaitinfo* a set containing the signals you wish to wait for; these signals should be already blocked from normal (handler-style) delivery.

Some signals (SIGSTOP and SIGKILL) cannot be blocked. If you set the signals in *new_mask*, they will be ignored by the system; it will block those signals it can, and then pause awaiting a signal arrival as described above.

Return Values

This function never returns unless a signal arrives. In the manner of all blocking POSIX functions which are interrupted by signals, *sigsuspend* returns –1, with *errno* set to EINTR, when it is interrupted by a signal.

sigsuspend (continued)

Errors

When *sigsuspend* returns, it returns −1 and sets *errno* to the following:

EINTR   An unblocked signal interrupted your wait.

Current UNIX Practice

sigsuspend is modeled on the standard UNIX *sigpause*.

See Also

sigprocmask (to block signals)
sigemptyset
sigfillset
sigaddset
sigdelset
sigismember (manipulation of signal sets)
sigqueue
sigaction (information on *siginfo_t*)
sigwaitinfo (dual of *sigsuspend*)

Name

sigwaitinfo, sigtimedwait — Synchronously await signal arrival; avoid calling handler.
sigtimedwait is a version of *sigwaitinfo* with a timeout value.

Synopsis

```
#include      <unistd.h>
#ifdef        _POSIX_REALTIME_SIGNALS
#include      <signal.h>
int           sigwaitinfo(const sigset_t *these_sigs, siginfo_t *infop);
int           sigtimedwait(const sigset_t *these_sigs, siginfo_t *infop,
                    const struct timespec *timeout);
```

Conditionality

```
#ifdef _POSIX_REALTIME_SIGNALS
```

Description

The *sigwaitinfo* and *sigtimedwait* functions provide the ability to synchronously await a signal's arrival. Unlike *sigsuspend*, which also awaits a signal's arrival, these functions eliminate the call to the signal handler function when the signal does arrive. Instead, the number of the signal is returned. Due to the lack of the handler call, *sigwaitinfo* and *sigtimedwait* can be more efficient than *sigsuspend*.

For both functions, the set of signals to await is passed in *these_sigs*. If the function delivered is a signal for which SA_SIGINFO has been set, then that signal is queued and carries extra information with it; such information will be returned in the area pointed to by *infop*. If *infop* is NULL, then any extra information associated with a queued signal will be discarded, but the signal number will still be returned.

The signals in *these_sigs* should be blocked from normal delivery so that they are not asynchronously delivered before a call to *sigwaitinfo*. You can use *sigprocmask* for blocking these signals from normal asynchronous delivery.

While *sigwaitinfo* will wait indefinitely for a signal to arrive, *sigtimedwait* takes (and requires) a *timeout* parameter which specifies a maximum time interval to wait for signal arrival. If no signal arrives in that time, then *sigwaitinfo* will return with *errno* set to EAGAIN. The *timeout* argument must be passed to *sigtimedwait*; the effect of a NULL parameter is undefined.

The *struct timespec* is usually defined in *<time.h>*, and consists of a number of seconds (*tv_sec*) and nanoseconds (*tv_nsec*). The number of nanoseconds may not equal or exceed 1,000,000,000, or an error may be generated on particularly anal-retentive systems. By specifying *tv_sec* = *tv_nsec* = *0*, you can effect a poll for pending signals, without any blocking at all.

Signal Delivery Order

The real-time extended signals SIGRTMIN through SIGRTMAX are delivered in order, lowest-numbered signal to highest. The other signals are delivered in an unspecified order, and it is not specified whether the other signals are delivered before, after, or interleaved with the real-time extended signals.

Return Values

These functions are successful when they receive a signal they were waiting for. In that case, they return the number of the signal which arrived. In the case of error, –1 will be returned.

Errors

If these functions return –1, they set *errno* to one of the following values:

EINTR   Some signal which you were *not* waiting for arrived and was han-
               dled.

EAGAIN   No signal arrived in the specified time interval. (*sigtimedwait* only)

EINVAL   The value in *timeout* contained a number of seconds less than zero,
               or a number of nanoseconds greater than 1,000,000,000. (*sigtimed-
               wait* only, and only on some systems)

Notes

For detail on the contents of the *siginfo_t* structure, see the documentation for *sigqueue* and *sigaction*.

Current UNIX Practice

Standard UNIX systems do not provide functions of this nature. They are new for POSIX.4.

See Also

sigqueue
sigaction (information on *siginfo_t*)

<time.h> (information on the *struct timespec*)
sigprocmask (to block signals you will be waiting for)

sysconf

Name

sysconf — Query system options at run-time.

Synopsis

```
#include         <unistd.h>

long             sysconf(int option);
```

Conditionality

Unconditional.

Description

The *sysconf* function allows your application to determine information about the run-time system under which the application is running. This is to support the ability to reconfigure operating systems with or without various POSIX options, and with differently-sized data structures.

You can also determine these numbers statically, at compile time, by querying values in *<unistd.h>* and *<limits.h>*. However, you should be sure in that case that your run-time configuration is not going to change.

The *option* argument to *sysconf* indicates a particular POSIX option or limit you wish to query. Available options from POSIX.1 and POSIX.4 are:

Sysconf option name	System Value Returned	Standard
_SC_JOB_CONTROL	_POSIX_JOB_CONTROL (binary)	POSIX.1
_SC_SAVED_IDS	_POSIX_SAVED_IDS (binary)	POSIX.1
_SC_VERSION	_POSIX_VERSION (binary)	POSIX.1
_SC_ARG_MAX	ARG_MAX	POSIX.1
_SC_CHILD_MAX	CHILD_MAX	POSIX.1
_SC_CLK_TCK	clock ticks per second (a.k.a. HZ)	POSIX.1
_SC_NGROUPS_MAX	NGROUPS_MAX	POSIX.1
_SC_OPEN_MAX	OPEN_MAX	POSIX.1
_SC_STREAM_MAX	STREAM_MAX	POSIX.1
_SC_TZNAME_MAX	TZNAME_MAX	POSIX.1
_SC_ASYNCHRONOUS_IO	_POSIX_ASYNCHRONOUS_IO (binary)	POSIX.4
_SC_MAPPED_FILES	_POSIX_MAPPED_FILES (binary)	POSIX.4
_SC_MEMLOCK	_POSIX_MEMLOCK (binary)	POSIX.4

_SC_MEMLOCK_RANGE	_POSIX_MEMLOCK_RANGE (binary)	POSIX.4
_SC_MEMORY_PROTECTION	_POSIX_MEMORY_PROTECTION (binary)	POSIX.4
_SC_MESSAGE_PASSING	_POSIX_MESSAGE_PASSING (binary)	POSIX.4
_SC_PRIORITIZED_IO	_POSIX_PRIORITIZED_IO (binary)	POSIX.4
_SC_PRIORITY_SCHEDULING	_POSIX_PRIORITY_SCHEDULING (binary)	POSIX.4
_SC_REALTIME_SIGNALS	_POSIX_REALTIME_SIGNALS (binary)	POSIX.4
_SC_SEMAPHORES	_POSIX_SEMAPHORES (binary)	POSIX.4
_SC_FSYNC	_POSIX_FSYNC (binary)	POSIX.4
_SC_SHARED_MEMORY_OBJECTS	_POSIX_SHARED_MEMORY_OBJECTS (binary)	POSIX.4
_SC_SYNCHRONIZED_IO	_POSIX_SYNCHRONIZED_IO (binary)	POSIX.4
_SC_TIMERS	_POSIX_TIMERS (binary)	POSIX.4
_SC_AIO_LISTIO_MAX	AIO_LISTIO_MAX	POSIX.4
_SC_AIO_MAX	AIO_MAX	POSIX.4
_SC_AIO_PRIO_DELTA_MAX	AIO_PRIO_DELTA_MAX	POSIX.4
_SC_DELAYTIMER_MAX	DELAYTIMER_MAX	POSIX.4
_SC_MQ_OPEN_MAX	MQ_OPEN_MAX	POSIX.4
_SC_MQ_PRIO_MAX	MQ_PRIO_MAX	POSIX.4
_SC_PAGESIZE	PAGESIZE	POSIX.4
_SC_RTSIG_MAX	RTSIG_MAX	POSIX.4
_SC_SEM_NSEMS_MAX	SEM_NSEMS_MAX	POSIX.4
_SC_SEM_VALUE_MAX	SEM_VALUE_MAX	POSIX.4
_SC_SIGQUEUE_MAX	SIGQUEUE_MAX	POSIX.4
_SC_TIMER_MAX	TIMER_MAX	POSIX.4

Note

The *sysconf* function returns −1 without setting *errno* for a *different* reason than *pathconf* and *fpathconf* do. Be careful when programming using these three functions!

Return Values

sysconf returns the value of the given option for the currently running system. If an option is *not* supported on the currently running system, *sysconf* will return −1 *without* setting *errno*. Therefore, you should initialize *errno* before calling *sysconf* if it is possible that an option may not be present.

Errors

sysconf returns –1 when an option is not supported, but in this case it will not set *errno*. If *sysconf* fails for another reason (and there's only one other reason), it will return –1 and set *errno* as follows:

EINVAL   The option number you passed was not a reasonable option number.

Current UNIX Practice

This function is new for POSIX.

See Also

pathconf, fpathconf (file/pathname-variable run-time configuration)
<unistd.h>
<limits.h>

Name

timer_create — Create a POSIX.4 timer based on a particular clock.

Synopsis

```
#include        <signal.h>
#include        <time.h>
int             timer_create(clockid_t which_system_clock,
                        struct sigevent *timer_event_spec,
                        timer_t *created_timer_id);
```

Conditionality

```
#ifdef _POSIX_TIMERS
```

Description

timer_create is used to create an interval timer for the calling process. The created timer may then be set, using *timer_settime*, to provide periodic or one-shot timer interrupts to the process.

Standard UNIX timers, via the *setitimer* facility, do not require the step of creating the timer, because standard UNIX supports only a static, constant number of timers. Standard UNIX *setitimer* corresponds to the *timer_settime* function; *timer_create* has no analogue in standard UNIX practice.

Each timer used by an application is based on a particular system clock, chosen by the application when the timer is created. An operating system may support many different clocks, corresponding to dedicated hardware facilities or other sources of time information. The POSIX.4 conformance statement should indicate what clocks are available on a particular system. All systems must support at least the single real-time clock, CLOCK_REALTIME. When *timer_create* is called, specify the ID of the system clock to be used in *which_system_clock*.

Timer expirations result in signals being delivered to the process. When the timer is first created, you can specify what signal delivery should be performed, by passing in an appropriately-initialized *sigevent* structure as *timer_event_spec*. You can set *timer_event_spec* to NULL, in which case, for the clock CLOCK_REALTIME, SIGALRM will be delivered to the process on timer expiration.

If you want to specify a particular signal to be delivered on timer expirations, use the *struct sigevent*, as defined in *<signal.h>*:

```
struct sigevent {
        int sigev_notify;                /* notification mechanism */
```

```
            int sigev_signo;              /* signal number */
            union sigval sigev_value;     /* signal data value */
    };
```

This structure contains three members. *sigev_notify* is a flag value that specifies what sort of notification should be used upon timer expiration—signals, nothing, or something else. Currently, only two values are defined for *sigev_notify*: SIGEV_SIGNAL means to send the signal described by the remainder of the *struct sigevent*, and SIGEV_NONE means to send no notification at all upon timer expiration. *sigev_signo*, an *int*, specifies which signal number should be delivered on timer expiration. This number may be any of the defined POSIX signals. The signal may be subject to the real-time signals extension, depending on your application. If you have set SA_SIGINFO for the signal you wish to be delivered, then the real-time signal queueing extension applies to this signal. In this case, an extra data value is passed to the signal handler as a third argument when the timer expires. That value is specified statically in the *sigev_value* field of the *struct sigevent*. *sigev_value* is a union which has either an *int* value (*sival_int*) or a pointer value (*void *sival_ptr*).

If you set *timer_event_spec* to NULL, then a default signal is delivered on timer expiration. For CLOCK_REALTIME, the default signal is SIGALRM. If you have set SA_SIGINFO for the default signal, then that signal is delivered according to the real-time signals extension, with an additional data value. The data value in this case will be the ID of the timer created by this call.

If you do not set SA_SIGINFO for the signal, then the signal may or may not be queued.

Because one timer initialization can result in an indeterminate number of signals, it is difficult at best for an operating system to reliably queue them all to a process and still maintain real-time responsiveness. Therefore, signals delivered as a result of a timer expiration do not queue up. Instead, the *timer_getoverrun* call can be used to determine the number of times a timer has expired. Since all the signals for a particular timer are identical, this is a much lower-overhead means of dealing with timer overruns than trying to queue signals in the operating system.

Since timers are created dynamically, they should always be deleted when the application is done with them. *timer_delete* is used for this purpose.

Return Values

timer_create returns the ID of the timer it created in the *created_timer_id* parameter. When *timer_create* is successful, it returns 0. In this case, the timer ID can be used to set the interval timer and receive periodic interrupts. If *timer_create* fails, it returns –1.

Errors

If *timer_create* returns –1, it sets *errno* to one of the following:

EINVAL   The clock ID specified is not one that exists on this system. It's not specified in POSIX.4, but you will probably also get an EINVAL return if you try to specify a signal number that does not exist.

EAGAIN   The implementation cannot create any more timers for this process. Alternatively, the system does not have the signal queueing resources to set up this additional queued signal.

Notes

The interaction of the timer facility and the real-time signals facility is complex because there are two options involved: _POSIX_TIMERS and _POSIX_REALTIME_SIGNALS. The key to understanding this interaction is common sense. If real-time signals are supported, then signals can be set to pass an additional data parameter. If real-time signals are not supported, then signals can still be delivered on timer expiration, but the additional data value will not be passed along to the signal handler.

timer_create is allowed to return EAGAIN when "the calling process has already created all of the timers it is allowed by this implementation." However, the standard doesn't specify any minimum number of timers. When you examine the conformance of a system, it makes sense to determine exactly how many timers a process can create—how many per the various clocks, how many per process, and so forth.

Current UNIX Practice

Standard UNIX uses *setitimer* and *getitimer*, facilities which are similar in scope to *timer_settime* and *timer_gettime*. However, POSIX.4 timers allow higher resolution in the *struct timespec*, and support multiplexing of a single clock into multiple timers. Additional timers are also specified in a defined way (new clock IDs).

Both BSD and SVR4 support *setitimer/getitimer*.

See Also

timer_settime, timer_gettime (to set interval timers to expire and determine their settings)
timer_getoverrun (to determine the number of times a "queued" timer signal has expired, since the signal is not really queued)
sigaction (to set up signal actions, including SA_SIGINFO)

timer_delete

Name

timer_delete — Delete a POSIX.4 timer.

Synopsis

```
#include        <time.h>
int             timer_delete(timer_t timer_id);
```

Conditionality

```
#ifdef _POSIX_TIMERS
```

Description

timer_delete is used to free up the timers created by *timer_create*. Since POSIX timers are dynamically created, they must also be deleted in order to free up system resources that are occupied by each currently-existing timer. Deleting a timer is like closing a file when you are done with it.

If the timer you are deleting is currently set to expire, the *timer_delete* call will automatically turn it off so that you do not get any more timer expiration signals.

Return Values

timer_delete returns 0 if it successfully deletes the timer. Otherwise, it returns −1 and sets *errno* to indicate the error.

Errors

If *timer_delete* fails, it returns −1 and sets *errno* to the following:

EINVAL   The timer ID specified is not valid for this process. Either it's already been deleted, or it was never created.

Current UNIX Practice

Standard UNIX uses *setitimer* and *getitimer*, which do not require the timer to be created and deleted like in POSIX.4.

Both BSD and SVR4 support *setitimer/getitimer*.

See Also

timer_create

timer_getoverrun

Name

timer_getoverrun — Get overrun count for a POSIX.4 timer.

Synopsis

```
#include        <time.h>
int             timer_getoverrun(timer_t timer_id);
```

Conditionality

```
#ifdef _POSIX_TIMERS
#ifdef _POSIX_REALTIME_SIGNALS
```

Description

timer_getoverrun returns the current overrun count associated with the timer identified by *timer_id*. This is the number of timer expirations that have occurred between the time the timer expiration signal was queued to the process, and the time at which the signal was delivered to the process.

When a timer is set, an indeterminate and potentially large number of signals may be delivered to the process. The normal queueing semantics of POSIX.4 real-time extended signals are difficult to support under these conditions without causing undue resource consumption by the operating system. For this reason, timer expiration signals are not queued to the process. Rather, the system maintains a count of the number of times the timer has expired between the time when the expiration signal was queued to the process, and the time when the process dealt with the signal. The timer overrun count, as it is called, can be obtained by calling *timer_getoverrun*. If you wait long enough, the overrun count will overflow whatever container the operating system has set up for it. This overflow occurs when the overrun count reaches DELAY-TIMER_MAX. When this happens, the operating system will return DELAYTIMER_MAX.

Note especially that the timer overrun count is defined as occurring in an interval of time whose endpoint is when the queued signal is delivered to the process. If the signal is never delivered to the process, then the value of the overrun count is undefined. In other words, always handle the signal, one way or another, before you retrieve the overrun count.

Note, also, that the overrun count is only defined by POSIX.4 when the real-time signals extension is supported. If _POSIX_REALTIME_SIGNALS are supported, though, the overrun count is available for any signal being used for timer expiration—even if it has not been set up for queueing!

Return Values

timer_getoverrun returns the overrun count for the named timer. If it fails, the call returns –1 and sets *errno* to indicate the error.

Errors

If *timer_settime* fails, it returns –1 and sets *errno* to the following:

EINVAL   The timer ID specified is not valid for this process. Either it's been deleted, or it was never created. Alternatively, you specified a nanosecond value greater than or equal to 1,000,000,000, or less than 0.

Notes

There does not seem to be an airtight definition of what it means for a signal to be delivered to a process. Obviously, when a process handles a signal via a signal handler, the signal has been handled. It would seem to me that whenever a signal that was queued to the process is dequeued, that signal is delivered. Thus, if a process retrieves a signal by calling *sigwaitinfo* or *sigtimedwait*, that should be considered signal delivery as well. You can check this out when you determine the degree of POSIX.4 conformance in your operating system.

The minimum value allowed for DELAYTIMER_MAX is 32, which is so small as to be practically useless. An operating system should support a large value of DELAYTIMER_MAX. For instance, if the overflow count is maintained in a signed 32-bit integer, a DELAYTIMER_MAX of $2^{32} - 1$ would be reasonable.

Timers created in a process are not valid in any children created by that process calling *fork*.

Current UNIX Practice

Standard UNIX does not support queued signals. This function has no analog in standard UNIX.

See Also

timer_create
timer_settime
sigwaitinfo

timer_gettime

Name

timer_gettime — Time remaining on a POSIX.4 timer before expiration.

Synopsis

```
#include        <time.h>
int             timer_gettime(timer_t timer_id,
                    struct itimerspec *current);
```

Conditionality

```
#ifdef _POSIX_TIMERS
```

Description

timer_gettime fills in current with the current setting of the interval timer indicated by *timer_id*. The timer is set by *timer_settime*. The setting returned will contain the amount of time remaining until the timer expires next, and the interval between successive timer expirations.

If the *it_value* field of current is zero, then the timer is disabled. If the interval, *it_interval*, is zero, then the timer is set to go off only once.

timer_gettime returns a time interval relative to the current time, even if you set the interval timer to go off at an absolute time.

Return Values

timer_gettime returns 0 if it successfully retrieves the setting for the indicated timer. Otherwise, it returns –1 and sets *errno* to indicate the error.

Errors

If *timer_gettime* fails, it returns –1 and sets *errno* to the following:

EINVAL   The timer ID specified is not valid for this process. Either it's been deleted, or it was never created.

Notes

When you set a timer, the system rounds up your intervals to the resolution of the clock. The value the system maintains for your interval timer will be this rounded value. Therefore, if you set a timer and then immediately retrieve the setting of it, the set value may be greater than the value you passed in.

For the CLOCK_REALTIME clock, the operating system must support a resolution no greater than 20,000,000 nanoseconds, or 50 times a second (50 Hz). Finer resolutions are generally expected.

Timers created in a process are not valid in any children created by that process calling *fork*.

Current UNIX Practice

Standard UNIX uses *setitimer* and *getitimer*, which are quite similar to *timer_settime* and *timer_gettime*. However, *getitimer* only supports microsecond resolution.

Both BSD and SVR4 support *setitimer/getitimer*.

See Also

timer_create
timer_settime

timer_settime

Name

timer_settime — Set expiration time/interval for a POSIX.4 timer.

Synopsis

```
#include     <time.h>
int          timer_settime(timer_t timer_id,
                     int flags,
                     const struct itimerspec *new_setting,
                     struct itimerspec *old_setting);
```

Conditionality

```
#ifdef _POSIX_TIMERS
```

Description

timer_settime is used to set up a POSIX.4 interval timer to expire either periodically or once only. *timer_settime* is also used to turn off a timer that is currently set. The timer, identified by *timer_id*, must have been previously created by *timer_create*. Note especially that timer IDs are not inherited when a process calls *fork*!

To set a timer, set *new_setting->it_value* with the time interval after which the timer should expire the first time. Set *new_setting->it_interval* with the interval at which subsequent timer expirations should occur. When the timer expires, a signal is delivered. The signal delivery is defined by the call to *timer_create* that initialized *timer_id*. When you call *timer_settime* for a particular timer, you replace the previous setting for that timer with the new setting. The previous setting for the timer is returned in *old_setting*, so it can be restored when you are done using the interval timer.

If you set *new_setting->it_interval* to 0 seconds and 0 nanoseconds, then the timer will expire only once, at the time indicated by *new_setting->it_value*. If *new_setting->it_value* is 0, then the timer is disarmed, and will not expire at all. The nanoseconds part of a time value must be less than 1,000,000,000 and non-negative; the nanoseconds are meant to be a fraction of a second.

If the *flags* parameter is 0, then the *new_setting->it_value* field is taken to be a time relative to the current time. Thus, if you want to sleep for a second, set *new_setting->it_value* to 1 and *flags* to 0. If, on the other hand, *flags* has TIMER_ABSTIME set, then *new_setting->it_value* is interpreted as an absolute time. So, if you wanted to sleep until 9:01 and 3 seconds, September 5, 1997, you would set *new_setting->it_value* to that number of seconds (using *mktime*), and set *flags* to TIMER_ABSTIME.

old_setting, if it is not NULL, will be filled in with the previous setting of the timer. *old_setting->it_value* will contain the relative time until the timer would have expired; *it_interval* contains the previous interval setting. The value in *old_setting* is the same thing that would have been returned if you'd called *timer_gettime* instead of *timer_settime*.

If *old_setting* is NULL, then the old interval timer setting is simply discarded.

Timer expiration signals are not queued to the process. Rather, the system maintains a count of the number of times the timer has expired since the last time the expiration signal was delivered. The timer overrun count can be obtained by calling *timer_getoverrun*.

Return Values

timer_settime returns 0 if it successfully sets the timer. Otherwise, it returns –1 and sets *errno* to indicate the error.

Errors

If *timer_settime* fails, it returns –1 and sets *errno* to the following:

EINVAL   The timer ID specified is not valid for this process. Either it's been deleted, or it was never created. Alternatively, you specified a nanosecond value greater than or equal to 1,000,000,000, or less than 0.

Notes

Few, if any, systems actually support nanosecond resolutions for their interval timers. Therefore, values you specify for nanoseconds may need to be rounded to a number of nanoseconds that the operating system supports. The operating system will do this for you, and will round the numbers up in all cases, so you do not have to worry about premature timer expiration. The values returned in *old_setting* will probably be rounded appropriately already.

For the CLOCK_REALTIME clock, the operating system must support a resolution no greater than 20,000,000 nanoseconds, or 50 times a second (50 Hz). Finer resolutions are generally expected.

If you are writing a piece of code that uses a pre-existing interval timer, and which may be used in various pieces of software, you should make use of the *old_setting* parameter to save the previous setting of the timer and restore it when you are done.

Timers created in a process are not valid in any children created by that process calling *fork*.

Current UNIX Practice

Standard UNIX uses *setitimer* and *getitimer*, which are quite similar to *timer_settime* and *timer_gettime*. However, *setitimer* does not support absolute timers, and it only supports microsecond resolution.

Both BSD and SVR4 support *setitimer/getitimer*.

See Also

timer_create
timer_gettime
timer_getoverrun

Name

wait, waitpid — Retrieve status of terminated process and clean up corpse.

Synopsis

```
#include        <sys/types.h>
#include        <sys/wait.h>
pid_t           wait(int *status);
pid_t           waitpid(pid_t who, int *status, int options);

WIFEXITED(int status)
WEXITSTATUS(int status)
WIFSIGNALED(int status)
WTERMSIG(int status)
WIFSTOPPED(int status)
WSTOPSIG(int status)
```

Conditionality

Unconditional. However, WIFSTOPPED and WSTOPSIG are only useful if
_POSIX_JOB_CONTROL is supported.

Description

The *wait* functions wait for a child process to terminate or, in some cases, become
stopped. The *wait* function will wait for any child process to terminate; *waitpid* can be
made to wait only for particular processes, and its behavior can be modified by several
values for *options*.

The *waitpid* function can be used to wait for processes that become stopped, if POSIX
Job Control (_POSIX_JOB_CONTROL) is supported. This use of *waitpid* is discussed in a
separate section below.

When either *wait* or *waitpid* find a deceased process, they return the *exit* status for
that process in the location referenced by *status*. The interpretation of this status information is described below.

wait simply blocks until one child process terminates. It then returns the process ID of
the terminated process and sets its *exit* status in *status*.

waitpid is more complex. First, its blocking behavior can be modified by setting WNO-
HANG in *options*. If WNOHANG is set, then a call to *waitpid* will not wait; it will only
return status for a child that is already terminated when *waitpid* is called, or it will
return 0 instead of a process ID.

The *who* argument to *waitpid* further complicates it. The *who* argument specifies what
process to wait for, as shown in the following table.

wait, waitpid (continued)

who Value	Effect
−1	Wait for any child process, like *wait*
> 0	Wait only for the child process whose ID is *who*
== 0	Wait for any child process with a process group ID Equal to the parent's (caller's) process ID
< −1	Wait for any child process whose group ID equals the absolute value of *who*

Cleanup of Deceased Processes

The *wait* functions serve another purpose in addition to retrieving the status of dead child processes. The *wait* functions also clean up the remaining data structure left by those children. There are two impacts of this. First, you can only call *wait* once for any particular process. Second, the remaining data structures are left around until *wait* or *waitpid* happens to come across them. Given large numbers of child processes and no calls to *wait*, it is possible for a system to "clog up" due to an abundance of corpses left lying about. I suggest you call *wait* or *waitpid* fairly promptly for your exited child processes.

Status Information

The status returned by *wait* and *waitpid* is crammed into an integer. This value will be zero if the child process exited with 0 status, either by calling *exit(0)*, *_exit(0)*, or by returning 0 from the *main* function of a compiled ANSI C executable. Note that many programs *exit* implicitly by "falling off the end of *main*." In this case, the *exit* status of the process is likely to be random, possibly zero but more likely a large, nasty number with bits set in high-order locations.

A set of macros are defined in *<sys/wait.h>* for evaluating the process status. For more information see the manual page for *<sys/wait.h>*.

Return Values

wait and *waitpid* return the ID of the process for whom status was retrieved, and return the status of the named process in the location referenced by *status*. If you call *waitpid* with WNOHANG in *options* and there is no immediately-available child process, then *waitpid* will return 0. Otherwise, these functions return −1 on error.

Errors

wait and *waitpid* both return −1 and set *errno* to one of the following values:

ECHILD   There are no more children to wait for for this process. For *waitpid*, this also is returned if the process ID or group specified does not exist or has no relevant processes in it.

EINTR   The call was interrupted by a signal's delivery to the calling process. The area pointed to by *status* may or may not have been modified.

In addition, *waitpid* sets *errno* to the following:

EINVAL   The bits specified in *options* are not valid.

Current UNIX Practice

wait is standard in all UNIX systems; POSIX.1 introduced *waitpid*. Other UNIX systems also provide a *wait3* function, which serves basically the same purpose as *waitpid* but which is far more interestingly named. There is no *wait2* that I am aware of.

See Also

fork
exec
exit

PART

III

Solutions to Problems

Exercise Code

Here, you'll find code for the exercises in this book, organized by chapter. Several of the exercises build on each other; in these, I've just presented the final code, rather than duplicating programs. You can find the code for a particular exercise, or the exercise for a particular piece of code ("what is this code supposed to be *doing*?"), by looking under "exercises" in the index.

One further note: in many of these exercises, especially those that use signals to measure times, you'll see *printf* statements. Technically, this is a no-no. *printf* is not what's known as an async-safe function—you cannot always call it safely from within a signal handler. This is because it uses global data structures, and if you were in the middle of a *printf* when a signal came in, and you then tried to *printf* from the signal handler—well, bad things might happen. This is the reasoning behind async safety or the lack thereof. In practice, you can call *printf* pretty safely, especially if your main-line code is not calling *printf*. And if you hit a machine where it doesn't work, just take the *printf*s out (although they really *should* work).

And a final disclaimer: I've gotten these examples to work under LynxOS. Portability being what it is, real-time being what it is, and system software vendors being what they are, you may need to do some tweaking to get these examples to work under other systems. (Of course, they don't even have a chance on systems that don't claim POSIX.4 conformance!)

Chapter 3: The Basics of Real-Time: Multiple Tasks

sigs_sent_noswtch.c

```c
#include     <stdio.h>
#include     <unistd.h>
#include     <sys/types.h>
#include     <signal.h>

int nsigs = 0;
pid_t chpid;

main()
{
    struct sigaction sa;
    extern void null_handler(), alarm_handler(), child_terminate();

    sigemptyset(&sa.sa_mask);
    sa.sa_flags = 0;
    sa.sa_handler = alarm_handler;   /* Terminates experiment */

    if (sigaction(SIGALRM, &sa, NULL) < 0) {
        perror("sigaction SIGALRM");
        exit(1);
    }

    sa.sa_handler = null_handler;        /* Counts signals */
    if (sigaction(SIGUSR1, &sa, NULL) < 0) {
        perror("sigaction SIGALRM");
        exit(1);
    }

    sa.sa_handler = child_terminate;     /* Terminates child */
    sigfillset(&sa.sa_mask);/* Take no signals after experiment done */
    if (sigaction(SIGUSR2, &sa, NULL) < 0) {
        perror("sigaction SIGALRM");
        exit(1);
    }


    switch (chpid = fork()) {
        case -1:    /* error */
                perror("fork");
                exit(2);
                break;
        case 0:     /* child */
                be_a_child();
                exit(0);
                break;
        default:    /* parent */
                be_the_parent();
                exit(0);
                break;
    }
```

```
        fprintf(stderr, "Unexpected exit from test program!\n");
        exit(3);
}


be_a_child()
{
    sigset_t sigset;
    sigemptyset(&sigset);
    while (1) {
        sigsuspend(&sigset);
    }
}


be_the_parent()
{
    alarm(60);
    while(1) {
        if (kill(chpid, SIGUSR1) < 0) {
            perror("kill");
            return;
        }
        nsigs++;
    }
}


void
null_handler()
{
    nsigs++;
}


void
child_terminate()
{
    printf("%d signals received by child (%d/sec)\n", nsigs, nsigs/60);
    exit(0);
}


void
alarm_handler()
{
    printf("%d signals sent by parent (%d/sec)\n", nsigs, nsigs/60);
    kill(chpid, SIGUSR2);
    exit(0);
}
```

sigs_sent_swtch.c

```
#include    <unistd.h>
#include    <stdio.h>
#include    <sys/types.h>
#include    <signal.h>

int nsigs_sent = 0, nsigs_recv = 0;
pid_t chpid, parentpid;
```

```
main()
{
    struct sigaction sa;
    extern void null_handler(), alarm_handler(), child_terminate();
    sigset_t blockem;

    parentpid = getpid();
    sigemptyset(&blockem);
    sigaddset(&blockem, SIGUSR1);
    sigprocmask(SIG_BLOCK, &blockem, NULL);

    sigfillset(&sa.sa_mask);
    sa.sa_flags = 0;
    sa.sa_handler = alarm_handler;   /* Terminates experiment */

    if (sigaction(SIGALRM, &sa, NULL) < 0) {
        perror("sigaction SIGALRM");
        exit(1);
    }

    sa.sa_handler = null_handler;        /* Counts signals */
    if (sigaction(SIGUSR1, &sa, NULL) < 0) {
        perror("sigaction SIGUSR1");
        exit(1);
    }

    sa.sa_handler = child_terminate;     /* Terminates child */
    sigfillset(&sa.sa_mask);/* Take no signals after experiment done */
    if (sigaction(SIGUSR2, &sa, NULL) < 0) {
        perror("sigaction SIGUSR2");
        exit(1);
    }


    switch (chpid = fork()) {
        case -1:    /* error */
                perror("fork");
                exit(2);
                break;
        case 0:     /* child */
                be_a_child();
                exit(0);
                break;
        default:    /* parent */
                be_the_parent();
                exit(0);
                break;
    }

    fprintf(stderr, "Unexpected exit from test program!\n");
    exit(3);
}

be_a_child()
{
```

```
    sigset_t sigset;
    sigemptyset(&sigset);
    while (1) {
        sigsuspend(&sigset);
        if (kill(parentpid, SIGUSR1) < 0) {
            perror("kill");
            return;
        }
        nsigs_sent++;
    }
}

be_the_parent()
{
    sigset_t sigset;

    sigemptyset(&sigset);
    alarm(60);
    while(1) {
        if (kill(chpid, SIGUSR1) < 0) {
            perror("kill");
            return;
        }
        nsigs_sent++;
        sigsuspend(&sigset);
    }
}

void
null_handler()
{
    nsigs_recv++;
}

void
child_terminate()
{
    printf("%d/%d signals sent/received by child (%d sent/sec)\n",
        nsigs_sent, nsigs_recv, nsigs_sent / 60);
    exit(0);
}

void
alarm_handler()
{
    printf("%d/%d signals sent/received by parent (%d sent/sec)\n",
        nsigs_sent, nsigs_recv, nsigs_sent / 60);
    kill(chpid, SIGUSR2);
    exit(0);
}
```

sigs_sent_swtch.p4.c

```
#define      _POSIX_C_SOURCE 199309

#include     <unistd.h>
#include     <stdio.h>
#include     <unistd.h>
#include     <sys/types.h>
#include     <signal.h>

int nsigs_sent = 0, nsigs_recv = 0;
pid_t chpid, parentpid;

/* Send signals between processes using POSIX.4 real-time queued signals */

main()
{
    struct sigaction sa;
    extern void alarm_handler(), child_terminate();
    extern void handler(int, siginfo_t *, void *);
    sigset_t blockem;

    parentpid = getpid();
    sigemptyset(&blockem);
    sigaddset(&blockem, SIGRTMIN);
    sigprocmask(SIG_BLOCK, &blockem, NULL);

    sigfillset(&sa.sa_mask);
    sa.sa_flags = 0;
    sa.sa_handler = alarm_handler;   /* Terminates experiment */

    if (sigaction(SIGALRM, &sa, NULL) < 0) {
        perror("sigaction SIGALRM");
        exit(1);
    }

    sa.sa_handler = child_terminate;    /* Terminates child */
    if (sigaction(SIGUSR2, &sa, NULL) < 0) {
        perror("sigaction SIGUSR2");
        exit(1);
    }

    sigemptyset(&sa.sa_mask);    /* No particular signal blockage */
    sa.sa_flags = SA_SIGINFO;
    sa.sa_sigaction = handler;        /* Counts signals */
    if (sigaction(SIGRTMIN, &sa, NULL) < 0) {
        perror("sigaction SIGRTMIN");
        exit(1);
    }

    switch (chpid = fork()) {
        case -1:     /* error */
                perror("fork");
                exit(2);
```

```
                break;
        case 0:      /* child */
                be_a_child();
                exit(0);
                break;
        default:     /* parent */
                be_the_parent();
                exit(0);
                break;
    }

    fprintf(stderr, "Unexpected exit from test program!\n");
    exit(3);
}

be_a_child()
{
    sigset_t sigset;
    union sigval val;

    sigemptyset(&sigset);
    val.sival_int = 0;
    while (1) {
        sigsuspend(&sigset);
        if (sigqueue(parentpid, SIGRTMIN, val) < 0) {
            perror("sigqueue");
            return;
        }
        nsigs_sent++;
        val.sival_int++;    /* Send different extra information */
    }
}

be_the_parent()
{
    sigset_t sigset;
    union sigval val;

    sigemptyset(&sigset);
    alarm(60);
    val.sival_int = 0;
    while(1) {
        if (sigqueue(chpid, SIGRTMIN, val) < 0) {
            perror("sigqueue");
            return;
        }
        nsigs_sent++;
        sigsuspend(&sigset);
        val.sival_int++;    /* Send different information */
    }
}

/*
 * The handler here does the same as does the handler for a plain old signal.
 * Remember, though, that the handler is _receiving_ extra information in
```

```
 * the info parameter.  In this test, that information is discarded.
 * However, in most applications the data will probably be used.
 */
void
handler(int signo, siginfo_t *info, void *extra)
{
    nsigs_recv++;
}

void
child_terminate(int signo)
{
    printf("%d/%d signals sent/received by child (%d sent/sec)\n",
        nsigs_sent, nsigs_recv, nsigs_sent / 60);
    exit(0);
}

void
alarm_handler(int signo)
{
    printf("%d/%d signals sent/received by parent (%d sent/sec)\n",
        nsigs_sent, nsigs_recv, nsigs_sent / 60);
    kill(chpid, SIGUSR2);
    exit(0);
}
```

Chapter 4: Better Coordination: Messages, Shared Memory, and Synchronization

fifo.c

```
#define     _POSIX_C_SOURCE     199309
#include    <unistd.h>
#include    <stdio.h>
#include    <sys/types.h>
#include    <signal.h>

int nreads = 0, nwrites = 0;
pid_t chpid, parentpid;

char *progname;
char *whoami;

#define DEFAULT_NBYTES 4
int nbytes = DEFAULT_NBYTES;

char *buf;

void
usage()
{
    printf("Usage: %s {nbytes} (default nbytes is %d)\n",
        progname, DEFAULT_NBYTES);
```

```
        exit(1);
    }

/* Descriptive array indices for pipes */
#define WRITE_END    1
#define READ_END     0

main(int argc, char **argv)
{
    struct sigaction sa;
    extern void alarm_handler(int);
    int pe1[2], pe2[2]; /* Pipeage */

    progname = argv[0];

    if (argc == 2) {
        nbytes = atoi(argv[1]);
    } else if (argc > 2) {
        usage();
    }

    printf("Testing IPC through pipes using %d-byte reads/writes\n",
        nbytes);

    if ((buf = (char *)malloc(nbytes)) == NULL) {
        perror("malloc");
        exit(1);
    }

    /* Set up signals used for terminating the experiment */
    sigfillset(&sa.sa_mask);
    sa.sa_flags = 0;
    sa.sa_handler = alarm_handler;  /* Terminates experiment */
    if (sigaction(SIGALRM, &sa, NULL) < 0) {
        perror("sigaction SIGALRM");
        exit(1);
    }

    /* Create some pipes */
    if (pipe(pe1) < 0) {
        perror("pipe");
        exit(1);
    }
    if (pipe(pe2) < 0) {
        perror("pipe");
        exit(1);
    }

    /* Duplicate the process */
    switch (chpid = fork()) {
        case -1:    /* error */
                perror("fork");
                exit(2);
                break;
        case 0:     /* child */
```

```
                        whoami = "child";
                        be_a_child(pe1[WRITE_END], pe2[READ_END]);
                        exit(0);
                        break;
            default:    /* parent */
                        whoami = "parent";
                        be_the_parent(pe2[WRITE_END], pe1[READ_END]);
                        exit(0);
                        break;
        }

    fprintf(stderr, "Unexpected exit from test program!\n");
    exit(3);
}


be_a_child(int write_this, int read_this)
{
    int ret;

    while (1) {
        if ((ret=read(read_this, buf, nbytes)) != nbytes) {
        printf("Returned %d bytes trying to read %d\n", ret, nbytes);
            perror("child read from pipe");
            exit(1);
        }
        nreads++;
        if (write(write_this, buf, nbytes) != nbytes) {
            perror("child write to pipe");
            exit(1);
        }
        nwrites++;
    }
}


be_the_parent(int write_this, int read_this)
{
    alarm(60);
    while (1) {
        if (write(write_this, buf, nbytes) != nbytes) {
            perror("parent write to pipe");
            exit(1);
        }
        nwrites++;
        if (read(read_this, buf, nbytes) != nbytes) {
            perror("parent read from pipe");
            exit(1);
        }
        nreads++;
    }
}


void alarm_handler(int signo)
{
    printf("%d/%d reads/writes (%d bytes each) by %s (%d bytes sent/sec)\n",
        nreads, nwrites, nbytes, whoami, (nwrites * nbytes) / 60);
```

```
        if (getpid() != chpid)   /* Parent--kill child too */
            kill(chpid, SIGALRM);
        exit(0);


}
```

msg.c

```
#define       _POSIX_C_SOURCE      199309
#include      <unistd.h>
#include      <stdio.h>
#include      <sys/types.h>
#include      <signal.h>
#include      <mqueue.h>

int nreads = 0, nwrites = 0;
pid_t chpid, parentpid;

char *progname;
char *whoami;

#define DEFAULT_NBYTES 4
int nbytes = DEFAULT_NBYTES;

#define MQ_ONE  "/mq_one"
#define MQ_TWO  "/mq_two"

char *buf;

void
usage()
{
    printf("Usage: %s {nbytes} (default nbytes is %d)\n",
        progname, DEFAULT_NBYTES);
    exit(1);
}

main(int argc, char **argv)
{
    struct sigaction sa;
    extern void alarm_handler(int);
    mqd_t m1, m2;
    struct mq_attr ma;

    progname = argv[0];

    if (argc == 2) {
        nbytes = atoi(argv[1]);
    } else if (argc > 2) {
        usage();
    }

    printf("Testing IPC through POSIX.4 mqs using %d-byte sends/recvs\n",
        nbytes);
```

```
        if ((buf = (char *)malloc(nbytes)) == NULL) {
            perror("malloc");
            exit(1);
        }


        /* Set up signals used for terminating the experiment */
        sigfillset(&sa.sa_mask);
        sa.sa_flags = 0;
        sa.sa_handler = alarm_handler;  /* Terminates experiment */
        if (sigaction(SIGALRM, &sa, NULL) < 0) {
            perror("sigaction SIGALRM");
            exit(1);
        }


        /* Create some message queues */
        ma.mq_flags = 0;     /* No special behavior */
        ma.mq_maxmsg = 1;
        ma.mq_msgsize = nbytes;
        i = mq_unlink(MQ_ONE); /* Deal with possible leftovers */
        if ((i < 0) && (errno != ENOENT)) {
            perror("mq_unlink");
            exit(1);
        }
        i = mq_unlink(MQ_TWO);  /* Deal with possible leftovers */
        if ((i < 0) && (errno != ENOENT)) {
            perror("mq_unlink");
            exit(1);
        }
        if ((m1 = mq_open(MQ_ONE, O_CREAT|O_EXCL, MODE, &ma)) < 0) {
            perror("mq_open");
            exit(1);
        }
        if (pipe(pe2) < 0) {
            perror("pipe");
            exit(1);
        }


        /* Duplicate the process */
        switch (chpid = fork()) {
            case -1:   /* error */
                    perror("fork");
                    exit(2);
                    break;
            case 0:    /* child */
                    whoami = "child";
                    be_a_child(pe1[WRITE_END], pe2[READ_END]);
                    exit(0);
                    break;
            default:    /* parent */
                    whoami = "parent";
                    be_the_parent(pe2[WRITE_END], pe1[READ_END]);
                    exit(0);
                    break;
        }
```

```
        fprintf(stderr, "Unexpected exit from test program!\n");
        exit(3);
}


be_a_child(int write_this, int read_this)
{
        int ret;

        while (1) {
            if ((ret=read(read_this, buf, nbytes)) != nbytes) {
            printf("Returned %d bytes trying to read %d\n", ret, nbytes);
                perror("child read from pipe");
                exit(1);
            }
            nreads++;
            if (write(write_this, buf, nbytes) != nbytes) {
                perror("child write to pipe");
                exit(1);
            }
            nwrites++;
        }
}


be_the_parent(int write_this, int read_this)
{
        alarm(60);
        while (1) {
            if (write(write_this, buf, nbytes) != nbytes) {
                perror("parent write to pipe");
                exit(1);
            }
            nwrites++;
            if (read(read_this, buf, nbytes) != nbytes) {
                perror("parent read from pipe");
                exit(1);
            }
            nreads++;
        }
}


void alarm_handler(int signo)
{
        printf("%d/%d reads/writes (%d bytes each) by %s (%d bytes sent/sec)\n",
            nreads, nwrites, nbytes, whoami, (nwrites * nbytes) / 60);
        if (getpid() != chpid)  /* Parent--kill child too */
            kill(chpid, SIGALRM);
        exit(0);

}
```

shm.c

```
/* This program, called as "shm_1", creates a shared memory area which
is shared with a process created via fork.  The second
process also does an exec. */

/*
 * Compile with SHM_1 defined to get shm_1 executable.
 * Compile with SHM_2 defined to get shm_2 executable.
 */

#define    POSIX_C_SOURCE 199309L

#include    <unistd.h>  /* POSIX et al */
#include    <limits.h>  /* PAGESIZE */
#include    <sys/mman.h>    /* shm_open, mmap */
#include    <sys/types.h>   /* waitpid */
#include    <sys/wait.h>    /* waitpid */
#include    <signal.h>  /* sigaction */

#define PARENT_SHM_DATA "Parent Wrote This"
#define CHILD_PRE_EXEC_DATA "Child Wrote This Before Exec-ing"
#define CHILD_POST_EXEC_DATA    "Child Wrote This AFTER Exec-ing"

#ifdef SHM_1
#define SHMNAME     "/my_shm"
#define NEW_IMAGE   "shm_2"

void cleanup(int called_via_signal)
{
    (void)shm_unlink(SHMNAME);
    if (called_via_signal)
        exit(3);
}

main()
{
    int d;
    char *addr;
    int chpid;
    int w;
    struct sigaction sa;

    /*
     * In case of premature termination, we want to make sure to
     * clean up the shared memory region.  Hence, the signal handlers.
     */
    sa.sa_handler = cleanup;
    sa.sa_flags = 0;
    sigemptyset(&sa.sa_mask);
    (void)sigaction(SIGINT, &sa, NULL);
    (void)sigaction(SIGBUS, &sa, NULL);
    (void)sigaction(SIGSEGV, &sa, NULL);

    /* Create shared memory region */
```

```
    d = shm_open(SHMNAME, O_RDWR|O_CREAT|O_TRUNC, S_IRWXU);
    ftruncate(d, (off_t)PAGESIZE);  /* Make region PAGESIZE big */
    addr = (char *)mmap(NULL, (size_t)PAGESIZE, PORT_READ|PROT_WRITE,
        MAP_SHARED, d, 0);

    /* Put data in the shared memory region */
    printf("Parent stores in SHM: \"%s\"\n", PARENT_SHM_DATA);
    sprintf(addr, PARENT_SHM_DATA);

    /* Create a child process */
    switch (chpid = fork()) {
        case -1:    perror("fork");
                cleanup(0);
                exit(1);
        case 0:     /* child */
                break;
        default:    /* parent; await child */
                chpid = wait(&w, 0);
                /* Child is done:  see what's in SHM */
                printf("Parent sees in SHM: \"%s\"\n",
                    (char *)addr);
                cleanup(0);
                exit(0);
    }

    /* Code executed by child */
    printf("Child, pre-exec, sees in SHM: \"%s\"\n", addr);
    printf("Child, pre-exec, stores in SHM: \"%s\"\n", CHILD_PRE_EXEC_DATA);
    sprintf(addr, CHILD_PRE_EXEC_DATA);

    /* Exec a new process image */
    execlp(NEW_IMAGE, NEW_IMAGE, SHM_NAME, NULL);
    perror("returned from execlp");
    exit(2);
}
#endif /* SHM_1 */
#ifdef SHM_2
main(int argc, char **argv)
{
    int d;
    char *addr;

    /* Single argument is the name of the shared memory region to map in */
    d = shm_open(SHMNAME, O_RDWR);
    addr = (char *)mmap(NULL, (size_t)PAGESIZE, PORT_READ|PROT_WRITE,
        MAP_SHARED, d, 0);

    printf("Child, after exec, sees: \"%s\"\n", addr);
    printf("Child, post-exec, stores in SHM: \"%s\"\n",
        CHILD_POST_EXEC_DATA);
    sprintf(addr, CHILD_POST_EXEC_DATA);

    exit(0);
}
#endif /* SHM_2 */
```

shmmutex_flock.c

```
/*
 * This program benchmarks the bandwidth of shared memory when we use
 * standard POSIX file locks as a means of mutual exclusion.
 * Notice that this test doesn't do any actual synchronization;  there's
 * only one process.  We're benchmarking the case of mutual exclusion.
 * In this case, the majority of accesses are uncontested.
 *
 * Alternatively, you could fork a child and run two processes at once,
 * benchmarking total throughput.  This would not work well under a real-
 * time scheduler on a uniprocessor, though.
 *
 * Compare this code to code using semaphores.
 */

#define     POSIX_C_SOURCE 199309L

#include    <unistd.h>  /* POSIX et al */
#include    <limits.h>  /* PAGESIZE */
#include    <sys/types.h>   /* fcntl */
#include    <sys/mman.h>    /* shm_open, mmap */
#include    <signal.h>  /* sigaction */

#define SHMNAME     "/my_shm"
#define TIME_PERIOD 60      /* Run test for a minute */

int iterations = 0;
int nbytes;     /* Test, passing 4 bytes of information */

void timer_expired(int called_via_signal)
{
    printf("%d iterations for region of %d bytes\n", iterations, nbytes);
    exit(0);
}

main(int argc, char **argv)
{
    int d;
    char *addr;
    struct sigaction sa;
    struct flock fl;

    if (argc == 2)
        nbytes = atoi(argv[1]); /* Use #bytes passed */
    else
        nbytes = 4; /* Default of 4 bytes (a word on real machines :) */

    sa.sa_handler = timer_expired;
    sa.sa_flags = 0;
    sigemptyset(&sa.sa_sigmask);
    (void)sigaction(SIGALRM, &sa, NULL);

    /* Create shared memory region */
    d = shm_open(SHMNAME, O_RDWR|O_CREAT|O_TRUNC, S_IRWXU);
```

```
    ftruncate(d, (off_t)PAGESIZE);   /* Make region PAGESIZE big */
    addr = (char *)mmap(NULL, (size_t)PAGESIZE, PORT_READ|PROT_WRITE,
        MAP_SHARED, d, 0);
    shm_unlink(SHMNAME);     /* So it goes away on exit */

    lockfile = open("lockfile", O_RDWR|O_CREAT|O_TRUNC, S_IRWXU);
    write(lockfile, "A Couple Of Bytes", strlen("A Couple Of Bytes"));
    unlink("lockfile"); /* So it goes away on exit */

    /*
     * Begin test. Repeatedly acquire mutual exclusion, write to area,
     * and release mutual exclusion.
     */
    lockit.l_type = F_WRLCK;
    lockit.l_whence = SEEK_SET;
    lockit.l_start = 0;
    lockit.l_len = 1;

    unlockit = lockit;
    unlockit.l_type = F_UNLCK;

    alarm(TIME_PERIOD);
    while (1) {
        /* acquire parent's lock */
        if (fcntl(lockfile, F_SETLKW, &lockit) < 0) {
            perror("fcntl(F_SETLKW wrlock)");
            exit(1);
        }
        /* store data in shared memory area */
        for (i=0; i<nbytes; i++)
            addr[i] = 'A';
        /* release parent's lock */
        if (fcntl(lockfile, F_SETLKW, &unlockit) < 0) {
            perror("fcntl(F_SETLKW unlock)");
            exit(1);
        }
        iterations++;
    }

}
```

shmmutex_sem.c

```
/*
 * This program benchmarks the bandwidth of shared memory when we use
 * POSIX.4 semaphores as the mutual exclusion mechanism.
 * In this example, I'm using a named semaphore.
 *
 * Like before, this test doesn't do any actual synchronization;  there's
 * only one process.  We're benchmarking the case of mutual exclusion.
 * In this case, the majority of accesses are uncontested.
 *
 * Alternatively, you could fork a child and run two processes at once,
 * benchmarking total throughput.  This would not work well under a real-
 * time scheduler on a uniprocessor, though.
```

```
       *
       * Compare this code to code using file locking.
       */

      #define     POSIX_C_SOURCE 199309L

      #include    <unistd.h>  /* POSIX et al */
      #include    <limits.h>  /* PAGESIZE */
      #include    <semaphore.h>   /* sem_* */
      #include    <sys/mman.h>    /* shm_open, mmap */
      #include    <signal.h>  /* sigaction */

      #define SHMNAME      "/my_shm"
      #define SEMNAME      "/my_sem"
      #define TIME_PERIOD 60       /* Run test for a minute */

      int iterations = 0;
      int nbytes = 4;     /* Test, passing 4 bytes of information */

      void timer_expired(int called_via_signal)
      {
          printf("%d iterations for region of %d bytes\n", iterations, nbytes);
          exit(0);
      }

      main(int argc, char **argv)
      {
          int d;
          char *addr;
          struct sigaction sa;
          sem_t *s;

          if (argc == 2)
              nbytes = atoi(argv[1]); /* Use #bytes passed */

          sa.sa_handler = timer_expired;
          sa.sa_flags = 0;
          sigemptyset(&sa.sa_sigmask);
          (void)sigaction(SIGALRM, &sa, NULL);

          /* Create shared memory region */
          d = shm_open(SHMNAME, O_RDWR|O_CREAT|O_TRUNC, S_IRWXU);
          ftruncate(d, (off_t)PAGESIZE);  /* Make region PAGESIZE big */
          addr = (char *)mmap(NULL, (size_t)PAGESIZE, PORT_READ|PROT_WRITE,
              MAP_SHARED, d, 0);
          shm_unlink(SHMNAME);    /* So it goes away on exit */

          /* create semaphore */
          s = sem_open(SEMNAME, O_CREAT, S_IRWXU, 1); /* value 1==>unlocked */
          sem_unlink(SEMNAME);    /* So it goes away on exit */

          /*
           * Begin test. Repeatedly acquire mutual exclusion, write to area,
           * and release mutual exclusion.
           */
```

```
        alarm(TIME_PERIOD);
        while (1) {
            /* acquire parent's lock */
            sem_wait(s);
            /* store data in shared memory area */
            for (i=0; i<nbytes; i++)
                addr[i] = 'A';
            /* release parent's lock */
            sem_post(s);
            iterations++;
        }
        /* Semaphore is automatically closed on exit, as is shm */
}
```

shmmutex_semembed.c

```
/*
 * This program benchmarks the bandwidth of shared memory when we use
 * POSIX.4 semaphores as the mutual exclusion mechanism.
 * In this example, I'm using an unnamed semaphore embedded
 * in the shared memory area.
 *
 * Like before, this test doesn't do any actual synchronization; there's
 * only one process. We're benchmarking the case of mutual exclusion.
 * In this case, the majority of accesses are uncontested.
 *
 * Alternatively, you could fork a child and run two processes at once,
 * benchmarking total throughput. This would not work well under a real-
 * time scheduler on a uniprocessor, though.
 *
 * Compare this code to code using file locking.
 */

#define     POSIX_C_SOURCE 199309L

#include    <unistd.h>  /* POSIX et al */
#include    <limits.h>  /* PAGESIZE */
#include    <semaphore.h>   /* sem_* */
#include    <sys/mman.h>    /* shm_open, mmap */
#include    <signal.h>  /* sigaction */

#define SHMNAME     "/my_shm"
#define SEMNAME     "/my_sem"
#define TIME_PERIOD 60      /* Run test for a minute */

int iterations = 0;
int nbytes = 4;     /* Test, passing 4 bytes of information */

void timer_expired(int called_via_signal)
{
    printf("%d iterations for region of %d bytes\n", iterations, nbytes);
    exit(0);
}

main(int argc, char **argv)
```

```
{
    int d;
    char *addr;
    /* This structure is overlaid on the shared memory */
    struct fu {
        sem_t s;
        char beginning_of_data[1];
    } *p;
    struct sigaction sa;

    if (argc == 2)
        nbytes = atoi(argv[1]); /* Use #bytes passed */

    sa.sa_handler = timer_expired;
    sa.sa_flags = 0;
    sigemptyset(&sa.sa_sigmask);
    (void)sigaction(SIGALRM, &sa, NULL);

    /* Create shared memory region */
    d = shm_open(SHMNAME, O_RDWR|O_CREAT|O_TRUNC, S_IRWXU);
    ftruncate(d, (off_t)PAGESIZE);  /* Make region PAGESIZE big */
    addr = (char *)mmap(NULL, (size_t)PAGESIZE, PORT_READ|PROT_WRITE,
        MAP_SHARED, d, 0);
    shm_unlink(SHMNAME);    /* So it goes away on exit */
    p = (struct fu *)addr;

    /* create semaphore */
    sem_init(&p->s, 1, 1);  /* pshared == 1, value 1==>unlocked */

    /*
     * Begin test. Repeatedly acquire mutual exclusion, write to area,
     * and release mutual exclusion.
     */
    alarm(TIME_PERIOD);
    addr = p->beginning_of_data;
    while (1) {
        /* acquire parent's lock */
        sem_wait(&p->s);
        /* store data in shared memory area */
        for (i=0; i<nbytes; i++)
            addr[i] = 'A';
        /* release parent's lock */
        sem_post(&p->s);
        iterations++;
    }

    /* Semaphore is automatically destroyed when shm is closed on exit */
}
```

mksem.c

```
/*
 * This program makes a named semaphore, and leaves it lying around
 * when it exits.
 */
#define     POSIX_C_SOURCE 199309L

#include    <unistd.h>   /* POSIX et al */
#include    <semaphore.h>   /* sem_* */

main(int argc, char **argv)
{
    sem_t *s;

    if (argc != 2) {
        fprintf(stderr, "Usage: %s semaphore-name\n", argv[0]);
        exit(1);
    }

    /* create semaphore */
    s = sem_open(argv[1], O_CREAT, S_IRWXU, 1); /* value 1==>unlocked */
    if (s == (sem_t *)-1) {
        perror(argv[1]);
        exit(2);
    }

    exit(0);
}
```

rmsem.c

```
/*
 * This program removes a named semaphore.
 */
#define     POSIX_C_SOURCE 199309L

#include    <unistd.h>   /* POSIX et al */
#include    <semaphore.h>   /* sem_* */

main(int argc, char **argv)
{
    if (argc != 2) {
        fprintf(stderr, "Usage: %s semaphore-name\n", argv[0]);
        exit(1);
    }

    /* remove semaphore */
    if (sem_unlink(argv[1]) < 0) {
        perror(argv[1]);
        exit(2);
    }

    exit(0);
}
```

Chapter 5: On Time: Scheduling, Time, and Memory Locking

cpubound.c

```
/* This program is compute-bound.  Durr! */

main()
{
    alarm(30);
    while (1)
        ;

}
```

iobound.c

```
#define _POSIX_C_SOURCE     199309  /* POSIX 9/1993: .1, .4 */
#include    <unistd.h>

#include    <sys/types.h>
#include    <sys/stat.h>
#include    <fcntl.h>
#include    <stdio.h>
/*
 * This program continuously performs I/O to the device named DEV_FILE.
 * You should make this a serial line or some such;  avoid using disks
 * which may have useful data on them...
 */
#define DEV_FILE "/dev/com1"    /* First serial port on my machine */

main()
{
    int fd, ret;
    char byte;

    fd = open(DEV_FILE, O_WRONLY);
    if (fd < 0) {
        perror(DEV_FILE);
        exit(1);
    }
    alarm(30);
    while (1) {
        ret = write(fd, &byte, sizeof(byte));
        switch (ret) {
            case sizeof(byte):
                break;
            case -1:
                perror("write");
                exit(2);
                break;
            default:
                fprintf(stderr, "Write, ret %d?!?\n", ret);
```

```
                exit(3);
                break;
        }
    }
}
```

vsched.c

```c
#include    <sched.h>

/*
 * This is one implementation of the virtual scheduling interface I mentioned
 * in the scheduling chapter.  It allows you to use a range of priorities
 * based at 0, regardless of the underlying implementation's priority numbers.
 * This code is used in all three of the versions of "atprio".
 *
 * Note: this might get you in trouble if your system supports different
 * schedulers in different priority ranges.  Your virtual priority 0 for
 * SCHED_FIFO would not compete equally with your virtual priority 0 for
 * SCHED_RR, e.g., if the lowest underlying priorities were not the same.
 */
static int sched_rr_min, sched_rr_max;
static int sched_fifo_min, sched_fifo_max;

static int vsched_initialized = 0;

static void
vsched_init()
{
    sched_rr_min = sched_get_priority_min(SCHED_RR);
    sched_rr_max = sched_get_priority_max(SCHED_RR);
    sched_fifo_min = sched_get_priority_min(SCHED_FIFO);
    sched_fifo_max = sched_get_priority_max(SCHED_FIFO);
}


int
vsched_setscheduler(
    pid_t pid,                  /* Process to affect */
    int vsched_policy,              /* Policy to set */
    const struct sched_param *vsched_param)     /* Parameters to set */
{
    struct sched_param tmp;

    if (! vsched_initialized)
        vsched_init();

    tmp = *vsched_param;
    switch (vsched_policy) {
    case SCHED_FIFO:
        tmp.sched_priority += sched_fifo_min;
        break;
    case SCHED_RR:
        tmp.sched_priority += sched_rr_min;
        break;
```

```
        default:
            break;   /* Do nothing */
        }
        return (sched_setscheduler(pid, vsched_policy, &tmp));
}


int
vsched_setprio(
    pid_t pid,                      /* Process to affect */
    int vsched_prio)                    /* Priority to set */
{
    struct sched_param tmp;
    int sched_policy = sched_getscheduler(pid);

    if (! vsched_initialized)
        vsched_init();

    tmp.sched_priority = vsched_prio;
    switch (sched_policy) {
    case SCHED_FIFO:
        tmp.sched_priority += sched_fifo_min;
        break;
    case SCHED_RR:
        tmp.sched_priority += sched_rr_min;
        break;
    default:
        break;   /* Do nothing; function below will return error */
    }
    return (sched_setscheduler(pid, sched_policy, &tmp));
}


int
vsched_getprio(
    pid_t pid)       /* Process whose priority is desired */
{
    struct sched_param tmp;
    int sched_policy;

    if (! vsched_initialized)
        vsched_init();

    if ((sched_policy=sched_getscheduler(pid)) < 0) {
        return -1;
    }
    if (sched_getparam(pid, &tmp) < 0) {
        return -1;
    }
    switch (sched_policy) {
    case SCHED_FIFO:
        return tmp.sched_priority - sched_fifo_min;
    case SCHED_RR:
        return tmp.sched_priority - sched_rr_min;
    default:
```

```
            return -1;   /* Invalid virtual priority */
        }
    }
```

atprio.1.c

```
#include    <stdio.h>
#include    <sched.h>

/*
 * atprio, version 1:  implemented using POSIX.4 standard facilities
 * and virtual scheduling (based at 0, regardless of minima/maxima of
 * implementation).
 *
 * Simply sets priority to a given number, based at 0.
 */

char *progname;

usage() { fprintf(stderr, "Usage: %s <priority> <command>\n",progname); }

main(int argc, char **argv)
{
    struct sched_param cmd_sched_params;

    progname = argv[0];

    if (argc < 3) {
        usage();
        exit(1);
    } else {
        /* Set de (virtual) priority */
        cmd_sched_params.sched_priority = atoi(argv[1]);
        if (vsched_setscheduler(0, SCHED_FIFO, &cmd_sched_params) < 0) {
            perror("vsched_setscheduler");
            exit(2);
        }
        /* Run de command */
        if (execvp(argv[2], &argv[2]) < 0) {
            perror("execvp");
            exit(3);
        }
    }

}
```

atprio.2.c

```
#include    <stdio.h>
#include    <sched.h>

/*
 * atprio, version 2:  implemented using POSIX.4 standard facilities
 * and virtual scheduling (based at 0, regardless of minima/maxima of
 * implementation).
```

```
 *
 * Priority deltas, +-delta, are now supported.
 */

char *progname;

usage() { fprintf(stderr, "Usage: %s {<priority>|[+-]<prio delta>} <command>\n",progname); }

main(int argc, char **argv)
{
    struct sched_param cmd_sched_params;
    int delta, policy;

    progname = argv[0];

    if (argc < 3) {
        usage();
        exit(1);
    } else {
        policy = sched_getscheduler(0);
        if ((policy != SCHED_FIFO) && (policy != SCHED_RR)) {
            fprintf(stderr, "Cannot adjust priority under scheduler %d\n", policy);
            exit(2);
        }
        if ((*argv[1] >= '0') && (*argv[1] <= '9')) {
            /* Explicit priority assignment */
            cmd_sched_params.sched_priority = atoi(argv[1]);
        } else {
            /*
             * Priority delta from current priority.
             * Only works if this process is running
             * SCHED_FIFO or SCHED_RR
             */
            if (*argv[1] == '+') delta = atoi(&argv[1][1]);
            else if (*argv[1] == '-') delta = -atoi(&argv[1][1]);
            else {
                usage();
                exit(1);
            }
            cmd_sched_params.sched_priority =
                vsched_getprio(0) + delta;
        }
        if (vsched_setscheduler(0, policy, &cmd_sched_params) < 0) {
            perror("vsched_setscheduler");
            exit(2);
        }
        /* Run de command */
        if (execvp(argv[2], &argv[2]) < 0) {
            perror("execvp");
            exit(3);
        }
    }
}
```

atprio.3.c

```
#include    <stdio.h>
#include    <sched.h>

/*
 * atprio, version 3:  implemented using POSIX.4 standard facilities
 * and virtual scheduling (based at 0), supporting priority adjustment
 * and the ability to set/adjust the scheduling priority of the calling
 * process.
 */

char *progname;

usage() { fprintf(stderr, "Usage: %s {<priority>|[+-]<prio delta>} <command>\n",progname); }

main(int argc, char **argv)
{
    struct sched_param cmd_sched_params;
    int delta, policy;
    int pid_to_affect = 0;  /* self */
    char **exec_this;

    progname = argv[0];

    /* Figure out who to affect--us or our parent--and what to execute. */
    if (argc == 2) {
        /* atprio 3 or atprio +-7: affect caller's priority */
        pid_to_affect = getppid();  /* Parent PID */
        exec_this = NULL;
    } else if (argc >= 3) {
        /* atprio 16 ls -lR: run command at a priority */
        exec_this = &argv[2];
    }

    policy = sched_getscheduler(pid_to_affect);
    if ((policy != SCHED_FIFO) && (policy != SCHED_RR)) {
        fprintf(stderr, "Cannot adjust priority under scheduler %d\n", policy);
        exit(2);
    }
    if ((*argv[1] >= '0') && (*argv[1] <= '9')) {
        /* Explicit priority assignment */
        cmd_sched_params.sched_priority = atoi(argv[1]);
    } else {
        /*
         * Priority delta from current priority.
         * Only works if this process is running
         * SCHED_FIFO or SCHED_RR
         */
        if (*argv[1] == '+') delta = atoi(&argv[1][1]);
        else if (*argv[1] == '-') delta = -atoi(&argv[1][1]);
        else {
            usage();
            exit(1);
        }
```

```
                cmd_sched_params.sched_priority =
                    vsched_getprio(pid_to_affect) + delta;
            }
            if (vsched_setscheduler(pid_to_affect, policy, &cmd_sched_params) < 0) {
                perror("vsched_setscheduler");
                exit(2);
            }
            /* Run de command, if dere is one */
            if (exec_this != NULL) {
                if (execvp(*exec_this, exec_this) < 0) {
                    perror("execvp");
                    exit(3);
                }
            }
        }
        exit(0);
    }
```

periodic_timer.c

```
    /*
     * This program takes timer interrupts forever.
     * It uses Berkeley-style interval timers,
     * rather than POSIX.4 interval timers.
     * Therefore it doesn't need unistd.h, _POSIX_C_SOURCE, etc.
     */
    #include <signal.h>
    #include <sys/time.h>
    #include <stdio.h>

    char *getopt_flags = "t:v"; /* '-t': specify time interval in usec */
    extern char *optarg;

    #define DEFAULT_USECS 100000    /* 10 Hz */
    int verbose = 0;

    char *progname;

    void
    usage()
    {
        fprintf(stderr, "Usage: %s {-t usecs}\n", progname);
        return;
    }

    void timer_intr(int sig)
    {
        if (verbose) puts("ouch!");
        return;
    }

    main(int argc, char **argv)
    {
        int c;
        struct itimerval i;
        struct sigaction sa;
```

```
        sigset_t allsigs;

        progname = argv[0];

        i.it_interval.tv_sec = 0;
        i.it_interval.tv_usec = DEFAULT_USECS;

        while ((c=getopt(argc, argv, getopt_flags)) != -1) switch (c) {
            case 't':
                i.it_interval.tv_usec = atoi(optarg);
                i.it_interval.tv_sec = 0;
                while (i.it_interval.tv_usec > 1000000) {
                    i.it_interval.tv_usec -= 1000000;
                    i.it_interval.tv_sec++;
                }
                printf("Time interval: %d sec %d usec\n",
                    i.it_interval.tv_sec,
                    i.it_interval.tv_usec);
                break;
            case 'v':
                verbose++;
                break;
            default:
                usage();
                exit(1);
        }
        i.it_value = i.it_interval;

        sigemptyset(&sa.sa_mask);
        sa.sa_flags = 0;
        sa.sa_handler = timer_intr;

        if (sigaction(SIGALRM, &sa, NULL) < 0) {
            perror("sigaction");
            exit(2);
        }

        if (setitimer(ITIMER_REAL, &i, NULL) < 0) {
            perror("setitimer");
            exit(3);
        }

        sigemptyset(&allsigs);
        while (1) {
            sigsuspend(&allsigs);
        }
        exit(4);
}
```

periodic_timer.p4.c

```
/*
 * This program takes timer interrupts forever.
 * It uses POSIX.4 interval timers.
 */
#define _POSIX_C_SOURCE 199309
#include <unistd.h>
#include <signal.h>
#include <time.h>
#include <stdio.h>

char *getopt_flags = "t:v"; /* '-t': specify time interval in usec */
extern char *optarg;

#define DEFAULT_NSECS    100000000    /* 10 Hz */

int verbose = 0;

char *progname;

void
usage()
{
    fprintf(stderr, "Usage: %s {-t nsecs} {-v}\n", progname);
    return;
}

void timer_intr(int sig, siginfo_t *extra, void *cruft)
{
    if (verbose) {
        if (extra != NULL) {
            printf("sig %d code %d val (ptr) %x overrun %d\n",
                extra->si_signo,
                extra->si_code,
                extra->si_value.sival_ptr,
                timer_getoverrun(*(timer_t *)
                    extra->si_value.sival_ptr));
        } else {
            printf("No extra data\n");
        }
    }
    return;
}

timer_t mytimer;

main(int argc, char **argv)
{
    int c;
    struct itimerspec i;
    struct sigaction sa;
    sigset_t allsigs;
    struct sigevent timer_event;
```

```
progname = argv[0];

i.it_interval.tv_sec = 0;
i.it_interval.tv_nsec = DEFAULT_NSECS;

while ((c=getopt(argc, argv, getopt_flags)) != -1) switch (c) {
    case 't':
        i.it_interval.tv_nsec = atoi(optarg);
        i.it_interval.tv_sec = 0;
        while (i.it_interval.tv_nsec > 1000000000) {
            i.it_interval.tv_nsec -= 1000000000;
            i.it_interval.tv_sec++;
        }
        printf("Time interval: %d sec %d nsec\n",
            i.it_interval.tv_sec,
            i.it_interval.tv_nsec);
        break;
    case 'v':
        verbose++;
        break;
    default:
        usage();
        exit(1);
}
i.it_value = i.it_interval;

sigemptyset(&sa.sa_mask);
sa.sa_flags = SA_SIGINFO;    /* Real-Time signal */
sa.sa_sigaction = timer_intr;

if (sigaction(SIGRTMIN, &sa, NULL) < 0) {
    perror("sigaction");
    exit(2);
}

/* Create a timer based upon the CLOCK_REALTIME clock */

/*
 * This describes the asynchronous notification to be posted
 * upon this timer's expiration:
 * - use signals (not that there's any other alternative at present)
 * - send SIGRTMIN
 * - send extra data consisting of a pointer back to the timer ID.
 */
timer_event.sigev_notify = SIGEV_SIGNAL;
timer_event.sigev_signo = SIGRTMIN;
timer_event.sigev_value.sival_ptr = (void *)&mytimer;

if (timer_create(CLOCK_REALTIME, &timer_event, &mytimer) < 0) {
    perror("timer_create");
    exit(5);
}
if (verbose) printf("Timer id at location %x\n", &mytimer);
if (timer_settime(mytimer, 0, &i, NULL) < 0) {
    perror("setitimer");
```

```
            exit(3);
        }

    sigemptyset(&allsigs);
    while (1) {
        sigsuspend(&allsigs);
    }
    exit(4);
}
```

cpubench.c

```
#define _POSIX_C_SOURCE      199309  /* POSIX 9/1993: .1, .4 */
#include    <unistd.h>

#include    <stdio.h>
#include    <sys/types.h>
#include    <signal.h>

/*
 * Simple CPU usage benchmark.
 *
 * You are not likely to see any difference at all when running this
 * concurrently with a timer that goes off at 100, 1000, or even 5000 Hz.
 * The reason is that the majority of systems don't support such high
 * resolutions, and will quietly trim back your timer interval to the
 * maximum supported by the system, usually on the order of 100 Hz.
 * So, setting an interval timer higher than this maximum resolution
 * does not produce any further degradation of background computation--
 * because the timer just don't go no faster!
 */

#define INTERVAL_SECS 10

int niter;

main()
{
    struct sigaction sa;
    extern void alarm_handler();

    sigemptyset(&sa.sa_mask);
    sa.sa_flags = 0;
    sa.sa_handler = alarm_handler;  /* Terminates experiment */

    if (sigaction(SIGALRM, &sa, NULL) < 0) {
        perror("sigaction SIGALRM");
        exit(1);
    }

    alarm(INTERVAL_SECS);

    while (1)
        niter++;
}
```

```
void
alarm_handler()
{
    printf("%d iterations in %d sec = %d iter/sec\n",
        niter, INTERVAL_SECS, niter / INTERVAL_SECS);
    exit(0);
}
```

jitter.p4.c

```
#define      _POSIX_C_SOURCE      199309

#include     <unistd.h>
#include     <sys/types.h>
#include     <time.h>
#include     <sys/signal.h>
#ifdef Lynx
#include     <conf.h>          /* HZ */
#else
/* Most UNIX systems define HZ in param.h. */
#include     <sys/param.h>     /* HZ */
#endif

/*
 * This program measures the jitter using a 100-Hz
 * POSIX.4 interval timer.  SIGRTMIN is the timer signal used.
 *
 * A reasonable real-time system is hardly likely to
 * display any jitter at all at 100 Hz, especially if timestamps
 * are taken only with an accuracy of 100 Hz.  The pedal is more likely
 * to hit the metal at higher rates.
 *
 * The Berkeley-style timer-based jitter program only used the signal as
 * a means to terminate a call to sigsuspend;  nothing actually happened in
 * that signal handler.  In contrast, this program performs the jitter
 * calculation in the signal handler (just to add a little variety).
 */

#define DEFAULT_SECS 0
#define DEFAULT_NSECS (1000000000 / HZ) /* 100 times a second */

#define TIMEBUF_MAX 200
struct timespec start_time, end_time, ta[TIMEBUF_MAX];
int this, prev;
long secs, nsecs;


#define JITTERBUF_MAX 100
struct {
    int next;
    struct timespec j[JITTERBUF_MAX];
} jbuf;
int nsig;

extern void ctrlc(int);
```

```
extern void timer_expiration(int, siginfo_t *, void *);

main(int argc, char **argv)
{
    sigset_t block_these, pause_mask;
    struct sigaction s;
    struct itimerspec interval;
    timer_t tid;
    struct sigevent notification;

    /*
     * I assume this program is externally run at the highest priority
     * in the system.  A program like "atprio" can be used for this
     * purpose.
     */

    /* Lock all process memory down */
    if (mlockall(MCL_CURRENT|MCL_FUTURE) < 0) {
        perror("mlockall");
        exit(1);
    }
    sigemptyset(&block_these);
    sigaddset(&block_these, SIGRTMIN);
    sigprocmask(SIG_BLOCK, &block_these, &pause_mask);
    if (sigismember(&pause_mask, SIGRTMIN)) {
        printf("ALRM was part of previous mask\n");
        sigdelset(&pause_mask, SIGRTMIN);
    }
    /* Handler for SIGINT */
    sigemptyset(&s.sa_mask);
    sigaddset(&s.sa_mask, SIGRTMIN);
    s.sa_flags = 0L;
    s.sa_handler = ctrlc;
    if (sigaction(SIGINT, &s, NULL) < 0) {
        perror("sigaction SIGINT");
        exit(1);
    }
    /* Handler for RT signal SIGRTMIN */
    sigemptyset(&s.sa_mask);
    sigaddset(&s.sa_mask, SIGINT);
    s.sa_flags = SA_SIGINFO;
    s.sa_sigaction = timer_expiration;
    if (sigaction(SIGRTMIN, &s, NULL) < 0) {
        perror("sigaction SIGRTMIN");
        exit(1);
    }

    secs = DEFAULT_SECS;
    nsecs = DEFAULT_NSECS;
    /* Assure nsecs is modulo HZ (paranoia) */
    nsecs -= nsecs % HZ;

    interval.it_value.tv_sec = secs;
    interval.it_value.tv_nsec = nsecs;
    interval.it_interval.tv_sec = secs;
```

```
        interval.it_interval.tv_nsec = nsecs;

        jbuf.next = 0;
        nsig = 0;
        prev = -1;
        this = 0;

        clock_gettime(CLOCK_REALTIME, &start_time);
        notification.sigev_notify = SIGEV_SIGNAL;
        notification.sigev_signo = SIGRTMIN;
        notification.sigev_value.sival_ptr = (void *)&tid;
        if (timer_create(CLOCK_REALTIME, &notification, &tid) < 0) {
            perror("timer_create");
            exit(1);
        }
        timer_settime(tid, 0, &interval, NULL);
        while (1) {
            sigsuspend(&pause_mask);
        }

}


void ctrlc(int sig)
{
    int i;
    int total_sec, total_nsec;
    float totaltime;
    struct timespec jmax;
    int start_sec;

    gettimeofday(&end_time, NULL);
    total_sec = end_time.tv_sec - start_time.tv_sec;
    total_nsec = end_time.tv_nsec - start_time.tv_nsec;
    totaltime = (float)total_sec * 1000000000. + (float)total_nsec;
    if (total_nsec < 0) {
        total_sec++;
        total_nsec += 1000000000;
    }
    printf("Control-C\n");
    printf("%d signals in %d sec %d nsec = 1 signal every %f nsec\n",
        nsig, total_sec, total_nsec,
        totaltime / (float)nsig);
    jmax.tv_sec = jmax.tv_nsec = 0;
    totaltime = 0.;
    for (i=0; i<jbuf.next; i++) {
        if ((abs(jbuf.j[i].tv_sec) > jmax.tv_sec) ||
            (abs(jbuf.j[i].tv_nsec) > jmax.tv_nsec)) {
                jmax.tv_sec = abs(jbuf.j[i].tv_sec);
                jmax.tv_nsec = abs(jbuf.j[i].tv_nsec);
        }
        totaltime +=
            (((float)abs(jbuf.j[i].tv_sec)) * 1000000000.) +
             ((float)abs(jbuf.j[i].tv_nsec));
    }
    printf("Max jitter: %d nsec\n", jmax.tv_sec * 1000000000 + jmax.tv_nsec);
```

```
        /* Jitter wasn't measured on the first signal */
        printf("Average jitter: %f nsec\n", totaltime / (float)(nsig-1));
        if (jbuf.next) {
            /* There was jitter */
            start_sec = ta[0].tv_sec;
            for (i=0; i<prev; i++)
                printf("%-5d %-7d\n",
                ta[i].tv_sec - start_sec,
                ta[i].tv_nsec);
        }       \

        exit(0);
}


void timer_expiration(int sig, siginfo_t *info, void *extra)
{
    nsig++;
    /* Calculate jitter: difference between the actual
     * time and the expected time */
    clock_gettime(CLOCK_REALTIME, &ta[this]);
    if (prev >= 0) {
        if ((ta[this].tv_sec !=
            ta[prev].tv_sec + secs) ||
            (ta[this].tv_nsec !=
            ta[prev].tv_nsec + nsecs)) {

            /* There seems to have been jitter.  Verify. */

            if ((ta[this].tv_sec==ta[prev].tv_sec + 1) &&
                (ta[this].tv_nsec == 0))
                /* No jitter;  the seconds just clicked over. */
                goto skip;

            /* Calculate the amount of jitter. */
            jbuf.j[jbuf.next].tv_sec =
                ta[this].tv_sec - ta[prev].tv_sec;
            jbuf.j[jbuf.next].tv_nsec =
                ta[this].tv_nsec - ta[prev].tv_nsec;
            jbuf.next++;
            if (jbuf.next == JITTERBUF_MAX) {
                ctrlc(0);   /* Terminate */
            }
        }
        skip:
            prev = this;
            this++;
            if (this == TIMEBUF_MAX)
                this = 0;
    }
}
```

Chapter 6: I/O for the Real World

iopipe.c

```
#define _POSIX_C_SOURCE 199309L

#include <unistd.h>
#include <stdio.h>
#include <sys/types.h>
#include <fcntl.h>

/*
 * This program copies its standard input to standard output
 * using read and write BUFSIZE bytes at a time.
 */

#define BUFSIZE (64*1024)

char buf[BUFSIZE];

int
main(int argc, char **argv)
{
    ssize_t nbytes;

    fcntl(fileno(stdout), F_GETFL, &flags);
    flags |= O_DSYNC;    /* Just get the data down */
    fcntl(fileno(stdout), F_SETFL, flags);

    while (1) {
        nbytes = read(fileno(stdin), buf, BUFSIZE);
        if (nbytes <= 0)
            break;
        if (write(fileno(stdout), buf, nbytes) != nbytes) {
            perror("write to stdout");
            break;
        }
    }
    exit(0);
}
```

aiopipe.c

```
#define    _POSIX_C_SOURCE 199309
#include   <unistd.h>
#include   <stdio.h>
#include   <sys/types.h>
#include   <signal.h>
#include   <fcntl.h>

#ifdef _POSIX_ASYNCHRONOUS_IO
#include   <aio.h>
#else
Error: Need asynchronous I/O!
```

```
        #endif


        #define SIG_AIO_READ_DONE (SIGRTMIN)
        #define SIG_AIO_WRITE_DONE (SIGRTMIN+1)

        struct aiocb_plus {
            struct aiocb a;
            off_t curr_offset;
            char *buffer;
        } a1, a2;

        #define BUFSIZE 4096
        char buf1[BUFSIZE], buf2[BUFSIZE];

        int aio_to_go;  /* Global flag */

        /* Called when this read is complete. */
        void aioread_done(int signo, siginfo_t *info, void *ignored)
        {
            struct aiocb_plus *ap;
            ssize_t nbytes_read;

            ap = (struct aiocb_plus *)(info->si_value.sival_ptr);
            /* No need to call aio_error here -- know AIO's done */
            nbytes_read = aio_return(&ap->a);
            if (nbytes_read > 0) {
                /* Read some data, so turn around and write it out. */
                ap->a.aio_fildes = fileno(stdout);
                ap->a.aio_buf = buf1;
                ap->a.aio_nbytes = nbytes_read;
                ap->a.aio_offset = ap->curr_offset;
                ap->a.aio_reqprio = 0;
                ap->a.aio_sigevent.sigev_notify = SIGEV_SIGNAL;
                ap->a.aio_sigevent.sigev_signo  = SIG_AIO_WRITE_DONE;
                ap->a.aio_sigevent.sigev_value.sival_ptr = (void *)ap;
                aio_write(&ap->a);
            } else {
                aio_to_go--;
            }
        }

        /* Called when this write is complete. */
        void aiowrite_done(int signo, siginfo_t *info, void *ignored)
        {
            struct aiocb_plus *ap;
            ssize_t nbytes_written;

            ap = (struct aiocb_plus *)(info->si_value.sival_ptr);
            /* No need to call aio_error here -- know AIO's done */
            nbytes_written = aio_return(&ap->a);
            /* Fire up another aio_read, skipping the data being read by our peer. */
            ap->a.aio_fildes = fileno(stdout);
            ap->a.aio_buf = buf1;
            ap->a.aio_nbytes = BUFSIZE;
```

```
        ap->curr_offset += 2*BUFSIZE;
        ap->a.aio_offset = ap->curr_offset;
        ap->a.aio_reqprio = 0;
        ap->a.aio_sigevent.sigev_notify = SIGEV_SIGNAL;
        ap->a.aio_sigevent.sigev_signo  = SIG_AIO_READ_DONE;
        ap->a.aio_sigevent.sigev_value.sival_ptr = (void *)ap;
        aio_read(&ap->a);
}

main(int argc, char **argv)
{
        sigset_t allsigs;
        struct sigaction sa;

        /* Handler for read completions. */
        sa.sa_sigaction = aioread_done;
        sa.sa_flags = SA_SIGACTION;
        /* Prevent the WRITE signal from coming in while we're handling
         * a READ completion. Just to keep things more clean. */
        sigemptyset(&sa.sa_mask);
        sigaddset(&sa.sa_mask, SIG_AIO_WRITE_DONE);
        if (sigaction(SIG_AIO_READ_DONE, &sa, NULL) < 0) {
            perror("sigaction");
            exit(1);
        }
        /* Handler for write completions. */
        sa.sa_sigaction = aiowrite_done;
        sa.sa_flags = SA_SIGACTION;
        /* Prevent the READ signal from coming in while we're handling
         * a WRITE completion. Just to keep things more clean. */
        sigemptyset(&sa.sa_mask);
        sigaddset(&sa.sa_mask, SIG_AIO_READ_DONE);
        if (sigaction(SIG_AIO_WRITE_DONE, &sa, NULL) < 0) {
            perror("sigaction");
            exit(1);
        }

        /* Block these signals from the mainline code so we can safely
         * examine the global variable aio_to_go */
        sigemptyset(&allsigs);
        sigaddset(&allsigs, SIG_AIO_READ_DONE);
        sigaddset(&allsigs, SIG_AIO_WRITE_DONE);
        sigprocmask(SIG_BLOCK, &allsigs, NULL);

        aio_to_go = 2;  /* Global flag */

        fcntl(fileno(stdout), F_GETFL, &flags);
        flags |= O_DSYNC;   /* Just get the data down */
        fcntl(fileno(stdout), F_SETFL, flags);

        /* Set up asynchronous I/O. */
        a1.a.aio_fildes = fileno(stdin);
        a1.a.aio_buf = a1.buffer = buf1;
        a1.a.aio_nbytes = BUFSIZE;
        a1.a.aio_offset = a1.curr_offset = (off_t)0;
```

```
a1.a.aio_reqprio = 0;
a1.a.aio_sigevent.sigev_notify = SIGEV_SIGNAL;
a1.a.aio_sigevent.sigev_signo  = SIG_AIO_READ_DONE;
a1.a.aio_sigevent.sigev_value.sival_ptr = (void *)&a1;
aio_read(&a1.a);

a2.a.aio_fildes = fileno(stdin);
a2.a.aio_buf = a2.buffer = buf2;
a2.a.aio_nbytes = BUFSIZE;
a2.a.aio_offset = a2.curr_offset = (off_t)BUFSIZE;
a2.a.aio_reqprio = 0;
a2.a.aio_sigevent.sigev_notify = SIGEV_SIGNAL;
a2.a.aio_sigevent.sigev_signo  = SIG_AIO_READ_DONE;
a2.a.aio_sigevent.sigev_value.sival_ptr = (void *)&a2;
aio_read(&a2.a);

/* Let the signals take it from here! */

sigemptyset(&allsigs);  /* Mask no signals when we suspend */
while (aio_to_go) {
    sigsuspend(&allsigs);
}

exit(0);
}
```

Chapter 7: Performance, or How To Choose an Operating System

noswitch.c

```
#define _POSIX_C_SOURCE     199309  /* POSIX 9/1993: .1, .4 */
#include    <unistd.h>

#include    <stdio.h>
#include    <sys/types.h>
#include    <signal.h>
#include    <sched.h>

/*
 * Measure overhead of using the sched_yield call.
 */
int nyield = 0;

main()
{
    struct sigaction sa;
    extern void alarm_handler();

    sigemptyset(&sa.sa_mask);
    sa.sa_flags = 0;
    sa.sa_handler = alarm_handler;  /* Terminates experiment */
```

```
        if (sigaction(SIGALRM, &sa, NULL) < 0) {
            perror("sigaction SIGALRM");
            exit(1);
        }

        switcher(); /* with self ==> no ctxtsw */

        fprintf(stderr, "Unexpected exit from test program!\n");
        exit(4);
}

/* Should never wake up from the sigsuspend--SIGUSR1 is blocked */
switcher()
{
    alarm(60);
    while (1) {
        sched_yield();
        nyield++;
    }
}

void
alarm_handler()
{
    printf("%d yield calls in 60 seconds = %d yield calls/sec\n", nyield,
        nyield / 60);
    exit(0);
}
```

switch.c

```
#define _POSIX_C_SOURCE     199309  /* POSIX 9/1993: .1, .4 */
#include    <unistd.h>

#include    <stdio.h>
#include    <sys/types.h>
#include    <signal.h>

/*
 * Measure context switch time using the sched_yield call.
 */
int nswitch = 0;
pid_t chpid;

main()
{
    struct sigaction sa;
    extern void alarm_handler(), child_terminate();

    sigemptyset(&sa.sa_mask);
    sa.sa_flags = 0;
    sa.sa_handler = alarm_handler;  /* Terminates experiment */

    if (sigaction(SIGALRM, &sa, NULL) < 0) {
        perror("sigaction SIGALRM");
```

```
                    exit(1);
            }

            sa.sa_handler = child_terminate;     /* Terminates child */
            sigfillset(&sa.sa_mask);/* Take no signals after experiment done */
            if (sigaction(SIGUSR2, &sa, NULL) < 0) {
                perror("sigaction SIGUSR2");
                exit(1);
            }

            /* Should set scheduler here, or use atprio */
            switch (chpid = fork()) {
                case -1:    /* error */
                        perror("fork");
                        exit(3);
                        break;
                default:    /* parent, set alarm and fall through
                             * to common case */
                        alarm(60);
                case 0:     /* everybody */
                        switcher();
                        exit(0);
                        break;
            }

            fprintf(stderr, "Unexpected exit from test program!\n");
            exit(4);
    }

/* Should never wake up from the sigsuspend--SIGUSR1 is blocked */
switcher()
{
    while (1) {
        sched_yield();
        nswitch++;
    }
}

child_terminate()
{
    printf("%d switches in 60 seconds = %d switch/sec\n", nswitch,
        nswitch / 60);
    exit(0);
}

void
alarm_handler()
{
    printf("%d switches in 60 seconds = %d switch/sec\n", nswitch,
        nswitch / 60);
    kill(chpid, SIGUSR2);
    exit(0);
}
```

sending_sigs_self.c

```c
#include     <stdio.h>
#include     <unistd.h>
#include     <sys/types.h>
#include     <signal.h>

/*
 * Measure time sent just for one process to send signals to itself.
 * Avoid all signal-handling overhead by having the signal blocked.
 */
int nsigs = 0;

main()
{
    struct sigaction sa;
    sigset_t blockem;
    extern void panic_handler(), alarm_handler(), child_terminate();

    sigemptyset(&sa.sa_mask);
    sa.sa_flags = 0;
    sa.sa_handler = alarm_handler;   /* Terminates experiment */

    if (sigaction(SIGALRM, &sa, NULL) < 0) {
        perror("sigaction SIGALRM");
        exit(1);
    }

    /* Should never _receive_ SIGUSR1--it's blocked.
     * Setting up this handler is just paranoia. */
    sa.sa_handler = panic_handler;
    if (sigaction(SIGUSR1, &sa, NULL) < 0) {
        perror("sigaction SIGUSR1");
        exit(1);
    }

    sigemptyset(&blockem);
    sigaddset(&blockem, SIGUSR1);
    if (sigprocmask(SIG_BLOCK, &blockem) < 0) {
        perror("sigprocmask");
        exit(2);
    }

    send_sigs_self();

    fprintf(stderr, "Unexpected exit from test program!\n");
    exit(4);
}

send_sigs_self()
{
    pid_t self = getpid();

    alarm(60);
    while(1) {
```

```
            if (kill(self, SIGUSR1) < 0) {
                perror("kill");
                return;
            }
            nsigs++;
        }
    }

    void
    panic_handler(int sig)
    {
        char *signame;
        switch (sig) {
            case SIGUSR1:   signame = "SIGUSR1"; break;
            case SIGUSR2:   signame = "SIGUSR2"; break;
            case SIGALRM:   signame = "SIGALRM"; break;
            default:    signame = "<unknown signal name>"; break;
        }
        printf("ERROR: received signal %d (%s)\n",
            sig, signame);
        exit(5);
    }

    void
    alarm_handler()
    {
        printf("%d signals sent (%d/sec)\n", nsigs, nsigs/60);
        exit(0);
    }
```

sending_recving_sigs_self.c

```
    #include    <stdio.h>
    #include    <unistd.h>
    #include    <sys/types.h>
    #include    <signal.h>

    /*
     * Measure time sent just for one process to send signals to itself
     * AND handle those signals.
     */
    int nsigs_sent = 0;
    int nsigs_recv = 0;

    main()
    {
        struct sigaction sa;
        sigset_t blockem;
        extern void null_handler(), alarm_handler();

        sigemptyset(&sa.sa_mask);
        sa.sa_flags = 0;
        sa.sa_handler = alarm_handler;   /* Terminates experiment */

        if (sigaction(SIGALRM, &sa, NULL) < 0) {
```

```
            perror("sigaction SIGALRM");
            exit(1);
        }

        /* Should never _receive_ SIGUSR1--it's blocked.
         * Setting up this handler is just paranoia. */
        sa.sa_handler = null_handler;
        if (sigaction(SIGUSR1, &sa, NULL) < 0) {
            perror("sigaction SIGUSR1");
            exit(1);
        }

        send_sigs_self();

        fprintf(stderr, "Unexpected exit from test program!\n");
        exit(4);
}

send_sigs_self()
{
        pid_t self = getpid();

        alarm(60);
        while(1) {
            if (kill(self, SIGUSR1) < 0) {
                perror("kill");
                return;
            }
            nsigs_sent++;
        }
}

void
null_handler()
{
        nsigs_recv++;
}

void
alarm_handler()
{
        printf("%d signals sent (%d/sec)\n", nsigs_sent, nsigs_sent/60);
        printf("%d signals received (%d/sec)\n", nsigs_recv, nsigs_recv/60);
        exit(0);
}
```

sending_sigs.c

```
#include     <stdio.h>
#include     <unistd.h>
#include     <sys/types.h>
#include     <signal.h>

/*
 * Measure time sent just for one process to send signals to another process.
```

```
     * Avoid all overhead on the child side by having the signal blocked.
     */
    int nsigs = 0;
    pid_t chpid;

    main()
    {
        struct sigaction sa;
        sigset_t blockem;
        extern void panic_handler(), alarm_handler(), child_terminate();

        sigemptyset(&sa.sa_mask);
        sa.sa_flags = 0;
        sa.sa_handler = alarm_handler;  /* Terminates experiment */

        if (sigaction(SIGALRM, &sa, NULL) < 0) {
            perror("sigaction SIGALRM");
            exit(1);
        }

        /* No one should ever _receive_ SIGUSR1--it's blocked.
         * Setting up this handler is just paranoia. */
        sa.sa_handler = panic_handler;
        if (sigaction(SIGUSR1, &sa, NULL) < 0) {
            perror("sigaction SIGUSR1");
            exit(1);
        }

        sa.sa_handler = child_terminate;    /* Terminates child */
        sigfillset(&sa.sa_mask);/* Take no signals after experiment done */
        if (sigaction(SIGUSR2, &sa, NULL) < 0) {
            perror("sigaction SIGUSR2");
            exit(1);
        }

        sigemptyset(&blockem);
        sigaddset(&blockem, SIGUSR1);
        if (sigprocmask(SIG_BLOCK, &blockem) < 0) {
            perror("sigprocmask");
            exit(2);
        }

        switch (chpid = fork()) {
            case -1:    /* error */
                    perror("fork");
                    exit(3);
                    break;
            case 0:     /* child */
                    be_a_child();
                    exit(0);
                    break;
            default:    /* parent */
                    be_the_parent();
                    exit(0);
                    break;
```

```
    }

    fprintf(stderr, "Unexpected exit from test program!\n");
    exit(4);
}

/* Should never wake up from the sigsuspend--SIGUSR1 is blocked */
be_a_child()
{
    sigset_t sigset;
    sigfillset(&sigset);
    sigdelset(&sigset, SIGUSR2);      /* Wait for only SIGUSR2 */
    while (1) {
        sigsuspend(&sigset);
    }
}

be_the_parent()
{
    alarm(60);
    while(1) {
        if (kill(chpid, SIGUSR1) < 0) {
            perror("kill");
            return;
        }
        nsigs++;
    }
}

void
panic_handler(int sig)
{
    char *signame;
    switch (sig) {
        case SIGUSR1:    signame = "SIGUSR1"; break;
        case SIGUSR2:    signame = "SIGUSR2"; break;
        case SIGALRM:    signame = "SIGALRM"; break;
        default:    signame = "<unknown signal name>"; break;
    }
    printf("ERROR: Child received signal %d (%s)\n",
        sig, signame);
    kill(getppid(), SIGALRM);    /* Terminate experiment */
    exit(1);
}

void
child_terminate()
{
    exit(0);
}

void
alarm_handler()
{
    printf("%d signals sent by parent (%d/sec)\n", nsigs, nsigs/60);
```

```
        kill(chpid, SIGUSR2);
        exit(0);
}
```

sigs_sent_noswtch.c, sigs_sent_swtch.c

The code for these exercises can be found in the section for Chapter 3, earlier in this appendix.

Bibliography

Throughout the book, I've referred to several books for additional information or just plain fun bedside reading. Here are the complete references.

Bach, Maurice J.. *The Design of the UNIX Operating System*. Prentice-Hall. 0-13-201799-7.

This is one of the canonical references to how UNIX is put together.

Frisch, Æleen. *Essential System Administration*. O'Reilly & Associates. 0-937175-80-3.

Institute of Electrical and Electronics Engineers. *Portable Operating System Interface (POSIX)—Part 1: System Application Program Interface (API) [C Language]*. Institute of Electrical and Electronics Engineers. 1-55937-061-0.

This is POSIX.1, also known as ISO 9945-1 (1990).

Institute of Electrical and Electronics Engineers. *Portable Operating System Interface (POSIX)—Part 2: Shell and Utilities (volumes 1 and 2)*. Institute of Electrical and Electronics Engineers. 1-55937-255-9.

This is POSIX.2. It's not an ISO standard yet.

Institute of Electrical and Electronics Engineers. *Portable Operating System Interface (POSIX)—Part 1: Application Program Interface (API) [C Language]—Amendment: Realtime Extensions*. Institute of Electrical and Electronics Engineers. 1-55937-375-X.

This is POSIX.4.

Jain, Raj. *The Art of Computer Systems Performance Analysis*. John Wiley and Sons, Inc.. 0-471-50336-3.

If you're *really* serious about performance measurement, you should read this book.

Klein, Mark H., Ralya, Thomas, Pollak, Bill, Obenza, Ray, Harbour, Michael González. *A Practitioner's Handbook for Real-Time Analysis: Guide to Rate Monotonic Analysis for*

Real-Time Systems. Kluwer Academic. 0-7293-9361-9.

This book tells you everything you might want to know about Rate Monotonic Analysis.

Leffler, Samuel J., McKusick, Kirk, Karels, Mike, Quarterman, John. *The Design and Implementation of the 4.3BSD UNIX Operating System*. Addison-Wesley. 0-201-06196-1.

This is the other canonical reference to how UNIX is put together.

Lewine, Don. *POSIX Programmer's Guide*. O'Reilly & Associates. 0-937175-73-0.

Zlotnick, Fred. *The POSIX.1 Standard: A Programmer's Guide*. Benjamin Cummings. 0-8053-9605-5.

Index

About the Author

Bill O. Gallmeister has been writing operating system software for an alarming number of years. Initially trained in BSD code at Valid Logic Systems and Sun Microsystems, he was briefly exposed to System V, an experience which drove him screaming into the dank wilderness of real-time. At Lynx Real-Time Systems, he developed the first complete implementation of POSIX.4 and POSIX.4a threads. During this time, he was vice-chair of POSIX.4. Following this adventure, he took another look at the current state-of-the art in UNIX systems. This caused him to head for the multimedia frontier. He can now be found at First Virtual Corporation, doing high-velocity file system work for a networked monster multimedia machine.

Bill earned his bachelor's in computer science at UC Santa Barbara, which entitles him to work barefoot. He earned his master's in computer science at Chapel Hill, which entitles him to use large words like "avuncular."

When not occupied in programming, Bill engages in activities typical of BWGs (see preface) in Silicon Valley: hanging out with his wife and son, drinking expensive coffee drinks, cooking and eating strange foreign foods, reading, watching bad science fiction movies, and riding his bike around the hills above Los Gatos. His email address is b0g@netcom.com (that's "Bee Zero Gee," not "Bee Oh Gee").

Colophon

Edie Freedman designed the cover of this book. The graphic is adapted from an engraving explaining "Mechanics" that Edie found in a London print shop: "Published as the Act directs, 1829, by Longman, Hurst, Rees, Orme, & Brown, Paternoster Row, London." The cover layout was produced using Quark XPress 3.3 and Adobe Photoshop 2.5 software, in Adobe ITC Garamond font.

Jennifer Niederst designed the interior layout. Text was prepared in SGML using the DocBook 2.1 DTD. The print version of this book was created by translating the SGML source into a set of gtroff macros using a filter developed at ORA by Norman Walsh. Steve Talbott designed and wrote the underlying macro set on the basis of the GNU gtroff -gs macros; Lenny Muellner adapted them to SGML and implemented the book design. The GNU groff text formatter version 1.09 was used to generate PostScript

More Titles from O'REILLY™

Programming UNIX

UNIX Systems Programming for SVR4

By David A. Curry
1st Edition July 1996
620 pages, ISBN 1-56592-163-1

Any program worth its salt uses operating system services. Even a simple program, if practical, reads input and produces output. And, most applications have more complex needs. They need to find out the time, use the network, or start and communicate with other processes. Systems programming really means nothing more than writing software that uses these operating system services.

UNIX Systems Programming for SVR4 presents the nitty gritty details on how UNIX interacts with applications. If you're writing an application from scratch, or if you're porting an application to any System V.4 platform, you need this book. It offers a complete, thorough explanation of all UNIX system calls and library routines related to systems programming, working with I/O, files and directories, processing multiple input streams, file and record locking, and memory-mapped files. You'll also learn about reading, printing, and setting the system time and date, determining who is logged in, and setting user and group ID.

The book also shows you how to change system configuration parameters for resource limits and how to create processes, job control, and signal handling. Also discusses interprocess communication, serial line characteristics, network programming with Berkeley sockets, Transport Layer Interface (TLI), and the data link provider interface.

Programming Python

By Mark Lutz
1st Edition Fall 1996
900 pages (est.), ISBN 1-56592-197-6

This Nutshell Handbook® describes how to use Python, an increasingly popular object-oriented scripting language. This book, full of running examples, is the only user material available on Python. It's endorsed by Python creator Guido van Rossum and complements reference materials that accompany the software. Includes a disk containing the Python interpreter software.

Pthreads Programming

By Bradford Nichols, Dick Butler & Jackie Farrell
1st Edition Fall 1996
400 pages (est.), ISBN 1-56592-115-1

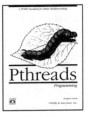

Computers are just as busy as the rest of us nowadays. They have lots of tasks to do at once, and need some cleverness to get them all done at the same time.

That's why threads are seen more and more often as a new model for programming. Threads have been available for some time. The Mach operating system, the Distributed Computer Environment (DCE), and Windows NT all feature threads.

One advantage of most UNIX implementations, as well as DCE, is that they conform to a recently ratified POSIX standard (originally 1003.4a, now 1003.1c), which allows your programs to be portable between them. POSIX threads are commonly known as pthreads, after the word that starts all the names of the function calls. The standard is supported by Solaris, OSF/1, AIX, and several other UNIX-based operating systems.

The idea behind threads programming is to have multiple tasks running concurrently within the same program. They can share a single CPU as processes do, or take advantage of multiple CPUs when available. In either case, they provide a clean way to divide the tasks of a program while sharing data.

A window interface can read input on dozens of different buttons, each responsible for a separate task. A network server has to accept simultaneous calls from many clients, providing each with reasonable response time. A multiprocessor runs a number-crunching program on several CPUs at once, combining the results when all are done. All these kinds of applications can benefit from threads.

In this book you will learn not only what the pthread calls are, but when it is a good idea to use threads and how to make them efficient (which is the whole reason for using threads in the first place). The author delves into performance issues, comparing threads to processes, contrasting kernel threads to user threads, and showing how to measure speed. He also describes in a simple, clear manner what all the advanced features are for, and how threads interact with the rest of the UNIX system.

FOR INFORMATION: **800-998-9938**, 707-829-0515; **INFO@ORA.COM**; **HTTP://WWW.ORA.COM/**
TO ORDER: **800-889-8969** (CREDIT CARD ORDERS ONLY); **ORDER@ORA.COM**

Power Programming with RPC

By John Bloomer
1st Edition February 1992
522 pages, ISBN 0-937175-77-3

A distributed application is designed to access resources across a network. In a broad sense, these resources could be user input, a central database, configuration files, etc., that are distributed on various computers across the network, rather than found on a single computer. RPC, or remote procedure calling, is the ability to distribute the execution of functions on remote computers outside of the application's current address space. This allows you to break large or complex programming problems into routines that can be executed independently of one another to take advantage of multiple computers. Thus, RPC makes it possible to attack a problem using a form of parallel or multiprocessing.

Written from a programmer's perspective, this book shows what you can do with Sun RPC, the de facto standard on UNIX systems. It covers related programming topics for Sun and other UNIX systems and teaches through examples.

POSIX Programmer's Guide

By Donald Lewine
1st Edition April 1991
640 pages, ISBN 0-937175-73-0

Most UNIX systems today are POSIX compliant because the federal government requires it for its purchases. Even OSF and UI agree on support for POSIX. Given the manufacturer's documentation, however, it can be difficult to distinguish system-specific features from those features defined by POSIX.

The *POSIX Programmer's Guide*, intended as an explanation of the POSIX standard and as a reference for the POSIX.1 programming library, helps you write more portable programs. This guide is especially helpful if you are writing programs that must run on multiple UNIX platforms. This guide also helps you convert existing UNIX programs for POSIX compliance.

"Posix Programmer's Guide belongs on the shelf of every Unix system programmer. Posix texts will be written, and Posix reference manuals will be produced, but it is rare to find such an interesting compromise between the two."
—Ed Gordon, BDataSystems, *IEEE Software Magazine*

POSIX.4

By Bill Gallmeister
1st Edition January 1995
570 pages, ISBN 1-56592-074-0

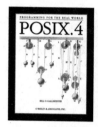

Real-world programming (typically called real-time programming) is programming that interacts in some way with the "real world" of daily life. Real-world programmers develop the unseen software that operates most of the world that surrounds you, software typically characterized by deadlines —and harsh penalties if the deadlines aren't met. When you've just rear-ended another car, it's no consolation that a sudden flurry of input slowed down your brake processor, so it couldn't react quickly enough when you hit the pedal.

This book covers the POSIX.4 standard for portable real-time programming. The POSIX.4 standard itself is a massive document that defines system interfaces for asynchronous I/O, scheduling, communications, and other facilities. However, this book does more than explain the standard. It provides a general introduction to real-time programming and real-time issues: the problems software faces when it needs to interact with the real world and how to solve them. If you're at all interested in real-time applications—which include just about everything from telemetry to transaction processing—this book will be an essential reference.

Includes problem sets, answers, and reference manual pages for all functions and header files.

Programming with curses

By John Strang
1st Edition 1986
76 pages, ISBN 0-937175-02-1

Curses is a UNIX library of functions for controlling a terminal's display screen from a C program. It can be used to provide a screen driver for a program (such as a visual editor) or to improve a program's user interface.

This handbook will help you make use of the curses library in your C programs. We have presented ample material on curses and its implementation in UNIX so that you understand the whole, as well as its parts.

FOR INFORMATION: **800-998-9938**, 707-829-0515; **INFO@ORA.COM**; **HTTP://WWW.ORA.COM/**
TO ORDER: **800-889-8969** *(CREDIT CARD ORDERS ONLY)*; **ORDER@ORA.COM**

Stay in touch with O'REILLY™

Visit Our Award-Winning World Wide Web Site

http://www.ora.com/

VOTED

"Top 100 Sites on the Web" —*PC Magazine*
"Top 5% Websites" —*Point Communications*
"3-Star site" —*The McKinley Group*

Our Web site contains a library of comprehensive product information (including book excerpts and tables of contents), downloadable software, background articles, interviews with technology leaders, links to relevant sites, book cover art, and more. File us in your Bookmarks or Hotlist!

Join Our Two Email Mailing Lists

LIST #1 NEW PRODUCT RELEASES: To receive automatic email with brief descriptions of all new O'Reilly products as they are released, send email to: listproc@online.ora.com and put the following information in the first line of your message (NOT in the Subject: field, which is ignored): **subscribe ora-news "Your Name" of "Your Organization"** (for example: **subscribe ora-news Kris Webber of Fine Enterprises)**

LIST #2 O'REILLY EVENTS: If you'd also like us to send information about trade show events, special promotions, and other O'Reilly events, send email to: **listproc@online.ora.com** and put the following information in the first line of your message (NOT in the Subject: field, which is ignored): **subscribe ora-events "Your Name" of "Your Organization"**

Visit Our Gopher Site

* Connect your Gopher to **gopher.ora.com**, or
* Point your Web browser to **gopher://gopher.ora.com/**, or
* telnet to **gopher.ora.com** (login: **gopher**)

Get Example Files from Our Books Via FTP

There are two ways to access an archive of example files from our books:

REGULAR FTP — ftp to: **ftp.ora.com** (login: **anonymous**—use your email address as the password) or point your Web browser to: **ftp://ftp.ora.com/**

FTPMAIL — Send an email message to: **ftpmail@online.ora.com** (write "help" in the message body)

Contact Us Via Email

order@ora.com — To place a book or software order online. Good for North American and international customers.

subscriptions@ora.com — To place an order for any of our newsletters or periodicals.

software@ora.com — For general questions and product information about our software.
  • Check out O'Reilly Software Online at **http://software.ora.com/** for software and technical support information.
  • Registered O'Reilly software users send your questions to **website-support@ora.com**

books@ora.com — General questions about any of our books.

cs@ora.com — For answers to problems regarding your order or our products.

booktech@ora.com — For book content technical questions or corrections.

proposals@ora.com — To submit new book or software proposals to our editors and product managers.

international@ora.com — For information about our international distributors or translation queries.
  • For a list of our distributors outside of North America check out:
  http://www.ora.com/www/order/country.html

O'REILLY™

101 Morris Street, Sebastopol, CA 95472 USA
TEL 707-829-0515 or 800-998-9938 (6 A.M. to 5 P.M. PST)
FAX 707-829-0104

Listing of Titles from O'REILLY™

INTERNET PROGRAMMING

CGI Programming on the
   World Wide Web
Designing for the Web
Exploring Java
HTML: The Definitive Guide
Web Client Programming with Perl
Learning Perl
Programming Perl, 2nd.Edition
   (Fall '96)
JavaScript: The Definitive Guide, Beta
   Edition (Summer '96)
Webmaster in a Nutshell
The World Wide Web Journal

USING THE INTERNET

Smileys
The Whole Internet User's Guide
   and Catalog
The Whole Internet for Windows 95
What You Need to Know:
   Using Email Effectively
Marketing on the Internet (Fall 96)
What You Need to Know: Bandits on the
   Information Superhighway

JAVA SERIES

Exploring Java
Java in a Nutshell
Java Language Reference
   (Fall '96 est.)
Java Virtual Machine

WINDOWS

Inside the Windows '95 Registry

SOFTWARE

WebSite™ 1.1
WebSite Professional™
WebBoard™
PolyForm™

SONGLINE GUIDES

NetLearning
NetSuccess for Realtors
NetActivism (Fall '96)

SYSTEM ADMINISTRATION

Building Internet Firewalls
Computer Crime:
   A Crimefighter's Handbook
Computer Security Basics
DNS and BIND
Essential System Administration,
   2nd ed.
Getting Connected:
   The Internet at 56K and Up
Linux Network Administrator's Guide
Managing Internet Information Services
Managing Usenet (Fall '96)
Managing NFS and NIS
Networking Personal Computers
   with TCP/IP
Practical UNIX & Internet Security
PGP: Pretty Good Privacy
sendmail
System Performance Tuning
TCP/IP Network Administration
termcap & terminfo
Using & Managing UUCP (Fall '96)
Volume 8: X Window System
   Administrator's Guide

UNIX

Exploring Expect
Learning GNU Emacs, 2nd Edition
   (Fall '96 est.)
Learning the bash Shell
Learning the Korn Shell
Learning the UNIX Operating System
Learning the vi Editor
Linux in a Nutshell (Fall '96 est.)
Making TeX Work
Linux Multimedia Guide (Fall '96)
Running Linux, 2nd Edition
Running Linux Companion
   CD-ROM, 2nd Edition
SCO UNIX in a Nutshell
sed & awk
Unix in a Nutshell: System V Edition
UNIX Power Tools
UNIX Systems Programming
Using csh and tsch
What You Need to Know:
   When You Can't Find Your
   UNIX System Administrator

PROGRAMMING

Applying RCS and SCCS
C++: The Core Language
Checking C Programs with lint
DCE Security Programming
Distributing Applications Across
   DCE and Windows NT
Encyclopedia of Graphics File
   Formats, 2nd ed.
Guide to Writing DCE Applications
lex & yacc
Managing Projects with make
ORACLE Performance Tuning
ORACLE PL/SQL Programming
Porting UNIX Software
POSIX Programmer's Guide
POSIX.4: Programming for
   the Real World
Power Programming with RPC
Practical C Programming
Practical C++ Programming
Programming Python (Fall '96)
Programming with curses
Programming with GNU Software
   (Fall '96 est.)
Pthreads Programming
   (Fall '96)
Software Portability with imake
Understanding DCE
Understanding Japanese Information
   Processing
UNIX Systems Programming for SVR4

BERKELEY 4.4 SOFTWARE DISTRIBUTION

4.4BSD System Manager's Manual
4.4BSD User's Reference Manual
4.4BSD User's Supplementary Docs.
4.4BSD Programmer's Reference Man.
4.4BSD Programmer's Supp. Docs.

X PROGRAMMING
THE X WINDOW SYSTEM

Volume 0: X Protocol Reference Manual
Volume 1: Xlib Programming Manual
Volume 2: Xlib Reference Manual
Volume. 3M: X Window System
   User's Guide, Motif Ed.
Volume. 4: X Toolkit Intrinsics
   Programming Manual
Volume 4M: X Toolkit Intrinsics
   Programming Manual, Motif Ed.
Volume 5: X Toolkit Intrinsics
   Reference Manual
Volume 6A: Motif Programming Man.
Volume 6B: Motif Reference Manual
Volume 6C: Motif Tools
Volume 8 : X Window System
   Administrator's Guide
Programmer's Supplement for Release 6
X User Tools (with CD-ROM)
The X Window System in a Nutshell

HEALTH, CAREER, & BUSINESS

Building a Successful Software Business
The Computer User's Survival Guide
Dictionary of Computer Terms
The Future Does Not Compute
Love Your Job!
Publishing with CD-ROM

TRAVEL

Travelers' Tales: Brazil (Summer '96 est.)
Travelers' Tales: Food (Summer '96)
Travelers' Tales: France
Travelers' Tales: Hong Kong
Travelers' Tales: India
Travelers' Tales: Mexico
Travelers' Tales: San Francisco
Travelers' Tales: Spain
Travelers' Tales: Thailand
Travelers' Tales: A Woman's World

TO ORDER: **800-889-8969** (CREDIT CARD ORDERS ONLY); **order@ora.com; http://www.ora.com/**
OUR PRODUCTS ARE AVAILABLE AT A BOOKSTORE OR SOFTWARE STORE NEAR YOU.

International Distributors

Customers outside North America can now order O'Reilly & Associates books through the following distributors. They offer our international customers faster order processing, more bookstores, increased representation at tradeshows worldwide, and the high-quality, responsive service our customers have come to expect.

EUROPE, MIDDLE EAST AND NORTHERN AFRICA *(except Germany, Switzerland, and Austria)*

INQUIRIES
International Thomson Publishing Europe
Berkshire House
168-173 High Holborn
London WC1V 7AA, United Kingdom
Telephone: 44-171-497-1422
Fax: 44-171-497-1426
Email: **itpint@itps.co.uk**

ORDERS
International Thomson Publishing Services, Ltd.
Cheriton House, North Way
Andover, Hampshire SP10 5BE,
United Kingdom
Telephone: 44-264-342-832 (UK orders)
Telephone: 44-264-342-806 (outside UK)
Fax: 44-264-364418 (UK orders)
Fax: 44-264-342761 (outside UK)
UK & Eire orders: **itpuk@itps.co.uk**
International orders: **itpint@itps.co.uk**

GERMANY, SWITZERLAND, AND AUSTRIA

International Thomson Publishing GmbH
O'Reilly International Thomson Verlag
Königswinterer Straße 418
53227 Bonn, Germany
Telephone: 49-228-97024 0
Fax: 49-228-441342
Email: **anfragen@arade.ora.de**

AUSTRALIA

WoodsLane Pty. Ltd.
7/5 Vuko Place, Warriewood NSW 2102
P.O. Box 935, Mona Vale NSW 2103
Australia
Telephone: 61-2-9970-5111
Fax: 61-2-9970-5002
Email: **woods@tmx.mhs.oz.au**

NEW ZEALAND

WoodsLane New Zealand Ltd.
21 Cooks Street (P.O. Box 575)
Wanganui, New Zealand
Telephone: 64-6-347-6543
Fax: 64-6-345-4840
Email: **info@woodslane.com.au**

ASIA *(except Japan & India)*

INQUIRIES
International Thomson Publishing Asia
60 Albert Street #15-01
Albert Complex
Singapore 189969
Telephone: 65-336-6411
Fax: 65-336-7411

ORDERS
Telephone: 65-336-6411
Fax: 65-334-1617

JAPAN

O'Reilly Japan, Inc.
Kiyoshige Building 2F
12-Banchi, Sanei-cho
Shinjuku-ku
Tokyo 160 Japan
Telephone: 8-3-3356-5227
Fax: 81-3-3356-5261
Email: **kenji@ora.com**

INDIA

Computer Bookshop (India) PVT. LTD.
190 Dr. D.N. Road, Fort
Bombay 400 001
India
Telephone: 91-22-207-0989
Fax: 91-22-262-3551
Email: **cbsbom@giasbm01.vsnl.net.in**

THE AMERICAS

O'Reilly & Associates, Inc.
101 Morris Street
Sebastopol, CA 95472 U.S.A.
Telephone: 707-829-0515
Telephone: 800-998-9938 (U.S. & Canada)
Fax: 707-829-0104
Email: **order@ora.com**

SOUTHERN AFRICA

International Thomson Publishing Southern Africa
Building 18, Constantia Park
240 Old Pretoria Road
P.O. Box 2459
Halfway House, 1685 South Africa
Telephone: 27-11-805-4819
Fax: 27-11-805-3648

O'REILLY™

TO ORDER: **800-889-8969** (CREDIT CARD ORDERS ONLY); **order@ora.com**; **http://www.ora.com**
OUR PRODUCTS ARE AVAILABLE AT A BOOKSTORE OR SOFTWARE STORE NEAR YOU.

O'REILLY

O'Reilly & Associates, Inc.
101 Morris Street
Sebastopol, CA 95472-9902
1-800-998-9938

Visit us online at:
http://www.ora.com/
orders@ora.com

O'REILLY WOULD LIKE TO HEAR FROM YOU

Which book did this card come from?

_____

Where did you buy this book?
- ❏ Bookstore
- ❏ Direct from O'Reilly
- ❏ Bundled with hardware/software
- ❏ Computer Store
- ❏ Class/seminar
- ❏ Other _____

What operating system do you use?
- ❏ UNIX
- ❏ Windows NT
- ❏ Macintosh
- ❏ PC(Windows/DOS)
- ❏ Other _____

What is your job description?
- ❏ System Administrator
- ❏ Network Administrator
- ❏ Web Developer
- ❏ Programmer
- ❏ Educator/Teacher
- ❏ Other _____

❏ Please send me O'Reilly's catalog, containing a complete listing of O'Reilly books and software.

Name _____ Company/Organization _____

Address _____

City _____ State _____ Zip/Postal Code _____ Country _____

Telephone _____ Internet or other email address (specify network) _____

Nineteenth century wood engraving
of a bear from the O'Reilly &
Associates Nutshell Handbook®
Using & Managing UUCP.

BUSINESS REPLY MAIL

FIRST CLASS MAIL   PERMIT NO. 80   SEBASTOPOL, CA

Postage will be paid by addressee

O'Reilly & Associates, Inc.
101 Morris Street
Sebastopol, CA 95472-9902

||I|ııı|ı|ıı|ı|ıı||ıı|ı|ı|I|I|ı|ı|ı|ıı||ıııı|ı|ıı|I|ı|